ABOUT THE BOOK

Differentiated staffing continues to be a highly controversial, much debated, and much misunderstood issue. It has been grossly oversold as a panacea for nearly all educational problems. It has been grossly undersold as a mechanistic reshuffling of old and new job titles in the schools, without reference to the content and spirit of education.

Differentiated staffing has profound implications for improving education. It promises individualized and more effective instruction to students, the elevation of the teaching profession to a higher professional status and competence, and the promise to a community that its educators and administrators can be held accountable for the results. This book is particularly valuable in illuminating some of the more thorny issues that accompany the proposal of this new concept.

The articles in section one discuss the rationale, theories, and functions of flexible staffing. Section two describes the case histories of four teacher training projects funded by the Office of Education's School Personnel Utilization Program. The last section correlates financial, political, and evaluative issues.

The editors and major contributors, Fenwick W. English and Donald K. Sharpes, have compiled this volume to increase interest in finding more flexible and effective ways to train and utilize educational personnel, and to raise the level of discussion about many of the problems and issues that the schools, the community, and the teaching profession face as they grapple with ways to improve educational services to children.

ABOUT THE AUTHORS

Fenwick W. English is assistant superintendent of the Sarasota County Schools in Florida. He was visiting lecturer at Arizona State University during 1970-72 and has served as differentiated staffing consultant to various national educational groups. Donald K. Sharpes is technical division director of the United States Office of Education and was program officer for its Office of School Personnel Utilization.

Strategies for Differentiated Staffing

Written and Edited by

Fenwick W. English

Assistant Superintendent
Sarasota County Schools
Sarasota, Florida

Donald K. Sharpes

Technical Division Director
United States Office of Education

McCutchan Publishing Corporation
2526 Grove Street
Berkeley, California 94704

DISCLAIMER

This book was edited by Donald K. Sharpes in his private capacity.
No official support or endorsement by the Office of Education is
intended or should be inferred.

Preface

Differentiated staffing continues to be a highly controversial, much debated, much misunderstood issue. It has been grossly oversold as a panacea for nearly all educational problems. It has been grossly undersold as a mechanistic reshuffling of old and new job titles in the schools, without reference to the content and spirit of education.

The concepts behind differentiated staffing do have profound implications for improving education and for the teaching profession. I believe that more flexible and differentiated approaches to training, utilizing, and paying school staffs offer promise for individualized and more effective instruction to students. These concepts also offer promise for the restructuring of the teaching profession in a way that will lead to higher professional status and competence, and promise to a community and its educators who seek appropriate ways to hold schools and their staffs accountable for the results.

The promise offered by the concept will be sustained or defeated, depending on execution of the ideas in practice and on the process through which the ideas are carried out.

This book is particularly useful because it provides the history of several attempts to execute differentiated staffing concepts in real schools. This history provided by the administrators and teachers who have contributed to the pages which follow will be valuable to those interested in the process of educational change. Similarly, the book is helpful in illuminating some of the thorny issues (salary differentiation and performance criteria, to name just two).

It is my hope that the book will increase interest in the search for more flexible and effective ways to train and utilize educational personnel, and that it will raise the level of discussion about many of the problems and issues that the schools, the community, and the teaching profession face as they grapple with ways to improve educational services to children.

Don Davies
Deputy Commissioner
U.S. Office of Education

Contents

Contributors

Don Davies is Deputy Commissioner, U.S. Office of Education

Fenwick English is Assistant Superintendent Staff Development of Sarasota County, Sarasota, Florida and formerly director of the Temple City, California and Mesa, Arizona DS projects.

Al Dobbins is Community School Project Officer, Portland Public Schools and formerly Director of Instruction at John Adams High School in Portland

John Parker is Coordinator of Teacher Education and Director of the Portland Urban Education Project

Patricia Wertheimer is Principal, Princeton High School, Princeton, New Jersey

Gene Pillot is Superintendent, Sarasota County Schools, Sarasota Florida

Miriam Simon is EPDA Coordinator, Kansas City Public Schools

James Zaharis is Director of Special Projects, Mesa, Arizona Public Schools

Donald Sharpes is Technical Division Director, formerly Program Manager, School Personnel Utilization, U.S. Office of Education

Gerald Krumbein is Assistant Principal, Madrone Intermediate School, Sunnyvale, California

Marshall Frinks is Senior Program Specialist, U.S. Office of Education

Michael DeBloois is Assistant Professor of Education at Florida State University

Section I:

Rationale, Theories, and Functions of Flexible Staffing

Section I is an introduction to the past seven years of the evolution of staff differentiation as an educational concept. It is a combination of success and failure, theory and practice, dream and reality. It provides a comprehensive overview for the reader prior to the case studies.

The section consists of four chapters by Fenwick English, former director of the Temple City, California, and Mesa, Arizona, staff differentiation projects. Chapter 1 reveals a rationale for changing school staffing patterns and an examination of a fundamental dilemma regarding an approach to such change. Staffing patterns are reviewed in their historical evolution, and the implications of that evolution on instruction, curriculum, and organization are shown. The differences between merit pay and standard salary schedules are highlighted and the early impetus of attempting to save money by changing traditional staffing is discussed. Chapter 1 closes with a review of generic models of staffing and an analysis of traditional staffing assumptions.

Chapter 2 explores the functions of staffing in a bureaucratic organization and delves into related organizational and sociological theories used in classifying staffing patterns. Implications of and relationships to the control system and the role of the school administrator from this vantage are presented.

Chapter 3 illustrates the controversial issues pertaining to the idea of staff differentiation and examines its early rationale as advocated by Dwight Allen. It separates the differentiated staffing movement into two generations for additional comparisons and analyses. Of particular interest should be English's comments on the AFT-NEA positions on staff differentiation. The chapter concludes with a presentation of an "organic" differentiated staffing model.

Chapter 4 deals with the problems of implementation. Teacher reaction, from the earliest AFT response in Temple City to big city implementation in the District of Columbia, is discussed. The practical problems of relating staffing to pupil needs are reviewed. A possible reconciliation is related between staffing and some principles of programmed instruction. Methods found partially successful in involving parents are also presented.

1 A Rationale for Change

Fenwick English

So what's *wrong* with the way we've been staffing schools? This question is always asked, whether directly or by implication. The voice inflection of defensive teachers, worried parents, uptight principals, and puzzled board members carries many messages, but they all boil down to a fear of change. So many project directors and teacher association leaders who have just negotiated a nonsalaried item stating, for example, "The Association and the Administration will cooperatively study the implications of differentiated staffing," ask: "How do you introduce the concept to colleagues and interested citizens for the first time?" Even introducing the concept is often construed negatively since to some it means that what we have been doing in education was somehow wrong.

There is nothing *wrong* with the way we have been staffing schools; no sacred principles have been violated or transgressed; no moral commandment has been broken. It is like asking, "What's wrong with a 1929 Ford?" Certainly, there is nothing morally wrong with a 1929 Ford, except that today, with increased knowledge of travel, a 1929 Ford is neither the safest, most economical, nor the most pleasurable automobile on the road. But it works and there is nothing *wrong* with it.

The second affective message sent by those who are broached with the idea of studying an alternative to present staffing of public schools is, "If you can *prove* it's better than what we have now, we will consider this alternative." The irony of this comment is that it is impossible to prove how efficient the present staffing patterns of schools are (except that they work and we have been using them for over 100 years) simply because they were not selected at some remote date in the past on the basis of any systematic comparison or study of alternatives.

Staffing patterns in schools evolved. Like Topsy, they just "growed." It is impossible to know whether their growth assumed any kind of desired or efficient form. So many of the assumptions that support our staffing patterns in schools arose by default because our educational ancestors never did examine the alternatives. They never brainstormed, set up research studies, tested theoretical alternatives, compared organizational inputs (salaries, books, equipment) to organizational outputs (what children can do, what they feel, how successful they were in society after leaving the school). No attempts were made to select the best combinations of time, space, and teacher/pupil relationships to achieve the highest form of organizational productivity. We don't know how effective our staffing patterns in public schools are today. We have good reason to suspect that they inhibit effective teaching and learning in schools. We can examine the assumptions that support present staffing practices, ascertain how they came into being, and examine their effects on teachers and students.

The best we can do perhaps is to "prove" that we need to search for staffing alternatives; then we can go about creating and implementing those alternatives and compare them to what exists. The creation of alternative staffing patterns is the only way to prove or disprove the merits of present practices. The traditionalist needs the alternatives as much as the innovator. Neither can demonstrate anything without a basis for comparison, which the other would provide. The professional is obligated, and every citizen with a stake in improving the schools should be interested, in exploring questions that pertain to making the schools become more humane, productive, and efficient in using resources provided by society. Regardless of the outcome, we are obligated to compare and analyze the alternatives as a first step toward implementing changes. But how do we go about implementing such changes?

CHANGE PEOPLE OR STRUCTURE?

Theodore White wrote a short piece on New York's Mayor John Lindsay when he changed his party affiliation from Republican to Democrat. White spoke of Lindsay's insight into human organization and change.

> What had he learned in the year? He answered in passion: the city was there for service—but to give service you had to fight with the tyrants of the bureaucracies who thought that government was there only to give them jobs. "The most difficult thing," he said, "is to change structures and people."[1]

If the word "city" were changed to "school district" and "government" changed to "education," the passage would accurately describe the major dilemma facing American public school systems today.

There appear to be two camps of thought on how to go about changing schools. The *humanist* camp ignores or plays down the effects of structure and emphasizes understanding, love, group process, greater sensitivity toward children, etc. The *structuralists* place their energies on building in flexibility, choice, and "openness" in schools, ignoring the tendency of people to make decisions without being influenced by organizational structure.

Any approach that ignores the importance of the other is not satisfactory. How many times have teachers in one set of organizational norms and assumptions been sent away to be "trained," and return to the home environment only to become resocialized and impotent to bring about desired changes. On the other hand, how many educators have been shown through a "modern" school built with flexibility in mind and observed lock-step teaching that negates the openness. Change may be initiated either from the environmental viewpoint or from concentrating upon adult-pupil or adult-adult relationships. Structure should emerge to suit the needs of people and foster better human relationships in the organization. Too often structure is assumed to be inviolate and unchangeable. Change from the structural viewpoint must be initiated by recognizing that only a limited amount of human behavior can be altered without working over the "people problems" at the same time. The greatest danger of the structural tack is that by concentrating upon the inanimate, people can become means to ends. In the most severe cases, people are manipulated and coerced in the name of "progress." The means to an end are as important as the end itself. At both ends of the people/structure continuum, incredible naivete prevails. If schools are structural prisons, all the love in the world cannot create missed opportunities. If no love or sensitivity to each other is present, the most modern facility with the most up-to-date concepts is cold, impersonal, and lifeless.

An early case by Snyder best illustrates this dilemma.[2] She defended the self-contained classroom structure because of its possibilities for permitting the teacher to perform certain functions, though "it is obvious that creating a self-contained classroom does not in itself result in positive gains in the teaching-learning process."[3] Snyder argued for the self-contained structure on the basis of what could transpire in it, and not because it was intrinsically a "better" type of structure (irrespective of the humans inhabiting that structure). It may be impossible to admit that a problem exists in such a structure, since "a closed system of truth, once established, is beyond internal correction because it is self-confirming even in its errors."[4]

In an insightful essay, Kuhn probed the structure of scientific revolutions and noted that various scientific fields develop paradigms, i.e., certain constructs, notions, and theories that those working in the field accept without much question as they solve "puzzles."[5] When the existing paradigm becomes cumbersome in explaining phenomena, the validity of the paradigm comes into question. In working with various paradigms or mind sets, some problems are

rejected as metaphysical, as the concern of another discipline, or sometimes as just too problematic to be worth the time. A paradigm can, for that matter, even insulate the community from those socially important problems that are not reducible to the puzzle form, because they cannot be stated in terms of the conceptual and instrumental tools the paradigm supplies.[6]

Educators and citizens who are concerned with improving schools most often prescribe solutions that accept the validity of the present structure of schools and their concomitant staffing patterns. Improvements are suggested around this structure. For example, a nonpartisan survey by various Republican women's units in Arizona (337 questionnaires returned) showed that Arizonans wanted more of the three Rs, more relevant courses, more vocational training, prayer and Bible in the schools, and physical education for all.[7] They expressed concern for more financial support for teachers and their training, more classroom aides, and less federal involvement. All of these are viewed as possible within the existing structure, since it is never questioned. This book and much of the topical literature on staff differentiation call into question the assumptions that support the current definition and presumed validity of traditional school staffing patterns. Some of these assumptions need to be challenged. Indeed, there is little sense in analyzing staffing alternatives unless one perceives a problem with the present structure.

THE BASIC BUILDING BLOCK OF PRESENT SCHOOL STAFFING PATTERNS

Snyder's work is cogent from another perspective because it highlights the most fundamental and pervasive barrier to change in public school staffing patterns—the concept of the single teacher per class. This idea has been firmly accepted and is at the root of a way of thinking about what teachers do with students in schools. Upon it have been promulgated generations of personnel policies, textbooks, procedural rules, parental expectations, and notions of advancement in teaching. Schools of education have formed training courses vis-a-vis this concept of student teaching and the definition of a "superior" teacher. The entire system of schools rests solidly on the concept of one teacher for thirty (or fewer) pupils, with the pupils sorted and grouped on the basis of their chronological ages.

Educators and citizens interested in pursuing staffing alternatives need to make a thorough study of how this single-teacher-per-class concept came into being and how completely it dominates the thinking of professionals in attempting to create more responsive human interrelationships in schools. Even modern critics often accept this structure without questioning its assumptions.[8] Many staffing studies have begun and ended with an examination of pupil-teacher ratios, never bothering to question more fundamental issues.

First, the idea of a single-teacher-per-age-graded-group is an invented concept that developed over a long period of time. It represents an evolutionary continuum of organizational development for schools in the absence of any rigorous research or data-gathering activities. Although the Quincy Grammar School of 1848 is usually cited as the beginning of the current definition, the roots of the idea can be found in the work of the German educator Johann Sturm (1507-89) when he founded the gymnasium at Strassburg. Cubberley notes that Sturm probably adopted his idea from the French colleges.[9] Sturm organized the gymnasium into ten classes, one for each year the pupil was in school and provided each class with a teacher. Sturm's gymnasium was visited by scholars and educators from all over Europe and the structure spread very rapidly, having been adopted by the Jesuits.[10] The significant difference between Sturm's gymnasium and the Quincy Grammar School was that in the latter, pupils were sorted and assigned to teachers within specialized subjects. Prior to that point teachers had been "differentiated" by subject or skill areas, but students remained a heterogeneous group. Cubberley observes how in the elementary schools the subjects of instruction were divided among the teachers rather than the children.

> A common division was between the teacher who taught reading, religion, and spelling, and the teacher who taught writing and arithmetic. Writing being considered a difficult art, this was taught by a separate teacher, who often included the ability to teach arithmetic also among his accomplishments.[11]

In the Lancastrian schools, which later came to dominate eastern and southern school systems in the United States, children were advanced individually and by subjects as their progress warranted, "until they had progressed as far as the instruction went, or the teacher could teach."[12]

The "modern" elementary school is the product of several organizational changes that began by having three separate schools coming together under one roof.

> The next step was the division of each school into classes. This began by the employment of assistant teachers, in England and America known as "ushers," to help the "master," and the provision of small recitation rooms, off the main large schoolroom, to which the usher could take his class to hear recitations. The third and final step came with the erection of a new type of school building, with smaller and individual schoolrooms. It was then possible to assign a teacher to each classroom, sort and grade the pupils by ages and advancement, outline the instruction by years, and the modern graded elementary school was at hand.[13]

Thus, the current definition of the role of classroom teacher was born, and with it were created a host of problems that have yet to be solved.

Instructional Implications

The instructional implications of the historical turn of events doomed any further teacher specialization by subject or skill areas at the primary levels. All teachers were expected to teach all subjects. It may have been possible to train teachers in the nineteenth century to be "master generalists." However, the proliferation of knowledge alone in the twentieth century and the juxtaposition of the teacher and the television set as dispensers of information have spelled the obsolescence of the self-contained classroom teacher. The lack of mastery of many discrete disciplines of knowledge also hampers current trends toward interdisciplinary teaching. It was the same difficulty that killed the idea of the *core* curriculum efforts in this country. Cross-disciplinary teaching, postholing, or whatever it may be called, requires the training of a skilled scholar. It requires someone who understands the inquiry structures of the particular discipline and who can relate such skills to teaching children in applied settings. Most teachers are still trying to compete with the mass media. Silberman deplores the fact that the teaching functions of the mass media have largely been ignored by the education professions.[14]

The single-teacher-per-class concept based on alleged pupil homogeneity of age was invented some fifty years prior to the concept of intelligence quotient (I.Q.), in which the concomitant notion of pupil mental age was established.[15] Early nineteenth-century educators were only dimly aware of vast differences among children and invented a structure which was impervious to such differences. It is ironic that this same structure now is sometimes advocated as one that best meets individual needs.[16]

Goodlad and Anderson aver:

> The realities of child development defy the rigorous ordering of children's abilities and attainments into conventional graded structure. For example, in the average first grade there is a spread of four years in pupil readiness to learn as suggested by mental age data. As the pupils progress through the grades, the span in readiness widens. Furthermore, a single child does not progress all of a piece: he tends to spurt ahead more rapidly in some areas than in others.[17]

The ordering of schools into classrooms based upon yearly, semesterly, or quarterly uniform progress defies all that is known about learning. It fosters practices that are oblivious to motivation or responsive teaching. Educational progress can be easily administered and scored. In the absence of real learning, pseudo-learning is assessed by the orderly accrual of units and credits, marks of time served rather than in actual learning. In this sense, the more primitive Lancastrian school was far more sensitive to students.

The single-teacher-per-class concept has promoted a type of instruction that is group based. Teaching to small groups for extended periods and regrouping by actual achievement is not a dominant form of instructional practice. Teaching consists mainly of talking or telling to groups of between twenty-five and thirty children for periods or segments of the school day, divided into time for spelling, arithmetic, social studies, physical education, and the like at the elementary level. The impact upon the instructional program has been a nonachievement-based school in which materials for one grade are jealously guarded by teachers for fear of encroachment into their "territory." Pupil interests and abilities are flattened out in order to make the system work smoothly. Promotion does not represent achievement; it represents time served.

If teachers were to pretest their classes on what they already knew, they would find a range of differences almost impossible to deal with for instructional purposes. Pretesting is not required; the teacher may pretest, but the system does not provide for differences or alternatives across grade levels. In some school systems teachers are forbidden to use materials above or below the grade in which they teach.

Curricular Implications

The Lancastrian school was perhaps the original differentiated staff in the United States. It contained a series of instructional positions occupied by both students and teachers. These were the tutor, the assistant, the teacher, the sub-usher, the usher, and the master. Responsibilities of these roles varied for teachers and students alike, i.e., they were *differentiated*. The pervasive influence of the Lancastrian school was not upon its personnel hierarchy, which was sacrificed to a flatter personnel structure embodied in the self-contained classroom, but upon the ruthless way the curriculum was cut into parts.

The spell of Lancaster has hindered all reform movements. Pestalozzian methods, which were supposed to be used in the infant schools, were cast in the Lancasterian mold. The imparting of information rather than training in observation and eliciting of thought became the aim. There was developed a catechetical method of teaching which could readily be acquired by the monitor or the unskilled teacher. With the introduction of the higher studies into the grammar grades, a similar adjustment was made to the capacity of the monitorial type of teacher. The chopping up of all subject matter into easy mechanical stages, and the estimation of the pupil's attainments on the basis of memory became the almost universal practice.[18]

The rigidity of the Lancastrian school, in which student learning positions were uniformly prescribed, lives on in the curriculums of today's schools. Many elementary school teachers still follow a standard subject-matter time schedule throughout the day and do not teach beyond the confines of the provided textbooks. This type of approach to curriculum development was preserved in the self-contained classroom where each teacher was virtually hidden and isolated from every other teacher. Interaction among teachers is strictly circumscribed, if not by design by default. Teaching has become known as the lonely profession and colleague interaction is confined to the faculty lounge. Teachers sometimes have difficulty dealing with each other. Indeed, one of the universal complaints by teachers when they begin moving toward a pooling of talents is the fear of offending each other or the expressed reservation of "ruining faculty morale," which can mean anything that disturbs the status quo. The complete absence of training in group dynamics at teacher preparatory institutions leaves teachers unprepared to face each other and work through, rather than avoid, professional conflict. The boxlike structure of the traditional school reinforces a strictly enforced (spatially and otherwise) egalitarianism that is largely indifferent to actual teacher performance or pupil need. The graded school demands a graded structure and a graded curriculum. The result is graded achievement and graded performance. What is lost with this system is the necessity for diagnosis of the pupil and the subsequent need of the organization to allocate resources (teachers) on the basis of that need. Diagnosis is unnecessary in graded schools. The most important thing one needs to know about the pupil is his birthday. One critic is said to have remarked that "astrology is the fundamental basis for public schools." It is no wonder that an individualized curriculum is largely mythical.

Organizational Implications

The movement toward graded schools happened at a time when the population of the cities was mushrooming. The single-teacher-per-class concept became embedded as the fundamental building block in the growth of schools as bureaucracies. It is easier to administer a system where there are fewer exceptions to policy than one in which diversity makes uniformity of operation more difficult. The need is for conformity by definition. As the desire for coordination and administrative organization became more and more apparent with size (a relationship now established empirically by Blau),[19] new roles became established in a hierarchical format. For example, the principal-teacher role eventually led to the position of superintendent. The lack of expertise with instruction by school principals led to formation of the role of supervisor.[20] What should be carefully observed is that, in the formation of new roles previously unknown in the organization, the self-contained definition of the teacher was the cornerstone. New roles were created to solve administrative and coordination problems, mostly for organizational needs (a trend followed in early models of staff differentiation), and were tacked onto the role of classroom teacher as organizationally defined. Substantial portions of the teaching role in the self-contained classroom did not become more specialized, but merely served as a base for expansion of administrative roles. One of the consequences was the lack of a teaching career ladder, a series of career offices by which the organization maintained some hold on its most talented practitioners. A promotion in education always did and still does lead away from the basic role definition of the self-contained classroom teacher, elementary or secondary. The monotony and drudgery of teaching stems not only from the maintenance of a punitive-centered, authoritarian, control-oriented posture by adults in the school, but also from repeating the same things, using the same textbooks, breaking open the same "canned" bulletin board displays year in and year out. For this reason the self-contained classroom has been facetiously labeled the "self-contaminated" classroom.

Another organizational implication is more subtle and perhaps more visible to students of organizational theory. In discussing the division of work, March and Simon note that it is "a problem of efficient allocation of activities among individuals and among organizational units."[21] They contend that there is a problem of specialization not only among people, but also among organizational units. Questions of economy and predictability of specialization arise as an aspect of deciding which programs can be repeated, simply because training (pre-service and in-service) represents a cost that is not practical unless well utilized. Schools are located far apart physically and coordination is potentially difficult. "The greater the specialization by subprograms (process specialization) the greater the interdependencies among organizational subunits.[22] The problem of interdependence does not cause difficulty, March and Simon note, "if the pattern of interdependence is stable and fixed. . . . Difficulties arise only if program execution rests on contingencies that cannot be predicted perfectly in advance."[23] A predictable situation is created between school units by age-grading pupils and assigning teachers by class and subject. Mandated materials further produce stability and order to match specified curricula and the problems of coordination and need for interdependency are reduced. Units may remain self-contained and autonomous physically with low administrative costs, with coordination achieved by standardization, i.e., interchangeable teachers, students and curricula. Schools have a low order of specialization. Greater specialization would increase coordination problems and problems of interdependency. There is an administrative need for maintaining a minimum level of teacher specialization, or at least an organizational "lid" over what the system will recognize and use. Put another way, the system which standardizes learning is easier to run. Standardization is achieved by placing limits on specialization, and by maintaining very little differentiation in teacher and pupil assignments.

Standard Salary Schedules and Merit Pay

Teachers have been serving on fixed salaries since 376 A.D. when the Roman Emperor Gratian fixed teacher salary schedules throughout the Empire.[24] The American standard salary schedule has come to be defined as ". . . based upon two elements—experience and preparation. It does not distinguish on the bases of grade levels or subjects taught, marital status or number of dependents or sex."[25] The standard salary schedule also evolved from an earlier time when each teacher would bargain for his salary with a board of education.

A teacher is not paid for performance or responsibility; he is paid to get older on the job and to collect Carnegie units which he exchanges for college degrees. In addition, extra pay for extra duty is usually attached to nonteaching responsibilities, except coaching, driver education, band, etc. Teacher salaries based on the standard salary schedule have been roundly attacked[26] and stoutly defended.[27] A frequent alternative posed is merit pay. Basically, under merit pay plans, the "superior" teacher is paid a higher wage. No distinction is made between paying him more for additional responsibilities, but only because his performance has been dubbed superior.

The standard salary schedule is a merit pay schedule without any qualitative indicators that are good predictors of quality teaching; in other words experience and college degrees are poor indicators of teacher effectiveness.[28] However, teachers are paid a vastly dissimilar amount for doing the same job on the basis of an automatic criterion, but on a qualitative basis nonetheless. While there is differentiation of salary, there is no differentiation of the basic job responsibilities. Steffensen felt that there are at least three bases other than the standard salary schedule which would provide additional salary differentiation. First, there should be differentiation on the basis of current imbalances in supply and demand. If current salary schedules cannot compete with industry for math or physics teachers, there should be extra factors added.[29] This consideration was earlier argued by Lieberman.[30] Secondly, Steffensen noted that greater differentiation of assignment within teaching staffs should be considered. "With such a differentiation—e.g., team teachers, teaching aides—there can be provided position specifications which establish different degrees of responsibility and hence, a differentiated salary on the basis of the level of responsibility."[31] Finally, the third approach was "differentiating salaries on the basis of differentiated levels of teaching effectiveness, with that effectiveness to be defined through an evaluation of the teacher's level of performance with respect to certain locally established criteria."[32] To this latter alternative the name "merit pay" is usually ascribed.

Steffensen raises the question of the efficacy of experience after five to seven years as a valid base for the differentiation of salary. "It can be assumed, for example, that with a strong recruitment program and a thorough evaluation program prior to placement on tenure, a district can establish a core of highly competent teachers. And, that after x number of years, the performance levels of these teachers are not distinguishable within the classroom."[33] Differentiated staffing and merit pay are frequently confused. Many teachers assume that differentiated staffing means the addition of more stringent qualitative criteria to the standard salary schedule which contains the essence of a merit pay approach without such criteria. In some cases differentiated staffing and merit pay have been proposed as joint innovations.[34] Experience has demonstrated that differentiated salaries, differentiated staffing, and differentiated instruction are not synonymous. Each may describe a separate and distinct practice. This will be worth comment later.

Much of the early impetus for differentiated staffing was the search for a salary alternative. The Council for Basic Education (CBE) has reviewed descriptions of current merit pay programs in Barrington, Illinois; Ladue, Missouri; Summit, New Jersey; and Ithaca, New York and contrasted those with a differentiated staff as represented in the Temple City model.[35] CBE preferred flat merit pay, but noted that critical support from the NEA (now on the wane) gave differentiated staffing a better chance of ultimate approval by teachers. "The attractiveness of the more-pay-for-more-responsibility schemes (differentiated staffing, team teaching, school improvement, etc.) reflects both the need to break out of the single salary schedule and the opposition to straightforward merit pay programs."[36]

The influential Citizens League of Minneapolis-St. Paul openly endorsed the concept of staff differentiation as a money-saving device which could also usher in needed new administrative and management practices. The Citizens League recommended the following:

1. Establish a differentiated staffing plan for the instructional staff in the public schools, by which personnel are classified according to their different jobs and levels of responsibility and compensated accordingly;

2. Establish a systematic method of evaluating the performance of personnel in various types of jobs to provide an acceptable basis for determining promotions and for granting tenure according to the caliber of performance;

3. After establishment of differentiated staffing, use the techniques of supervision and evaluation which were developed for the differentiated plan to determine the extent to which—within a given job classification—some compensation can be based on caliber of performance;

4. Abolish arbitrary salary levels for personnel who transfer from other school systems, to assure freedom of mobility for instructional personnel and freedom for a school board to hire personnel it desires;

5. Provide a mechanism, outside the framework of the teachers' council, which negotiates salaries whereby teachers can have a continuing, meaningful participation in the decision-making process on educational matters;

6. Adopt twelve-month salary schedules for teachers and adjust salaries for fewer months of employment;

7. Give greater emphasis to separating the roles of the professional educators from the business administrators in the public schools;

8. Develop improved budget-fiscal information systems to make possible the identification of program costs, the extent of program costs and the extent to which program objectives are achieved;

9. Provide for continuing, formal contact and area-wide planning among school boards in the Twin Cities metropolitan area on matters of mutual concern.[37]

The Citizens League was obviously concerned about the rising costs of education and the lack of accountability of personnel within the organization, particularly teachers. When the report was released, there was consternation in the Twin Cities by teachers who feared that the overwhelming motive of the League was to "save money." However, it appears the League's concern was also aimed toward relating teacher performance to pay and to some extent greater efficiency for the schools. The League's recommendations were stated some years earlier by school economist Charles Benson:

> The responsibilities of a professional position in education have not been clearly defined. In a school district it is often difficult to determine where the responsibility of the classroom teachers ends and the responsibilities of the directors, coordinators, supervisors, consultants, principals, and various catagories of superintendent begin. Such lack of classification can be distracting to those who are honestly seeking to carry on the work of the system; it can also be a subterfuge for the avoidance of responsibility. The most important effect of this lack of definition is that schools have never arrived at an effective division of labor, under which each person spends most of his working day at those tasks—but only those tasks—that call upon his highest skills (natural and acquired).[38]

A New Cult of Efficiency?

Raymond Callahan has documented rather dramatically how concerns of business and industry for "efficiency" produced a new cult in American education by applying public and professional pressure on school administrators.[39] Once "efficiency" was a means to an end; during some decades it became an end in itself. The only questions asked of school administrators were how much money was saved the taxpayers. No school administrator working with differentiated staffing has made such claims, though at least one said several times that differentiated staffing should not cost "more" than traditional staffing.[40] The question raised here is, is efficiency a bad word? Does an economic motive rule out examining alternatives? Some teacher leaders believe that to be the case. That differentiated staffing may be more efficient makes it a new panacea since any saving would necessarily affect teachers' salaries—that is where 80-90 percent of the costs of education occur. We believe, however, that Callahan is right when he notes that efficiency must be judged in terms of an institution's functions. The functions of a school as a social institution are to serve a special type of client (nonadults). Efficiency must not be based chiefly on how to give students a mass dosage of something called "education," but rather on determining what students need to function in our society, grow up to be self-actualizing persons and lead productive lives. The means toward those ends may be judged on many criteria, chiefly on the outcomes of how well they actually produce the results in terms of costs, harmony with approved social means, and other related benefits to clients and/or community.

When staffing patterns are measured as to whether they are "efficient," any ultimate judgment must be based on how well the school is achieving its purposes, not on how much money was saved. Schools can become more sensitive to their clients if they possess the capacity of specialization based upon the needs of those clients. The degree of specialization required in a school must first be determined by analyzing its clients and the peculiar functions of the school itself, as well as its objectives.

Too often, educators are left to define the base of specialization necessary, irrespective of purpose, objectives, or the needs of the students in question. Because increased specialization may cause a serious reexamination of present staffing and teaching practices, it is argued that specialization is detrimental to the "best" interests of children. Some educators hide behind the children they believe they are serving adequately without any further specialization. Some elementary teachers deny the need for any further specialization by labeling all such concerns attempts to "departmentalize" the elementary school.

There is a relationship between the degree of labor specialization in an organization and its productivity. Burkhead contends that every economic system becomes more efficient as it becomes more specialized. "Specialization brings the increase in productivity that characterizes a developing economy."[41] Burkhead summarizes the level of specialization in the schools:

> In elementary and secondary education, contrasted with other professions, there has been relatively little specialization of skills, particularly in the teaching process itself. The failure of elementary and secondary education to develop such specialized teaching inputs gives rise to suspicion that there has been very little improvement in the productivity of education over time.[42]

Burkhead hypothesizes that team teaching would permit salary differentiation in accordance with responsibility and would help to boost salary ceilings for teachers. He supports the allegation that schools currently have a low level of specialization, noting that specialization creates a need for more interdependence. We have already pointed out that schools as self-contained units are kept interdependent with a uniform curriculum and lock-step grouping of students by age grading. Such a posture mandates that teachers be utilized within uniform personnel policies. There is a direct relationship between recognizing much client diversity and providing the necessary organizational specialization to meet such diversity. Teacher assignments are impervious to client differences. Teachers are thus overwhelmed with "unrecognized" diversity which is presented in an undifferentiated student body. Students are already differentiated. It is the schools which are not; they seek to avoid recognizing the need for diversity because many of the school problems with discipline, attendance, boredom, and antipathy are symptoms of schools that are organized and responsive only to the age of the student. Although schools recognize many other indicators of learning, the 1848 criterion of chronological age is still the dominant force behind placement, promotion, or "success." The assignment of a single teacher to groups of age-graded pupils sterilizes the potential utilization of staff talent in forming teacher/student groups. Current assumptions about what a school is and how it should be organized are the most crippling and debilitating barriers to more humane and effective school staffing.

Are Schools Less Productive?

Part of the problem in determining whether schools are more or less productive is that "productivity" is very difficult to define. A shoe factory could be judged on the number of shoes it produces and the cost per shoe. Chris Argyris' definition, from the organization's viewpoint, is that an organization is effective if, when outputs are increased, inputs stay the same or even decrease.[43] An ineffective organization is one in which increased inputs produce the same or decreased outputs. Woodhall and Blaug constructed alternative measures of output for British secondary schools during 1950-1963, including an economic index of how much school students earned upon leaving the institution, the length of schooling index, and an academic index of the "academic" achievement level of students.[44] The "inputs" were teacher time in terms of salaries, pupils' time, costs of school buildings, and the use of books, stationery and other materials. The authors concluded their analyses as follows:

> If our index adequately measures the output and quality of secondary education the productivity of education is declining, whereas the productivity of most other sectors of the economy is rising. This means that education is becoming increasingly costly relative to other goods and services. As schools have to compete with other sectors of the economy for resources, they will find it increasingly expensive even to maintain present standards and doubly difficult to raise standards or expand provision.[45]

A Labor Intensive Hangup

To increase the quality of education, most educators think immediately of smaller classes. Yet there is a conspicuous lack of solid research indicating that smaller classes will alone result in greater productivity. Most of our solutions to the question run along the lines of hiring "more" people to augment the present organizational structure. We do not usually conceptualize the need to reexamine who is doing what in the organization and redistribute task responsibilities on the basis of skill or need. Teachers and administrators do not look beyond the confines of the self-contained classroom, but instead hire more "specialists." More people doing the same thing holds little promise for educational improvement. Perhaps the same people doing different things will prove more promising. It seems candid to admit that an approach whereby tasks are redistributed will be resisted. The temptation to simply hire more teachers to do the same thing will be increased as teacher groups pressure legislatures. Such an approach should be resisted without evidence that merely repeating the same assumptions and practices of the last one hundred years is justified.

Bowman has reviewed methods by economists used in educational planning which are germane to the assertions of the authors in this text.[46] If staffing patterns are indeed means to ends and to be considered "inputs," it behooves educational planners to become as sophisticated as possible with economic concepts. For example, Bowman lists "manpower planning models" which attempt to focus projection on manpower requirements at some future target date. Another type of model employed is the one previously discussed, i.e., "the input-output model." The stress of these models is on the "supply side; indeed some models assume that the supply of skills from the educational system is independent of any sort of economic decision making."[47] The third type of model is a "social benefit/cost analysis" one. "These are essentially rate-of-return or present-value methods applied to analysis of investments in the expansion of one or another level of schooling, type of curriculum, or scheme of compensatory education."[48] Bowman cites "linear programming models" as the fourth type of model which attempts to "maximize attainment of some 'objective function' subject to linear constraints."[49] Another function of model comparison is to illustrate that the elementary "black-box" design model is only a starting point in the examination of the effectiveness of a staffing pattern. Sociology, psychology, social psychology, management and organizational theory, economics and related disciplines need to be analyzed for their relationship to staffing schools.

Models of Staffing Patterns

The first conceptual model presented is an attempt to identify the elements of a staffing model. Together the components compose a school. The model in Figure 1 identifies content, process and structure as the three major variables.[50] A staffing pattern is a combination of time, space and people. A staffing pattern is invisible. The closest approximation to a staffing pattern is a schedule which incorporates time, place (or space) and people (teachers, pupils, aides, etc.). Process refers to the modes of instruction and various types of pupil/teacher interaction patterns. These patterns have been barely developed with such primitive devices as micro-teaching or the Flanders interaction analysis system. Content represents the "what" of the school. No one learns in a vacuum. The hinging activities, units, constraints, is the "what."

FIGURE 1

Model Showing Relationship of a Staffing Pattern to
Structure and Other School Related Components

Structure
(time, space, staff)

The
School

Process
(modes and interaction
pupil/teacher-patterns
of school)

Content
("subject matter" or "curriculum")

The second generic model of a staffing pattern appeared in the
ISR Journal.[51] In this paradigm Roger Kaufman's system model[52]
served as a base from which one of the results was the creation of a
specific type of organizational atmosphere or "climate" employing
Halpin's empirical definition.[53] From the climate, which was under-
girded by a host of managerial assumptions, some founded on principles such as McGregor's theory X, theory Y bifurcation, was
derived the control system.[54] This system of rewards and non-
rewards was used to attain desired organizational behavior from
which would emerge a staffing pattern. A staffing pattern was therefore a representation of:
(a) assumptions regarding the utilization of time, space, people,
    curricular content and a selection of a methodology;
(b) assumptions regarding man and what motivates man;
(c) a system of "controls" to accompany assumptions from "a" and
    "b";
From the model in Figure 2, it can be seen that staffing patterns are
a series of interrelated parts, each dependent upon the other. It is
possible to install flexible scheduling, large/small group instruction,
programmed instruction and other "technological" innovations
without actually changing anything. The fundamental value captured
in the procedures has not changed, only the technology. It is possible

FIGURE 2

Generic Model Showing Relationship Between Critical Assumptions/
Organizational Climate/Control System and a Staffing Pattern

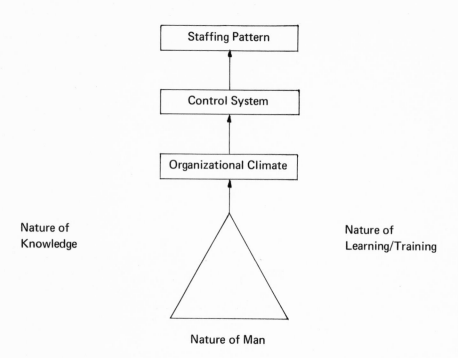

Nature of Man

for increased specialization to become more rigid and authoritarian. Figure 3 attempts to reconcile the first two models.[55] In Figure 2, it appears that the organizational climate and the control system are two sides of the same coin, extremely difficult to separate. What is missing is the entire mechanism by which the informal and formal organization is joined, or the social communication network of the informal organization. In Figure 3, a closer relationships is drawn between the control system and a staffing pattern, since it would be impossible to install the latter when it is not congruent with the former. Deployment can be a reward or a punishment. It can unlock the key to status and power in an organization. Generic Model III appears to separate the ambiguity between "power" and "authority." Too often conceptualizations of models were begun from only the viewpoint of changing the "formal" organization—the

FIGURE 3

Model Showing Relationship Between Critical Variables
and Assumptions in Viewing a Staffing Pattern

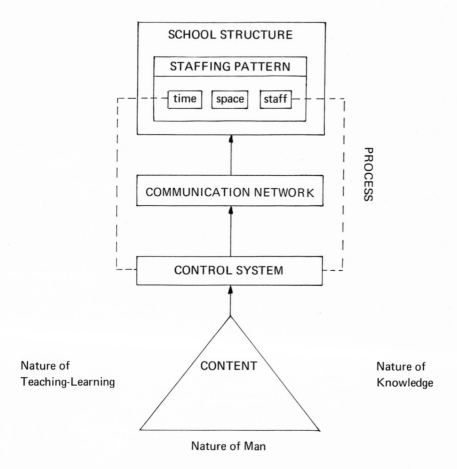

positions of the organizational flow chart. This change is a form of bureaucratic office shuffling which most people know results in little, if any, real behavioral change. Within the communication network are various subgroups, professional, social and others. The way an organization runs on paper and the way it really functions may not be the same. The former is the formal organization and the latter the informal. The formal organization is the legitimate, the legal organization, which is set into ranks and clear-cut divisions of authority contained in offices. Such authority may be distinguished from power, which is the force which "gets things done." In some professional and scientific organizations the force which gets things done is more spontaneous and emergent than in other organizations, and the people comprising the actual work force may cut across many levels of the organization.

The informal organizational structure moves the organization. It can facilitate or hinder the goals of the organization. As such it exerts tremendous influence. This often unrecognized social matrix can be ignored only at great risk. Paul Lawrence stated that the reason why innovation was unpopular in some quarters of the organization was that it threatened a social change.[56] If innovations will not alter social relationships, they are often adopted rapidly. If they threaten such relationships, they may be rejected or severely resisted. Resistance may take many forms, from overt and open hostility to widespread apathy. One measure of organizational "health" may be the extent to which the formal and informal organizations represent the same set of offices and positions. The response by administrators and those in charge of implementing differentiated staffing is often to marshal more organizational muscle when groups appear to be stubborn, hostile, or apathetic. As Lawrence notes, this makes little sense.

The key to the problem is to understand the true nature of resistance. . . . To use a rough analogy, signs of resistance in a social organization are useful in the same way that pain is useful to the body as a signal that some bodily functions are getting out of adjustment. The resistance, like the pain, does not tell what is wrong but only that something is wrong. And it makes no more sense to try to overcome such resistance than it does to take a pain killer without diagnosing the bodily ailment . . . What is needed is not a long harangue on the logics of the new recommendations but a careful exploration of the difficulty.[57]

There have been "flaps" in districts moving toward staff differentiation. Indeed, they have followed a rhythm of early resistance due to proposed changes in the social structure, changes in the salary mechanism, antagonism toward the innovators due to personality differences, and professional jealousies. What is difficult to separate is resistance due to the "normal" reluctance by people to accept change, and resistance against the innovation's violating fundamental laws of human nature. The latter are not always visible, and they may be invisible during the early stages of implementing something new. When resistance is encountered, a careful review is necessary.

Some types of resistance can be plotted, others will develop over a long period. Even those, however, must be carefully scrutinized. For example, continuous anxiety and fatigue may result from a transitional problem of "keeping up" or not anticipating each day what the demands may be. These are temporary longitudinal problems typical with project or model prototyping activities which lessen the second and third years.

What often leads administrators astray in implementing change is their ignorance of the fundamental mechanisms of the informal organization. What appears sometimes as irrational behavior is rather logical when knowledge regarding this aspect of organizational life is understood. Administrators may have difficulty relating to feelings because there is such an overemphasis at the administrative level on rationality as the dominant mode of problem solving. The rational mode need not be abandoned, but using logical reasoning to explain why something is better is useless if the person hearing it does not understand. If one of a teacher's great concerns is a fear for his status if new teacher roles come into existence, no amount of reasoning about the need for career ladders for the profession, the need for professional self-regulation of colleagues, or notions of "advanced" opportunities for *some* teachers are logical, because none of them directs itself to his "reasons" for resistance. A logical presentation which ignores his psychological state is mere semantics. Add to this another level, that of trust in the presentor himself, and he may indeed address his reasons to the teacher's feelings, but the teacher's suspicions of his motives can still outweigh the presentor's logic.

Our experience tells us that, time after time, administrators can out-argue teachers, intellectually out-point or intimidate them in their arguments against changing staffing patterns, but no change really occurs. People may adopt the new terminology to avoid being embarrassed or publicly chastened, but an analysis of their behavior indicates they have not changed at all. In actuality, the administrator "lost" because his verbal discourse resulted in closing off and silencing the opposition rather than in actually convincing them that the new approach was better. The administrator, then, will believe his arguments were effective because he hears no more opposition. Thus the repercussions will puzzle him. He may even feel they did not have the courage of their convictions to stand up and fight. Many times "feeling" problems cannot be verbalized, either because they are embarrassing or because the person does not know what is really bothering him. Such feelings may attach themselves to some issues, perhaps an extremely small issue. It is what is *not* being said that is the problem. A logical problem-solving approach is to probe for the deeper understanding of the meanings of teachers' perceptions. Perhaps there is no such thing as irrational behavior; what is really being said is that the observer doesn't understand the reasons for the behavior and therefore is revealing more about his own ignorance than the individual being observed.

The ultimate test for judging an innovation is whether it actually caused a behavioral change. Too often, an innovation is judged only if it has been implemented and maintained itself over a period of time. Too often the costs in human labor and money which are necessary to maintain what has been implemented are ignored or only partially costed. Too often we are insensitive or ignorant of the enormous personal costs which do not appear on the ledgers: poor morale, fatigue, subversion or discontent. This is a particular problem with a structural change. A successful change is not whether the new structure came into existence, but whether the behavior for which a new structure was created has changed. Schools can adopt modular-flexible scheduling or differentiated staffing without altering teacher behavior unless the behaviors desired are determined in advance and a structure created to facilitate their development.

A Closer Look at Traditional Staffing Patterns

What is wrong with traditional staffing patterns is that they meet some kinds of needs and ignore others. Alternatives should be judged as to what needs they meet and what needs they ignore. Perhaps the most damaging criticism of traditional staffing patterns is that they are contradictory to what we understand about how human beings learn. They are the products of an unscientific age, an age basically unaware of the range of diversity of human ability and talent. Consequently human needs, both student and teacher, are bypassed or dismissed. The natural need for humans towards spontaneity is virtually lost in the schools. Spontaneity is closely aligned with the motivation to learn. The apparent natural bent of the human being to follow his curiosity, to find out why, cannot easily be scheduled, nor does it lend itself to report cards, lectures, term papers, or workbooks. The elaborate standardizations of schools which satisfy basic needs of an organizational bureaucracy run counter to learning. Some youngsters lose their motivation for school in the third grade. One of the lessons they learn in grades K-3 is that they cannot follow their natural desire to learn what interests them. What students learn is that they must learn what the school, their teachers and their parents want them to learn first, and occasionally follow their own interests. However, if a priority has to be developed, the school prevails. The student learns to supress his own natural curiosity. He learns that a good student is dependent and does what he is told.

Variations from the traditional notion of the single-teacher-per-class concept began as early as 1862, but none has succeeded in replacing it on a large-scale basis. Despite at times a vociferous criticism of its Procrustean qualities, the self-contained classroom and the secondary departmentalized self-contained classroom are as strongly entrenched today as ever. The following is an exploration into some of the reasons for this:

1. *It is manageable.*

The self-contained, single-teacher-per-class concept is easy to administer, organize and fund. It is simple to translate to public school patrons who must invest in bonds to build schools and pay taxes for their support. Unfamiliar structures with a concomitant type of deviant architecture are subject to community criticism. The system is workable and taxpayers are familiar with its basic structure.

2. *Alternatives are not attractive.*

Many of the educational alternatives to this basic structure cost more money. Funds for teacher aides, subject area resource centers, media centers, small group rooms, etc., are still considered frills in many communities. Basic education is somehow translated into basic classrooms of four walls each. Callahan reviews the rise of the Platoon School as a serious challenger to the traditional school conceived from 1900 to 1925. The Platoon School, while economically cheaper, was shown not to be as educationally sound as its predecessor.[58]

3. *It is simple.*

Alternatives not only appear to be more costly, but they are more difficult to understand since they attempt to deal with many more variables. Translating the supposed advantages of varying school structures to the public is a risky business, running into professional language barriers and criticism of "progressivism."

4. *It is surrounded by "the good old days" ethos.*

A kind of myth has been built up about the self-contained classroom. Parents tend to forget their unpleasant experiences and remember "dear old Mrs. Peacock" in the fourth grade, or some other pleasant memory which serves to justify the entire structure being perpetuated.

5. *It is familiar.*

If teachers were convinced that some alternative was better, they could probably change the structure. The problem is the known is preferable, though flawed, to the unknown in which there is no promise or security. To a teacher who has functioned for many years in one structure and has learned how to get around or to get lost in that structure, proposals for change are not welcomed.

6. *Lack of "proof" something else will be better.*

Teachers and administrators often ask for "proof" that the alternative proposed is better than the traditional methods. However, in order to obtain such proof, the outputs of the system will need to be defined so as to provide a comparison of means to those ends. Spelling out the outcomes of education means a pinpointing of responsibility for producing such outcomes. These are resisted so that proof can never become a reality. In some places teacher groups have protested the writing of behavioral objectives and negotiated such activities out of existence.

7. *It is cheap.*

Looking at just the costs on the ledger of maintaining self-contained schools with a uniform set of textbooks and expectations, it is clearly the cheapest solution, since such costs are reimbursed by state aid. Moving toward alternatives with richer sources of materials to provide a greater diversity of learning materials for children is more expensive.

8. *There is a vested interest in perpetuating it.*

Millions of dollars are spent in textbooks alone which undergird the basic staffing patterns of public schools. State laws have been passed on assumptions regarding the proper role definition of a teacher. Probably, more importantly, administrative bureaucracies have proliferated on confining the scope of the teachers' responsibilities to four walls. Virtually all of the middle management positions were founded on the assumptions, once fact, that teachers needed a great deal of support services in minimum, basic ways. Such positions as supervisor, coordinator, and consultant continue to function on this much muted assumption. Proposing reexamination of the role of teacher to include a broader and more authoritative base makes many administrators become stout defenders of the traditional school. Changes in the role of teacher cause ripple effects throughout the system and will necessitate a redefinition of everyone's responsibilities.

9. *It is invisible.*

The assumptions of traditional staffing are rarely discussed; they are not visible like books, walls, lesson plans, report cards, and curriculum guides, all of which are established on those assumptions. We are used to dealing with the manifestations of staffing patterns rather than with them directly. It is like dealing with atoms; their properties are knowable, perhaps observable, but the atom itself is invisible. And that which is invisible tends not to be questioned. Inventing new solutions to problems is usually based on beginning from the same set of assumptions about what the role or responsibility of the teacher is within existing confines, rather than on beginning to question the assumptions which hold the present lock box structure together.

10. *It is safe.*

Traditional staffing patterns do meet some needs, for example, security needs. This should not be dismissed as unimportant, or scoffed at. Security needs are basic to professional operation. It is ironic that college professors often ridicule public school staffing patterns and salary schedules on one hand as offering a haven for the incompetent and the low-risk takers, but, on the other hand, do not propose abolishing a system of academic ranks, tenure, and faculty decision-making prerogatives that are basic to their security.

Security is necessary for several reasons. First, a professional must be somewhat unbiased in the recommendations he makes for a client. A certain amount of detachment is required for a professional to function most effectively. If a professional is too dependent upon the client, he may only prescribe what the client may accept, and not what he actually feels is in the best long-range interests of the client. Engel explored the degree of professional autonomy exercised by medical doctors noting that, "The professional should be able to alter typical procedures or instigate changes necessary for the solution of the specific problem."[59] Engel concluded her research by illustrating that physicians in moderately bureaucratic settings perceived themselves to be more autonomous than those physicians in private practice or in highly bureaucratic settings.

The organizational physicians probably had more control than the solo physicians because they did not depend directly upon patients for their income. Since the solo physicians' clients paid for each service rendered and were not bound to a single group of physicians, they were probably less docile and more demanding than those who had prepaid.[60]

While some professional detachment is necessary, professionals cannot be allowed to take over an organization. Some professionals' interests are selfish, and concerned only with issues of status, welfare, and control, which may exclude issues central to a high level of services for society. There is a difference between professional detachment and professional disinterest and indifference. If the client has no choices, as he does not in schools, what mechanism does society have to insure some concern for client progress other than the professional conscience? In too many cases, teachers shroud their indifference and hostility to students in the cloak of "doing what is best for them" which may actually mean, "doing what I want to do." Teachers' organizations seem overwhelmedly concerned with improving their own status and financial positions and in continuing the form of traditional staffing in self-contained classrooms with lower class loads as the only acceptable alternative for "improving" education. A preoccupation with security in some cases has shut off considering the consequences of allowing client choices or options, or providing the client with any more authority to make his own educational decisions, if by doing that it would mean giving him the right to select or evaluate his own teacher. Some teachers do not care about students because their jobs are such that they do not have to care or be concerned to maintain their positions or to be advanced on the salary schedule. If clients are powerless they must accept the quack and the charlatan as well as the dedicated professional. In this case the client's education is determined more by chance than by intelligent decision making or consideration of his needs. If a student gets a "dud" he is stuck, sometimes for a whole year. A professional group which continues to ignore the plight of the client is bound to incur the public wrath. Much of the accountability movement of this decade may be based on the public's chronic inability to choose teachers for their children within their schools, in the same way they choose their doctors, dentists or auto mechanics.

What Is Wrong with Traditional Staffing

The place to begin an analysis of traditional school staffing is an examination of the assumptions which support their continuance. If we decide we will not accept assumptions based on evidence to the contrary, we must create alternatives. Traditional staffing must be questioned.

1. *Learning is linear and proceeds on an inclined plane.*

While a half-century of research on learning has indicated that it is a nonlinear phenomenon, traditional staffing patterns assume it is a regular event. Since it is not, however, teaching is made linear and regular and the word "instruction" is substituted to encompass both activities. A series of box-like learning environments which children enter and remain in each year has to assume that learning accrues in annual units and that all children in that room need the same thing at the same time. If it were not assumed, the entire framework on which most classroom teaching occurs would be invalidated. This assumption alone contradicts the thousands of words written on the individualization of instruction in self-contained classrooms. For a teacher to vary the pace alone (only one aspect of instructional individualization) would require a diversification of effort beyond the ability of one individual. Because the single-teacher-per-class concept is accepted, increased subject-matter specialization has crystallized in roles *outside* that of classroom teacher—music specialist, physical education specialist, reading specialist—at the elementary level. This type of division of labor is neither economical nor permanent since the basic teacher's role is not redefined but augmented, and when school budgets need to be pared, the specialists are released.

2. *Pupil needs and diversity must be "contained".*

Since pupil needs cannot be met, they must be controlled and "contained." Much teacher energy is consumed keeping the lid on the energy of students to maintain teachable groups. The accumulated frustration of being subjected to "teaching" year in and year out is nerve-racking and draining, not to mention dehumanizing. In the truest sense, pupil energy which might naturally go toward learning is instead involved in creating a hundred different control problems for the teacher. Hostility, apathy and alienation become more common as the child progresses from elementary to secondary school. In traditional schools with traditional staffing patterns, both students and teachers are captives. It is not only the students who are "contained," it is also their teachers. Human difficulties in a contained organization can only be weathered but never solved. This is because solutions are always envisioned within the same constraints —uniform walls, uniform spatial relationships, uniform time, routines, and equal division of responsibility regardless of talent or performance on the part of teachers and students.

3. *Teachers and pupils are interchangeable parts.*

The confinement of differences to age-grades of blocks of pupils and the assignment of teachers on that basis means that both are interchangeable. A teacher is a teacher is a teacher because a third grader is a third grader is a third grader.[61] While teachers often resent being treated as numbers in school systems, present assumptions perpetuate that practice. Numbers do quite well in the absence of any other type of differentiation.

4. *Achievement is time served.*

Since learning cannot be measured without precise objectives, pseudo-measurement practices are created in which grades stand for attendance, tests passed or failed, and semesters or years put in. Schools do not do much with real pupil achievement, for to do so would be to invalidate the implied assumptions which hold the organization together. Changing the school so that real learning is assessed would be to question and/or abolish the grading system and time-based definitions of achievement and instruction.

5. *All subjects are of equal value.*

The strict period designation of equal time for each "subject" taken by students must be translated that each is of equal difficulty and of equal importance, not only to the student but also to society. Thus, driver training and Latin are equally important as are mathematics and physical education. At present, some deviation is granted for athletics.

6. *Organizational conformity is equal to excellence in teaching.*

There are no promotions in teaching simply because schools are indifferent to teacher performance. The basic factor for advancement on salary schedules is conformity—doing what the system and the principal desire. Since it is assumed that salary can be equated with excellence, excellence is reserved for those teachers who maintain "quiet" classrooms. Education is indifferent to real indicators of quality. An organization indifferent to performance values conformity in its stead. Creative teachers are not compensated any differently than uncreative ones. In short, those values which are prized verbally are not recognized nor compensated any differently. What is valued in education is not reinforced. What is not reinforced ceases to occur over a sustained period of time. It is small wonder that teaching is characterized as an insipid, trivial and repetitive type of work on a longitudinal basis where life is subverted to routine, to schedules and the dictums of the policy and procedure handbooks.

Attempting To Create Alternatives

It is harder to work out staffing alternatives than it appears to be. We have gone through two generations of basic models of differentiated staffing in which the first generation resulted in supporting many of the assumptions we have listed as being a rationale for dissatisfaction with traditional staffing. What may appear to be workable on paper, moving the educational organization around to reinforcing contrary principles, is easily corruptible in practice, especially if the implementors do not know more subtle forms of organizational behavior.

Early alternatives were too structure-oriented, that is, too concerned with changing offices and role responsibilities, and not enough concerned with predictors of normative behavior of the total social system of the school. Early efforts ignored the sets of norms in constellation with each other and concentrated upon changing one rule at a time. Patterns were not studied; roles were altered singularly and the effects of such changes on other rules were not recognized. Role expectations quickly reestablished original norms. Training activities concentrated on preparing teachers to fill newly created roles, but not to deal with the pressures which would force a return to the existing role and normative pattern of organizational behavior. Teachers thus went back into the traditional social setting and became resocialized.

The teacher social system is efficiently geared to coincide with the student social system. Few models have even considered the reinforcing effects of student expectations in changing staffing patterns. This is based upon the faulty assumption that the teacher is the most important part of the teacher-pupil dyad, or that students can be left out of the analysis. Innovators who concentrated solely on changing teaching and teaching related roles deluded themselves. They were dealing with only one subsystem of the total organization. This is perhaps the most fundamental reason leading to a study of organizational theory as an attempt to conceptualize the *gestalt* of school structure in order to place staff differentiation in larger operational perspective and relate it to other important organizational subsystems. Unless the interaction of staffing patterns can be anticipated and predicted, we may never understand their importance or how to move away from assumptions we cannot accept. Five years of national efforts and many millions of dollars later, educators are learning how complicated and intricate is the social system in which they try to carry on the business of learning and teaching. A staffing pattern is only one manifestation of the system itself. It is firmly anchored to a host of other variables which are interdependent and interrelated. As yet we do not fully understand the ramifications of proposing to adopt a different set of assumptions, nor do we know the full implications of how to change such patterns. We are clearly groping. We are not doing much better than hoping to eliminate unproductive efforts by trial and error. If we know what doesn't work, we are one step closer to ascertaining what may work. The end result must always be what is actually happening between teachers and pupils. Changes in the school system are means to those ends. We must be hard-nosed about that. Francis Keppel puts it in the same manner.

The end of education is learning; if teaching does not achieve that consequence it is futile. Each new program for reform must finally stand or fall on its proven quality of attainment. Too often a plan for improving the effectiveness of teaching is judged on the basis of its intrinsic appeal, its inner logic; too rarely is it judged in terms of the actual learning of children, the intended product of the educational enterprise. In the necessary revolution of education, the means must become consistent with the end.[62]

Innovations which cannot stand analysis are not worthy of replication, no matter how interesting they may be to those conducting the investigation. After investigation and study, we must also admit that pursuit of staffing alternatives for schools may be unproductive and should not be analyzed further, no matter what the investment has been. If we accept that role of the social scientist, we may assist ourselves in adopting a posture which will allow us to conduct an investigation which in the long run may be fruitful. To adopt a contrary posture may mean spending time and effort just to save face and possibly discrediting the concerns which first led to the examination. Our best guarantee of a full exploration is objectivity about the outcomes. We pass it along as a watchword to those who may seek to improve staffing patterns in schools in the future.

Footnotes

1. Theodore H. White, "The Lindsay Choice Now To Preach or To Run," *Life*, August 20, 1971, p. 66.

2. Edith Roach Snyder, *The Self-Contained Classroom* (Washington: Association for Supervision and Curriculum Development, National Education Association, 1960).

3. Ibid., p. 7.

4. William O'Neill, *Reading, Ritin, and Rafferty: A Study of Educational Fundamentalism* (Berkeley: Glendessary Press, 1969), p. 111.

5. Thomas S. Kuhn, *The Structure of Scientific Revolutions* (Chicago: University of Chicago Press, 1962).

6. Ibid., p. 37.

7. "Arizonans Quizzed On Schools," *Phoenix Gasette*, August 6, 1970.

8. Herbert R. Kohl, *The Open Classroom* (New York: Vintage Books, 1969).

9. Ellwood P. Cubberley, *The History of Education* (Boston: Houghton Mifflin, 1948), pp. 272-74.

10. Ibid.

11. Ibid., p. 757.

12. Ibid.

13. Ibid.

14. Charles Silberman, Crisis in the *Classroom* (New York: Random House, 1970).

15. By Simon and Binet in France in 1905 as cited in Karl C. Garrison and Dewey G. Force, Jr., *The Psychology of Exceptional Children* (New York: Ronald Press, 1959), p. 26.

16. Snyder, *Self-Contained.*

17. John I. Goodlad and Robert H. Anderson, *The Nongraded Elementary School* (New York: Harcourt, Brace & World, 1963), p. 3.

18. John C. Reigart, *The Lancastrian System of Instruction in the Schools of New York City* (New York: Teachers College, Columbia University, 1916) p. 90, as cited in Charles J. Brauner, *American Educational Theory* (Englewood Cliffs, N.J.: Prentice-Hall, 1964), pp. 24-26.

19. Peter M. Blau, "A Formal Theory of Differentiation in Organizations," *American Sociological Review*, 35, April 1970, pp. 201-18.

20. Henry J. Otto, *Elementary School Organization and Administration* (New York: Appleton-Century-Crofts, 1954), p. 653.

21. James G. March and Herbert A. Simon, *Organizations* (New York: John Wiley, 1958), pp. 158-61.

22. Ibid.

23. Ibid.

24. Stephen Duggan, *A Student's Textbook in the History of Education* (New York: Appleton-Century-Crofts, 1948), p. 62.

25. James P. Steffensen, *Merit Salary Programs*, U.S. Department of Health, Education, and Welfare Bulletin 1963, no. 5 (Washington, D. C.), p. 3.

26. Aaron Chodes, "Are Teachers Underpaid—Or Overindulged?" *Nation's Schools,* June 1967, p. 35.

27. Robert Bhaerman, "A Paradigm for Accountability," *American Teacher,* November 1970, pp. 18-19.

28. Bruce J. Biddle, "The Integration of Teacher Effectiveness Research," *Contemporary Research on Teacher Effectiveness* (New York: Holt, Rinehart, and Winston, 1964), pp. 1-40.

29. Steffensen, *Merit Salary.*

30. Myron Lieberman, *The Future of Public Education* (Chicago: University of Chicago Press, 1960).

31. Steffensen, *Merit Salary,* p. 15.

32. Ibid.

33. Ibid.

34. Metropolitan Applied Research Center, Inc., "A Possible Reality: A Design for the Attainment of High Academic Achievement for the Students of the Public Elementary and Junior High Schools of Washington, D.C.," mimeographed (New York: MARC Corporation, 1970), 83 pp.

35. George Weber and William H. Marmion, "Merit Pay and Alternatives: Descriptions of Some Current Programs," Occasional Paper No. 16 (Washington, D. C.: Council for Basic Education, 1969), 32 pp.

36. Ibid., p. 30.

37. Citizens League of Minneapolis-St. Paul, "Stretching The School Salary Dollar: or How a Re-definition of the Teacher's Job Can Ease Problems for Minnesota Teachers and Taxpayers," mimeographed, August 1969, 28 pp.

38. Charles S. Benson, *The School and the Economic System* (Chicago: Science Research Associates, 1966) pp. 114-15.

39. Raymond E. Callahan, *Education and the Cult of Efficiency* (Chicago: University of Chicago Press, 1964).

40. From a speech given by Dr. Edward Pino of Cherry Creek, Colorado, to the New York State Regents Advisory Board on Teacher Education and Certification in New York City, April 16, 1970.

41. Jesse Burkhead, *Public School Finance, Economics and Politics* (Syracuse: Syracuse University Press, 1964), pp. 82-84.

42. Ibid.

43. Chris Argyris, *Integrating the Individual and the Organization* (New York: John Wiley, 1964).

44. Maureen Woodhall and Mark Blaug, "Productivity Trends in British Secondary Education, 1950-63," *Sociology of Education,* Winter 1968, pp. 1-35.

45. Ibid., p. 25.

46. Mary Jean Bowman, "Economics of Education," *Review of Educational Research,* December 1969, pp. 641-70.

47. Ibid., pp. 666-67.

48. Ibid.

49. Ibid.

50. Fenwick W. English, "Differentiated What?" mimeographed, unpublished position paper, Mesa Public Schools, January 1970, 8 pp.

51. Fenwick W. English, "Differentiated Staffing: Refinement, Reform, or Revolution?" *ISR Journal*, Fall 1969, pp. 220-34.

52. Roger A. Kaufman, "A System Approach to Education: Derivation and Definition," *A V Communication Review*, Winter 1968, pp. 415-25.

53. Andrew W. Halpin, *Theory and Research in Administration* (New York: Macmillan, 1966).

54. Douglas McGregor, *The Human Side of Enterprise* (New York: McGraw-Hill, 1960).

55. Fenwick W. English, "A Short Laboratory Manual to Understanding Differentiated Staffing," mimeographed, AASA-NASE, May 1970, 26 pp.

56. Paul Lawrence, "How To Deal With Resistance to Change," *Harvard Business* Review, 47, January-February, pp. 41-100.

57. Ibid.

58. Callahan, *Education*.

59. Gloria V. Engel, "Professional Autonomy and Bureaucratic Organization," *Administrative Science Quarterly*, March 1970, pp. 12-21.

60. Ibid., p. 17

61. Dwight W. Allen, "A Differentiated Staff: Putting Teaching Talent to Work," NCTEPS Occasional Paper No. 1, National Education Association, 1967, 11 pp.

62. Francis Keppel. *The Necessary Revolution in American Education* (New York: Harper and Row, 1966), p. 103.

2   The Functions of Staffing

Fenwick English

Whether one is examining the way a department store, a hospital or a school are staffed, he will find staffing patterns function on an even larger organizational scale. Both innovators and traditionalists have largely ignored these functions. Innovators have concentrated upon building elaborate personnel hierarchies to capture an earlier objective with staff differentiation—that of building a "teacher career ladder." Traditionalists have denied the need for a career ladder and concentrated upon human relations within self-contained classrooms. In both cases, the functions of staffing have not been changed.[1]

A staffing pattern is an overt or extrinsic manifestation of the division of labor within an organization. As such, in a bureaucratic organization the division of labor is closely connected to the partitioning of authority. In other words, a staffing pattern is the glue which holds the hierarchy of authority and the formal power structure together. A staffing pattern is part of the total organizational control system because it defines the functions of distribution (the allocation of resources), coordination (the degree of reciprocal relations between parts, divisions or units) and integration (the degree of various blends of organizational units or divisions in the decision-making process) which determine the mode of distribution and the type of coordination employed.

The covert or intrinsic functions of a staffing pattern are that it maintains a given partitioning of rank and authority within an organization. (Thus, it is a measure of organizational stability.) In the case of the schools, the lack of differentiation between teachers acts as a counterbalance to administrative authority by negating the manipulation of financial incentives as an organizational control mechanism.[2] The degree to which the organizational decision-making structure is integrated (a definition of organizational pluralism) may be represented with the name Control Index (CI). A high Control Index would place a heavy emphasis upon uniformity achieved by a formula as the most efficient method of distribution, thus insuring ease of coordination. Coordination is more difficult in specialized organizations engaged in highly technical or professional work. The size of the organization itself is a factor mitigating against extreme technical differentiation, since a person performing those particular technical tasks may use his knowledge to provide himself with some independence. In such organizations coordination and distributive activities become more costly,[3] especially in highly bureaucratic settings which serve as a focus for organizational conflict. This presents a dilemma to school systems. To become more effective with clients, a good deal more role specialization will be necessary to solve client problems. However, by meeting these needs, serious internal problems will be created, especially if school administrators are adverse to forming new working relationships with teacher specialists in the decision-making process. What is suggested here is that a tightly controlled bureaucratic line/staff school organization will not be able to solve the social-educational problems of our society. The control of the schools via authoritarian means by that society is a major inhibitor itself to improved organizational effectiveness. Tight control (a high CI) is inimical to unstandardizing school budgets and personnel allocation on the basis of task specialization to meet diagnosed client differences. A staffing pattern is the Gordian knot to untying the resources of the school with these aims in mind.

Bidwell has called the division of labor in schools "a temporal division of labor" because at the elementary level particularly there is no real task or structural difference in what teachers do in schools.[4] They are divided not on tasks but on the basis of how clients are grouped, by chronological age. Charters has labeled this same practice the "duplication of labor" as contrasted with an actual division of labor based upon task specialization and separation.[5] For this reason, a real differentiation of the skills of teaching is impossible within the present structural arrangement of classrooms. True, flexible staffing based upon student diagnosis first and an actual specialization of skills by teachers is minimized in the self-contained classroom structure of almost all schools. The role definition of "teacher" is thus held in perpetuity at a very low level of specialization, inhibiting a truly viable response to student differences. Ironically, this same skill weakness for students is a source of strength by teachers and administrators in an authoritarian organization. This suggests that the democratization of the school system is a basic step toward greater humaneness and sensitivity by individual schools and individual teachers toward students.

Another covert function of a staffing pattern is transactional. When there is interaction with elements in the managerial system and with assumptions regarding the nature of learning, pupils and teaching, a staffing pattern reinforces all of those assumptions. While it is the product of those assumptions, it serves as an excuse for their perpetuation. Thus, if the managerial system were proposed to be changed, the staffing pattern of the organization would then become a barrier to such change.

THE PARADOX OF FUNCTION

The paradox of the situation regarding staffing schools appears to be this: the manner in which educators have gone about solving the problem is part of the problem itself, i.e., the "solution" makes the problem worse. In the field of medicine such a situation is called "iatrogenic," and refers to a situation where the medical treatment makes the patient more ill. The schools are failing to meet the needs of students in part because they are not organized to be sensitive to student needs. Such external pressures on schools to meet student needs increases social expectations upon school boards. The boards press the administration for solutions via the line/staff command, drawing a teacher counter-response which forces the implementation of similar solutions or "more of the same" answers. Teachers cannot respond differently since to do so would be to lose all autonomy and independence within the school system. Administrators will not press for greater role specialization if it would endanger their current decision-making prerogatives. Boards of education are caught up in a balancing act between restive constituents, militant teachers and students, and defensive administrators. The cycle of action/reaction does not solve the problem itself, rather it extends and perpetuates the problem. At the broadest level the paradox of function is illustrated by the insistence of prototyping remedies for the schools instead of prototyping basic reforms. For example, the federal government funds dropout centers instead of creating legislation for new school systems which don't produce dropouts. To break from the cycle which worsens the problem, a high level of sophistication and knowledge of such chains of action are required. Given the nature of organizations, the cooperation and consent of all parties will be required to avoid becoming trapped in an escalating paradox which does not solve the problem. Within a traditional structure, coordination, integration and distribution remain essentially set within a downward pattern of authority, from top to bottom. Changing the pattern is not the solution; the solution lies more in a process than in replacing one pattern with another, hierarchical or not.

CLASSIFYING STAFFING PATTERNS

Four broad types of staffing patterns may be classified on two continuums creating four quadrants, i.e., the degree of integration of the staffing pattern and the degree of coordinating activities required to maintain the pattern of units as a whole. This is illustrated in Figure 4. Using the quadrants of degree of integration (high-low) and the degree of coordination activities required (high-low) it is possible to classify four types of staffing patterns. The first is the traditional self-contained staffing pattern which requires a low degree of integration and coordination, the latter condition being assured through standardized curriculum. The second represents a more open space, flexible team teaching situation in which several teachers are contained within a larger than single classroom area (usually a "pod"). Greater coordination is required which also requires some changes in the distributive functions of the school system. The third represents a type of staffing model best illustrated in the Temple City type of staff differentiation, which is a stair step permanent hierarchical ranking of teacher based roles. This type of model was developed during 1966-1970. It requires more integration because the new hierarchy serves as a definite forcing function to break up the line/staff dyads of traditional bureaucratic structures. The fourth

FIGURE 4

Classification of Generic Staffing Patterns

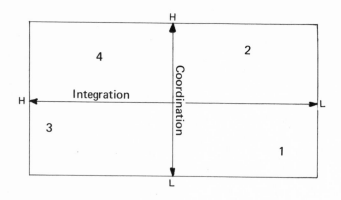

Legend
1 = traditional self-contained staffing pattern;
2 = team teaching/open space staffing pattern;
3 = Generation I models of DS;
4 = Generation II models of DS;

model represents a different type of staffing best exemplified in the Mesa, Arizona, approach based on task analysis derived from a pupil needs assessment, with built-in role and position fluidity. The Mesa type requires even greater coordination, but less formal integration in the school system than the Temple City variety.

To the extent that a staffing model falls in the upper left or lower left quadrant, it would indicate a greater degree of organizational pluralism, or low Control Index. The degree of downward decision making would indicate a tendency to fall in the lower or upper right quadrants which would indicate a high control index for the staffing pattern. Coordination costs do not exactly parallel either, but generally increase with greater organizationl pluralism. Figures 5 and 6 illustrate the opposite but parallel nature of organizational pluralism and the degree of downward decision making employed. A high degree of downward decision making would be indicative of a high Control Index and a low degree of organizational pluralism. The latter condition would witness a large amount of diffused decision making or participative management. The seventh figure shows that the degree of coordination required does not exactly follow the same

FIGURE 5

Degree of Organizational Pluralism

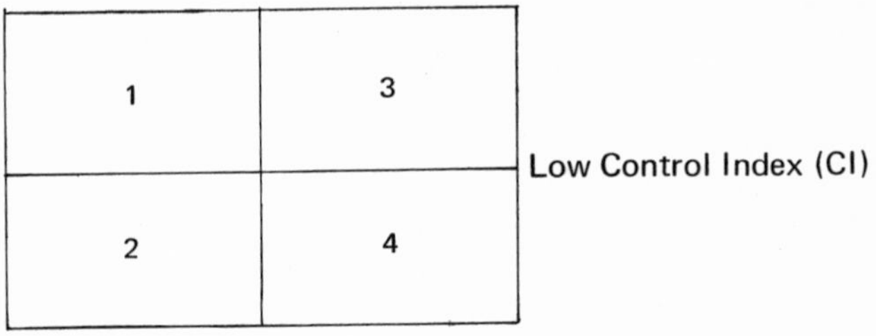

1	3
2	4

Low Control Index (CI)

FIGURE 6

Degree of Downward Decision Making

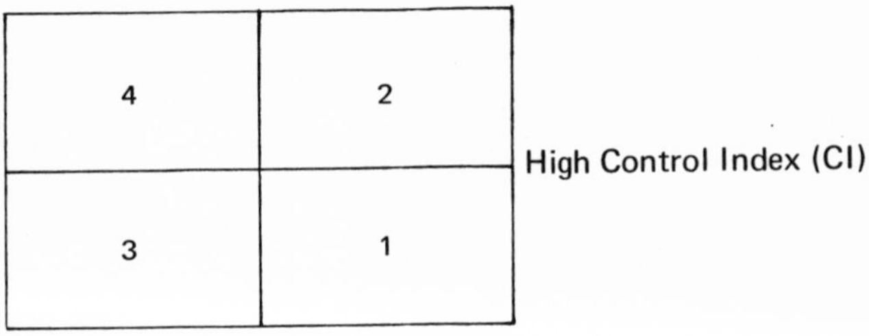

4	2
3	1

High Control Index (CI)

FIGURE 7

Degree of Coordination Required

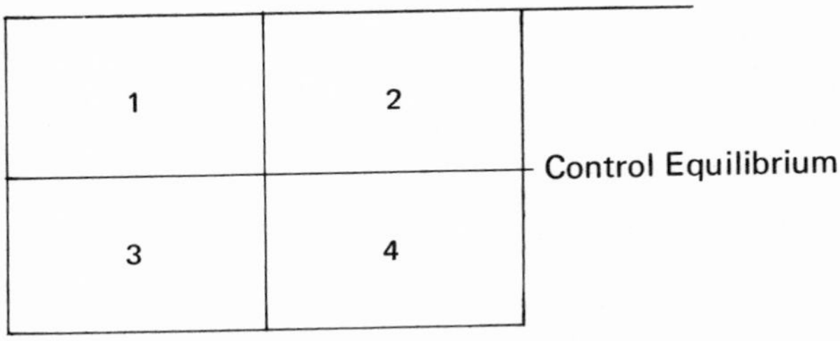

1	2
3	4

Control Equilibrium

pattern. If a more fluid series of roles is created at the school unit level, but none of the roles forces a reanalysis and subsequently a redistribution of functions at the middle management level, coordination at those levels beyond the schools is not substantially more difficult. It may be more costly at the school level in the case of the role of the school principal, but little else may change. This idea assumes that the same level of organizational control achieved by the former control system is still necessary, and this may not be true. Some coordination is always necessary or no system would be possible. The requirements for control may vary and with it the necessary expenditure of organizational talent and time in order to achieve it.

A STAFFING PATTERN AND THE ORGANIZATIONAL CONTROL SYSTEM

The Control Index is really a hypothetical measure of a series of often unstated assumptions about human motivation and human behavior. In simple terms, if one believes that man is basically lazy and must be forced or coerced to work (McGregor's Theory X idea) then the authority envisioned by administrators as necessary to operate school systems will be coercive and punitive, risking the creation of a counter force perhaps just as arbitrary and abrasive.[6] In such a situation a staffing pattern is a mechanism of reinforcement for the control system (a transactional function). Those promoted are those who have learned how to fit into the system. Promotions are rarely offered to rebels. On the other hand, if the administration believes that work is a meaningful part of someone's life, and if that person is convinced it will be meaningful, he will naturally work hard. Rules and procedures are not made to coerce, manipulate, or control, but to create harmony and maximum coordination (McGregor's Theory Y notion). Furthermore, they will be founded on a profound trust between all parties. A staffing pattern can contain the mechanism of great intrinsic motivation, such as the factors of achievement, responsibility, and recognition that Herzberg, Mausner, and Snyderman researched and concluded were more important job satisfiers than salary.[7]

A staffing pattern can fulfill some of the needs of teachers when they follow a Maslow-type list of needs. Carver and Sergiovanni reported a study of 1,593 high school teachers in which they indicated that the lower order needs pertaining to security and social areas were relatively well met in their working environments.[8] However, teachers reported less satisfaction with the higher order needs of esteem, autonomy and self-actualization. As long as school system administrators perceive teacher autonomy as a threat, the present staffing pattern which places a lid on autonomy and self-actualization will be retained. Teachers must recognize that what they may gain in security by not recognizing differences between them in performance and ability, they lose in the organization's capacity to recognize competence, and bestow additional autonomy as a reward for superior performance. Teachers might also forfeit the keys to full professionalization.[9] To illustrate the transactional function of a staffing pattern and the organizational control system, Figure 8 attempts to show how a staffing pattern may reward two contrary ideas on a view of man, utilizing McGregor's Theory X and Theory Y assumptions. Each view of man is self-reinforcing and it has a number of ramifications for the total school system. The maintenance of the organizational or the controlling functions are enclosed in the dotted lines and further reinforced, usually with legislation. State laws regarding the privileges of teachers, supervisors, or administrators define the scope of power of each role. State statutes regarding class size ratios, restrict utilization of paraprofessionals, etc. Organizational distribution of resources is often spelled out with ADA formulas, books per child, penalties for exceeding certain teacher-pupil ratios, and textbook allocation. A staffing pattern is logically congruent with the other elements maintaining or controlling the organization. It would be naive to assume that changing a staffing pattern to reward the Theory Y view of man would have much success without recognizing and similarly assaulting the other reinforcing elements of the school system. Instead, the staffing pattern would become quickly socialized to fit in. Changing the organizational Control System from X to Y is only hypothetically possible. The system has learned to respond to a given set of stimuli which are self-reinforcing.

The maintenance functions of the organization deal with a fundamental lever of the total organization, that of sustaining equilibrium.[10] Herbert Simon observes that even business organizations are not as quick to change as they might be. He offers some reasons why this may be so. First he refers to "sunk" costs as those involved in change, which means that the organization must acquire new know-how, and posits:

FIGURE 8

The Transactional Nature of a Staffing Pattern
and the Organizational Control System

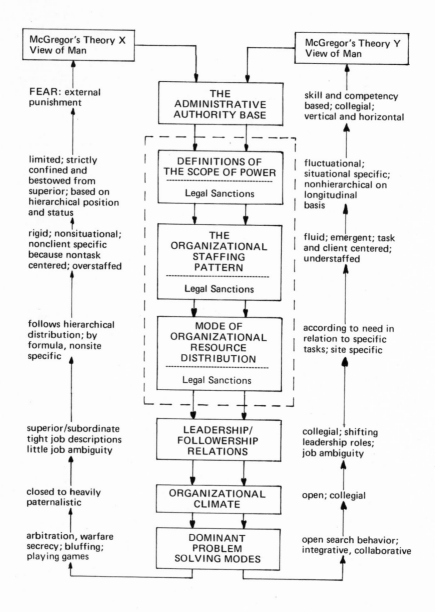

the organization acquires goodwill, which is also a sunk asset that may not be readily transferable to another area of activity. Stated differently, a change in organization objectives ordinarily entails decreased efficiency in use of resources (sunk costs and know-how) and a loss of incentives otherwise available to maintain a favorable balance (goodwill).[11]

In short, the stabilizing functions of the organization are very powerful. One representation of this function is that of a staffing pattern. At the roots of staffing patterns lie often unstated but encompassing theories of motivation. From these theories definitions of power, organizational patterns and modes of distribution of the organization's resources emanate. In a Theory X or mechanistic view of man,[12] the scope of power is contained by a hierarchy of authority and has limitations which are not necessarily defined in terms of skills needed to solve problems, but in tasks needed to maintain the organization via the chain of command. A Theory Y organization bases roles on functional authority which is limited by the nature of the problem and the skill of the person, and not on the basis of strict organizational definitions of competence. The roles in a Theory Y organization fluctuate in relation to one another and are fluid over an extended period of time. The staffing patterns which emerge from these bases will be inherently different, one being hierarchical, fixed and relatively diffident to specific situational demands, and the other being limited to a hierarchical format bound by specific objectives and the nature of the problem at hand. A Theory Y staffing pattern is always, at the abstract level, a relatively impermanent structure but always task centered. At the present time it is possible to describe it completely only in theoretical terms since in its entirety it has not been implemented anywhere. A Theory Y based staffing pattern is essentially a nonbureaucratic one in that the most important professional roles are in a state of flux in relationship to other roles. Some organizational roles would be necessary purely for administration and coordination, but these would be subservient to the professional roles. The other outcomes of a Theory Y staffing pattern are a collegial or reciprocal role to role relationship. It would be more common to find an understaffed organization functioning under a Theory Y structure since the redistribution of tasks could occur with frequency only in an open climate. Rigid, organizationally defined roles lead to overstaffing; organizational problems cannot be solved since roles are not based on skills necessary to resolve assessable and defined problems. Two difficulties are apparent. First, problems are not really described; solutions are substituted for problem identification. Thus, one hears, "the problem around here is that we don't have flexible scheduling," or "differentiated staffing." The problem has not been identified but the solution has been proposed. This approach leads to overstaffing. The most blatant example is the proliferation of middle-management positions to "solve" coordination problems. Thus, coordinators of programs, areas, and units are created to dispense with problems which remain undefined. The anachronism is that if coordination problems were solved in actuality there would be no need for coordinators. The problem is not defined in terms of how it can be solved, but in terms of a given solution. One result is that the costs of the problem increase, first because it remains unsolved and unidentified and second because personnel are being paid to perpetuate it. It is perhaps twice as expensive as before. Worse, the organization is seduced into believing it has responded in a meaningful way and ceases to further define problems or seek alternative solutions. School systems thus engage in a kind of organizational self-hypnosis which creates dangerous and often explosive gaps between the institution and its society and its clients. A Theory Y based staffing pattern engages in problem solving in a more realistic search for alternatives. There are no intense bureaucratic pressures for preconceived solutions to fit the existing hierarchical structure or to be advanced or defended on the basis of maintaining organizational homeostatic needs. There are peculiar problems with bureaucratic hierarchies which will be explored in more detail in Chapter 3.

PARADOX RESOLUTION: THE FUNCTION
OF THE ADMINISTRATION

In resolving the paradox of solutions reinforcing problems, breaking the cycle would be a refusal to reinforce the cycle of causative events. In a bureaucratic organization with forces which reinforce the problem, the administration must interpose itself so it does not reinforce those events which perpetuate the problem. This means creating an open-climate system by which roles can become unencumbered from each other, and opening up greater organizational ambiguity (thereby being able to redefine the problem and search again for alternatives). Keeping school going though students form a powerful force which may affect the whole process and shielding forces out of the organizational field which reestablish the causative cycle are difficult objectives. Knowing that interposing between field forces within the cycle will intensify pressures to re-establish it.[13] Such interpositions are limited in terms of how long it may take to break the cycle and set in motion a different series of events before external and internal forces become overwhelming. This interposition is illustrated in Figures 9, 10, and 11. The

FIGURE 9

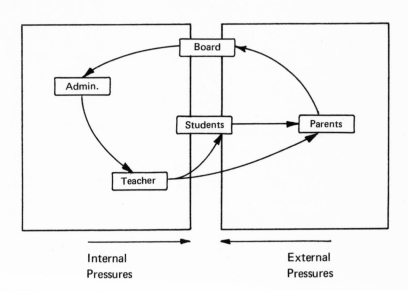

administration must create the conditions of ambiguity (unloosen some of the structural bonds) and create incentives for a different type of structure. As such, if the external environment is threatening, the threat must be reduced or suspended in order that full energy may be devoted to internal affairs. School systems functioning in hostile social situations may find so much energy used to cope with the environment that the cycle of internal events is left untouched, thus perpetuating the external problem. If a balance with the external environment can be reached, at best it will be tenuous and short term. Careful planning is necessary to use the time provided. The pivotal role of students is often the swaying factor for the time duration. An increase in student freedom can be extremely threatening to a conservative community and a traditional teaching staff. It could lead to parental reaction, a change in board membership and

FIGURE 10

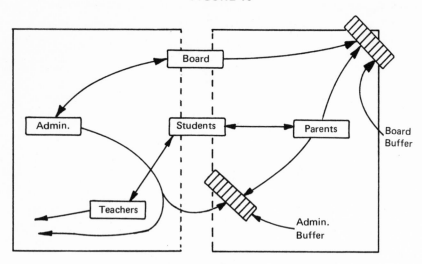

Administrative/Board
Interposition to Disengage
or Weaken Traditional
Internal/External Pressures

FIGURE 11

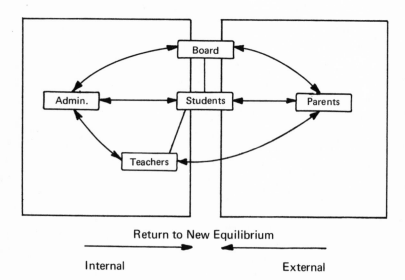

Return to New Equilibrium

Internal   External

subsequent closing down of the innovation before it has been fairly evaluated. The administration and the board must prepare for intensive reaction and prepare to maintain an interpositional stance until interim objectives have been reached. Maintaining student enthusiasm by capitalizing on at least the Hawthorne effect will extend the time limits for this period. The buffer role is critical and the administration and the board must work together. A divided school board will not provide the umbrella necessary for internal changes; the opposite usually happens. The system becomes less flexible internally and it is more difficult to bring about organizational changes. The separation of the parts of the system may strike some as a diabolical scheme to interfere with teacher/parent relationships. Experience indicates and some research shows that teachers regard parents and board members with the greatest fear and resent internal interferences in what is regarded as professional matters.

Ziegler's work states that teachers view parents as competitors with students and resent internal interference.[14] Serious discussion, in which teachers and administrators must analyze their abilities and admit shortcomings are not likely to occur with citizens present. The role of citizens is for goal setting and outcome (output) specification, what the new system must do better than the old. The board and the administration must create buffer zones to reduce external pressure on the system. This will enable the system to redirect energies towards internal change, normally expended in maintaining equilibrium externally. As stated earlier, this is a redirection of internal/external equilibrium and is limited since the buffer zones cannot be perpetuated indefinitely. *Buffer zones* may be described as a period of time which is protected from criticism, attack, or premature evaluation from external pressures.

THE SLOWNESS OF STRUCTURAL CHANGE

Because structural change of an organization involves almost everyone in the organization, it is the slowest type of change schools may undergo. Jones' model of innovation types yields a fairly quick analysis of two variables: time needed to implement the change and the number of people involved.[15] Figure 12 illustrates that methodological changes are the easiest since they involve the least number of people and the shortest time, whereas instructional and organizational changes become more difficult as the factors of time and people become enlarged.

FIGURE 12

Jones' Model of Innovation Types

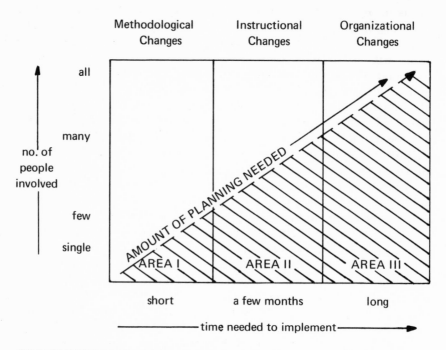

STAFF DIFFERENTIATION AND EDUCATIONAL MANPOWER

Staff differentiation was the product of the close of the decade of the teacher shortage.[16] With the teacher surplus of the seventies, the problem of initial career attraction has lessened; that is, the recruitment problem has dwindled. The idea of the differentiated staff was that a career ladder to the teaching profession would retain quality teachers, cut the turnover rate—still a valid solution to the turnover problem—and place the effects of turnover on the lower levels of the career ladder. This latter solution would reduce the costs of training and the loss of highly trained personnel.[17]

A teacher surplus merely masks the real problem. The fact is that teaching itself, the chores, responsibilities and factors which drive out many creative, talented and energetic people are still present. While more bodies are available to fill in the gaps, it is perhaps the loss of these personnel which is most damaging to the teaching profession. People of dedication, creativity and ability are too rare in any occupational group. They will always be at a premium. The problem which initially led to an examination of the necessity for staff differentiation is a little less obvious, but certainly no less compelling or important.

Sooner or later educators will have to face the fact that problems with the teaching profession must be seen as related to the environment and organizational setting in which teachers work, and in which administrators have some authority to act.

> . . . my reading of the history of educational reform leads to the position that the reformulation of educational purposes cannot be accomplished within current educational structures. Bureaucracy, as I hope I have made clear, is more than a form of organization: it is the crystallization of particular values. . . . School structure communicates particular norms; the learning of those norms has priority to the learning of skills. Those norms that are crystallized into contemporary educational forms reflect the purposes of education that have dominated American schools. Any radical reformulation of educational objectives, it follows, requires a radical restructuring of educational forms.[18]

Administrators must recognize that solutions to problems arise when they conceptualize the problem differently. Staff differentiation must be related to the organizational setting and that in turn to the larger educational questions. Problems do not arise in isolation and they cannot be solved in isolation. A sound understanding of the many forces at play is fundamental to meaningful change.

SOME MODERN HISTORICAL PRECEDENTS

It has been noted earlier that the original differentiated staff in American education was the Lancastrian school. A true personnel hierarchy of both students and teachers served in the Lancastrian school. Costs were greatly reduced by paying for the salary of only one or two fully qualified personnel and then arranging a straited series of lesser qualified roles to perform the more ministerial or perfunctory tasks. The demise of the Lancastrian school witnessed the end of its personnel hierarchy and pupil grouping plans and the permanent replacement of the graded school single-teacher-per-class-concept with all instruction taking place in what had been the recitation rooms adjoining the large Lancastrian lecture hall. Although various types of school plans have been offered before and since, nothing so far appears to have the potential widespread acceptance of any further structural changes for American schools.

Heathers reviews three modern alternatives in nongrading, the dual progress or Stoddard plan, and team teaching.[19] Nongrading is the practice of abolishing grades and the utilization of assumptions about learners supporting grades, usually with concomitant movement towards some sort of progress by achievement. Stoddard proposed his semidepartmental concept for the elementary school in 1956 in which he maintained the self-contained classroom for some subjects and installed semidepartmentalization for others. Team teaching represents the rudiments of a differentiated staff with only the role of team leader above that of regular teacher. What occurs in a team situation is the identification at a rudimentary level of teacher abilities and specialization usually by subject area or sometimes on the ability to handle one type of instructional mode, i.e., large group, small group, or tutorial instruction. The essence of team teaching in terms of group planning and the conceptualization of a more liberal utilization of time, space, and classroom group size is necessary for differentiated staffing.[20] Where differentiated staffing and team teaching separate, however, is that differentiated staffing is a more drastic separation of teacher responsibilities and in theory aims at reconceptualizing the role of the school principal and the entire decision-making structure. Team teaching may or may not propose to go that far.

The weakness of team teaching may be that it does not go far enough; that is, it does not separate and parcel out teaching skills in such a way as to actually make a difference in the lives of learners. Indeed, there is no guarantee that staff differentiation will either. Furthermore, both concepts may be engaging in an irrelevant analysis of the definition of tasks and their subsequent specialization by teachers is not based upon a pupil needs assessment. Too often only the teachers' perception is represented in a definition of roles which are needed in the school. In too many cases, job responsibilities are assigned on the basis of what exists in the light of present staff talents. The redistribution of such talents may not make an effect at all; indeed, it may be harmful if the staff is already overbalanced with certain skills.

The question of staff balance must be situational and based upon an analysis of the type of client the school serves. One schools' balanced staff may be another's overbalanced staff. This situation already exists since all staffs are essentially staffed in exactly the same way. In most cases, an analysis would reveal that schools are terribly overstaffed with some teaching skills, and others are neglected or not recognized at all. The redistribution of skills is merely a process which can go on even if the outcomes are irrelevant. This is why data gathering activities of system analysis by assessing needs is a critical activity before reinforcing assumptions about what students need. It is here that the variable of school structure is linked to learning. Critics of the structural approach argue that it is unimportant because good teaching can happen anywhere and indeed it can. But when structural biases are laid aside and the needs of learners are examined and related to the most economic utilization of staff talent available, it will quickly become apparent that such utilization is dependent upon joint usage of available skills and that self-containedness is uneconomical. It is uneconomical now, but those kinds of questions are rarely asked. The present school staffing pattern is not subject to the same scrutiny as we often ask of potential alternatives. The status quo often wins by default.

SOME THEORETICAL PRECEDENTS FOR ROLE DIFFERENTIATION

The division of labor has formed the basis of intensive scholarly investigation of organizational functioning since Adam Smith. Writing in the *Wealth of Nations* published in 1776, Smith described how ten men, each performing one or more of the eighteen operations necessary to make a pin, together produced 48,000 pins a day, whereas working individually they could only make 200.[21]

Adam Smith posited that the differentiation of roles or the division of labor was promoted by: (1) the inability of one person to perform all the job tasks required, (2) the limitation of knowledge by the worker to solve problems, and (3) the achievement of efficiency of a smaller margin of tasks with work standardization.[22] The first great work on the division of labor was that of the French sociologist, Emile Durkheim (1858-1917), a professor at the Sorbonne. Durkheim saw the division of labor, or work specialization, as an organic process with biological roots. Examining the complexities of living organisms, he saw the division of labor as a phenomenon in the distant past of the world. In human life, the division of labor was caused by human density in the cities, since population growth stimulated specialization and interdependency and a higher degree of human culture. Durkheim did not envision the ultimate lengths of human specialization in the factories of industrialized nations subject to the clock watch inspections of a Frederick W. Taylor; rather he postulated that the phenomenon would increase human solidarity even though functions and tasks became divided.[23]

Modern sociologists accept without much difficulty the fact that the degree of social mobility within a society is the degree to which it has become specialized. In fact, the specialization and modernization are viewed as synonymous terms, two sides to the same coin. Eisenstadt summarized this relationship.

... It is possible to talk about stages of modernization in terms of the degree of social mobilization and differentiation, and of some structural corollaries of such stages—for instance, the greater the scope of such mobilization the greater also will be the tendency to develop large scale organizations.[24]

Eisenstadt reviewed the impact of the general social momentum towards specialization upon education. From the societal pressures towards more skilled manpower came a variety of institutions. "The supply side of educational services also became greatly diversified and differentiated," observed Eisenstadt;

... among those characteristics, the most important were the growing specialization of educational roles and organizations, on the one hand, and growing unification and interrelation of the different educational activities and organizations tended to become more widespread and a continuous differentiation between the different levels of the educational system—between primary, secondary, vocational, adult, and higher education—took place. Each of these "systems" and even many subsystems of each, has gradually become more autonomous, specialized and organized in its own framework.[25]

It was precisely the evolvement of society into more specialized units in all aspects of social life which led to the establishment of the bureaucracy. Since education as an institution has been subject to the same pressures towards the division of labor, sociological analysis of bureaucratic behavior, structure and effects would appear especially germane to an adequate understanding of staff differentiation.

German sociologist Max Weber (1864-1920) coined the name bureaucracy after describing its characteristics. These are:

1. organization tasks distributed among offices in clean-cut division of labor which promotes a high degree of staff specialization;

2. offices and/or positions are organized into a hierarchy which takes on the shape of a pyramid;

3. a system of rules and regulations which governs the decision-making power of the offices is developed;

4. officials are expected to assume an impersonal orientation in their contacts with clients;

5. employment in the organization is construed to become a career for officials of the organization.[26]

Early sociological literature attempted to describe what was happening in organizations much the same way the early writings on staff differentiation were descriptive of how the educational organization needed to change and what the effects might be of those changes.

An introduction to organizational theory is necessary to acquaint the schoolman with at least a working vocabulary of ideas of schools, staffing patterns, and principles of schools as social systems. Perhaps basic to a discussion of organizational theory are some related ideas such as one's view of man, what motivates man and the extent to which one changes organizations by changing the organizations' norms, or by working on individuals irrespective of those norms.

What has been called classical organization theory differs from more modern theories. The latter attempt to bring in more knowledge regarding man's psychological needs and are considerably more sophisticated regarding the impact on people of institutionalized behavior than the older models. What is central to understanding classical theory has been identified by Hutchinson as "line and staff."[27] The line and staff concept is a way of looking at specialization. If the division of work is separated by a process known as a scalar relationship, the result is the formation of superior and subordinate dyads. The scalar process "provides a scale or grading of duties according to degrees of authority and responsibility."[28] Classical organizational ideology is based upon a line and staff or superior/subordinate relationship in which, in theory, no subordinate has more than one superior and there are no unassigned or overlapping responsibilities. This principle is often expressed in the term "unity of command"[29] which means that subordinates should not be subjected to the conflicting views of two superiors. An extension of the unity of command notion is the "chain of command" which designates "a single line of authority from the top to the bottom of the organization."[30]

. . . a single chain of command is desirable because multiple chains necessarily involve multiple sources of authority, thus violating the principle of unity of command.[31]

With the chain of command comes "the system of roles—the roles of subordination and superordination—arranged in a chain so that role one is subordinate to role two; and two is superordinate to one but subordinate to three."[32] This system of roles is commonly referred to as a hierarchy. A hierarchy of roles is related to several other concepts such as departmentation, jobs, and the notion of "span of control."[33] A hierarchy implies a vertical type of organizational differentiation. Filley and House note that the horizontal differentiation, or organizational function, is that of departmentation, job definition and span of control, as well as line and staff.[34] Hutchinson has identified seven types of departmentation; functional, territorial or geographical, product, equipment or process, customer service or customer expectation, clean-break and alphabetical or numerical.[35] The grouping of tasks or functions into clusters called jobs represents what may be assigned to one man to perform. The term "span of control" is concerned with a theoretical number of subordinates any superior may effectively supervise. Obviously this concept is closely aligned with unity of command, chain of command, and hierarchy.

Classical theory has been challenged on a number of grounds. It has been of a descriptive nature, rather than derived from empirical testing or experimentation. As such generalizations from these observations usually follow rather obvious structural qualities, but are extremely weak predictors of organizational behavior.[36] March and Simon have also criticized classical theory on the basis that many of the assumptions regarding human behavior on which classical theories are expounded are false or incomplete.[37] For example, classical theory ignores intraorganizational conflict caused by its definitions and the complexity of humans in such systems is not recognized.

The practicing administrator cannot help but bump into the sociological theories of Talcott Parsons in some way as he attempts to grasp the significance of some gestalt of organizational theory.[38] Parsons was a master descriptor. He carefully analyzed social phenomena and has written extensively. Parsons' framework of social and organizational structure has carried over into a myriad of other works, some in business and industry, others in educational administration.

SOME THEORETICAL PROBLEMS AND ISSUES

The practicing school administrator may become bored or frustrated wading through what may appear to be some rather abstract concepts which do not have much to do with field problems. Nothing could be further from reality. Too often school administrators have avoided the use of theory as a predictor or in establishing a conceptual framework for implementation. A good example may be provided by the work of Hills.[39] Hills doubts whether schools can be significantly changed at all. The author's reasons pertain to the earlier discussion regarding the functions of staffing. Beginning with Parsonian theory as a base, Hills hypothesized four types of organization: pattern maintenance, integration, goal attainment, and adaptation. Schools were examples of a pattern maintenance type. In discussing the function of the educational organization in society, Hills states that schools are differentiated around the pattern-maintenance of "institutionalized normative culture."

Pattern-maintenance activity is, by definition, activity which leaves the system, i.e., the society, in the same patterned state, and unless the value pattern of the society places an emphasis on change and improvement, there is no basis for a conception of the educational organization as a progressively improving entity . . . the flexibility with which improvements may be made is reduced by the very values the organization is obligated to maintain.[40]

Hills examines the ability of the educational organization to adopt innovations in terms of adapting it to ways which are compatible with the maintenance of its unit value patterns. "The same point can be made with respect to the recruitment and selection of personnel. The primary concern is not how competent, but how committed the individual is to the values of the organization."[41] Furthermore, Hills points out a rather dismal prediction which dampens earlier rationale by some who argued that increased technical expertise would serve as a forcing function to change the orientation of the school.

. . . the most important consequence of increased levels of technical training for operative personnel in pattern-maintenance organizations is not, as one might expect, more rapid change, or improvement in the ordinary sense of greater control over, or responsiveness to, environmental changes, but greater organizational stability. Thus, increasing levels of technical training for public school teachers seems a doubtful way of 'modernizing' educational practices.[42]

Hills' work is part of a growing doubt about earlier claims which promoted a differentiated staff via the creation of a teacher hierarchy.[43] While the American Federation of Teachers and the Association of Classroom Teachers of the NEA appeared to react negatively to the concept of the teacher's hierarchy because of what it would do to teacher bargaining power and teacher strength generally, earlier innovators are disenchanted with staff differentiation and its potential for improving learning.[44] While salary schedules and career attractiveness have been linked to a career hierarchy to reducing teacher turnover (arguments used for decades by teachers to improve their general working conditions), none is the direct link to improved learning. In the vocabulary of Hills, the solution of these problems does not appear to have much to do with changing the basic patterns of staffing schools. There is some evidence that the opposite may be true as Hills avers, a career hierarchy which is permanent reinforces the same value orientations more deeply than before. If these value orientations reinforce the dominant values of a bureaucratic setting, professionalism would run counter to more sensitive and nurturant teacher-pupil relationships. This means that if "professionalism" is construed to mean the addition of career offices and collegiality between offices based on bureaucratic roles, such offices must be grounded on assumed common grounds between students, thus precluding students being treated as persons. "It is the apparent paradox, noted earlier, of the professional ideology of teachers occurring as one important factor working against a professional relation between teachers and students."[45] Thus, the self-contained classroom, by being relatively isolated from the bureaucratic setting, provides the teacher with the autonomy to deal with pupils individually. In this perspective, it stands as a counter-force to further bureaucratization. This is discussed in more detail later. If schools were rigid, Procrustean and insensitive before, there are now (with a rigid career hierarchy) more reasons for maintaining them in such a state. In other words, solutions to teacher problems are not necessarily solutions to learner problems. This area will prove to be rather sensitive since it is so closely aligned with arguments for teacher welfare. Hills' rationale and presentation need to be considered carefully. Will renewed emphasis on a bureaucratic career hierarchy for teachers result in a system of schools which is more sensitive to learners than is the present model?

In line with Hills' statements are those of Davis who cited trends within organizational structure as a result of employing scientific and professional personnel.[46] David mentioned three peculiar trends:

organizational pluralism, matrix organization and nonstructured management. Organizational pluralism was defined as "diverse groups which maintain semiautonomous participation and influence in the organization."[47] The result of such pluralism was to spread the power over a broader base within the organization. This was accomplished through jointly narrowing the scope of command authority and widening the scope of authority through expertise."[48] Matrix organization is also called project organization since it is the organization of a separate group of people with a temporary function competitive for the organization's resources. This is particularly true of federal project staffs in school districts, projects within the aerospace or defense industries. The matrix organization is superimposed over the permanent organizational hierarchy. Davis cites the advantages of the matrix organization:

1. it effectively focuses resources on a single project, permitting better planning and control to meet deadlines;

2. it is more flexible than a traditional functional hierarchy;

3. its distribution of authority and status is more in agreement with democratic norms;

4. more emphasis is given to authority of knowledge as it relates to the contribution a specialist can make to a particular project;

5. specialists can contribute according to their talents regardless of their rank in the hierarchical structure;

6. it helps a specialized employee become more of a generalist.

The matrix organization is a functional, time specific structure; it is not permanent, but situationally anchored. By nonstructured management Davis means, "its members determine among themselves how the work will be organized and performed.[49] A parallel concept is the "underdefinition of roles" for jobs. When a person is given an underdefined job he has to create the more finite lines of his role and is apt to be more creative in breathing life into it and be committed to it than if it were handed to him during a job interview.

A similar idea is Chris Argyris' "understaffing" concept.[50] Developed within an educational context, settings can serve as a forcing function only when they are underpopulated or undermanned. When there are more tasks and fewer people to perform them, "the individuals tend to experience a greater feeling of responsibility, a greater sense of challenge, and a higher evaluation of their functional importance in the system."[51] One of the drawbacks of undermanning an organization acknowledged by Argyris is that of fatigue. Some experienced educators have commented that certain schools have been undermanned historically, like ghetto schools, where class sizes ran exceedingly high. However, undermanning can be effective only if a more fluid working environment is created by which the most effective level of skills and skill interchange can be ascertained. As such, to effectively adopt the spirit of undermanning with the concomitant utilization of staff in a variety of settings, the self-contained classroom structure has to be abandoned almost totally. Argyris cautions that undermanning should only be attempted under the following conditions:

1. if the tasks available permit individuals to use their important abilities;

2. if the employees believe that the undermannedness is legitimate;

3. if they are sharing the fruits of increased productivity.[52] Argyris underlines the fact that the motive for undermanning must be "to increase the probability for self-expression, self-responsibility, commitment in individuals, and the flexibility in, and vitality of, the organization."[53]

Argyris also proposes a more unified view of organizations and people in solving individual and organizational problems, a theme delineated briefly in Chapter 1. Argyris proposes a "mix" model of incorporating concern for the individual and the organization into a unified whole. Using a simplified model of input-output ratio, Argyris notes that the way to increase organizational effectiveness is to increase the available amount of human energy in the organization. Thus, we must be concerned with the individual psychological states of the employees. Those responsible must be interested in organizational norms and procedures which frustrate and alienate employees and result in the creation of work environments which produce norms counterproductive to those of the goals of the organization itself. Attitudes of fatalism, withdrawal, goldbricking, cheating and noninvolvement indicate that the organizational energy of people is being channeled into counterproductive activities. Argyris is careful to qualify his theme in this regard. ". . . we maintain that increased opportunities for employees to experience psychological success does not mean a completely people-centered organization."[54] He maintains that such concerns are legitimate because they lead to the diminution of counterproductive values. Similar views have been advocated by Davis in reexamining the potential benefits to large corporations of sensitivity training for top management.[55] It is fine if the individuals involved in such training activities become more acutely aware of their behavioral styles and influence upon others, but, if the organization itself does not become more effective in problem-solving, such activities cannot be justified. The organization must become more sensitive to the people charged with carrying out its objectives because those objectives cannot be realized if it does not recognize their individual needs.

The "mix" model can be applied to educational organizations. As such it will require a more precise definition of purpose than is currently available in most. A kind of mushy and nondefinitive terminology which permeates school activities, especially those related to child-centered practices, may be extremely worthwhile, but the tendency for its advocates to engage in educational sentimentalism prohibits it from being analyzed and compared at the empirical level to other practices. This results in an argument which cannot be resolved rationally—what is actually best for students and learning—because of the intrusion of philosophical biases that has led to an unproductive and confusing debate regarding educational practice. The exhortative remedies advocated by a Max Rafferty are sustained because the events which produced such solutions are equally exhortative.[56] To avoid a reaction which may be destructive and unproductive, it is imperative that efforts towards change be offered from an empirically defensible position. Advocates of flexible scheduling have fallen into the same trap, with an equally vociferous counterattack by conservatives. Potential implementors of other educational innovation must be couched in language that stems from what students will be able to do that they cannot do now in terms of organizational purpose and direction.

SCHOOLS AS BUREAUCRACIES

A comparison of public school characteristics to Max Weber's list of bureaucratic indicators or an updated list by Blau and Scott will reveal that school systems have all of the classic earmarks of a bureaucracy.[57] There already are roles and offices, and a very definitive hierarchy of power, status and privilege. The basic division of labor remains the historic role of the classroom teacher, surrounded by quasi-teaching roles such as teaching-principal, supervisor, coordinator and consultant, with a myriad of nonteaching roles such as directors of curriculum, instruction, personnel and assistant and associate superintendents. The visibility and power of roles within the educational organization increase with distance to classroom teaching. This is not unlike other occupations such as social work and nursing, for example.[58]

Bidwell documents that schools indeed possess characteristics of bureaucracies in that they have a functional division of labor, a definition of staff roles as offices, offices which are ordered hierarchically and officers who function according to rules of procedure.[59] Anderson has conducted extensive research into the bureaucratic function of rules in schools in this regard.[60] One function of rules is to insure predictability in a system in which the organizational subunits are physically separated, often at great distances. Operating without precise criteria of organizational effectiveness, rules are directed to prescribing functions of teachers rather than dealing with teaching per se. "In the minds of many administrators, unfortunately, conformity and effectiveness are synonymous," admits Anderson.[61] This is true because what is measurable is conformity by the teacher and not his performance. Bidwell further states that the division of labor, a temporal division, is attached to the practice of the age-grading of pupils in schools. It appears that age-grading practices, though not educationally sound, fulfill the bureaucratic need for control and predictability in an administrative sense and compound the issue of examining the teacher's role. While Bidwell noted the existence of a career ladder, he commented that, "the internal career line of a school system thus consists of movement into and through the administrative ranks."[62]

Despite the functional and temporal differentiation of teaching activities, the teaching cadre typically does not contain specialized teacher offices. Thus, teachers' salaries usually are tied to training and seniority rather than to function or position. Within the teaching cadre there is no bureaucratic career.[63]

The creation of a bureaucratic career line for teachers ends with the role of classroom teacher and proceeds into quasi and then full-time administrative positions. Thus, there is in school systems an already differentiated staff with a career line set firmly into hierarchical format. The low-level status of the teacher in school systems is thus cemented, and promises to seek an alternative structure do not look encouraging. Even if the administrative hierarchy would be amenable or could be unencumbered, the essential ingredients for building a ladder of sophisticated and senior teaching skills is conspicuously absent.

In a penetrating and somewhat discouraging analysis, Etzioni and colleagues set about investigating the *semi-professions:* the occupations of teaching, social work and nursing.[64] Of these groups, only social work appeared to have any chance at all for full professionalization in the future. At the core of the problem is the lack of an esoteric knowledge base regarding teaching, a value set which acts against establishing such a base on the part of the teaching majority, which are overwhelmingly female. The feminine role in teaching is a major barrier to professionalization as it has been defined from the more masculinized professions of law, medicine, college teaching and the ministry (all male-dominated professions). The lack of an esoteric knowledge base does not provide teachers with the force they need to confront the public and win the rights of full professionals. To alter the bureaucratic decision-making structure in which a colleague group could form, it is necessary to maintain independence. Established professions maintain their independence with the possession of esoteric knowledge. Teachers have attempted to win professionalization with collective bargaining, but this does not extend to entry privileges to the occupation itself, nor has it meant colleague evaluation or the identification of superior teaching performance. Furthermore, the essentially bureaucratic and administrative structure of school systems has not been replaced or altered, it has been augmented by the collective bargaining machinery and reinforced. The basic value set against recognizing teaching tasks as different and the specific collection and refinement of teaching skills has not occurred either.

There is little opportunity for purely professional recognition because there is little basis for it in distinctive skills to be judged by an audience of colleagues, there is little development of orientations to colleagues as the primary audience, and there is little feeling among clients or the public that specifically professional skills might deserve more rewards than administrators receive. Lacking a genuinely professional basis for recognition, semi-professional organizations create a proliferation of hierarchical levels which provide status badges. Each level guards its badge jealously. A result is still further reduction of professional colleague solidarity.[65]

Since teaching is still a feminine-dominated occupation, the values which females possess in the organization have an important bearing on what the occupation will embrace in the way of change. Simpson and Simpson find that feminine values are contradictory to winning teachers' independence and power in an organization. Noting that women tend to have stronger desires than men for pleasant social relations on the job, they argued, "They (women) are more fearful of conflict that might endanger it, and less interested in the long-range career goals that might make the risk of conflict seem worthwhile."[6][6] The feminine predisposition to avoid conflict, a predisposition towards deference regarding men (the overwhelming majority of whom are administrators), and a value complex which places service above self to the client preserve teachers as a docile and subordinate group. Simpson and Simpson argue that the service-above-self ethic is substantively different than a professional orientation.

> Professional activity is sometimes expressive, but the rewards are derived more from the exercise of skills, than from the response of the client, who may sometimes be seen essentially as an object to whom skills are applied."[6][7]

Simpson and Simpson label this orientation a holistic orientation which is endemic to the professional's "task orientation." The holistic orientation inhibits the refinement of peculiar skills to an occupation. This is especially noticeable in training institutions where holistic training programs are not aimed at training teachers with specific skills to accomplish specific objectives. The college graduate entering the semiprofessions is generally there because she seeks to avoid the more highly competitive, intellectually rigorous training of the established professions. Thus, the lack of an esoteric knowledge base is perpetuated by the values of those entering the occupation. The high turnover of women in teaching leads to the necessity for further administrative bureaucratic control to achieve stability of the organization. Thus, feminine problems and the feminine value orientation to the occupation place a set of strong inhibitors to full professional status.

Teachers live in an authoritarian organization which maintains its authoritarianism by the types of people attracted to it in the first place. Teachers are dependent upon the administration. As McGregor pointed out a decade ago, dependent relationships are explosive ones.[6][8] In an authoritarian organization, control is limited to the degree of the ability of that organization to reward or punish employees. McGregor confines this largely to punishment. "The effectiveness of authority as a means of control depends first of all upon the ability to enforce it through the use of punishment."[6][9] Control is limited, says McGregor, to the availability of countermeasures and he points to collective bargaining, restriction of output, featherbedding, etc., as countercontrol mechanisms.

Through collective bargaining, teachers deny to the administration the ability to control their behavior through the utilization of extrinsic rewards, namely salary.

The patterning of extrinsic rewards in teaching differs from the patterning of such rewards in most occupations. As we have seen, in-school effort has no effect on money rewards for classroom teachings, since money is increased by course-taking and longevity. The package of formal prestige and power meted out to teachers is highly standardized—the absence of hierarchy among teachers neutralizes extrinsic rewards as an important incentive for individuals.[70]

As Lortie notes from his analysis, the neutralization of extrinsic rewards from the organization provides the teacher in a bureaucratic setting with a measure of independence, a measure of countercontrol to balance their dependence on the administrative power structure. Teachers resist further differentiation, asserts Lortie, because they perceive additional ranks as strengthening the ability of the administration and board to control extrinsic rewards. The teacher's delicate state of independence would be lost. Lortie finds a true dilemma in the teacher's stance on further differentiation. On the one hand, "the resistance to differentiation within teaching ranks inhibits the emergence of senior colleagues in the field. This impedes the development of organizational arrangements found in established professions."[71] On the other hand, Lortie hypothesizes that to create a hierarchy would indeed strengthen the hand of the administration. In the present organizational framework, "Equality is the foundation of autonomy."[72]

The major conclusions of the semiprofessions by Etzioni, Lortie, and Simpson and Simpson were underscored by a study of 755 classroom teachers in Mesa, Arizona.[73] Female elementary teachers were found to be the group least in favor of differentiated staffing. Secondary and beginning elementary male teachers were the most positive toward the idea. When position on the salary schedule was considered, teachers generally on the first and middle salary ranges were most positive. Teachers on the top levels were least inclined towards differentiation. The pattern is illustrated in Table 1.

It appears that the present bureaucratic control system within school systems is a powerful barrier against further role differentiation. The control mechanism of most school systems demands conformity. The countermeasure by teachers to live in an authoritarian system is rigid egalitarianism to limit administrative control. The success of differentiated staffing, a series of new teacher career offices, appears linked to (1) the growth of a substantial esoteric knowledge base regarding pedagogy which actually makes a difference with clients and in the eyes of the public, (2) the wholesale abandonment of authoritarian management styles by public school

TABLE 1

A Rank Order Summary of Teacher
Response to Staff Differentiation
on the Factor of School Level

School Level	Sex	Mean	Standard Deviation	Salary Level	Number Responding
elementary	male	10.852	4.950	1	54
junior high	male	10.683	4.351	1	63
high school	male	10.385	4.093	3	13
junior high	male	10.233	3.892	2	30
junior high	female	10.141	4.093	1	13
junior high	female	10.000	3.584	2	20
high school	male	9.982	4.889	1	55
elementary	male	9.667	5.785	3	6
high school	female	9.593	4.069	1	27
high school	female	9.500	6.245	3	4
high school	female	9.476	4.082	2	21
elementary	female	9.178	4.856	1	208
elementary	male	8.543	3.492	2	35
high school	male	7.982	4.742	2	57
junior high	male	7.625	4.373	3	8
elementary	female	7.260	4.042	2	73
elementary	female	6.556	4.978	3	9

administrators which is demanded by boards of education, and reinforced by collective bargaining agreements, and (3) the removal of
the egalitarian straitjacket of the basic tasks comprising the classroom teacher's role. The effects, forces and reactions are difficult to
separate in practice. Cause and effect are muddled. The real reasons
for being for or against DS are sometimes not stated. In untangling
the threads, the problem becomes considerably more messy and complicated. This will undoubtedly frustrate the action-oriented administrator. We should remind him at this point that if he desires to
succeed, a thorough understanding of the forces at play is vital for
success. We hope, in the analysis, that planning will take on a more
serious tone and more deliberate consideration of some of the factors
discussed will occur. This is one of the lessons of implementing staff
differentiation models learned from 1967-1970. Simple solutions do

not fail because they were applied to the wrong problems, but most often because the problem was over-simplified in the first place to the point of being unsolvable.

SOME PSYCHOLOGICAL ASPECTS OF STAFFING

Even though tasks may be ferreted out and divided on criteria upon which all can agree, two persons performing the same job on paper may be performing a different job in reality. Too rational an approach to studying staffing may lead to some disillusionment. There is an aspect which may be called the psychological half of staffing schools. The criteria for staffing psychologically to maximize human talent is hypothesized to overlap the needs of the organization as an entity, i.e., that there is some congruence between individual and organizational needs. Research is needed to be more precise in this regard.

The degree of compatibility between the needs of the organization and those of the individual may be partially judged on the following criteria:

1. the degree to which the staffing relationships promote individual involvement and independence;

2. the degree to which the assumptions of staffing contribute to mutual trust, openness, and lack of manipulation;

3. the degree to which the staffing roles promote the incumbent's identity, sense of self and self-awareness;

4. the degree to which the staffing pattern distributes the psychological rewards of achievement, recognition, responsibility, and visibility of accomplishment;

5. the degree to which the staffing pattern capitalizes upon emergent abilities and is rooted in skill and role competence as the final base of organizational authority.

A staffing pattern which indeed contained these aspects would to the largest extent be nonbureaucratic. In a time of rapid social and environmental change, Bogue has postulated the need for what he terms "disposable organizations."[74] The characteristics of disposable organizations are that they are:

1. problem or issue-centered rather than function-centered;

2. temporary structures containing a built in self-destruct mechanism which concludes the resolution of the problem for which it was organized;

3. staffed so that the authority of competence replaces the authority of position;

4. shortening the line of communication which exists in present, bureaucratic hierarchies.

The time may come when it is possible through disposable organizations to arrive at competency based staffing which is maximally congruent with the individual's needs to contribute to the goals of the organization. In that case, many of the symptoms of our ailing school systems will have vanished.

Footnotes

1. Fenwick English and Larry E. Frase, "Making Form Follow Function in Staffing Elementary Schools," *The National Elementary Principal*, 51:3, January 1972.

2. Dan C. Lortie, "The Balance of Control and Autonomy in Elementary School Teaching," *The Semi-Professions and Their Organization* (New York: The Free Press, 1969), p. 31.

3. For a highly detailed account of the relationship between organizational size, degree of differentiation, and cost of coordination, see Peter M. Blau, "A Formal Theory of Differentiation in Organizations," *American Sociological Review*, 35:2, April 1970, pp. 201-18.

4. Charles E. Bidwell, "The School As A Formal Organization," *Handbook of Organization*, James G. March, ed. (Chicago: Rand McNally, 1965), p. 974.

5. W. W. Charters, Jr., "An Approach To the Formal Organization of the School," *Behavioral Science and Educational Administration*, Daniel E. Griffiths, ed., 63rd Yearbook of the National Society to Study Education, Part II (Chicago: University of Chicago Press, 1964), pp. 243-61.

6. Douglas McGregor, *The Human Side of Enterprise* (New York: McGraw-Hill, 1960).

7. Frederick Herzberg, Bernard Mausner, and Barbara Snyderman, *The Motivation to Work* (New York: John Wiley, 1967).

8. Fred D. Carver and Thomas J. Sergiovanni, "The School as a Complex Organization: An Analysis of Three Structural Elements," mimeographed, Department of Educational Administration, University of Illinois, June 1968. As cited in Thomas J. Sergiovanni and Robert J. Starrett, *Emerging Patterns of Supervision: Human Perspectives* (New York: McGraw-Hill, 1971), pp. 142-43.

9. Fenwick W. English, "Et Tu Educator: Differentiated Staffing?" Occasional Paper No. 4. National Commission on Teacher Education and Professional Standards, (Washington, D.C.: National Education Association, 1969), 23 pp.

10. For some insights into this concept see Herbert Simon, *Administrative Behavior* (New York: The Free Press, 1945), pp. 110-22.

11. Ibid., p. 120.

12. A term used to describe bureaucratic organizational behavior by Tom Burns and G.M. Stalker in *The Management of Innovation* (London: Tavistock, 1961).

13. Andrew W. Halpin, *Theory and Research in Administration* (New York: Macmillan, 1966), p. 131.

14. Harmon Ziegler, *The Political World of the High School Teacher* (Eugene, Oregon: Center for the Advanced Study of Educational Administration, 1966), p. 141.

15. Richard W. Jones, Jr., "Tuning Up The Staff for Organizational Change," *Journal of Secondary Education*, December 1968, pp. 339-45, as adapted from Richard I. Miller, *Perspectives on Educational Change* (New York: Appleton-Century-Crofts, 1967), p. 369.

16. "The Education Professions: A Report On The People Who Serve Our Schools and Colleges—1968," U.S. Department of Health, Education, and Welfare, Office of Education (Washington, D.C.: U.S. Government Printing Office, 1969), 377 pp.

17. A point of view argued much earlier by Myron Lieberman in *The Future of Public Education* (Chicago: University of Chicago Press, 1960).

18. Michael B. Katz, "The Present Moment in Educational Reform," *Harvard Educational Review*, August 1971, p. 357. Article adapted from the book, *Class, Bureaucracy, and Schools: The Illusion of Educational Change in America* by Michael B. Katz (New York: Praeger Publishers, 1971).

19. Glen Heathers, "School Organization: Nongrading, Dual Progress, and Team Teaching," *The Changing American School*, NSSE Yearbook, John I. Goodlad, ed. (Chicago: University of Chicago Press, 1966), pp. 110-34.

20. See "Organizing For Learning, A Report of the Commission on Public School Personnel Policies in Ohio," published by the Greater Cleveland Associated Foundation. June 1971, 54 pp.

21. *The Columbia Encyclopedia*, William Bridgewater and Elizabeth J. Sherwood, eds. (New York: Columbia University Press, 1956), p. 547.

22. Thomas A. Marshcak, "Economic Theories of Organization," *Handbook of Organization*, James G. March, ed. (Chicago: Rand McNally, 1965), pp. 423-50.

23. Frederick W. Taylor, *The Principles of Scientific Management* (New York: W. W. Norton Company, 1967).

24. S. N. Eisenstadt, *Modernization: Protest and Change* (New Jersey: Prentice-Hall, 1966), p. 45.

25. Ibid.

26. H. H. Gerth and C. Wright Mills, *From Max Weber: Essays in Sociology*, trans. and ed. (New York: Oxford University Press, 1946), pp. 196-204.

27. John G. Hutchinson, *Organizations: Theory and Classical Concepts* (New York: Holt, Rinehart & Winston, 1967), pp. 62-63.

28. Keith Davis, *Human Relations at Work* (New York: McGraw-Hill, 1957), p. 161.

29. Victor A. Thompson, *Modern Organization* (New York: Alfred A. Knopf, 1961), p. 104.

30. Alan C. Filley and Robert J. House, *Managerial Process and Organizational Behavior* (New York: Scott, Foresman, and Company, 1969) p. 298.

31. Ibid.

32. Thompson, *Modern Organization*, p. 58.

33. Filley and House, *Managerial Process*, p. 213.

34. Ibid.

35. Hutchinson, *Organizations*, pp. 67-69.

36. Marcus Alexis and Charles Z. Wilson, *Organizational Decision Making* (Englewood Cliffs: Prentice-Hall, 1967), p. 4.

37. James G. March and Herbert A. Simon, *Organizations* (New York: John Wiley, 1958), p. 33.

38. Talcott Parsons, *The Social System* (New York: The Free Press, 1951).

39. R. Jean Hills, *Toward A Science of Organization* (Eugene, Oregon: Center for The Advanced Study of Educational Administration, 1968).

40. Ibid., p. 98.

41. Ibid., p. 100.

42. Ibid., p. 107.

43. For a good synopsis of this earlier thinking, see Bruce G. Caldwell, "Differentiated Staffing: A Probe or a Plunge?" *Educational Technology*, April 1971, p. 6.

44. For a broader discussion of the NEA/AFT response, see Fenwick English, "AFT/NEA React to Staff Differentiation," *Educational Forum*. To be published 1971-72 volume.

45. Bidwell, "The School," p. 1013.

46. Davis, *Human Relations*, pp. 285-299.

47. Ibid., p. 294.

48. Ibid., p. 298.

49. Ibid.

50. Chris Argyris, *Integrating the Individual and the Organization* (New York: John Wiley, 1964), p. 222.

51. Roger Barker, "Big School—Small School," Midwest Psychological Field Station, University of Kansas, Lawrence, Kansas, 1962.

52. Argyris, *Integrating the Individual*, p. 228.

53. Ibid.

54. Ibid., p. 146.

55. Sheldon A. Davis, "An Organic Problem-Solving Method of Organizational Change," *Behavioral Science and the Manager's Role* (Washington, D.C.: NTL Institute for Applied Behavioral Science, 1969), pp. 285-99.

56. Max Rafferty, *Suffer Little Children* (New York: Signet Books, 1962).

57. Peter M. Blau and W. Richard Scott, *Formal Organizations* (San Francisco: Chandler, 1962).

58. For a comparison see Amitai Etzioni, et. al., *The Semi-Professions and Their Organizations* (New York: The Free Press, 1969).

59. Bidwell, "The School," p. 974.

60. James G. Anderson, *Bureaucracy In Education* (Baltimore: Johns Hopkins Press, 1968), pp. 18-19.

61. Ibid.

62. Bidwell, "The School" p. 977.

63. Ibid.

64. Etzioni, *Semi-Professions.*

65. Richard L. Simpson and Ida Harper Simpson, "Women and Bureaucracy in the Semi-Professions," in *The Semi-Professions and Their Organization,* Amitai Etzioni op. cit., p. 246.

66. Ibid.

67. Ibid., p. 235.

68. Douglas McGregor, *The Human Side of Enterprise* (New York: McGraw-Hill, 1960).

69. Ibid., p. 21.

70. Dan C. Lortie, "The Balance of Control and Autonomy in Elementary School Teaching," in *The Semi-Professions and Their Organization* (New York: The Free Press, 1969), p. 31.

71. Ibid., p. 41.

72. Ibid.

73. Fenwick W. English, "Assessing Teacher Attitudes Towards Staff Differentiation," unpublished Ph.D. dissertation, (Department of Secondary Education, Arizona State University, September 1971), 277 pp.

74. E. G. Bogue, "Disposable Organizations," *Phi Delta Kappan,* 53, October 1971, pp. 94-96.

3   Models and
Issues

Fenwick English

Whether or not the building of models is a process which qualifies education as a discipline remains conjectural.[1] However, it has been an integral part of staff differentiation since Dwight Allen, then Associate Professor at Stanford, and Jack Rand, Superintendent of Temple City, first brainstormed a model of a teacher's hierarchy in December 1965 on a napkin.[2] In discussing the functions of model building, Belth identifies scale models, analogue models, mathematical models and theoretical models. Models of staff differentiation to date have assumed properties of scale models and analogue models.[3] According to Belth a scale model reproduces "an event which is being studied by reproducing exactly its important or relevant features, for the purpose of making possible closer scrutiny and manipulation."[4] An analogue model is also representative but "they are more abstract and more selective, and their form permits the development of hypotheses about the event being examined."[5] The ability to hypothesize from a model is perhaps its major function, especially in the initial stages of the development of an idea.

This possibility of hypothesizing is important. In fact, because the event itself which confronts us does not always easily yield answers to direct inquiry, we find that we have no other way to think about it than by first constructing a model.[6]

Elements of staff differentiation dot the literature of education. Some important aspects of the idea such as the freeing of teachers from routine job responsibilities, incorporating teacher training into the school itself and paying discriminative salaries on the basis of performance were advocated by Preston W. Search in 1901.[7] Trump described aspects of the problem and prescribed various solutions for it.[8] Prior to Dwight Allen, probably the man who came closest to actual model building was Myron Lieberman.[9] Lieberman is largely forgotten today for his pioneering ideas, some of which were basic to staff differentiation. For example, Lieberman argued against the single salary schedule showing that it was discriminatory against teachers. He advocated paying teachers on market supply and demand conditions. If it cost more to hire a physics teacher, Lieberman advocated that salary schedules should permit school districts to be competitive. He pointed out the need for a personnel hierarchy of teachers within disciplines, and averred that teacher turnover could be reduced in its severity by copying a medical model in which there were teacher doctors and teacher nurses. Turnover could be largely confined to the nurse level; thus its most damaging effects, such as a loss of trained manpower, could be offset. It is ironic that Lieberman, once the darling of the AFT intellectuals, should have predated others like Allen and that today the American Federation of Teachers has taken an obdurate stand opposed to "verticalism" in teaching.[10] Lieberman anticipated the objections of his own union colleagues.

> Whenever I have suggested to teachers that one of our educational frontiers is the development of a hierarchical personnel structure, the character of their objections has tended to confirm my conviction that such a structure is feasible . . . in general, the intellectual level of the objections to a personnel hierarchy in education shows clearly that teachers have never even considered a personnel structure different from the prevailing one.[11]

THE CONTRIBUTION OF DWIGHT ALLEN

While many educational innovators both described and prescribed the problems and solutions relating to the lack of career incentives for teachers, it was Dwight Allen who provided major impetus for the movement which culminated in the national thrust by the United

States Office of Education toward staff differentiation. Professor Allen spoke at hundreds of conferences from 1966-69 and made several films about various aspects of the concept. In addition, he persuaded the Kettering Foundation to underwrite the costs of prototyping a model of staff differentiation at Temple City, California.[12] The major contribution of Dwight Allen was his ability to separate school staffing as an entity of national focus instead of having it be antecedent to other practices such as nongrading, team teaching, flexible scheduling, and continuous progress curriculum.

Some aspects of Professor Allen's model appeared in *A New Design for High School Education* (with Robert Bush).[13] The model represented in Figure 13 soon became nationally famous.[14] When school administrators and teachers began their work on actually developing a model in Temple City, California, the model was rejected. First, they took umbrage that the advanced functions did not show a common root in classroom teaching responsibilities. There was fear that the positions above would become supervisory in nature or quasi-administrative. The Teachers Job Analysis Task Force, headed by AFT local President Allen Shuey redrafted the model which was reported to the total staff in September, 1967.[15] This is represented in Figure 14. Model II was also reported by Reinertsen[16] and erroneously labeled "The Florida Model," in at least one publication.[17] From the beginning the emphasis of the Temple City Model was structural. It boldly proclaimed that teachers should have a more active role in the school district. It demanded an end to the role of supervisor, a drastic revamping of the role of school principal, and an augmented district decision-making structure. Several years later this remained the most viable and visible impact of staff differentiation on the structure of the school district. The involvement of teachers at all levels in decision making was ignored by both the national AFT and the NEA in their adopted positions on staff differentiation.

Cost projections soon forced a further revision of the Temple City plan. Figure 15 shows the model as it was during the school year 1970-71. The Temple City model was copied with some variations in Kansas City, Missouri, and Beaverton, Oregon. It has been debated and discussed. Its concepts and rationale formed the basis for the guidelines for national models of the School Personnel Utilization Program of the Education Professions Development Act and were reflected in the subsequent platforms by the AFT and the NEA. Differentiated staffing became synonymous with Temple City. Yet staff differentiation has undergone both theoretical and practical alterations which represent as dramatic a shift as did the idea when it was introduced.[18] Mann has labeled the difference in approaches Generation I and Generation II approaches to staff differentiation.[19] A review of these differences is important in grasping the implications of staff differentiation for public schools.

FIGURE 13

Temple City Differentiated Staffing Plan
1965-66 (Model 1 - Dwight Allen)

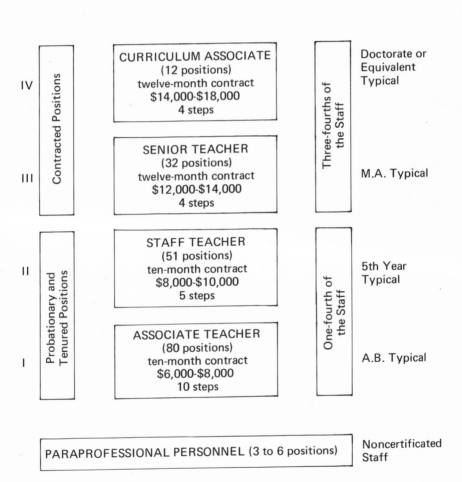

IV	Contracted Positions	**CURRICULUM ASSOCIATE** (12 positions) twelve-month contract $14,000-$18,000 4 steps	Three-fourths of the Staff	Doctorate or Equivalent Typical
III		**SENIOR TEACHER** (32 positions) twelve-month contract $12,000-$14,000 4 steps		M.A. Typical
II	Probationary and Tenured Positions	**STAFF TEACHER** (51 positions) ten-month contract $8,000-$10,000 5 steps	One-fourth of the Staff	5th Year Typical
I		**ASSOCIATE TEACHER** (80 positions) ten-month contract $6,000-$8,000 10 steps		A.B. Typical

PARAPROFESSIONAL PERSONNEL (3 to 6 positions)	Noncertificated Staff

FIGURE 14

Model of Temple City Differentiated Staffing Plan 1967-68 (Model 2)

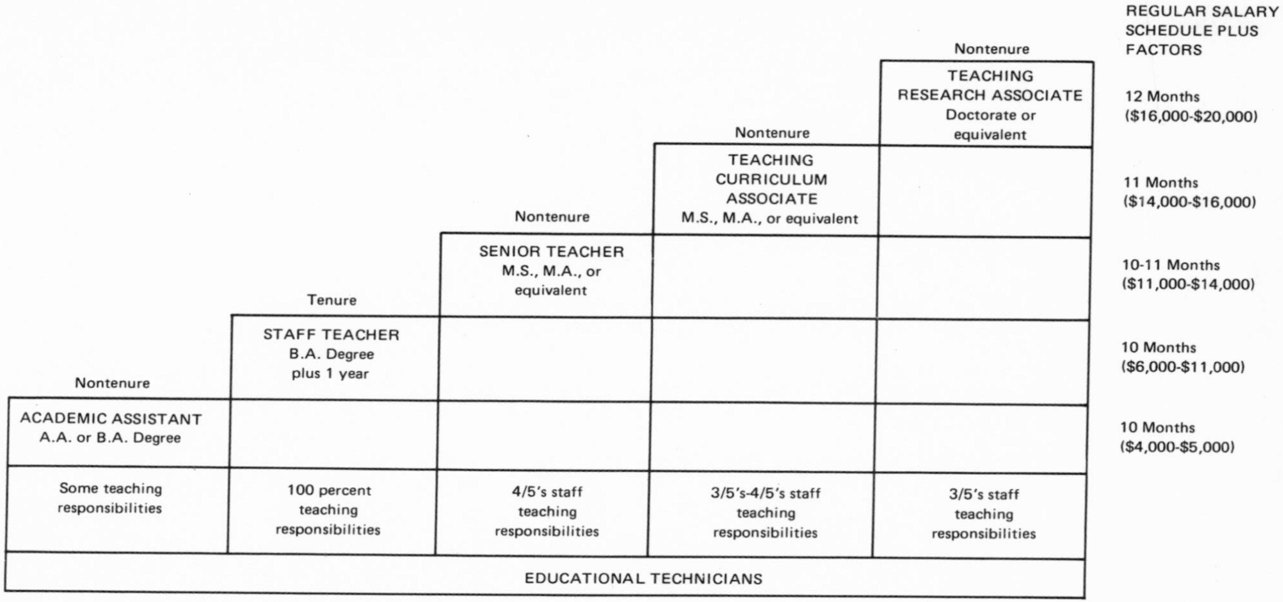

	STAFF TEACHER B.A. Degree plus 1 year	SENIOR TEACHER M.S., M.A., or equivalent	TEACHING CURRICULUM ASSOCIATE M.S., M.A., or equivalent	TEACHING RESEARCH ASSOCIATE Doctorate or equivalent	REGULAR SALARY SCHEDULE PLUS FACTORS
	Tenure	Nontenure	Nontenure	Nontenure	12 Months ($16,000-$20,000)
					11 Months ($14,000-$16,000)
					10-11 Months ($11,000-$14,000)
					10 Months ($6,000-$11,000)
ACADEMIC ASSISTANT A.A. or B.A. Degree	100 percent teaching responsibilities	4/5's staff teaching responsibilities	3/5's-4/5's staff teaching responsibilities	3/5's staff teaching responsibilities	10 Months ($4,000-$5,000)
Nontenure					
Some teaching responsibilities					
EDUCATIONAL TECHNICIANS					

The second model illustrates that the roots of staff differentiation begin in the classroom and that all teachers maintain regular contacts with students. The initial staff reaction was most critical of the Senior Teacher role as presented in September of 1967.

FIGURE 15

Temple City Differentiated Staffing Plan
1969-71 (Model 3)

			Nontenure
		Nontenure	**MASTER TEACHER** Doctorate or equivalent
	Tenure	**SENIOR TEACHER** M.A. or equivalent	
Tenure	**STAFF TEACHER** B.A. and Calif. Credential		
ASSOCIATE TEACHER B.A. or Intern			
100% teaching responsibilities	100% teaching responsibilities	3/5's staff teaching responsibilities	2/5's staff teaching responsibilities
10 Months $6,500-9,000	10 Months $7,500-11,000	10-11 Months $14,500-17,500	12 Months $15,646-25,000
INSTRUCTIONAL AIDE II $6,000-7,500			
INSTRUCTIONAL AIDE I $4,000-7,500			
CLERKS $5,000-7,500			

Model 3 saw the renaming and combination of the Teaching Curriculum Associate and Teaching Research Associate into the Master Teacher-Research and Curriculum. The Academic Assistant of Model 2, originally a semiprofessional position, became the Associate Teacher which was fully professional and certificated. Model 3 was the one implemented in the Fall of 1969 at Oak Avenue Intermediate School.

A REVIEW OF GENERATION I MODELS

The differences between Generation I and Generation II are rooted in assumptions, points of view, and some related research. Allen hypothesized the following advantages to a four-level teacher hierarchy:[20]

1. automatic promotions regardless of competence would be eliminated;

2. school districts would have better control over dollars for staffing than before;

3. younger teachers would be encouraged to stay in teaching with "ceilings" removed;

4. the pool of available teaching talent would be expanded since school systems could recruit teachers who do not wish to accept a full professional role (i.e., housewives, etc.);

5. the differentiated staff would eliminate the labor-management connotations in staff negotiations by making it possible for teachers to receive greater compensation than administrators;

6. a differentiated staff would facilitate innovation;

7. the educational organization could become more flexible because more alternatives could be considered than before.

Allen foresaw these problems regarding staff differentiation in 1966:

1. working relationships between teachers would be more difficult;

2. the total school program would have to be modified;

3. educational decision making would have to be altered;

4. teacher education programs at universities and colleges would have to be substantially changed;

5. some teachers who were afraid of performance criteria would reject the idea.

In a later position paper distributed nationally by the NCTEPS of the National Education Association, Allen repeated the rationale of his earlier paper and added the criteria which he felt would be necessary to call a staff "differentiated."[21] These later became a part of the SPU guidelines.[22]

1. a minimum of three differentiated staff teaching levels, each having a different salary range;

2. a maximum salary at the top teaching category that was at least double the maximum at the lowest;

3. substantial direct teaching responsibilities for all teachers at all salary levels, including those in the top brackets.

A SECOND LOOK AT ALLEN'S ASSUMPTIONS

Underlying Allen's proposals which were adopted almost *in toto* in Temple City were a number of unstated but pervasive assumptions.

Assumption I: A Labor-Intensive Solution

Because he proposed a new task analysis and grouping of tasks by differentiation, Allen assumed that having more general classroom teachers would not improve educational productivity substantially. However, the addition of new teaching roles (a more labor-intensive solution) would enable the organization more effectively to utilize and retain teaching talent. Most educational economists would agree.[23, 24] However, Allen did not delve into *less* labor-intensive solutions with man/machine relationships.[25] He never proposed reducing the number of people in schools, but did propose the addition of more roles which were "differentiated" within the same dollar constraints. For example, he wrote in 1966:

> I would rather that you would take the position that there might be a number of teachers that would be able to occupy a senior position, but because you only have a limited number of senior positions available, you'll not be able to give senior recognition to more than a certain number of your staff. Otherwise, your mean salaries will never work out.[26]

The pursuit of less labor-intensive solutions to school staffing was not popular in 1966 and today, with the present teacher surplus, it is even less so. Nonetheless, the assumption of only a labor-intensive solution led to early models of differentiated staffing following the Temple City lead by adding on new teaching roles rather than redistributing tasks within teaching roles.

Additive models of differentiated staffing meant that the role of the classroom teacher formed a base to which other responsibilities were grouped, such as curriculum construction, research activities and administrative duties, each with a separate range of pay.[27] The significance of this approach to building a staffing model was that the actual range of teaching responsibilities with children was not substantially altered. This led to the removal of the teachers at the upper end of the hierarchy from pupil contact, a fact pointed out by Rose in 1968.[28] This criticism was answered at the time by assuming a broader definition of teaching than simply daily contact with pupils.[29] Allen's foresight led him to pointing this out while working in Temple City in the summer of 1967, but Temple City teachers rejected it on the grounds that it was too close to merit pay. If Allen had won the argument, Generation I models of differentiated staffing would have had a more profound impact on instructional programs than they have. The additive approach resulted in a change in roles, role structure and relationships, and organizational decision making, but only a very crude improvement of instruction by separation of instructional modes in flexible scheduling of the schools (large group, small group, tutorial). One of the attractive assumptions here is that *differentiated staffing* is synonymous with *differentiated instruction.* Almost any seasoned bureaucrat could testify to the inability of structural change alone to change real organizational behavior. This was especially true with differentiated staffing because the single-teacher-per-class-concept was not altered much by building career offices on the generic role responsibilities of classroom teachers. Figure 16 illustrates a further refinement of Allen's original hierarchy developed by an undergraduate seminar at Stanford in March 1967.[30] Allen consistently used the term "professor" for his top teaching role which was just as consistently rejected in Temple City and elsewhere. Some critics used the term to show that what Allen really had in mind was the superimposing of the university faculty hierarchy on the public schools. Figure 17 indicates an example by the author showing varying role responsibilities in a differentiated teaching staff. The same assumptions had to be accepted of nondifferentiating the actual teaching responsibilities in a differentiated staff. This is simpler to conceptualize doing than really doing. The fact is the teaching act is enormously complex. The derivation of a true base of "senior" skills based on either training or experience or both is very difficult to identify and to use as predictors of pupil performance.[31]

Assumption II: The "Salutary Effects" of the Career Ladder

Allen foresaw many salutary effects of a teacher career ladder embraced in the concept of a teacher's hierarchy. Among those were the added incentive for younger teachers to stay in teaching, greater leverage for change in the organization and greater ability of the organization to undergo changes, i.e., the organization would become more flexible than before. It is perhaps here that Allen made his worst prognostications about staff differentiation. During this time some research was beginning to emerge regarding the effects of hierarchies on organizations. First, the stratification of labor in an organization tends to crystallize upon divisions already in existence. The pattern was followed in Temple City. The addition of roles in Model II (Figure 18) such as Teaching Research Associate and Teaching Curriculum Associate were not brand new roles either to public school systems or education. The first redistribution of power in the school district was proposed under Model II and is shown in Figure 18. It was never implemented since the model was changed. The changed model resulted in a blend between what Parsons has called

FIGURE 16

ACADEMIC CABINET
Chairman—Principal   Members—Professors and Senior Teachers
Duties: Hiring and firing; evaluation of school, staff, and departments. Interdepartmental Communication

TITLE & SALARY	TEACHING DUTIES	CO-ORDINATING DUTIES	PLANNING DUTIES	QUALIFICATIONS	PROFESSIONAL DUTIES
PROFESSOR $14-18,000 $16,000 (average) (4)	Maximum pupil contact — large group teaching Conferences with small groups of teachers Remediation specialist	Anticipate needs Innovate to meet needs Coordinates tasks of cabinet Works with student advisory group	Special programs for exceptional students Overall school and curriculum goals	Ph.D. Multiple discipline orientation Demonstrated excellence in specialty	Guest lectures Liaison with college or university
SENIOR TEACHER $11-14,000 $12,500 (average) (7)	Prime candidate for large group instruction Teaches pilot program	Coordinates department Supervises and evaluates Coordinates pilot program	Unit plans with staff and associate teacher Responsible for departmental innovations	M.A. degree Must have teaching credential Outstanding teaching competence	Develops innovations in field
STAFF TEACHER $7500-9000 $8,200 (average) (19)	Maximum use of particular specialty Diagnosis and routine remediation Conducts in-service training. Teaches different grade and ability levels	Supervises associate teacher	Weekly planning with associate teacher. General course planning Responsible for pupil placement	Must have teaching credential Demonstrated teaching competence	Keep ahead in field and in education
ASSOCIATE TEACHER $5800-7500 $6,700 (average) (22)	Discussion leader Gives makeup tests Advisor to students	Coordinates own classes	Daily planning and evaluation	B.A. degree Provisional or full credential (Ex. Intern)	Parent Conferences
$2,500 (average)	Clerical Staff — Educational Technician				

FIGURE 17

ROLE RESPONSIBILITIES IN A DIFFERENTIATED TEACHING STAFF

TEACHING ROLE	RESPONSIBILITY	FUNCTIONS	EXAMPLE(S)
Master Teacher	District-wide; subject area responsibilities, K-12.	Classroom teaching; application of research to curriculum design by subject discipline and structure.	Development of experimental-research design of social studies units utilizing "post-holing" approach to solving contemporary social science problems at junior high school level.
Senior Teacher	School responsibilities, K-6, 7-9, 10-12.	Classroom teaching; application of new methodologies, learning and teaching strategies; media applications.	Concomitant development of experimental teaching strategies and tactics with new social studies "post-holing" units in pilot situations; evaluation; in-service with staff; revision; development of resource banks for new units.
Staff Teacher	Grade responsibilities, K-6, 7-9, 10-12.	Classroom teaching; individualized instruction; large/small group presentations, tutorial sessions.	Adaptation, adoption, evaluation of new social science units with suggestions made after extensive pupil monitoring in various instructional settings and modes for alternative strategies.
Associate Teacher	Grade responsibilities; K-6, 7-9, 10-12.	Beginning teacher. Classroom teaching; team-teaching partner; large group instruction assistance.	Implementation of new social science units with variations appropriate to teaching team strategies and assignment; evaluation of units regarding relevancy and content validity.

the "technical" and "managerial" organizational subsystems.[32] This blend of corporate decision making is illustrated in Figure 19.[33] Perhaps the most favorable aspect of this definition of a career ladder was that it served a tremendous forcing function toward integration of teachers in the decision making process in the schools at all levels. Of course, the involvement of teachers was not an automatic guarantee of better decisions, though experience showed that this was usually the case, but the process did take longer. Another criticism was that it was not possible to tell who made decisions any more, since the system had become fuzzy. The worst feature of the hierarchy as it began to take on longitudinal effects was that it made the organization more rigid than flexible.

Hierarchical relations overemphasize the veto and underemphasize approval of innovation. . . an hierarchical system always favors the status quo . . . the advantage is on the side of those who oppose innovation.[34]

FIGURE 18

Temple City Unified School District Differentiated Staffing Project
District Organization Under a Differentiated Staffing Plan
(Model 2)

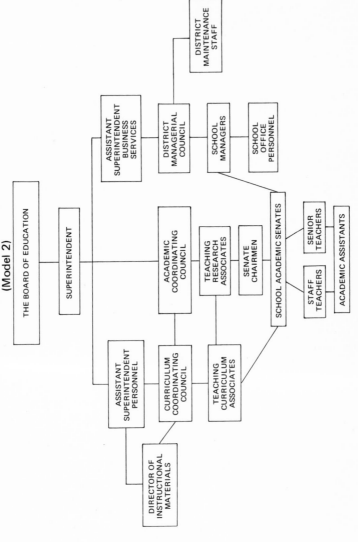

FIGURE 19

A Model of Evaluation and Decision Making in a
Differentiated Teaching Staff

Board Policy (Institutional Subsystem)

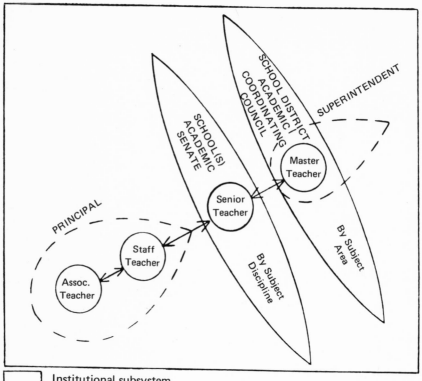

☐ Institutional subsystem

⟵⟶ Technical subsystem (evaluative and decision-making responsibilities)

⟨ ⟩ Managerial Subsystem (evaluative and decision-making responsibilities)

⬭ Corporate decision-making subsystems (technical/managerial groups)

Thompson notes two factors with specialization and hierarchy:
the restriction of communication and the division of employees into

labor and management camps, the latter condition offered by Allen to ameliorate staff differentiation. A reexamination of the Temple City project reveals some of the phenomena mentioned by Thompson. First, the deference system. Notes Thompson:

> Prolonged enactment of a role reacts upon the personality. People become what they do. Thus the deference accorded a person who performs a hierarchical role gradually modifies his self-characterization and hence his self-projection.[35]

In Temple City some older staff teachers became chronic complainers about their loss of status and prestige. They were depressed about a loss of status, saying that the visibility and the fruits of labor appeared to go to the senior teacher. Additional data on this point was provided by the Florida State evaluation completed in the spring of 1970. The FSU findings showed that staff teachers at Oak Avenue in Temple City identified three problems which related to the perceived loss of status. They were: (1) rivalry among faculty members, (2) loss of collegiality between peers due to hierarchical differentiation, (3) the lack of skills for interpersonal relations on the part of teachers.[36] The evaluation team commented on the plight of the staff teacher:

> Staff teachers displayed considerably greater concern with problems related to interpersonal relations than did associate teachers. Since the rank of staff teacher was automatically given to all personnel who were teaching in the school at the time the staffing project began and since all faculty additions were given the position of associate teacher, greater rivalry and competition for advancement to positions of responsibility would be expected among staff teachers during the initial years of implementation.[37]

This phenomenon was discussed some six months after staff differentiation was implemented in Temple City, "Staff teachers have expressed disappointment over the slipping status of the staff teacher role. Probably the role has not lost any of its authority, it just doesn't look as good when compared to the senior or master teacher positions."[38] Two years later, the Florida State evaluation revealed that the feeling was still present. Although teachers were not demoted in salary or any other visible loss of role prerogatives, some staff teachers felt they had lost something. Hierarchies of a permanent nature may have certain endemic problems which may never be solvable. The problem was predicted by Barbee:

> . . . it should be recognized that additional status levels may provide more opportunity for undesirable hierarchical distinctions to be made. Where position and title are overemphasized, where prerogatives of "office" are abused, and where respect of one's colleagues is derived from position rather than performance, professional relations will be unnecessarily encumbered and vital, everyday communication, with its essential flow of ideas, could be seriously impeded.[39]

These conditions were documented as existing in various forms by Stout and Burke earlier in Temple City.[40] They commented as follows after spending several days interviewing teachers:

1. the flow of information in the district was predominantly vertical;

2. what teachers knew derived from the administration;

3. teachers had no clear perception of how information reached the decision process. They were quite ignorant of the upward flow of communication;

4. the vast amount of "stuff" produced by the project staff did not facilitate teacher needs in the field;

5. the limits of teacher influence were deliberately set at a very low level;

6. teachers were unwilling to give deference to other teachers on the basis of their organizational responsibilities (because what most teachers—senior teachers—did was not regarded as important, except in the negative);

7. the program was resisted with little effort, it required only passive acceptance;

8. there was a lack of rewards to active participants; few rewards from colleagues were available for participation in the staffing model;

9. senior teachers had not built powerful bases of influence;

10. staff and associate teachers anticipated little impact on them by senior teachers.

Stout and Burke's onsite observations in Temple City were reaffirmed by research of Harrell Carpenter[41] of six school systems randomly selected from among ten in the Houston area. Carpenter hypothesized that the "taller" the school system in terms of hierarchical positions was, the less the perceived job satisfaction of classroom teachers. His data confirmed that teachers in "tall" school systems found less community prestige, professional authority, and participation in determining school goals than those in "flat" systems.

What became apparent with the Temple City experience was that the status system attached to some roles created in some teachers a morale problem, was ignored by others, and was a source of hostility for still others. Thompson comments on the status system:

> The inflation at the upper end of the status system results in deflation at lower levels. Since the status system controls distribution, the organization gives a great deal at the top and very little at the bottom. It has often been observed that at the middle and lower-middle reaches of the hierarchy concern with status and the symbols of status reaches an almost pathological intensity. At these points people with great dominance and status needs find less than enough to satisfy their needs because so much has been allocated to the positions above. The status system skews the distribution system.[42]

To return to an earlier notion, one definition of an organizational equilibrium is the extent to which the individual is willing to invest his energies to attain organizational objectives. If he is indifferent to those objectives, the organization must be able to offer him sufficient inducements to make it matter, such as salary, status and prestige.[43] Since most teachers were left out of the hierarchical structure with its skewed status system, there were little inducements for them to care what happened. A hierarchy actually underdevelops talent in this regard. Instead of offering career incentives it actually constricts the development of teacher talent and aspirations.

> The data suggest that differentiated formal positions in independent work groups may have negative consequences for performance. The occupants of lower positions may not be motivated to accomplish managerial objectives. If group members have an equal opportunity to engage in more challenging work, however, this lack of motivation may be eliminated. . . . formal position differentiation kept those in the lower formal positions underskilled and thus created a loss in potential group resources.[44]

Herbert Simon reinforces the findings that suggest teacher acceptance of the objectives of the school system depends on the nature and magnitude of the incentives the organization offers:

> In addition to the salary he receives, he may value the status and prestige that his position in the organization gives him, and he may value his relations with

the working group of which he is a part. In setting his task, the organization must take into consideration the effect that its order may have upon the employees' realization of these values.[45]

Simon insists that the return for mixing the organization goals and employee inducements is the degree to which employees can proclaim to be loyal to the organization. A person is loyal to an organization if he is committed to its objectives and purposes. A static hierarchy of fixed positions may act contrary to these objectives by limiting the distribution of status and prestige and actually impede the equilibrium of the organization.

Serious disturbances in the spring of 1971 in Temple City saw some defection by the teaching staff. A new board hostile to staff differentiation and flexible scheduling assumed leadership. The hostile element was fed informally by some disgruntled teachers and administrators who for six years had been replaced, moved or lost out on any of the new differentiated positions. One board member's wife was a high school teacher who had been turned down twice for leadership training and a senior teacher position. This board member's supporters launched a bitter and acrimonious vilification of the superintendent and the administration.[46] The effort was fueled by the county office who refused to pay the teacher her salary on the grounds that having her husband on the board was a conflict of interest. This latter obstacle was removed by a legal opinion in favor of the teacher.

While the school district has weathered the storm, the extent of damage is not known. For longitudinal observation upon teachers, pupils and parents of this model, it would be beneficial to continue it several more years. While other projects have experienced some difficulties, none has been as pronounced. This is because few extended the career ladder to offer substantial salary and status differentials beyond the role of classroom teacher which were really competitive with the administrative career ladder. It is easy when armed with hindsight to second guess a courageous educational experiment. It should be remembered that the findings and opinions presented here are still preliminary. Without Temple City there would have been no Generation II models. Like breaking the four minute mile, before most educators and school board members would actually consider a radical staffing alternative, it had to become a reality. That fact is owed to Temple City.[47]

ORGANIZED TEACHERS REACT TO THE HIERARCHY APPROACH

Probably the most heated response by organized teachers, the American Federation of Teachers, and the Association of Classroom Teachers of the NEA was reserved for the concept of a teacher's hierarchy. The American Federation of Teachers was consistent in its response: a teacher's hierarchy was divisive and destructive to the goals of organized teachers. In January 1968 David Seldon reviewed the newly funded Education Professions Development Act and its implications for classroom teachers.

Regardless of the validity of the systems analysis approach to school staffing from an engineering standpoint, it is obvious that the point of view is managerial . . . it is obvious that the master plan of the USOE runs counter to the present goals of organized teachers. . . . Improvements sought by organized teachers are viewed as possible within the present structure without major alteration of prevailing tables of organization except, perhaps, for a bit of team teaching here, and restricted use of paraprofessionals there.

The last thing education needs is more bureaucracy, nor can teachers permit the introduction of merit rating and a rank system into what is now a reasonably cooperative and egalitarian work group.[48]

AFT literature was from the beginning highly skeptical, often petulant and finally downright negative. Seldon and Bhaerman[49] in "How High, O Lord, How High?" listed the AFT position on staff differentiation.

1. The AFT, through the process of teacher negotiations, reiterates the necessity for teacher involvement in all phases of decision making on matters of educational policy and process. Academic senates should not be viewed as substitutes for comprehensive collective bargaining.

2. The AFT reiterates its opposition to merit-pay scales and to other methods which may be elusive disguises for merit salary ratings.

3. The AFT reiterates its long-time goal for the limitation of maximum class size and opposes the attempt to increase teacher-student ratios. Nevertheless, within the context of collective bargaining, the AFT supports all forms of legitimate educational experimentation.

4. The AFT supports the position that teaching is not competitive. It is a cooperative and communal effort and so it should remain. Nothing must be injected to create divisiveness.

5. The AFT supports legitimate and comprehensive research efforts in order to evaluate various differentiated staffing models. Such evaluatory research must take into consideration the effects of these models upon educational productivity.

The AFT has denied that teachers can be ranked—that one is more important than the other. This view is contained in Bhaerman's, "Several Educators' Cure For the Common Cold, Among Other Things, or One Unionist View of Staff Differentiation."[50] Bhaerman alleges that (1) differentiated staffing was created to serve not student needs but administrator convenience, (2) differentiated staffing embodies the philosophy and weaknesses of merit pay, and (3) differentiated staffing does not reward all qualified teachers who seek advancement.

Claffey feared that differentiated staffing was used by some school systems to save money.[51] Seldon spoke on differentiated staffing at the AFT's 1969 Convention:

> The idea of differentiated staffing—separating faculty members into specialized functional and status categories—originated outside the governing bodies of the teaching profession—either NEA or AFT—and, it was thrust upon us without discussion or vote. Now we have to deal with it. . . . We have avoided an outright negative response but, at the same time, we have made it clear that we will not support the introduction of ranks into elementary and secondary school teaching. We consider this merely a device to introduce merit rating in disguise.[52]

It came as no surprise that the following year Resolution 39 of the American Federation of Teachers voted that differentiated staffing tends to:

1. create a vertical hierarchy with job responsibilities commensurate with a rate of pay which could eventuate in merit pay scales;

2. destroy the cooperative and communal effort necessary for effective teaching;

3. create divisiveness within the teaching staff and;

4. be of dubious value in improving the learning process.[53]

The AFT's objections center on the effects of staff differentiation on teachers and teacher power. Virtually none of their objections relates to greater specialization because children are in need of such specialization. The greatest fear of the AFT is the creation of ranks which would weaken teachers at the bargaining table. In commenting on the union theory of collective bargaining, Millis and Montgomery noted that three important assumptions undergird the concept, the first of which is "that the members of the worker group have an important common interest rather than conflicting, competitive interests.[54] The reasoning behind collective effort to secure wages is that, "the individual bargain, or individual contract, between employers and men means that the condition of the worst and lowest man in the industry will be that which the best man must accept."[55]

One of the major differences in the past between the NEA affiliates and the AFT affiliates is that the latter would not accept administrators as members. The union has assiduously avoided accepting anybody but teachers since they argue that, "teachers can hardly be expected to gain redress with those who are the source of their grievances."[56] Homogeneity is strength. To the extent that members differ markedly, and heterogeneity increases, so does the possibility of divisiveness. The union believes that the "interests of employers, as seen and acted upon by them, and the interests of the workers of the group are frequently, if not generally, conflicting."[57] Since school administrators are extensions of the authority of the employer, to accept them in the membership would be self-defeating, especially if conflict is inevitable.

Teacher union response is couched in the union's historical movement towards confrontation. "The great majority of unions are interested above all else in the worker's position in his trade or industry. This is especially true of unions of the business type, which have limited interest in matters of reform and no active interest in effecting radical changes in the essentials of the existing economic order ... they are immediately interested in jobs, wages, and working conditions."[58] To bring about compliance by boards of education, unions must preserve the unity of the ranks, establish a monopoly so that school systems cannot go elsewhere for a supply of labor or radically change the labor supply (with the mass introduction of paraprofessionals), and must depend heavily upon established order and procedures to bring the full weight of numbers to bear on recalcitrant school systems. The AFT will not only be resistant to a vertical division of labor, but any type of radical change or reform which threatens to disrupt those same sets of conditions upon which the strength of the union is perceived to rest. The union's response must therefore be perceived in light of its own organizational needs and goals as opposed to those of school systems, or children, generally. What the AFT position means is that they recognize more clearly than others the essential stabilizing functions of present school staffing patterns. Collective bargaining fits neatly into the quality in the division of labor and the present bureaucratic model of education. For this reason, the AFT has as much interest in the status quo as any single group within education.

Bhaerman summarized the Union position for the Commissioner of Education in March of 1971 by commenting on the following resolution passed by the AFT Executive council:[59]

Vertical Staffing

Whereas, vertical staffing patterns (sometimes called "differentiated staffing") threaten to become a common administrative practice in U.S. education, and

Whereas, vertical staffing patterns create a hierarchy of salary ('levels' of job responsibilities commensurate with a rate of pay), status and authority, and thus tend to destroy the cooperative and communal effort necessary for a successful teaching effort, and

Whereas, vertical staffing patterns create arbitrary and artificial "levels" of responsibility in terms of salary differentials and thus result in a new version of the merit salary system, and

Whereas, vertical staffing patterns create a divisiveness within the teaching staff and are of dubious value in improving the learning process among students; there, be it

Resolved, that the AFT go on record as opposing any vertical staffing patterns which reduce the total number of fully certificated staff responsible for the education of pupils, which results in an arbitrary reduction of financing for education, and which is a movement away from the concept of the single salary schedule, and, be it further

Resolved, that any plan dealing with staff utilization must be developed in consonance with the teachers union through the process of negotiations in all phases of decision making in matters of policy and process, and be it further

Resolved, that all AFT locals investigate thoroughly any and all plans promulgated by school districts which violate the above precepts.

The resolution is based upon the following eight tenets:

1. We hold that it is imperative to *distinguish between* the concept of "differentiated staff" (differentiated roles and responsibilities) and the concept of "verticalism" (the creation of a hierarchy of authority, salary and status). While we support the former, we reject the latter. We hold that teaching must be viewed as a cooperative and communal effort.

2. We hold that the concept of verticalism is a negative strategy in that it tends to destroy the single salary schedule and injects a new version of merit salary which is equally abhorrent to classroom teachers, namely, that "levels" of responsibility can be distinguished in terms of salary differentials.

3. We hold that the single salary schedule must be maintained. Significant increases in salary should be the means by which teachers are attracted to and retained in the profession.

4. We hold that differentiated roles and responsibilities on a *horizontal* basis, that is, with salaries based on experience and education, implies the use of such positive elements as flexible staff assignment, individualized in-service programs, cooperative team approaches, interdisciplinary curriculum, cross-age grouping and the like. We hold that these innovations can be achieved without the encroachment of verticalism.

5. We hold that the arbitrary designation of vertical levels between specialists and generalists, one group of specialists and another, or any personnel designated on such ladders as "master teacher," "senior teacher," and "staff teacher" leads to divisiveness in the schools and should be rejected.

6. We hold that the concept of *horizontally* differentiated roles and responsibilities is consistent with the union principle of extra pay for extra work. This does not assume the inflexible levels common to most vertical models. We reject the attempt at institutionalizing, rigidifying, and bureaucratizing staff utilization patterns. The union alternative, extra pay for extra work, bases extra salaries upon the performance of additional tasks (e.g., supervision of interns, committee work, teaching in-service courses) rather than upon designated, locked-in "levels" of responsibility. Since these extra jobs may vary from time to time, rigid ladders of any kind are rejected.

7. We hold that, within the context of collective bargaining, we will support legitimate experimentation and comprehensive research into all patterns of staff utilization.

8. We hold that so-called educational solutions which are of dubious value in encouraging the learning process among students, or which create more problems than they are intended to resolve, or which promote divisiveness in the teaching ranks are not worthy of our support.[60]

The Gemini Posture of the NEA

For several years the NEA spoke out of two sides of its mouth. First, NCTEPS supported and advanced the concept while Gary D. Watts, Head of the Division of Field Services, called it ". . . camouflaged merit pay of the highest order and I'm against it for all the reasons that I'm against merit pay."[61] At the beginning of the decade TEPS was abolished after a prolonged in-house fight. It was no secret to anyone that TEPS' support of staff differentiation was one of the major issues between the two NEA divisions. In its own position paper on staff differentiation, the Association of Classroom Teachers noted certain "unresolved issues." Of the six unsettled questions, four dealt with the problem and antagonism towards the concept of a teacher hierarchy. Cautioned ACT:

1. Can differentiated staffing be accomplished only by establishing a new hierarchy within the school system? Might there not be horizontal movement for the teacher rather than vertical movement or a plan of rotating assignments that could be equally effective?

2. Will differentiated staffing foster greater teamwork and solidarity among teachers, or will specialization and differentiation be a divisive factor?

3. If teaching is the primary function of the teacher and since status is so closely related to remuneration in today's society, can any plan be successful if it is implemented on the basis of the hierarchy described in most differentiated staffing plans?

4. Are the various assignments identified in differentiated teaching so specialized and so individualized that they fall automatically into hierarchic pattern? If one accepts the premise that each individual has both strengths and weaknesses, does a hierarchic system maximize strengths and minimize weaknesses?[62]

Later the NEA's Division of Field Services released a very negative blast about staff differentiation and reiterated the NEA's Resolution No. 69-4 on Differentiated Staffing.

The Association insists that any design for differentiating staff to be successful:

a. must meaningfully involve classroom teachers and the local associations from the initial stages of development through implementation and evaluation, and

b. must clearly define roles and responsibilities of certificated and noncertificated staff so that the actual process of teaching rests in hands of individuals having sound educational preparation, and

c. must keep the community informed and seek its cooperation in order to prevent misunderstanding of the educational values to be gained from differentiated staffing.

Available funds must be sufficient both to assure maintenance of manageable loads and to guarantee remuneration for all staff-auxiliary personnel, teachers, and administrators—based upon well grounded criteria and not reflective of a merit pay plan for teachers.[63]

The AFT and ACT remain solidly opposed to differentiation of function and salary, for reasons which pertain to the power and autonomy of organized teachers within bureaucratically defined and operated school systems: They are destined to defend and support traditional staffing patterns, particularly if they threaten to change the present salary structure, or the present administrative structure.[64] As David Seldon said, the union supports the present table of organization. It supports it because arrangements for collective bargaining function on it. The only approach which appears hopeful for innovators is to demonstrate the need in the classroom that advanced expertise is necessary to meet the specified and clearly differentiated needs of children for differentiated instruction. The irony is that, while the AFT proposes an assessment based upon productivity, it denies to school districts definitions of productivity by opposing behavioral objectives when they are related to pupil accomplishment and teacher pay.[65] The AFT's "Paradigm for Accountability" is in actuality a slick new euphemism for the present model of school staffing and an endorsement (more by default than design) of the traditional line and staff bureaucracy of education.[66] As mentioned by Millis and Montgomery earlier, teacher unions are not agents of reform. Their own interests preclude the necessity for reform.[67]

Generation II Models: "Contingency" Staffing

The bridging model between Generation I and Generation II was that of Bernard McKenna.[68] McKenna's interest in staffing patterns can be traced back to his earlier works at Columbia with the late Paul Mort.[69] McKenna rejected the idea of a professional staff based upon "a hierarchy of professional development," and took the stand that differentiation should be based upon the learning tasks of pupils. He proposed five teacher types accompanying five learning task categories. McKenna's first teacher type was the Teacher Technologist who possessed skill in administering basic skills and knowledges with children. The learning tasks essential for the student were the mastering of basic skills and knowledges, e.g., reading, historical data and computational skills. McKenna's second teacher type was dubbed the Liberal Enlightener, who possessed skill as a master presenter. The learning task for the student was enlightenment in areas in which knowledge of the general population was considered important but in which every person was not required to be proficient. The third teacher type was the Identifier of Talents, an instructor who had skill in promoting exploration in broad fields. The learning task accompanying this teacher would be having students identify their interests and aptitudes in music, creative writing, and earth science. The fourth teacher type was the Developer of Talents and Aptitudes. This teacher helped develop a potential talent in specialized areas such as proficiency in dealing with higher mathematical concepts, or writing plays. The last and highest teacher type was the Facilitator of Attitudes. This teacher's expertise consisted of human relations attitudes and skills as he attempted to develop in pupils acceptance and appreciation of cultural differences, group process, and group leadership roles. There are a number of theoretical and practical problems with the McKenna approach. To actually staff schools, policies, procedures, and pay scales would ultimately have to accompany this model. For the hierarchy to have any validity or fairness, one must be able to screen out learning behavior not due to the behavior of the teacher. Another difficulty is that McKenna uses as one method of separating tasks breaking them into cognitive or affective domains, following the approach of the Bloom and Krathwohl *Taxonomies*.[70,71] While this may be instructive for the purposes of analysis, in reality the two domains are so intertwined that to rank and pay teachers on the basis of this separation would be fallacious.

One of the major criticisms of the present staffing pattern employed is that it assumes the existence of a universal student. Individual differences between students, though certainly real enough, do not form the operational procedures of an organization that denies their existence in the manner in which both students and teachers are assigned to deal with one another. The McKenna approach changes the once generic role of the teacher, but not of the student. The fundamental assumption remains that student needs are about the same for all students. If they were not, the idea of arranging a permanent ranking of teachers based upon a common set of learning tasks would be an impossibility. To admit much pupil diversity would be to throw the teacher ranking into confusion. Figure 20 shows the assumptions of the McKenna paradigm graphically.

FIGURE 20

Building a Model of Staff Differentiation on Learning Tasks:
The McKenna Approach

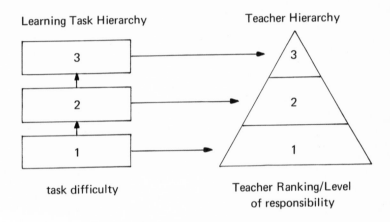

N. L. Gage has likewise disputed this approach on the grounds that

We have assumed for too long that if we understood how learners learned, we would automatically understand how teachers should teach. Too much of educational psychology makes the teacher infer what he needs to do from what he is told about learners and learning . . . theories of teaching would make explicit how teachers behave, why they behave as they do, and with what effects. Hence theories of teaching need to develop alongside, on a more equal basis with, rather than by inference from, theories of learning.[72]

The McKenna model was later modified by Fantini and Weinstein in their concept of the three-tiered school, though its actual implementation of that model is not known.[73] English collected and classified twelve models of staff differentiation, of which only three placed primary emphasis upon the student as the central focus of staff differentiation.[74] He introduced in theory what was later to become in practice the Mesa staff differentiation model.[75] It was called then the Learning Stage Model. There was in this model no permanent hierarchy of positions, those being contingent upon pupil needs. (This is the source of the term "contingency" staffing.)

The model would concentrate its energies on establishing measurable learning objectives and arranging its teaching talents to accomplish those objectives, and in building a tightly knit group of teachers. . . . Vertical hierarchical relationships are shaped by the major tasks of each learning stage. They might be:

STAGE I: The building of data banks
STAGE II: Establishing assessable, valid objectives
STAGE III: Pupil diagnosis
STAGE IV: Learning prescriptions (sequence of activities)
STAGE V: Implementation (teaching/learning)
STAGE VI: Evaluation/feedback/diagnosis

In theory the advantages of a model stressing such "fluidity" appeared to be:

1. the teacher hierarchy was made to "fit" the pupil rather than the opposite with preformed professional hierarchies;

2. hierarchical problems of status can be played down;

3. hierarchical position is the function of the task rather than a preconceived idea of what services are of the most worth for all students;

4. the overspecialization problem (and later "deadwood" problem) can be dealt with much more quickly;

5. organizational "rewards" can become congruent with "results" and the relationship between a staffing pattern (deployment) and pupils (learning) can become discernable and assessable;

6. a collaborative atmosphere between teaching professionals is emphasized rather than individual competition for hierarchical positions;

The learning stage model was revolutionary, since it focused staffing positions and functions on pupil performance objectives. Fixing salary to the fluidity of the staffing pattern thereby avoided the problem of salary ceilings. In the learning stage model, the salary accompanied performance and the salary model moved to what has been called "baseline plus commission"[76] and led to the creation of an internal educational performance contracting system.[77] This latter salary idea introduced the concept of teaching teams in the field submitting educational bids to the administration to accomplish specific instructional objectives. With the exception of the notion of a fluid hierarchy, the Mesa model closely parallels AFT specifications. Baseline plus commission is simply an expansion of the acceptable extra pay for extra duty concept. The idea of fluidity due to fluctuating factors was already mentioned in the AFT position. The Mesa position is that a teacher's hierarchy is never permanent since the needs of pupils are not permanent. A vertical ranking of roles is (or is not) necessary in order to parallel a hierarchy of pupil need.

Some credence was given to the Mesa approach of "fluidity" as a result of the Florida State evaluation. The FSU study revealed that of the two concepts which were statistically significant (in this case "collegiality" and "professional practices of the school") Mesa was the highest of four models compared on both items.[78] [The exact breakdown was as follows: on "collegiality" with a mean of 3.37, Mesa = 3.70; Sarasota = 3.45; Temple City = 3.41 and Leon = 3.17. For "professional practices of the school" the mean was 2.72. Mesa = 3.54; Sarasota = 2.79; Temple City = 2.71; and Leon with 2.44] It may be hypothesized that the nonhierarchical model did in fact "play down" status differentials.

Probably the most damaging criticism of Generation I models of staff differentiation is that if they represented a concrete bridge to pupil need (and few made any attempt to do this) and if instruction had been effective, pupil needs could not be static. Roles must have the possibility of moving in relationship to one another. The perpetuation of static hierarchies can only be continued at the risk of promoting a teacher solution at the expense of a pupil problem.[79] Generation I models were never initiated on the basis of a pupil needs assessment. They began from the assumption of the necessity for a career ladder. Even if they had been based initially upon a needs assessment of pupils, a static career ladder would cease to be functional over a period of time due to the fluctuating basis of pupil needs interacting with the instructional program. When pay scales and personnel policies are similarly established on the basis of a permanent hierarchy of positions, pupil needs must exist in approximately the same proportion as the teacher hierarchy in order to continue paying a consistently higher wage for some responsibilities. Generation I models promoted a structural, not necessarily a behavioral change in the schools.

As I look back now at our unbridled optimism, our efforts and accomplishments take on a new perspective. I think now that we overestimated the effect of an innovation like differentiated staffing in bringing about the fundamental kind of changes in schools that matched our dreams. We saw the emergence of fresh levels of specialization ushering in new institutional vitality and to some extent it did happen. On the other hand, changes in teacher behavior have been much slower, though here too, there is real evidence of change.

What has become very apparent is the deep realization that unless staff differentiation is accompanied by a substantial working of the system towards reconciliation of "people" problems via group dynamics and other types of conflict resolution techniques, a structural change is quite limited as a forcing function for real behavioral change.

In short, we have returned from utopia, that is, believing that the mere alteration of the administrative structure and the establishment of new or refined instructional roles would alone dramatically upgrade the quality of education in the public schools.[80]

A type of staffing which *is* responsive to pupil needs and derives its shape from specific instructional objectives is referred to as contingency staffing. Contingency staffing is based upon the following:

1. it is envisioned as a means to an end, and not as an end in itself; it is based upon a diagnosis first of learners; Figure 21 illustrates that when staff differentiation is viewed as an end in itself, pupils become means to that end. If viewed as a means to an end, specific changes in pupil behaviors become the goal.

2. that staff are hired and deployed *after* diagnosis and not before;

3. that staffing positions and salary are contingent upon per-

FIGURE 21

MEANS/ENDS ANALYSIS

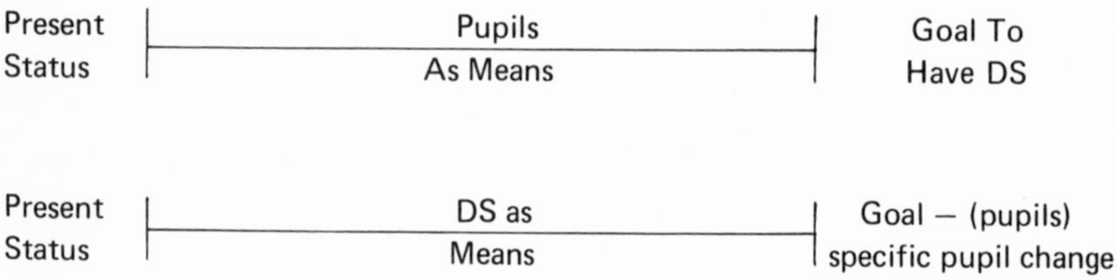

Present Status	Pupils As Means	Goal To Have DS

| Present Status | DS as Means | Goal — (pupils) specific pupil change |

forming activities (1) and (2) and are considered "hierarchical" only for the time period designated to reach specified, performance objectives;

4. may be considered "balanced" by beginning first with a statement of output, and then resources are distributed where needs assume a hierarchy; balanced staffing is roughly a parallel to pupil need and as such is highly situational and fluid.[81]

The Mesa Model: The Second Generation

The Mesa, Arizona, model of staff differentiation has been called a second generation paradigm. It is described in more detail elsewhere in this volume. Its theoretical predecessor was the Learning State Model previously described. The Mesa approach is based upon the following ideas:

1. all new teaching roles (and indeed the perpetuation of old roles) must be based upon a needs assessment of learners. Whatever else a staffing pattern must be, it must be learner centered;

2. no *permanent* ranking or hierarchy of roles is envisioned in the schools. Some roles may assume some static aspects during a transitional stage and especially during training periods;

3. a hierarchy of roles must parallel a hierarchy of student need as revealed in the schools needs assessment; roles are established for a specific period of time and in relationship to specific objectives. When objectives have been met the hierarchy is abolished. All roles are objective and situationally specific.[82]

4. the pay mechanism for such a fluid arrangement is a secondary aspect to the project, subject to the involvement of all parties concerned. The focus of the project is on *output*, or student behavior and growth, rather than on input.

5. there is no overall (generic) model in the Mesa project. Rather, all models of staff differentiation are site specific, time specific and objective specific. Differentiated staffing is a *process*, not a thing. The emphasis of the project has been upon teaching teachers how to build models based upon sound theoretical practices, and from a pupil data base since teachers will continually be having to build models from contracting period to contracting period.[83]

Figure 22 is a classification of three models of staff differentiation of ten continuums. Indeed, for the most part, the models represent the opposite and middle of those continuums. Temple City represents the most famous and successful of the Generation I models, the purest Generation I model. Sarasota, Florida, is midway between Mesa and Temple City. The Sarasota model was constructed by Pillot after extensive analysis of the Temple City experience, but prior to the Mesa project.[84] Pillot explicates the Sarasota model in another chapter of this book.

FIGURE 22

Tentative List of the Characteristics of Three Differentiated Staffing Models on Ten Basic Continuums of Project Development

CONTINUUM	TEMPLE CITY, CA.	SARASOTA, FLA.	MESA, ARIZONA
1. Hierarchy of roles	fixed-static	semistatic	fluid; shifting; impermanent
2. Degree of teacher-centeredness	almost wholly teacher centered	semi-teacher centered	student needs form basis for task analysis and role development;
3. Basis of role structure	analysis of teacher tasks	analysis of teacher tasks	learning objectives for pupils;
4. Model site (school) specificity	very little model site adaptability	units are interchangeable or equated	wholly site specific
5. Salary structure	fixed/hierarchical and parallels administrative career ladder	semihierarchical	salary base plus (+) role contribution during "bid" period;
6. Utilization of output as feedback to change model of DS degree of closed-loop provisions;	roles and role numbers are not dependent upon feedback (student) utilization	not a planned part of model, but adaptable	dependent upon feedback on pupils from performance contract to contract
7. Role of pupil objectives in model	ancillary	generalized pupil tasks form role base	dependent upon pupil objectives based on needs assessment;
8. Curriculum focus	disciplined centered or subject matter centered	same as Temple City	product centered within and across existing disciplines
9. Evaluative criteria	means centered/incidental data gathered	means centered	criterion and product centered
10. Model priorities and "mix"	(a) structural change; (b) people; (c) curriculum (d) outcomes;	(a) structural (b) curriculum (c) people (d) outcomes	(a) outcome centered; (b) people centered; (c) curriculum centered (d) structural change

Hierarchy of Roles

The diagram illustrates that roles in Temple City were fixed and remain static in relationship to one another over long periods of time.[85] The hierarchy is set. Personnel and salary policies in Temple

City reflect its permanency. In Sarasota roles may be swapped via a standardization procedure developed by Pillot for role exchange in relationship to school needs and budget considerations. In Mesa, roles are fluid, both in relationship to one another and in their very existence as roles. Some functions may extend from performance contract to performance contract, but hierarchical relationships are extremely situational.

Degree of Teacher Centeredness

Temple City teachers designed the Temple City differentiated staffing roles. They were centered on an analysis of teacher tasks and were ordered by teachers. In Sarasota teacher tasks were grouped in roles which were interchangeable. The Mesa approach demands that teacher tasks and functions follow and must be based upon an assessment of learner needs. Learner needs are not exclusively defined by teachers or educators.

Basis of Role Structure

The basis of role structure follows and reflects the degree of teacher centeredness. Role structure in Temple City followed an analysis of teacher tasks and is flexible but still system centered in Sarasota. In Mesa, role structure is client-centered.

Model Site Specificity

The exportability and adaptablility of a model depend largely on its site specificity, or how sensitive the process of model building is to local conditions and characteristics. In Temple City a model was developed centrally by groups in the district with minor variations from elementary to secondary in terms of actual role responsibilities. In Sarasota staffing units are viewed as interchangeable separately or in combinations. Thus, combinations of roles can be utilized at particular buildings, but roles are defined centrally. The Mesa approach is wholly site specific. Roles come and go. Schools are held accountable for the results of their staffing pattern by performance contracting.

Salary Structure

The salary structure in Temple City was fixed by salary ceilings created for each hierarchical position. Salary for the advanced teacher positions closely matched that of the administrative position to which it was paired on the career ladder. Salary for teaching positions was fixed in Sarasota to ranges for particular positions, some with varying responsibilities. The salary structure in Mesa was based upon the idea of a flatter teacher salary schedule which encompassed some recognition for training and experience, but beyond which teachers earned "a commission" by performance contracting role responsibilities. This aspect was being modeled at the time of publication.

Degree of Closed-Loop Provisions

In system analysis the term "closed-loop"[86] connotes the fact that the model developed is self-correcting since it enjoys the capacity of gathering data about how well it met specified objectives and is able to initiate activities to come closer to the target. In Temple City, the staffing model was created before the needs assessment was undertaken and in Mesa the needs assessment preceded the development of staffing roles at the schools. Roles are maintained in Temple City irrespective of how well target objectives were met (though the person occupying the role might be removed for incompetency); whereas roles, tasks and personalities may change in Mesa as a result of obtaining feedback information. This provision is in reality part of a larger process of implementing a closed-loop school. English, Zaharis, and Kaufman proposed a three-sided needs assessment model developed by Kaufman and used extensively in education.[87,88] (See Figure 23). Figure 24 illustrates how the needs assessment model may be employed to build four basic organizing centers of the school, including a professional self-renewal center in which staffing patterns could be studied and evaluated and in which staff could be trained for new roles onsite. The closed-loop school is built and organized around specific pupil objectives in the cognitive and affective areas. It possesses the capacity to alter its methodologies to reach those objectives within specific performance requirements. From the basic needs-assessment model, four generic organizing centers are formed. Specific curriculum content, staffing, teaching methodologies, and materials are formed after the needs assessment in which specific student and teaching objectives have been developed. The ongoing feasibility study insures that costs are kept under control.[89]

FIGURE 23

SCHOOL GOALS

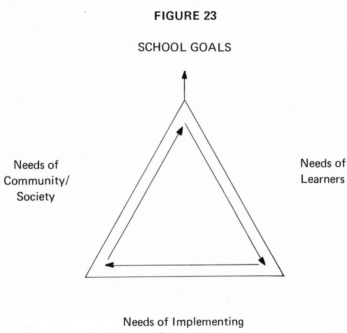

Needs of Community/Society

Needs of Learners

Needs of Implementing Educators

ROLE OF PUPIL OBJECTIVES IN THE MODEL

The difference between Generation I and II models is very clear here. Pupil objectives were not established first in Temple City or elsewhere prior to an analysis of teaching tasks. Rather, it was assumed that what teachers were doing was essentially correct and that a redistribution and addition of functions was necessary. Generation II models begin with an analysis of pupil needs. These are then formed into goals and performance objectives from which teaching functions are derived.

FIGURE 24

The Closed-Loop or Self-Correcting School

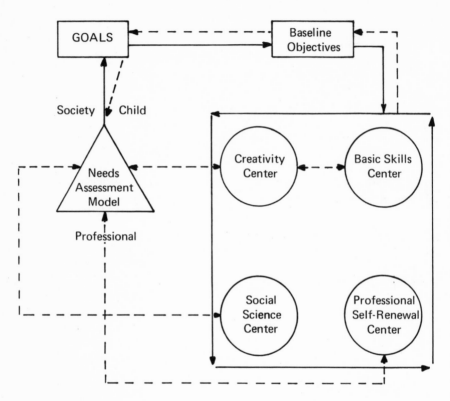

Curriculum Focus

Generation I models accepted current notions of the curriculum disciplines—mathematics, history, English—and worked almost exclusively within them. Thus, in Temple City there was a senior teacher of mathematics and a master teacher of social studies, for example. Generation II models are more product centered, though even in Mesa there has not been a significant movement away from the traditional disciplines.

Evaluative Criteria

Evaluative criteria refers to whether differentiated staffing has been envisioned as a means or an end. A view of staff differentiation as an end limits data to whether or not the model was implemented. A product centered emphasis accompanies Generation II models because they stem from outcomes stressed in terms of things produced by students or teachers. If staff differentiation has been conceived as a means, it is possible to ascertain what has occurred after it has been implemented. Better yet, staff differentiation should have been selected as the best methods-means available to reach specified objectives. Then it may be determined to what degree desired objectives have been reached.

The Model Mix

The model mix refers to the relative priorities models give to four critical areas: structure, people, curriculum and/or outcomes. Generation I models were almost exclusively concerned with structural changes and alternatives. Generation II models placed more emphasis upon process and people with heaviest emphasis on outcomes stated in terms of pupil behaviors. There is almost a complete reversal from GI to GII models on the point of structure.

Toward Generation III Models

The essential differences between Generation I and II models is a matter of emphasis, philosophical approach and outcome-feedback provisions. Generation II resolved the hierarchy problem and correctly placed staff differentiation as a means to an end (student outcomes), while providing a process whereby models were continually created and abolished. The shift is important and fundamental. However, Generation II models are still limited because they have not yet been able to become fully sensitized to client differences nor based upon any type of comprehensive learning theory; they lack a sound psychological base. If our study and experimentation of staffing patterns ends with Generation II, we may have merely created a system whereby improved learning can take place, but by which it cannot be guaranteed with any certainty or predictability. Bluntly, we do not have, with staffing flexibility, a scientific staffing of the schools; we merely have the vehicle and the process by which one might be defined. In considering the alternatives several issues are raised.

How Specialization of Work Relates to Instructional Improvement

The historic division of labor (work specialization) in education occurred in the splitting off of the role principal-teacher from teacher, and later from principal-teacher to superintendent.[90] Although new roles have been created (such as supervisor, coordinator, counselor, vice-principal), the basic role differentiation has remained teacher-principal-superintendent. The role of paraprofessional has often been confused with differentiated staffing. It is true that the addition of teacher aides or paraprofessionals[91] does represent a kind of work specialization. But it is not true that the addition of such roles increases the sophistication of the instructional staff; it merely represents a reallocation of talent with existing time frames. This can be illustrated in a series of figures (25, 26, 27). Job depth and job scope have been borrowed from Filley and House and slightly changed in meaning.[92] In this context, "job depth" refers to the range of tasks that a role incumbent is required to perform, from simple to complex. "Job scope" refers to the degree to which the incumbent performs those tasks *across* the organization. Figure 25 shows a self-contained classroom teacher. The teacher ranks high on the depth continuum and low on the scope continuum. While the self-contained classroom teacher is infinitely responsible for a plethora of duties (from nose wiping to reading diagnosis), her ability to perform any of those tasks is contained within the four walls of her classroom.

Figure 26 shows the addition of a paraprofessional. The paraprofessional reduces the lower quadrant of the self-contained teacher's functions, thus enabling the teacher to concentrate her time on other functions. However, it does not raise the depth or scope of the teacher's responsibilities. The addition of teacher aides in self-contained classrooms is uneconomical since it is possible for one aide effectively to service more than one teacher. Secondly, a one-on-one situation, which is duplicated with all teachers in a school, ignores the fact that what teachers are "freed" to do is more of the same. The addition of aides on an indiscriminate basis reinforces existing skills and functions and ignores those which should be developed (It perpetuates present inequities in teacher skills). Aides should be

FIGURE 25

The Self-Contained Classroom Teacher

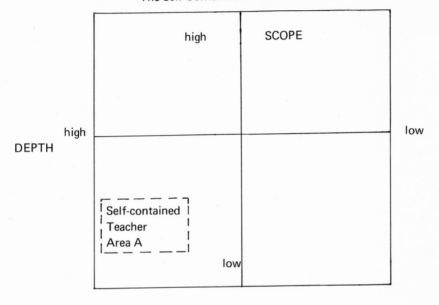

FIGURE 26

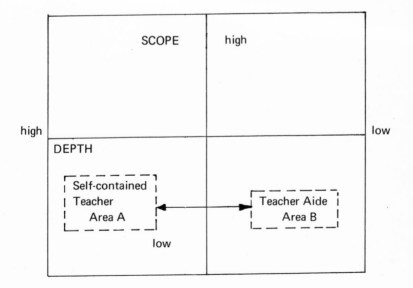

FIGURE 27

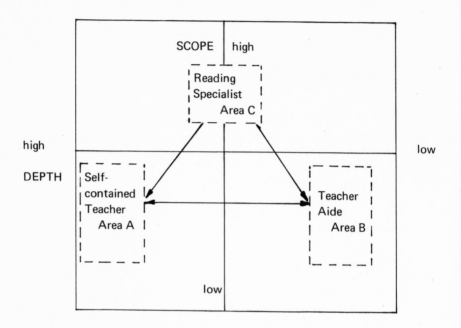

assigned on a differentiated basis matching teacher differentiated responsibilities. Some teachers, because of the kind of instructional responsibilities they bear, may have three or four aides, while others may not have any. Such assignments only make sense when a teaching staff is functioning in an open space work environment.

The significant point of this analysis is that instructional sophistication is not increased unless more specialization is added in the form of upgrading some staff roles/skills or in the addition of roles as in the example, a reading specialist shown in Figure 27. Such specialization on top of self-contained classrooms is likewise somewhat uneconomical (Witness the release of many music, art and physical education specialists in elementary schools in big city school systems.) Unless the specialists and generalists are meshed together, additional specialization is more costly than it needs to be. This is also illustrated in Figure 27 where, to increase the specialization of the reading program, a reading specialist is added. Coordination problems are created as specialists and generalists compete for the time of the same children, one resenting the other's encroachments. In California, this model represents the approach of the mandated

Miller-Unruh primary reading program, where reading specialists are created on top of the existing elementary school structure. Aided by teacher association and union lobbies, this approach represents a refinement of existing practices and structures rather than a reform. Its assumptions automatically make more specialization costly and there are no tradeoffs. Furthermore, the implementation of the Miller-Unruh program reinforces the self-contained school.

Different Foci of Specialization

There are several different foci of organizational specialization. Curriculum has been probably the most obvious and worked-over area. It is assumed that increased specialization of teachers as represented in subject matter knowledge will increase the effectiveness of the schools. Teachers can be differentiated on the basis of their own knowledge regarding a subject matter discipline. However, unless there is also a concomitant carry-over to pupils, the acquisition of such knowledge may be negligible. While traditional salary schedules reinforce our beliefs about the legitimacy of paying more for more teacher knowledge, the resulting schedule of schools is not responsive to increased pupil knowledge. Other areas of specialization may be learning theory, methodological or pedagogical skills, group dynamics, or specialized skills in preparing learning materials for children. For the most part, the merits of each focus can be argued by its own special brand of advocate; however, unless a needs assessment of clients is included, it is unlikely to be resolved satisfactorily. Without the needs assessment as validating criterion, the AFT assertion that any vertical ranking of roles is essentially arbitrary is correct. It would be impossible to resolve an argument over which medical specialization was more important until the patient is inserted into the diagnosis. Only then may priorities be determined. It is time that increased specialization is tied to needs and student outcomes instead of the dominant philosophical or political power at any particular time in education. However, there is an interesting phenomenon with organizational specialization.

Specialization and Rising Expectations

As organizations acquire specialization, they find an increase of problems as a result of such acquisition. This is because many problems go unrecognized simply because untrained professionals do not identify some types of problems. This is one danger in having teachers provide the sole input in the design stages of a differentiated staff. Other data sources must be utilized to prevent a kind of professional myopia which can result in needed specialization going begging. Of course, there are those that argue that this is not so much a fault of the classroom teacher, but a lack of help for the teacher and time. While some of this may be true, the acquisition of a fully qualified reading specialist will reveal to even experienced classroom teachers problems they did not know existed. Furthermore, once identification has been made, the specialist is often better able to prescribe the solutions for the teacher to implement. In all probability organizations concerned with human beings as the central focus of their specialization (like medicine and education) will always be underspecialized. This is why a feedback loop in a needs assessment model is essential. It is assumed that the human being is sufficiently complex to be a study of infinite magnitude. It needs to be determined what needs are being met with what level of specialization. How much more specialization can be added? Are there personnel tradeoffs? How much in-service training does it take to reach a level where the new specialization can become effective? Since not all needs can be met, it will be necessary to establish priorities. These will reflect social, economical and political emphasis as well as educational values.

An Organic Approach to Staffing

Organic or contingency staffing has been posed as an alternative in which the same benefits of fluidity (Generation II definitions of unequal time, space and staff and the continual movement of those elements) are present but in which teacher tasks emerge from a psychological theory.[93] First, an organic approach has organizational implications in terms of creating the necessary climate for change. These two approaches (Generation I and Generation II) are illustrated and adapted from Burns and Stalker's discussion of mechanistic and organic forms of management.[94] These are illustrated in Figure 28.

FIGURE 28

A Comparison Between Differentiated Staffing
and Contingency Staffing

Differentiated Staffing (mechanistic)	*Contingency Staffing* (organic)
The separation of teaching tasks into a permanent hierarchy of superior-subordinate relationships with precise rights and obligations for each role;	The adjustment and continual redefinition of teaching roles and role priorities through interaction with students;
Control is exercised through the hierarchy solely;	The abolition of a narrow definition of rights, obligations and methods; control rests in the total social/professional network (community);
Expertise is increased and almost exclusively located in the upper positions;	Knowledge of how to accomplish a task may rest anywhere in the organization; control is client-centered and client specific therefore continually "ad hoc."
Communication is chiefly vertical, between superior and subordinate;	Communication is vertical and *lateral* as a function of the formation of new clusters of roles;
Roles are set into a permanent rubric in order to create a career ladder;	A career ladder is present but it depends upon utilization more than arbitrary ranking via position;

In Search of a Psychological Theory of Staffing

One of the first to conceptualize a model of staff differentiation on a psychological basis was that of Zaharis, *et al.*[95] Zaharis adopted Robert Mogar's psycho-social model which represented a combination of the ideas of Abraham Maslow and Carl Jung.[96] Jung hypothesized that there were four basic perceptual models representing four basic preferences for life responses. They are:

1. Sensing-Thinking, ST
2. Sensing-Feeling, SF
3. Intuition-Thinking, IT
4. Intuition-Feeling, IF

There are two ways people can become aware of things, people, events and ideas. The first (1) is through the *senses* or conscious processes and (2) through *intuition* or unconscious inner perception. After the stimulus has been perceived, then the evaluating or judging mode makes conclusions about the perceptions. One *thinking* mode is a rational, logical way to come to conclusions about the perceived reality. The *feeling* mode discriminates and integrates perceptions into self on the basis of whether one values or feels good, or is drawn to the stimulus. The two perceiving modes, *sensing* and *intuition*, are completely independent of the two judging modes, *thinking* and *feeling*. Therefore, the four combinations can be described as the four dominant "perceptual filters" by which we make sense of our environment.

Figure 29 illustrates how we view the client as a whole and diagnose his dominant perceptual filter. When this has been assessed, we attempt to discover at what need level the client is functioning. Based on this information we build with the client an educational experience that dictates the human resources needed (staffing pattern), time necessary (schedule) and space (physical requirements). This model assumes the individual is undifferentiated; he exists in the *gestalt* not in various segments we use to describe self. Staffs and curriculum must be sensitive to this fact. Maslow's picture of human needs coupled with Jung's life style provide a base for relating teaching tasks to human needs. This is essential to humanizing a staffing pattern. Such an approach is the epitome of an organic concept of school staffing and provides a more defensible and worthwhile goal from which specialized teaching-learning tasks can be related to the whole and integrated into the individual needs of clients. This process provides for continual renewal of teaching goals, methods and needs of students.

The Gestalt Approach

In this approach the goal is integration of curriculum and of self so the student can move to the level of self-actualization. Many of the

FIGURE 29

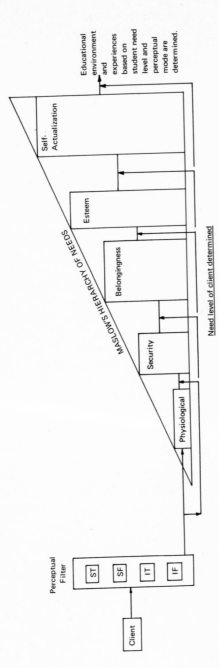

assumptions of present staffing patterns envision a fragmented body of curriculum and self. Figure 30 indicates the process the model provides to achieve the Gestalt.

FIGURE 30

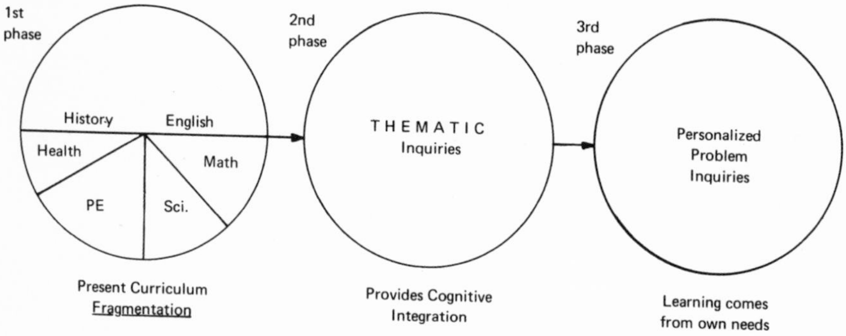

In the third phase the student's educational experiences are diagnosed by himself. He is the best diagnostician for determining what educational experiences and human resources are necessary for accomplishing his goals. A student in this phase would be evidencing a need at least at the esteem level. He is becoming self-directed. From a curriculum point of view, an organic staffing model would move from a fragmented curriculum approach in which present subject matter divisions are developed into a thematic framework and ultimately move to a problem-centered approach that emerges through the student. A student or client-centered staffing model would promote and develop all human resources (professionals, support staff, students) into the teaching-learning role. This would enable variations in teacher-student-paraprofessional learning arrangements. (Students are staff in the model, for example). An organic staffing model would derive learning and teaching tasks from the child's needs. As discussed in the previous chart, needs would be assessed from the perceptual mode of the child and the need level at which he is living. The following illustrations will provide examples.

PHYSIOLOGICAL NEEDS

Child's Needs	*Learning/Teaching Tasks*
1. Normal physiological function	1. Writing
2. Respiratory	2. Large and small muscle coordination as in writing and drawing

3. Normal nutrition

4. Normal developmental process

5. Organic presence

6. Physical boundaries

3. Stamina and strength (a function of attention span)

4. Communication skills (speech development)

5. Psychomotor-tactile-kinesthetic

Example 1. This precludes no diagnostic tools. If the person is having a short attention span, and if he were diagnosed as an intuitive-feeling type of person, he might react with withdrawal behavior. If his short attention span was broken by aggressive behavior, his perceptual mode would seem to be sensing-feeling. Therefore, in order for the instructor to utilize appropriate techniques, he must be sensitive to the dominant perceptual mode of the child. If the child is not able to meet his needs at this level it is useless to try and carry on instruction of any higher level.

SECURITY NEEDS

Child's Needs	Educational Environment	Tasks
1. Acceptance	1. Successful experience	1. Self-paced materials and packets
2. Responsible freedom	2. Freedom to implement own ideas, inquiry methods, problem exploration	2. Programmed instruction with positive reinforcement
3. Support	3. Consistency of reinforcement (positive)	3. Professional and peer acceptance through verbal and nonverbal communication
4. Consistency	4. Structure of curriculum	4. State objectives and structure
5. Congruency	5. Physical and psychological boundaries	

Example 2. On the security level, the person who is a sensing-thinking type needs to feel involved. The intuitive-feeling person needs personal warmth plus support. If this need level is not diagnosed correctly we often find either withdrawal from the educational environment or an attack upon it in order to establish his place.

BELONGINGNESS OR LOVE NEEDS

Self	Educational Environment	Tasks
1. Sense of personal warmth	1. Accepting individual contributions	1. "Student turf" concept for peer identification
2. Need for acceptance	2. Staff, peer and individual acceptance	2. Curriculum contracts
3. Need for role identification	3. Provide alternatives such as groups to join. Also provide fluidity so students can interchange roles.	3. Group problem-solving
		4. Feedback sessions
		5. Simulated games

Example 3. Many roles are provided in the schools for sensing-thinking people. Intuitive-thinking and intuitive-feeling people have been neglected as far as providing roles for them and for staff and peer acceptance. Hippies are predominantly deficiency motivated, S-F, I-T, and I-F types. There is little place for them in the schools as they have few opportunities for staff and peer acceptance within the school. Therefore they tend to go outside the institutions and set up subcultures that meet the individuals need for belonging.

ESTEEM NEEDS

Self	Educational Environment	Tasks
1. Need for personal recognition	1. Opportunity to develop excellence in some area	1. Individual responsibility given for choosing learning tasks
2. Need for self-discipline	2. Opportunity to develop self-discipline	2. Thematic curriculum approach
3. Need to master an environment	3. Opportunity to make decisions and take responsibility	3. Opportunity to overcome barriers and develop mastery in an area

Example 4. At this level need for recognition of individual abilities and strengths must be allowed to emerge. Curriculum that provides for individual growth with concomitant time, space and resources that are flexible enough to support the student in his quest for self-esteem.

SELF-ACTUALIZING NEEDS

Self	*Educational Environment*	*Tasks*
1. Need for aesthetic beauty	1. Self-initiated learning activities	1. Karate
2. Need for finding meaning in life	2. Intrinsically valuable learning	2. Outward Bound program
3. Need for fulfillment	3. Integration of knowledge and being	3. Drama and dance
4. Need for creative expression	4. Integration with the sources of life	
5. Need for holistic understanding	5. Appreciation of oneness with mankind	
	6. Weaving one's life with the infinite	

At this point therapy and curriculum are virtually the same activity. The essence of a contingency staffing model is that the child, the curriculum, and the resources of the school (human and machine) can be integrated by focusing on the client first as the central point of the origin of the deployment system.

Three Staffing Patterns as Alternatives

The utilization of Mogar's synthesis creates in theory three different types of staffing patterns based upon client need as perceived from Jung's perception-judgment preference and Maslow's modal need level concept.[97] For example *uniformity staffing* would mean that irrespective of client need or perception-judgment preference, all students would be subjected to the same educational experiences, with standardized curriculum, staffing and scheduling. This is not changed even with the installation of such innovations as team teaching or flexible scheduling. There may be legitimate points in the educational experience of children that they should have common experiences. However, a daily diet of common experiences ignores the diversity of the educational clientele. *Congruity staffing* would envision a staffing system where individuals identified as one particular life style would be exposed to comparable life styles. The deployment system would capitalize upon the strengths of the clients and not worry about the weaknesses. Some potentialities would not be developed except by accident. A third approach would be *compensatory staffing* in which the school would place students and teachers together in a deployment system which would expose students to life styles and perceptual modes other than their own. Mogar's writings provide a fertile field where more educational experimentation and research is needed to fully explore the various staffing alternatives which could improve school systems.

Staff Differentiation and Democratization

Much of the early impetus of staff differentiation was couched in terms of the apparent need to democratize school systems, that is, redistribute the power and authority within the school systems. Democratized decision making became a watchword of the staff differentiation movement to the extent that it incurred the suspicion of school administrators who were fearful of being supplanted and/or replaced and of teacher unions who felt that academic senates were a management counterforce to legitimate collective bargaining.

After several years of implementation, the following generalizations are offered regarding the ability of a teacher's hierarchy, as couched in the Generation I approach, to "democratize" an educational system.

1. *A hierarchy does not democratize the system.*

It is a misnomer that a teacher's hierarchy, even though extended into previously sacrosanct administrative dominated circles, democratizes school systems. Democracy implies equality of influence, formally and informally. In Temple City, while senior teachers and principals possessed equality, the senior teacher never did outrank the principal in informal authority within the system. Staff and associate teachers did not vote in the academic senate at all. Furthermore, senior teachers were not representative, they were selected on the basis of their ability to fulfill job responsibilities. They were not elected to office. It would be fairer to call the system an educational oligarchy, in which the sole power of administrators to make decisions was abrogated with a select corps of teachers. Furthermore, the teacher's hierarchy did not decentralize the system any more than did the individual principal functioning alone in a single school. It is a fact validated by Lippitt that differentiation leads to centralization. "Power, in the sense of capacity to influence behavior, becomes more and more central as positions become more differentiated."[98] While more teachers were involved in decision making in Temple City, the control system was extended to include larger groups than before.

Organizations are cooperative instrumental systems assembled out of the usable attributes of people. They are also places in which people compete for advancement. Similarly, members of a business concern are at one and the same time cooperators in a common enterprise and rivals for the material and tangible rewards of successful competition with each other. The hierarchical order of rank and power, realized in the organization chart, that prevails in all organizations is both a control system and a career ladder.[99]

2. Decision making is enhanced with expert participation.

Although teacher involvement was not necessarily a true democracy (perhaps no school system could ever become one in this sense) teacher involvement did improve the quality and acceptance of decisions made. This follows the idea presented by March and Simon on "bounded rationality."[100] This term connotes the reality that the more variables a decision can encompass, the better the decision. Since one man cannot know all the possible ramifications of a decision, involvement of expertise should lead to a larger sphere of "knowns" than a group which was smaller. Participative group decision making did enhance the decision-making process in Temple City in senates where senior teachers had been trained and were fully paid for additional decision-making responsibilities. It also increased the degree of staff involvement (at least the senior teachers) and staff acceptance (to the degree that senior teachers genuinely commanded respect from staff and associate teachers.

3. A hierarchy impedes problem solving and risk taking.

If hierarchical relationships are likewise inserted into the counsel of experts involved in decision making, the effects are considerably less than if there were no hierarchical relationships at all. For example, in Temple City, where senior teachers had not achieved a commensurate status with the school principal, Stout and Burke commented on the effectiveness of the academic senate:

Although it is generally conceded that the academic senates represent a potential influence over decisions, they are not yet perceived as having much impact. There is general agreement that teachers have a major voice in some kinds of decisions: they can choose to cooperate with one another; they have the ability to develop methods of student control; they can manipulate certain budget categories within the constraints of a school budget; they have some collective influence over curricular matters. However, there is wide-spread belief that they operate within parameters set by the administrators. They do not believe they are able to consider all the options; rather, that options are limited before their consideration. This is manifest to them by agenda control, by a virtual monopoly of information among administrators, and of course, by law.

. . . the general pattern is that teachers believe that the limits of influence are well-defined at a low level. Teachers do not believe that their decisions will have much effect on the direction of the district. For example, in our limited observation of senate meetings, perusal of minutes, and discussions with senators, we were struck with the virtual absence of discussion about purpose or major alternatives to reach those purposes. The senators were not making important policy decisions; they were embroiled in rule-making exercises. In retrospect, the teachers are sophisticated analysts of the phenomenon. In practice, they expend much energy in resolving issues which seem unimportant in perspective.[101]

Research by Bridges, Doyle and Mahan on the effects of hierarchy on group productivity, efficiency and risk taking showed that the presence of formally based status differences among group members inhibited the risk-taking behavior of the members of those groups.[102] The reason for this was hypothesized to be that members of the groups with status differentials did not mobilize their energies fully and that the low level of mobilization reduced the groups' overall productivity. In a repeated experiment, Doyle discovered that:

Fewer ideas were generated by subordinates in groups with leaders having high achieved status and a higher percentage of their ideas were ignored. There was also distortion in the error-correcting and social-supporting mechanisms. These social conditions seem dysfunctional in the analyzing productivity of the groups.[103]

Both experiments involved the solving of a problem with elementary principals and elementary teachers comprising the decision-making groups.

In a letter to Allan Shuey, chairman of the Teachers Job Analysis Task Force in Temple City, Homer Hurst prophetically responded to that body's eager request for a reaction to the ideas so far developed, including that of a teacher's hierarchy.

The differentiated staff proposal will have a chance if you retain fluidity and flexibility, not just toward a new order, but sometimes back to the old order. It is patently experimental and idealistic, and it is up against almost a century of indigenous public school articulation. The years are clogged with the remains of promising proposals. Fortunately, the winnowing has left us with a lot of fine practices. Your efforts will, in the long run, be rewarded. The short haul may be more trying. Not only is the institution grinding alone in a (for the moment) set pattern; teachers' and administrators' career patterns are also set.

There are some pertinent questions: Will the old routine persist despite renaming positions and indicating new channels of communication on an organizational chart? Will the usual bulges in the power structure develop after the new wears off? The apathetic personnel now on tenure may continue so. Early enthusiasm will wane. Many professional people make a move, consolidate a new position, and resist further inroads on time devoted to personal activities such as home, church, and recreation even for more compensation. They may want the salary, but sacrifice, even in the name of professional advancement, may not be alluring beyond a certain point. If this happens, authority and responsibility will gravitate to the spots where it currently rests.[104]

It appears very doubtful now that a full-blown Generation I model of staff differentiation like Temple City will become a dominant type of staffing in public education. Not because it could not be replicated—the fact is that a teacher's hierarchy appears now not to have the urgency of a teacher shortage as a rationale.[105] Nor does the creation of a career ladder have the professional support from the NEA and AFT it would need to win success.[106] Teachers themselves doubt its efficacy and will resist further bureaucratization on a large scale without tying new roles specifically to client need, promoting their desire for greater control of organizational decision making and without retaining role and salary flexibility. So long as females comprise the largest group of teachers at work, efforts to change the teaching profession to a system of higher and lower ranks will not have the power to capture the support of teachers themselves.[107] [Later in September 1968, pre- and post-test data on a semantic differential attitude inventory confirmed that females, particularly primary teachers, were least positive of any groups of teachers towards staff differentiation. The Mesa study by English also confirmed the Temple City experience regarding elementary females.] Before a concept which demands the support of teachers can be effectively implemented, teachers must endure long periods of denial and frustration to realize that idea. That kind of dedication is not to be found at the present time in sufficient force, nor does it appear to be the posture of any teacher leader. Meanwhile Generation II and III models appear to have the capacity to appeal to the same constituents by avoiding the teacher's hierarchy issue.

There are many positive and needed benefits from a full study of the implications of differentiated staffing. Of prime importance is the need of pupils in public schools for a diversified and highly specialized teaching staff that avoids or negates the historic assumptions of age-grading and Procrustean standards of equality. What boards, administrators, teachers and parents must realize is that they are all part of the problem. Our ideas and concepts regarding what education is and how we can reach the goals of a truly public school system must undergo some fundamental changes before solutions are possible to envision, let alone implement.

A study by Guthrie, Kleindorfer, Levin and Stout in Michigan concluded that state aide formulas and the distribution of federal funds reinforced present inequalities in per pupil expenditures:

> Where is the school money going? The answer for Michigan, and by extrapolation, probably for most other states as well, is that it is going to those who already have it. School resources are presently distributed in a manner which tends to reinforce existing patterns of inequality, inequality of knowledge, opportunity, income, and social standing. This is true despite an overwhelming belief on the part of the public that schools are the great social equalizer.[108]

There is a growing realization that simply throwing open the schoolhouse doors to all the children of all the people is not synonymous with equality of opportunity. Equality does not mean treating all pupils as equals, it implies, within the concept of social opportunity, a redistribution of resources to those with the most needs. To accomplish this objective traditional school staffing patterns will have to be abolished since it is by them that teacher resources are deployed on the present rigidly deceptive egalitarian basis.

Footnotes

1. A point of view advocated by Marc Belth in *Education as a Discipline* (Boston: Allyn and Bacon, Inc., 1965).

2. Recounted in Fenwick English, "A Handbook of the Temple City Differentiated Staffing Project, 1965-1970," mimeographed, Temple City Schools, Temple City, California, 44 pp.

3. Belth., *Education* p. 87. Derived from M. Black, *Models and Metaphors* (Ithaca: Cornell University Press, 1962), Ch. 13.

4. Ibid.

5. Ibid.

6. Ibid., p. 88.

7. Preston W. Search, *An Ideal School: or, Looking Forward* (New York: D. Appleton and Company, 1901), International Education Series.

8. J. Lloyd Trump and Dorsey Baynham, *Guide to Better Schools: Focus on Schools* (Chicago: Rand McNally, 1967).

9. Myron Lieberman. *The Future of Public Education* (Chicago: University of Chicago Press, 1960).

10. Robert Bhaerman, "A Paradigm for Accountability," *American Teacher*, November 1970.

11. Lieberman, *Future*, p. 99.

12. Temple City Unified School District, "A Project Proposal to the Kettering Foundation," offset, Temple City, California, August 1966, 22 pp.

13. Robert N. Bush and Dwight W. Allen, *A New Design for High School Education: Assuming A Flexible Schedule* (New York: McGraw-Hill, 1964).

14. Dwight W. Allen, "A Differentiated Teaching Staff," mimeographed, Stanford University, 1966, 12 pp.

15. Allen Shuey, William Schmidt, Tad Root, Janice Peet and Fenwick English, "A Proposal for a Differentiated Teaching Staff," mimeographed, Temple City Unified School District, Temple City, California, September 1967, 59 pp.

16. Robert Reinertsen, "Let's Talk Kettering," offset, Publication of the Temple City Schools, Kettering Project, September 1967, 20 pp.

17. "Differentiated Staffing: The Strategy of Deployment," *Nation's Schools*, 85, June 1970, pp. 43-46.

18. M. John Rand and Fenwick English, "Towards a Differentiated Teaching Staff," *Phi Delta Kappan*, 49, January 1968, pp. 264-68.

19. Peter B. Mann, "Differentiated Staffing: The Second Generation," *Arizona Teacher*, 59, January 1971, pp. 13-17.

20. Allen, "Differentiated Teaching."

21. Dwight W. Allen, "A Differentiated Staff: Putting Teacher Talent To Work," Occasional Paper No. 2, NCTEPS-NEA, Washington, D. C., December 1967, 9 pp.

22. Department of Health, Education and Welfare, Office of Education, Bureau of Educational Personnel Development, October 2, 1969. "Clarification of Criteria for the Selection of Prospectuses Under School Personnel Utilization," xeroxed, 4 pp. These same criteria were also repeated by Dwight Allen and Lloyd W. Kline, "Differentiated Staffing," xeroxed, ERIC, ED 051 119, 32 pp. See page 21 for a reiteration.

23. Jesse Burkhead, *Public School Finance: Economics and Politics* (Syracuse: Syracuse University Press, 1964).

24. Charles S. Benson, *The School and the Economic System* (Chicago: Science Research Associates, 1966).

25. Joseph M. Conte and Fenwick W. English, "The Impact of Technology on Staff Differentiation," *Audiovisual Instruction* 14, May 1969, p. 108.

26. Dwight W. Allen, letter to Fenwick W. English, typed, June 10, 1966, 2 pp.

27. Fenwick W. English, "Field Testing A Differentiated Teaching Staff," *Educational Manpower,* James Olivero and Edward Buffie, eds., (Bloomington: Indiana University Press, 1970), pp. 189-225.

28. Anthony L. Rose. Letter to M. John Rand, Western Behavioral Sciences Institute, April 26, 1968, 4 pp., ditto. Rose commented, "The way your model is now designed, you are providing greater monetary reinforcement for assuming nonteaching responsibilities. That model seems likely to encourage good teachers to move away from the classroom." p. 2.

29. Fenwick W. English, "Et Tu Educator: Differentiated Staffing?" NCTEPS-NEA, Write-In Papers on Flexible Staffing No. 4 (August, 1969) 23 pp. "It is important to note that all personnel in the staffing model function as teachers. . . . Current definitions of a teacher as anyone who teaches more than 50 percent of the school day will be inadequate to describe the job in a differentiated staff. New concepts of what a teacher is and does are no more apparent than here. Since the staffing model rests upon flexible scheduling, teachers will not be with children all day long even though they perhaps are teaching 100 percent. Definitions of what teaching is, or what a teacher is, instead will describe what happens with students and in what situations professional judgments are required." p. 16.

30. "Differentiated Teaching Staff," mimeographed, Product of Intern Seminar, Stanford University, March 15, 1967, 26 pp.

31. English, "Et Tu Educator," p. 14.

32. Talcott Parsons, *Essays in Sociological Theory* (Glencoe, Illinois: Free Press, 1964).

33. English, "Et Tu Educator," p. 17.

34. Victor A. Thompson, *Modern Organization* (New York: Alfred A. Knopf, 1961), p. 61.

35. Ibid., p. 73.

36. Evaluation Training Center, Department of Educational Research, Florida State University, "An Evaluation Paradigm for Flexible Staffing Patterns and Its Application to the Temple City, Mesa, and Florida Network Projects," Volume IV, Tallahassee, Florida, 1971, p. 95.

37. Ibid., p. 96.

38. Fenwick W. English, "Temple City: From Theory to Practice," *Florida Education*, February 1969, pp. 12-15.

39. Don Barbee, "Differentiated Staffing: Expectations and Pitfalls," TEPS Write-In Papers on Flexible Staffing Patterns, No. 1 (Washington, D. C.: National Education Association) March 1969, p. 4. Barbee called this phenomenon "status hiatus."

40. Robert T. Stout and David Burke, "The Dilemmas of Difference," dittoed, Claremont Graduate School, Claremont, California, May 1970, 20 pp. This report was submitted by Stout and Burke to the Temple City District Senate in the spring of 1970. It was inaccurate in some respects in that it failed to separate the effects of roles at the pilot school (Oak Avenue) and those in nonpilot schools. However, it provided much insight into the problems caused by adherence to the hierarchical approach.

41. Harwell H. Carpenter, "Formal Organizational Structural Factors and Perceived Job Satisfaction of Classroom Teachers," *Administrative Science Quarterly*, 16:4, pp. 460-65.

42. Thompson, *Modern Organization*, p. 73. Thompson feels that the status system has a certain "quasi-neurotic" character and that it has both structural and psychological determinants.

43. Herbert A. Simon, *Administrative Behavior* (New York: Macmillan, 1945).

44. Gerald I. Susman, "The Concept of Status Congruence as a Basis to Predict Task Allocations in Autonomous Work Groups," *Administrative Science Quarterly*, June 1970, p. 173.

45. Herbert Simon, *Administrative*, p. 116.

46. "Citizens for Education Bring You Chris and Jack, A Tale of Three Conflicts," Paid Political Advertisement, *Temple City Times*, November 28, 1971. See also "Citizens for Education Present Jack In Sac. (a playlet)—A Tale of Funding," Paid Political Advertisement, *Temple City Times*, December 12, 1971.

47. English, "Handbook of Temple City Project," p. 44.

48. David Seldon, "The Future of Teachers According to the USOE," *American Teacher*, 18:4, January 1968, pp. 12-13.

49. David Seldon and Robert Bhaerman, "Climbing That Career Ladder, How High, O Lord, How High?" *American Teacher*, 53:9, pp. 8 and 17.

50. Robert D. Bhaerman, "Several Educators' Cure For the Common Cold, Among Other Things or One Unionist View of Staff Differentiation," AFT Quest Paper, No. 7, Department of Research, American Federation of Teachers, Washington, D. C., 13 pp.

51. Quote by AFT Vice-President Rose Claffey of Salem, Massachusetts in "Differentiated Staffing Said Used by Some School Systems to Save at Teachers' Expense," *The Forum*, Fargo, North Dakota, November 13, 1969, p. 21.

52. David Seldon as quoted in AFT Quest Paper, No. 2, Edited by Robert D. Bhaerman, (Washington, D. C.: Department of Research, American Federation of Teachers), p. 12.

53. Resolution 39 of the American Federation of Teachers, adopted in annual convention, Washington, D. C., August 1970.

54. Harry A. Millis and Royal E. Montogmery, *Organized Labor*, vol. III of a series, *The Economics of Labor* (New York: McGraw-Hill, 1945), p. 356.

55. Ibid.

56. Harmon Ziegler, *The Political Life of American Teachers* (New Jersey: Prentice-Hall, 1967), p. 76.

57. Millis and Montgomery, *Organized Labor*.

58. Ibid.

59. Robert D. Bhaerman, "American Federation of Teachers' Statement on Vertical Staffing," xeroxed, 77 pp., March 1971.

60. Ibid.

61. As quoted by Joseph Stocker in "Differentiated Staffing in Schools," *Education U.S.A. Special Report*, National School Public Relations Association (Washington, D.C.: National Education Association, 1970), p. 2.

62. Association of Classroom Teachers, "Classroom Teachers Speak on Differentiated Teaching Assignments," Report of the Classroom Teachers National Study Conference on Differentiated Teaching Assignments for Classroom Teachers, (Washington, D. C.: National Education Association, 1969), 32 pp.

63. NEA Division of Field Services, "About Differentiated Staffing and Trojan Horses," *The Washington Memo*, Sylvia Brotman, ed., April 1970, 17 pp.

64. One example of an education association taking the same stand as the AFT on salary schedules was reported by Milan Wall, "Schools Act Cautiously on Differentiated Plan," *The Lincoln Star*, Lincoln, Nebraska, June 1, 1971.

65. See Gayle Tunnell, "Teachers Defending Security," *Washington Post*, May 30, 1971. Teachers were reacting very negatively here to the Clark Plan which proposed basing salary on pupil gain as assessed on standardized achievement tests.

66. Bhaerman, "Paradigm."

67. Millis and Montgomery, *Organized Labor.*

68. Bernard H. McKenna, "School Staffing Patterns and Pupil Interpersonal Behavior: Implications for Teacher Education " (Burlingame: California Teachers Association, 1967), 27 pp.

69. Bernard McKenna, *Staffing the Schools* (New York: Teachers College Columbia, 1965).

70. Benjamin S. Bloom et. al., *Taxonomy of Education Objectives: Cognitive Domain* (New York: David McKay Company, 1956.).

71. David R. Krathwohl, et. al., *Taxonomy of Educational Objectives: Affective Domain* (New York: David McKay Company, 1964.)

72. N. L. Gage, "Paradigms for Research on Teaching," *Handbook of Research on Teaching* (Chicago: Rand McNally, 1963), p. 133.

73. Mario Fantini and Gerald Weinstein, *Making Urban Schools Work* (New York: Holt, Rinehart, and Winston, 1968).

74. Fenwick W. English, "Differentiated Staffing: Refinement, Reform, or Revolution?" *ISR Journal,* 1:4, Fall 1969, pp. 220-34.

75. Mesa Education Association, "Differentiated Staffing: The Mesa Approach," offset, Clarence Huber, ed., Mesa Public Schools, Mesa, Arizona. August 1971, 24 pp.

76. Gail Pew and Jerry Melton, "Baseline Plus Commission: An Experimental Salary Paradigm," mimeographed, Fremont Junior High School, Mesa Public Schools, Mesa, Arizona, April 1971, 9 pp.

77. Fenwick W. English and James K. Zaharis, "Are Accountability and Governance Compatible?" *Phi Delta Kappan,* 52:6, February 1971, pp. 374-75.

78. Evaluation Training Center, Department of Educational Research, Florida State University, "An Evaluation Paradigm," p. 105.

79. Fenwick W. English, "A Short Laboratory Manual to Understanding Differentiated Staffing," mimeographed, National Academy of School Executives, American Association of School Administrators, Washington, D. C., May 1971, 26 pp.

80. Fenwick W. English, "Back From Utopia: Some Reflections On Ṣtaff Differentiation," *Educators Advocate,* October 22, 1970, South Dakota Education Association, Pierre, S. D., p. 16.

81. Fenwick English, "A Tentative and Partial Report Regarding the Feasibility of Staff Differentiation in the Public Schools of the District of Columbia Considered with the Implications of Hobson vs. Hansen. Civil Action, No. 82-66 of May 25, 1971." Report to Dr. Hugh J. Scott and the Board of Education, District of Columbia, July 1971, xeroxed, 11 pp. The decision of Judge J. Skelly Wright meant that, by October 1, 1971, teacher salaries per pupil could not deviate more than 5 percent from elementary school to elementary school. The ·

impending transfer of teachers was not contrary to movement towards staff differentiation.

82. See also a brief discussion of "situational staffing," as discussed in Robert J. Mockler, "Situational Theory of Management," *Harvard Business Review,* May-June 1971, pp. 146-55. For a more in-depth look at this concept as it was applied in Mesa, Arizona, see Fenwick English and James Zaharis, "Staff Differentiation the Right Way," *Arizona Teacher,* 60:2, November 1971, pp. 6-9, 35.

83. Fenwick W. English, James K. Zaharis and Clarence E. Huber, "A Brief Progress Report to Mesa Educators," mimeographed, Mesa Public Schools, Mesa, Arizona, April 1971, 9 pp.

84. Gene M. Pillot, "A Conceptual Design of a System Model of Differentiated Staffing," unpublished Ed.D. dissertation, Department of Educational Administration, University of Florida, June, 1970, 152 pp.

85. Adapted from Fenwick W. English, "A Tentative List of the Characteristics of the Three Major Differentiated Staffing Models on Ten Basic Continuums of Project Development," from "Differentiated Staffing," p. 5.

86. Fenwick English, James Zaharis and Roger Kaufman, "Educational Success Planning: Reducing Chance as An Aspect of School Innovation," *Audiovisual Instruction,* May 1971, pp. 20-22.

87. Ibid.

88. Roger A. Kaufman, "System Approaches to Education: Discussion and Attempted Integration," *Social and Technological Change: Implications for Education* (Eugene, Oregon: Center for the Advanced Study of Educational Administration, 1970), pp. 121-81.

89. English, Zaharis, and Kaufman, "Educational Success," p. 22.

90. Fenwick W. English and James K. Zaharis, "How To Build A Model of Staff Differentiation," offset, A Step by Step Guide in the Development of a Situational Specific Site Model of Differentiated Staffing. Center for Differentiated Staffing, Claremont Graduate School, Claremont, California. Second Printing, March 5, 1971. 38 pp.

91. National Education Association, "Teacher Aides at Work," Washington, D. C., 1967.

92. Allan C. Filley and Robert J. House, *Managerial Process and Organizational Behavior* (New York: Scott Foresman, 1969), p. 215.

93. Based on an earlier discussion presented in an unpublished paper, "Contingency Staffing: An Alternative to Staff Differentiation," xeroxed, by Fenwick W. English and James K. Zaharis, Department of Secondary Education, Arizona State University, Tempe, 20 pp.

94. Tom Burns and G. M. Stalker, *The Management of Innovation* (London: Tavistock, 1959), p. 7.

95. James Zaharis, Larry Simmons, Keith Tucker, and Wayne Johnson, "A Self-Actualizing Staffing Model: Opportunity Hall," mimeographed, unpublished manuscript, Mesa Public Schools, Mesa, Arizona, 1970, 12 pp.

96. Robert E. Mogar, "Toward A Psychological Theory of Education," *Journal of Humanistic Psychology*, Spring 1969, pp. 17-52.

97. Abraham Maslow, *Motivation and Personality* (New York: Harper and Row, 1954).

98. Gordon L. Lippitt, *Organization Renewal* (New York: Appleton-Century Crofts, 1969) p. 51.

99. Burns and Stalker, *Management*, p. xii.

100. James G. March and Herbert A. Simon, *Organizations* (New York: John Wiley, 1958), pp. 137-42.

101. Stout and Burke, "Dilemmas of Difference," p. 5.

102. Edwin M. Bridges, Wayne J. Doyle and David J. Mahan, "Effects of Hierarchical Differentiation on Group Productivity, Efficiency, and Risk Taking," *Administrative Science Quarterly*, September 1968, pp. 305-19.

103. Wayne J. Doyle, "Effects of Achieved Status of Leader on Productivity of Groups," *Administrative Science Quarterly*, March 1971, pp. 40-50.

104. Letter to Allan Shuey from Homer Hurst, Whittier College, Department of Education, Whittier, California, July 20, 1967, 6 pp.

105. By Legislative Mandate in California, Temple City was subjected to an extensive financial analysis by the California State Department of Education during the spring of 1970. The report later released indicated the cost factors were negligible. See also *Education USA* (Washington, D. C.: National Education Association, March 15, 1971), p. 153.

106. See Alan Rosenthal, *Pedagogues and Power: Teacher Groups In School Politics* (Syracuse: Syracuse University Press, 1969).

107. The lack of interest on the part of elementary females was reported on the basis of empirical data in Temple City by Rand and English in "Towards A Differentiated Teaching Staff," *Phi Delta Kappan*, January 1968, p. 267.

108. James W. Guthrie, George B. Kleindorfer, Henry M. Levin, and Robert T. Stout, "Dollars for Schools: The Reinforcement of Inequality," *Educational Administration Quarterly*, Autumn 1970, pp. 32-45.

4   From Intervention to Implementation

Fenwick English

Implementing staff differentiation has been a haphazard process, more successful in some places than others. Where in one place model schools have been isolated from the regular school system, and in another, the step toward prototyping has been aborted, it is virtually impossible to understand what has happened. Not only has there been a lack of uniformity of approach (a necessity during the experimental stages), but also directors cannot recall the precise nature of any particular treatment nor what observable effects it had upon the ongoing system. Nor can they ascertain precisely what alternatives were available to them at critical decision-making junctures along the road from intervention to implementation.

A universal malady has been the tendency for directors to oversimplify the nature of school systems. Schools are viewed as simple combinations of teachers and students. Overlooked are the facets of interorganizational dependencies, rivalries, imbalances in power distribution and problems with interpersonal jealousies. To admit to such problems is often considered a weakness, since solving them brings out emotional counterparts which must be confronted openly. Educational personnel lack such skills and motivation to deal with organizational problems at this level which means that reform is stalled and ultimately killed. The problem is compounded by the simplistic manner in which large segments of the public, reflected in their elected members of boards of education, continue to press for unidimensional solutions to these multi-faceted organizational dilemmas.

PRELIMINARY CONSIDERATIONS

The implementer responsible for carrying staff differentiation from theory to reality must be well grounded in organizational sociology. The working of the system, formally and informally, by groups must be preeminent in the planner's mind. As Sarason[1] has explained in a revealing discourse about previous failures of school innovation, the psychology of the individual is totally inadequate as a base in which to plan or implement organizational change. The uniqueness of the school culture is a sociological phenomenon. The school culture defines the permissible ways that problems can be conceptualized and solved. Staff differentiation is the systematic introduction of a new structure into that culture. In many cases it purports to reshape the culture itself, and the roles and role relationships within the system.

The question is often asked, "who should initiate the probe for staff differentiation?" The answer is that it makes little difference. What does make a difference is who "owns" staff differentiation after it has been introduced. Various groups own an idea when they have helped shape it. This is a time-honored principle which is overlooked just as much as it is recognized. Administrators repeatedly find themselves coming to boards, community, and particularly teachers' unions with ready-made proposals. Those groups are placed in ratifying positions rather than in positions to help with developmental proposals. There are as many excuses for not seeking broad involvement as there are situations. Staff differentiation which was introduced hastily has rarely, if ever, been implemented. Equally pertinent is that there are no known cases where staff differentiation was successfully developed in a teacher union—board or administration confrontation in collective bargaining. There are those who argue that collective bargaining can be creative; however, teachers and administrators are still too unskilled and unsophisticated with it to be able to do much more than whittle away at previously held static positions. The free give and take in which ideas can be proposed, abandoned, and developed in a nonthreatening atmosphere does not seem possible. Introducing anything more than the request by the administration or the union for a study committee on staff differentiation or the union ratifying an experiment as in Kansas City and later denying its spreading to other parts of the system is about all the process has so far yielded. While the idea may be initiated in bargaining sessions, the establishment of entrenched positions does not permit bold and innovative solutions being implemented.

Informal discussion with union or teacher association leaders, administrators, and board members appears to be conducive to a frank interchange without the necessity to defend hard and fast positions. For those early innovators of staff differentiation who viewed it primarily as a "thing," little negotiation is possible. After several years of trying to implement teacher hierarchies some were complaining that the idea had been "prostituted."[2] This was a common theme among members of the SPU-LTI Panel on the "state of the art" on staff differentiation before it was phased out by the office of education. Clearly only a *thing* can be prostituted. Such a view of staff differentiation negates negotiation and leads to the formation of steadfast positions. If, however, staff differentiation is regarded as a process of matching people skills to people needs, there is much room for negotiation. Furthermore, the process can be laid on the table, subjected to criticism and public and professional scrutiny. A priori model building usually initiates a series of power moves which provokes suspicion. A negative reaction, particularly by teacher groups, can be predicted. Throughout the brief and early developmental period of staff differentiation (1966-1970), teacher strikes in Montgomery County, Maryland, and militant action in Washington, D. C. were over issues pertaining to staff differentiation.

We can no longer shrug our shoulders and say, "You can't change people." Research shows we can change people. In fact, people *like* change. What they resist are the *methods* which are used to put changes into effect. The word and concept of "change" is feared because it upsets a way of doing things and threatens security. This feeling is balanced by a desire for new experiences and for the benefits that may come as a result of change.[3]

Only recently did one large city school system undertake the joint involvement of union, board and administration that was necessary for a productive study of staff differentiation.[4] The study was made of the public schools of the District of Columbia. At the time of this writing, there has been bitter controversy regarding the Academic Achievement Plan and the fate of the young superintendent; the work regarding a joint study committee on staff differentiation has not been an issue. We can only recount some of their problems and planned activities at this point. Since they are representative of many large urban school systems, there may be value in reviewing the work accomplished. After spending some time in the school system, the following "Open Memorandum" was filed with the board of education, the administration, and the teachers' union.

AN OPEN MEMORANDUM[5]

The following is a list of proposed steps by which each group would enter into a working relationship pertaining to staff differentiation. It is the hope of the consultant to return and discuss this report with the Board, Administration, and the Union and to redraft the suggestions made as a working guideline for cooperative action.

1. Cooperation of all Parties

Without the support of all parties concerned toward an honest and straight-forward analysis of both the problem and the solutions together with the formulation of alternative implementation strategies, little real change will be effected. All parties must recognize that they are *part* of the problem. In a complex and interrelated organization, everyone must share in both the diagnosis of the problem and in its solution.

2. Preservation of Independence

Each party must respect the autonomy and independence of the other. Engaging in discussion must be seen not as tactics to trap or co-opt the other, but as attempts to find common understanding on common grounds. The developmental process is not only the step-by-step building of alternatives, but the establishment of sufficient trust to be able to effectively implement a collectively defined solution.

3. Mixing Individual and Organizational Needs

A particular solution is viable because it meets the identified needs of those who are to be affected by it and because all breathed life into it. In this sense, the process *is* the product. What people do not develop they do not own; what they do not own has little but nuisance value and cannot command their energies and loyalty, except in a negative sense. This is as applicable for teachers as it is for principals, board members or parents and the larger community.

4. Staff Differentiation is Neutral

Staff differentiation is in its purest form the process of work specialization which is a natural and evolutionary form of organization building. It can lead to further organizational bureaucratization or it can be a form of organization renewal and reform if it is clearly related to client (pupil) needs. Staff differentiation is neither inherently good nor bad. It is rather a process which must be intelligently directed toward mutually desired ends. Staff differentiation is inevitable; it happens in organizations whether we like it or not. It is artificial and abrasive when it assumes a form which is counterproductive to human interaction and understanding, when it frustrates, alienates, and inhibits human energy rather than freeing and maximizing that same energy.

5. Minimizing Risk and Maximizing Change

Organizational reform is a process of maximizing change and minimizing risk. To maintain maximum loyalty during change, participants must envision the change as personally and professionally desirable. Advantages may be salary, visibility, status, travel, involvement, and prestige. In many cases the selection of inappropriate means to implement desired ends negates those same ends. In such cases resistance may be encountered.

Resistance is a combination of many factors and it assumes a variety of forms. Judson has identified a spectrum of possible behavior towards a change. This is identified in Figure 31.[6]

School administrators most often assume that a logical explanation as to why a certain change is necessary is the best method of introducing a change. This rationale, however, may completely ignore the power struggle of groups within the organization. No matter how appealing the logic to the individual or even the leader of a group, the group's position within or without the system, its agenda and past history may not be amenable to that same logic. An idea which is offered by some groups, or endorsed by others may endanger the reactions of other groups. It is important to assume that resistance is *always* logical. If it appears to be irrational, it is because the causes for the behavior are unknown or in some cases camouflaged, usually because of fear.

Lawrence compares resistance to pain and advises:

The key to the problem is to understand the true nature of resistance. Actually, what employees resist is usually not technical change but social change—the change in their human relationships that generally accompanies technical change. . . When resistance does appear, it should not be thought of as something

FIGURE 31

Judson's Spectrum of Possible
Behavior Towards a Change

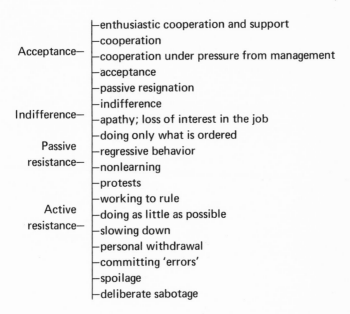

Acceptance—	⊢enthusiastic cooperation and support
	⊢cooperation
	⊢cooperation under pressure from management
	⊢acceptance
	⊢passive resignation
Indifference—	⊢indifference
	⊢apathy; loss of interest in the job
Passive resistance—	⊢doing only what is ordered
	⊢regressive behavior
	⊢nonlearning
	⊢protests
Active resistance—	⊢working to rule
	⊢doing as little as possible
	⊢slowing down
	⊢personal withdrawal
	⊢committing 'errors'
	⊢spoilage
	⊢deliberate sabotage

to be overcome. Instead, it can best be thought of as a useful red flag—a signal that something is going wrong. To use a rough analogy, signs of resistance in a social organization are useful in the same way that pain is useful to the body as a signal that some bodily functions are getting out of adjustment. The resistance, like the pain, does not tell what is wrong but only that something is wrong. And it makes no more sense to try to overcome such resistance than it does to take a pain killer without diagnosing the bodily ailment . . What is needed is not a long harangue on the logics of the new recommendations but a careful exploration of the difficulty.[7]

It is a natural reaction to exert more energy into overcoming resistance than it is to disengage from the reaction and backtrack by diagnosis. There are times when nothing can be done about resistance, as when internal politics of a teachers' union inhibit the group from making anything but an obdurate stand until things are stabilized internally. There are times when understanding the causes cannot be discussed openly because public disclosure would endanger a tenuous balance between groups. Understanding does not always lead to a change in a course of action, though it usually leads to a more sensitive human interaction and less aggressive and dogmatic behavior between parties. The memo continues:

6. The Utilization of Conflict

Conflict is inevitable; it should be used to enhance understanding and serve as a binding rather than a divisive force. It can be so if there is honest dialogue and confrontation where emotions are viewed as a legitimate part of dialogue and not submerged behind issues. Trust is an emotional tie, not an intellectual system of logic. Logic can weigh, measure, analyze, develop a plan. Trust stems from an open climate. Energy must be expended to initiate and maintain an open climate. Planning activities should be aimed at anticipating and utilizing conflict rather than in avoiding it. Anticipatory administration means that all sides listen to each other. Listening involves the heart and dialogue is possible. Hearing implies receptivity, but not necessarily understanding. The public schools have been plagued with conflict. It has led to a healthy reassessment in some cases and resentment in others. There are visible signs that groups have ceased to communicate except formally. Reopening face-to-face informal communication is a necessity for the establishment of a climate conducive to developmental activities.

7. Confusion of Means and Ends

Prototyping is a process of successive approximation, which means a precise definition of required outcomes and the selection and continued refinement of means to reach those outcomes. Means are flexible, expendable; ends are not. The greatest danger in prototyping (during the developmental stages) is that means have a habit of usurping ends. The purpose of differentiated staffing is not to improve student learning along definitive lines, but to have differentiated staffing per se, or to pay teachers differently, as if the innovation were valuable for its own sake.[8] The difference between means and ends is the difference between differentiated staffing as a refinement of present staffing patterns or as a reform to those practices.

8. Democratization and Structure

Differentiated staffing is a process, a process of matching people skills with people needs. As such, it is an investment in people; a secondary emphasis is placed on structure. This is not to negate the importance of structure on human behavior but to recognize the supremacy of people who can in their personal relationships overcome administrative structures. People can overcome inhibitory structures; on the other hand, structure can always be subverted by people.

Structure is important chiefly by its ability to limit human activity, either by compartmentalization as in a bureaucratic hierarchy of organizational offices and/or because it serves to lower the aspirations and level of expectations of people within those hierarchies. Structural changes are the most difficult type of organizational change because the key to the organization's control system is locked into it and thus the dispersion of power. The process of unlocking human potential is thus aimed at structural changes for the specialization of talent and the equalization of authority. For this reason, democratization often accompanies specialization.[9]

9. A Commitment to Retrain

An investment in people implies an organizational commitment to retrain, transfer, or reassign the human resources of that organization so that they are capable of maximum contribution to the objectives of the organization. The concept of understaffing means that contributions can be maximized, particularly at the middle-management level which is traditionally overstaffed. Overstaffing creates a cycle of inefficiency which leads to further discontent and an excuse for more overstaffing. The proliferation of administration in school systems is caused by a lack of performance standards. . . . If a problem is defined adequately the conditions for its solution are knowable and can be assigned to specific roles for specific time periods. These may then be subcontracted (priced and assigned) and solved (permanently). The psychology of overstaffing is the cycle of adding administrative units to solve problems. With precise problem definition, administrative units are added, but at the conclusion of the problem, they are subtracted, as in temporary or "project" administration. In most cases, added personnel become permanent. Differentiated staffing can help solve or perpetuate this problem.

10. Avoiding "Instant" Solutions

Given the intense pressures on school systems for instant solutions to chronic problems, people will want results faster than they can be made available. If simple, one-time solutions could solve education's problems, they would not now be causing trouble. In too many cases we merely massage the problem or treat the symptom. In all probability the proper treatment for our problems is now available. The real problem has been our inability to adequately define the dimensions and interrelationships of the problem itself.

11. Prototyping and Internal Reform

Even a cursory glance at the millions of dollars spent on educational innovation will reveal little real change in school systems. This is partly due to the nature of financial support; that is, it has been categorical itself, leading to piecemeal change. However, the defense mechanism of a bureaucratic organization serves to fence off innovations into separate entities, thus avoiding the necessity for serious and sustained reform.

To avoid this mechanism from again functioning, much leverage can be gained by prototyping staff differentiation at selected school sites and, at the same time, using the same energy in a different direction for internal organizational reform. [The Board of Education and the Washington Teachers Union were most receptive regarding the necessity for internal reform and adjustments made in the distribution of power and authority. The least responsive group was that of the central administration to such suggestions. It is the bureaucratic structure of large city school systems which is a major barrier to reform. John Gardner's notion of internal educational reform or self-renewal may be unworkable without enlightened management.] Thus, not only is "fencing" denied the organization, the school system itself is undergoing a similar process. For this reason, the consultant recommends that the efforts of prototyping be aimed in two directions simultaneously.

The School Reform and Action Task Force (SRATF)

The consultant recommends the formation of an in-house action task force to accomplish the dual purposes previously specified. This group shall possess organizational, fiscal and authoritative independence, include equal representation of the major parties involved, and be *abolished* when the objectives for its creation are met.

The SRAFT should be composed of the following members:

a. Two members of the board of education or board designates;

b. Two teachers appointed by the union;

c. Two administrators appointed by the Superintendent (can be a principal's representative and central office person);

d. An in-house executive secretary and staff (internal change agent);

e. An external change-agent (the consultant); The composition of this group was later changed. First, principals became unionized via the creation of a Council of School Officers. The CSO desired four seats. The WTU countered that the current contract did not separate principals and administrators and therefore the teachers would not be equally represented. The final agreement reached included six administrators (two central office and four principals) and six teachers. Two board members sat ex officio. (From a memorandum to Mrs. Anita F. Allen, President, Board of Education, filed by Hugh J. Scott and Fenwick W. English, August 27, 1971.)

Recommended Functions of the SRATF

The tentative and recommended functions of the SRATF would be as follows:

1. the definition and articulation of prototyping activities at selected pilot schools;

2. the definition of appropriate training activities for pilot school personnel;

3. the identification of system-wide organizational talent and application of that talent in the pilot schools and in planning for organizational reform;

4. the coordination of federal funding into a sustained organizational thrust;

5. the definition and derivation of plans for specifying the output of the public schools, i.e., the definition of baseline student behaviors and performances which comprise the school system's basic responsibilities to the pupil (i.e., pupils don't fail, schools fail pupils); to ultimately include provisions for recycling, specification of minimum entry behaviors, etc.

6. the definition and specification of plans of changing the organizational structure from bureaucratic to organic or fluid.[10] This latter structure is far more conducive to rapid change, internally and externally. In brief, the characteristics of these two types of structures are listed below.

Bureaucratic Structure

a. every official is subject to an impersonal order by which he acts. His instructions have authority only insofar as they conform with this generally understood body of rules; obedience is due to his office, not to him as an individual;

b. each person has a specified sphere of competence, with obligations, authority, and powers to compel obedience strictly defined;

c. the organization of offices follows the principle of hierarchy; that is, each lower office is under the control and supervision of a higher one;

d. the system serves as a career ladder.[11]

Organic Structures[12]

a. the adjustment and continual redefinition of individual tasks through interaction with others;

b. the spread of commitment to the concern beyond any technical definition;

c. the shedding of responsibility as a limited field of rights, obligations and methods (problems may not be posted upwards, downwards, or sideways as being someone else's responsibility);

d. situational and emergent leadership; omniscience no longer imputed to offices; knowledge about the technical or commercial nature of the here and now task may be located anywhere in the organization; this location becoming the ad hoc center of control authority and communication;

e. a lateral rather than a vertical direction of communication through the organization, communication between people of different rank, also, resembling consultation rather than command;[13]

7. the initiating of a systematic plan for "organizational development," a method whereby the school district invents a process to intervene in its own affairs and change directions rapidly. This is a planned program of organizational training and analysis;[14]

8. the development of a communication procedure which keeps all parties informed via briefings, reports, etc.

9. the development of position papers on critical issues and controversial topics for resolution and consensus;

10. the development of data gathering and evaluation filing by which the system is able to ascertain how well it is or is not fulfilling the objectives of the organization (the self-correcting function).

The school system cannot return to the "good old days." Power is shared, the three groups in question have achieved a kind of tenuous balance in this regard, though perhaps not realized. New situations demand new solutions. Joint leadership is the only route possible since none of the parties appears to be willing to abandon its present positions. A frank appraisal of the new type of situation is necessary, both to begin on a realistic base and to promote the kind of cooperation necessary to discover, define, and implement new types of solutions. Frustrations are perhaps the symptoms of having arrived at a new balance of power distribution, but it will be unproductive unless the power is used to solve the school system's problems.

While the Washington Teachers Union Executive Committee empowered their president to enter into the study committee for staff differentiation in August of 1971, the union had not appointed its six teacher members by December of 1971, prompting a letter by the superintendent to the WTU president.[15] While the rest of the task force has met a number of times, the school system is seeking an alternative to securing teacher involvement rather than waiting indefinitely. School officials report that this has been a tactic of the union—to agree to participate and then to refuse to name their representatives. The important point, however, is that the union was not shut out and it cannot take the position that it opposes an innovation merely because it was not involved in the deliberation process.

Furthermore, such a position on a significant educational innovation erodes public confidence and support for the Union, and pits it against reforms which are aimed at improving public schools for their clients, rather than purely for teacher comfort and security.[16]

TENTATIVE PERT FOR DEVELOPMENTAL ACTIVITIES FOR STAFF DIFFERENTIATION 1971-72

Background and Assumptions

PERT stands for *Program Evaluation and Review Technique* and is a useful method for illustrating the activities involved in a project which must occur simultaneously so the major steps can be completed within a given time frame. (See Figure 32.) Assumptions regarding the preparation of the PERT are listed below.[17]

1. The proposal is based upon the concept of model or prototype schools—schools which have been identified by all parties as sites conducive to developmental activities;

2. Time estimates are based upon the assumption of a five-day work week and based on days as the unit (.5 would equal one-half day). A day is assumed to be eight hours including lunch;

3. The PERT is independent of the recommendations for the School Reform and Action Task Force; it is therefore independent of any other consensus making group at the present time;

4. The PERT does not include days allocated for "start-up" time;

5. It is assumed that funds are or can be made available for training activities, principally activities related to needs assessment and task analysis;

6. Sufficient autonomy is assumed to exist in the functioning of the prototype schools within the school system;

7. Salaries specified in the PERT are considered as commission, and for developmental activities are above the standard salary schedule.

Time Estimates

Three time estimates are included in the PERT. Optimistic Time represents an estimate of the least amount of time it would take to complete the activity given optimum conditions. Pessimistic Time

FIGURE 32

Tentative PERT Network for Developmental Activities for Staff
Differentiation Public Schools District of Columbia
August, 1971
F. English

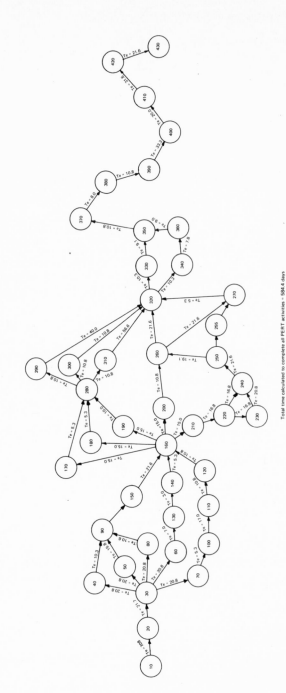

Total time calculated to complete all PERT activities = 584.4 days

represents the least likely time given the fact that almost everything that could go wrong will go wrong. The Most Likely Time is an estimate as to how much time the activity will take under normal conditions. A description of PERT activities is in Table 1.

Network Calculation

From the three time estimates an average or Expected Elapsed Time (t_e) is calculated via formula below.[18]

$$t_e = \frac{a + 4m + b}{6}$$

TABLE 1

Tentative Description of PERT Activities

Network #	Activity	Opt. Time	Pes. Time	MLT
10	Needs Assessment Training	2.5	20.0	5.0
20	Develop needs assessment model	10.0	40.0	20.0
30	Select/Develop needs assessment instruments	5.0	40.0	20.0
40	Gather School System Goals	2.0	20.0	10.0
50	Involve school community	5.0	30.0	15.0
60	Develop faculty inventory	2.0	20.0	5.0
70	Select Pupil Assessment Instruments	2.0	10.0	5.0
80	Gather larger societal data	4.0	20.0	10.0
90	Develop school baseline goals	2.0	10.0	5.0
100	Buy/develop pupil instruments	2.0	40.0	15.0
110	Administer instruments	5.0	20.0	10.0
120	Collate data	5.0	20.0	10.0
130	Administer faculty inventory	1.0	5.0	3.0
140	Collate/graph faculty skill levels	2.0	10.0	5.0
150	Develop school baseline student objectives/cog/aff/p-m/	10.0	40.0	20.0
160	Match-mismatch student discrepancies	5.0	25.0	15.0
170	Compare #160 with present school curriculum and materials	2.0	10.0	5.0
180	Compare #160 with inadequacies of school schedule/assumptions	2.0	10.0	5.0
190	Compare #160 to school facilities	5.0	15.0	10.0
200	Examine role structure with skill levels	5.0	20.0	10.0
210	List staff/skill discrepancies	5.0	30.0	15.0
220	Formulate generic training program	5.0	30.0	15.0
230	Transfer/reassign personnel	5.0	40.0	20.0
240	Cost/fund training program	10.0	40.0	20.0
250	Implement training program	5.0	30.0	20.0

Network #	Activity	Opt. Time	Pes. Time	MLT
255	Training activities	20.0	80.0	40.0
260	Create alternative staffing models	10.0	40.0	20.0
270	Evaluate training program	2.0	10.0	5.0
280	Formulate plans for upgrading	5.0	20.0	10.0
290	Revise curriculum	20.0	60.0	40.0
300	Create schedule alternatives	5.0	20.0	10.0
310	Modify school facilities	20.0	80.0	60.0
320	Determine total readiness	2.0	20.0	10.0
330	Definition of learning units	5.0	20.0	10.0
340	Create salary criteria	2.0	15.0	5.0
350	Prototype schools submit units (costs)	5.0	20.0	10.0
360	Consensus on salary criteria	2.0	20.0	8.0
370	Units negotiated	2.0	20.0	5.0
380	Units let by central group/board	5.0	20.0	10.0
390	Units implemented in prototype schools	20.0	60.0	30.0
400	Units evaluated	10.0	30.0	20.0
410	Salary distributed by staff	10.0	60.0	30.0
420	New student diagnosis	10.0	40.0	20.0
430	Recycle/refine/repeat			

Funding Prototype Schools

Prototype schools will be funded via an internal system in which all parties collectively define "learning units." These units are stated in terms of desired outcomes for a given population of students. Objectives include cognitive, affective and psychomotor outcomes. Objectives may well cut across disciplines or be confined to skill areas or some combination of both. The time frame for learning units remains to be determined.

After prototype schools have been selected and they are trained and in a state of readiness, learning units are submitted for consideration. These units have been developed according to mutually agreed upon criteria. These are then awarded to the prototype schools for a given period of time. Learning units include all related costs pertaining to instruction including salary in the form of commission, materials, tests. The school as a unit is in effect a subcontractor. Part of the learning unit is the specification of a staffing pattern based upon pupil needs and differentiated according to pupil need. A staffing pattern is hierarchical only to the extent that it may parallel a hierarchy of pupil need and reflects the value of some skills in meeting required objectives based upon the school needs assessment. No staffing pattern is ever permanently hierarchical since it could not be so if it is relevant to constantly changing pupil needs. This is what is meant by client-centered staffing, or contingency staffing rather than differentiated staffing.

An integral aspect of the entire process is a high degree of participative management at the prototype schools. Principals must be highly skilled in group dynamics and be confident professionals who are not threatened by a high degree of staff decision making which is almost wholly dependent upon skills and emergent leadership. Each school's staffing pattern will be different since it will emphasize and follow the needs of the local students and community expectation. Pluralism and diversity will be the hallmark rather than conformity and uniformity of design. The methods-means are wide open, the outcomes are jointly defined and less so. Staffs must be given maximum ability to create educational and instructional alternatives and be held accountable for the outcomes within a broad framework at first, which becomes more and more specific as expertise is gained and new relationships formed. The process is one of successive approximation towards the objectives.

The PERT closely follows activities of the Mesa approach to staff differentiation in that model building is a continual process because student needs form the requirements for role and staffing pattern formation and reformation. Figure 33 by Vance illustrates another model at a higher generalization level.[19] Vance envisions a unique school profile for each unit which is client specific. A school staff is balanced to the extent that teacher tasks match derived learning objectives which have been site validated.

Developing a Needs Assessment Model

Melton developed a complete school wide needs assessment model for a junior high school. This model was based on a system approach developed by Kaufman.[20, 21]

System analysis is a process for determining the requirements for getting from "what is," to "what should be" ... The outcome of a system analysis is a delineation of feasible "whats" for problem solution, and a listing of possible strategies and tools for achieving each "what."[22]

Several critical terms are defined by Melton of the Kaufman model:

Need: The discrepancy between "what is" and "what should be" or what is desired.

FIGURE 33

Vance's Model for Balanced Staffing

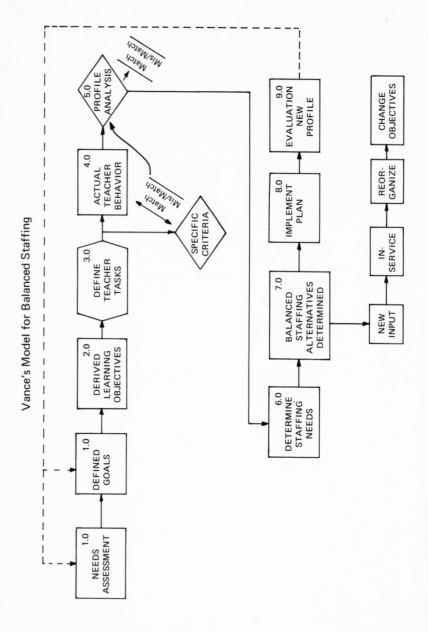

Methods means: Tools and strategies that when implemented produce specific outcomes as defined by performance objectives.

Performance requirements: The specific performance objectives for a given segment of the model, or measurable specifications concerning (a) ground rules for achievement and (b) what the product will look like or do.

Reconciliation: A process to arbitrate the discrepancies created by different approaches to a specific problem.

Mission Objective: The overall statement or need in performance terms.

Melton's mission profile shows the major steps involved in developing a needs assessment model. From the mission profile, the model is refined to levels of functions and finally to individual tasks. Figure 34 shows a function analysis approaching the task level. It should be obvious that training administrators and teachers in the techniques of system analysis and PERT are basic to almost all other skills. System analysis provides a logical and precise way of working through a definition of a problem and considering alternatives. If a staffing pattern is a process of continuous adjustment, system analysis provides a vehicle for the orderly examination and creation of variations.

Performing A Needs Assessment

Once a validated needs assessment model has been developed for a school (see Figure 35), the needs assessment itself needs to be done. In Mesa, Arizona, this was accomplished by subcontracting back to the teaching staff the major responsibilities for instrument selection and/or development with consultant help. Teachers took a random sample of approximately one-third the student body at one school and all the pupils at another. Parents were likewise sampled. Teachers at Fremont Junior High School administered the Mooney Problem Checklist to the entire student body prior to the summer of 1971. The compilation of the data was presented to the staff in initial training sessions and translated into goals. The staff discovered that there was an important change going on from grade six to nine of which they were unaware. The teachers underestimated the importance of boy-girl relationships as problems and student problems pertaining to money, work, and future. Parents underestimated home-family problems and boy-girl relations as problems. The eighth grade was the time when several problem areas became more intense. They were related to home and family, money, work and future, and problems related to self. Sixth graders led all others in relation to

FIGURE 34

0.0 MISSION OBJECTIVE:

By the end of the semester (Fall 70-71), a valid Needs Assessment Model will be designed to obtain a consensus of student needs from learner, parents, educator and district-state policies. The student needs derived will be used to evaluate and revise, if required, the present school goals and policies. If 60% of the learners, parents, educators, etc., agree that the revised school goals meet student needs, then the criteria have been met.

PERFORMANCE REQUIREMENTS:

1. Existing Conditions at Fremont Jr. High

MISSION PROFILE:

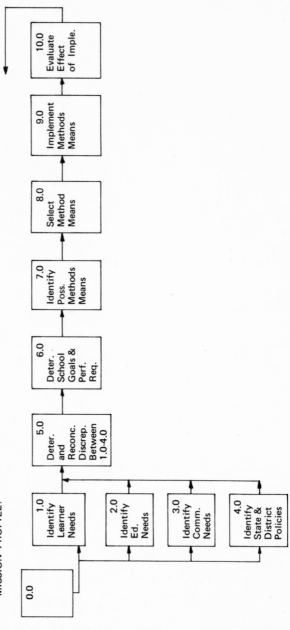

FIGURE 35

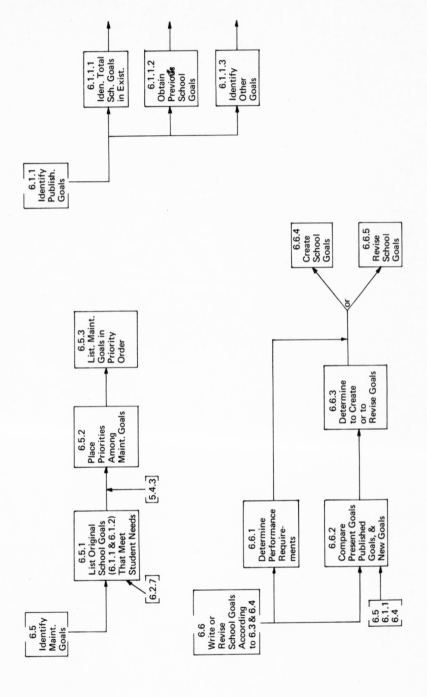

problems regarding health and physical development, boy-girl relations and relating to people in general. All grades indicated that school problems led all others. The steps involved in this needs assessment process were as follows:

1. Gather baseline data regarding cognitive, affective, and psychomotor growth of the students;

2. Compile and reconcile the data into a series of goals based on school and societal "what should be" conditions;

3. From the goals derive a series of baseline objectives which are terminal from the last grade that the pupils are in school. Once these goals have been specified into a series of performance objectives (irrespective of discipline or skill area at first) then each department may take them and derive strands in their respective disciplines;

4. Develop curriculum units based upon the needs assessment (the "what");

5. Define teacher tasks based upon what is to be accomplished;

6. Analyze existing teacher skills to reach the objectives;

7. Train, transfer, hire personnel to arrive at the necessary balance of staff skills to implement the objectives;

8. Diagnose pupils to delineate learning groups and learning strategies;

9. Develop total system plan for implementing learning unit including material deployment, scheduling, facility modification;

10. Implement/evaluate/recycle;

A needs assessment model provides a systematic method of making an alternative staffing pattern self-correcting by establishing a channel whereby fresh data can alter the methodology of the system.[23] The goals of instruction are continually influenced by facts from each source of data.

An Examination of Programmed Instruction and Staffing Patterns

It is possible to connect a methodology of programming classroom instruction with staffing pattern so that both may represent harmonious means towards the same instructional objectives resting on a valid needs assessment design. A methodology to attain compound objectives has been proposed by Bert Y. Kersh and rests upon these characteristics:[24]

1. It should provide a notation and charting technique which the programmer can use to prepare in advance a detailed outline of the learning experience in

terms of practice and reinforcement, schedules, branching criteria, and related characteristics without attending to the specifics of frame writing;

2. It should outline a procedure for preparing a basic program aimed at objectives which are amenable to automated instruction and then for weaving in programs involving human instruction, or vice versa. It should be possible to maintain one part of the overall program intact while changing the other part. In this way, different processes of learning could be employed simultaneously in a single program, or a single program could be systematically altered for purposes of research and development;

3. The methodology should enable the programmer to deal separately with problems of program design, frame writing, and materials development so that these operations can be accomplished by different individuals concurrently.

Kersh provides the TRAC procedure as an example. Basically, the steps are as follows:

a. specifications of objectives in terms of both content and process;
b. preparation of a hierarchy of subordinate facts and processes;
c. preparation of flow charts for each subordinate fact and process;
d. combination of separate flow charts;
e. development of specific instructions and materials;

The TRAC procedure provides an excellent series of first steps if a needs assessment design precedes the derivation of objectives. In linking the development of an alternative staffing pattern to the TRAC steps, an overlapping model which has been used in developing site specific differentiated teaching staffs and enumerated by Wretha W. Wiley and Sidney A. Fine can be employed.[25, 26]

In discussing methods for manpower analysis, Wiley and Fine suggest a six-step model:

1. State the overall purpose (long-term goals) of the agency;
2. Set specific objectives for the agency;
3. Identify major subsystems;
4. Define tasks into "what gets down" and "what the worker does;"
5. Organize tasks into jobs;
6. Organize jobs into career ladders or lattices.

This procedure has been used in the construction of a differentiated teaching staff at three Mesa public schools. One school, the Holmes Elementary School, built its model as follows:[27]

Identified Need

What is: 50 percent of students are reading at least one year below grade level;

What should be: 80 percent of students should be reading within one year of grade level;

Measurable discrepancy: 30 percent of students scored outside tolerance limits.

Objectives:

1. At the end of 150 days of instruction 80 percent or more of the students will score within one year of their grade level on the Gates-McGinite reading test;

2. At the end of 150 days students in grades 4-6 will score 85 or better on the Holmes Reading Attitude Inventory.

Tasks To Be Performed

1. Identification of students scoring outside of tolerance limits;

2. Selection and administration of diagnostic skills test to target group;

3. Identification of students with sight, hearing, visual perception problems, etc.

4. Selection of strategies to be used to meet specific skill deficiencies;

5. Ordering of materials and supplies;

6. Large and small group instruction;

7. Grouping and scheduling of students;

8. Periodic evaluation (30 days);

9. Coordination of above activities;

10. Selection and administration of evaluative instruments;

11. Interpretation of evaluative data;

12. Feedback-correction.

At this point Holmes teachers are drawn from a school directory, where their skills and interests have been classified according to ability. These are grouped into broad skill areas. From the directory the relative strength of a school staff may be assessed. It is likely that schools are overstaffed on some skills and lack talents in others. Such a continual comparison to pupil objectives and instructional tasks provides the basis for continual in-service training and a realistic policy of hiring teacher replacements to match needed skill levels in the school.

Suppose that Teacher A possesses skills in coordinating (administration), scheduling, and small group instruction; Teacher B has skills in art, music, and writing behavioral objectives; Teacher C has skills in constructing diagnostic instruments in reading and large group instruction; Teacher D is skilled in visual perception and public relations; Teacher E is an experienced reading teacher, a media specialist, and excellent in small group instruction; and Teacher F is an evaluation specialist.

Implementing the Holmes reading program and the 1-12 skills above requires the formation of four stages in which teacher tasks are grouped and regrouped and teacher roles shifted accordingly. From such stages a staffing hierarchy is formed. The stages are:

1. Diagnosis;
2. Selection of various implementation strategies;
3. Implementation;
4. Evaluation, which is divided in data gathering and interpretation;
5. Feedback and self-correction;

Hierarchical position among teachers (Teacher A-F) is a result of determining a hierarchical level of tasks which in turn are based upon criteria according to need and resources available. No arbitrary hierarchy is established into which are placed both resources (teachers and materials) and clients (pupils).

The present public school staffing pattern is neither objective specific, time specific, nor achievement specific. It makes no attempt to diagnose pupils and match teacher skills, interests or abilities to them in any kind of system. School is established as a solution before pupils are diagnosed. Criteria for grouping pupils for instruction is based upon nonachievement variables, impervious to need, pacing or achievement prior to the initiation of instruction.

The mere application of sophisticated banks of media or programmed texts, set within a nonspecific, nonclient-centered staffing pattern misses the potential of changing both. To maximize an investment in programmed instruction, the entire school program and its human resources must be made student and site specific. Until these requirements are met, long a hallmark of good programmed materials, significant school improvement will be tied to panaceas, politics, and charismatic protagonists, each with his own bill of goods. Real change is backed by a lot of prosaic and tedious examination. Part of that menu is the beginning of a needs assessment model with a strategy for building in the capacity for change.

Until school staffing patterns become congruent with more defensible and systematic instructional specifications and more easily altered as the requirements change, fitting programmed instruction into current staffing models will be impossible.[28]

Toward an Index of Organizational Productivity

Through system analysis and related tools, it is possible to see how changing a staffing pattern can set off a total change in school systems. The definition of outputs is the first step toward a radical alteration of school budgeting. At this point, both in planning and execution of staff differentiation, it is possible to tie in the concept of PPBS, or program planning and budgeting systems. The fundamental shift toward outputs means a thorough alteration of budget building. James reinforces this shift:

> I suppose the main reason PPBS has so upset school officials is that it changes their perception of the school as a stable, static organization with its solid objectives rooted in its history of past performance, their view of the future as an orderly and conservative projection by extrapolation into the future.[29]

James argues that traditional budget building is largely "incremental," and begins with last year's budget as a base. When some budget categories are cut, it is impossible to ascertain exactly how specific programs in the schools will be affected. James observes that in the traditional budget building process small programs have a habit of becoming increasingly larger through the years and eventually may become permanent. PPBS means that budget building begins each year from ground zero:

> ..attention is focused on choosing from many possible objectives to be achieved, and then choosing from alternative courses of action that plan which will accomplish the chosen objectives at the lowest possible cost, or accomplish some more optimum set of objectives at a specified cost.[30]

A move toward client-centered staffing will demand greater budget flexibility than traditional budgets allow. Ground zero budget building accompanies ground zero staffing. Certain legal provisions will inhibit a completely free hand in staffing schools according to need, since transfer rules, tenure, certain mandated staffing ratios (based on the traditional budget concept) will imply that all alternatives cannot be considered just on cost-benefit merits. Nonetheless the process of alternative selection can be made public and solutions can be costed in terms of the benefits they produce. It is not difficult to imagine the usual stormy and acerbic board budget sessions becoming a more rational review of the types of methods-means available to produce the desired student outcomes instead of citizens making obdurate demands about cutting a very nonspecific budget.

Adult taxpayers also have begun to demand more say about teacher salaries and fringe benefits—the huge budget category that is usually lumped under "instruction."

Shorewood voters last year sent their board packing until September 1 when a cut budget was approved in adjourned session. Taxpayers were disgruntled over "instruction" costs making up about 80% of the budget and demanded that administrators, whose salaries are also in that category, make sacrifices.[31]

So far, measures of educational productivity indicate that the schools are costing more but are becoming less productive.[32] Without specific measures to gauge productivity, school districts will continue to depend on standardized testing as a substitute. Even this is preferred over the usual habit of school personnel dodging any sort of professional responsibility, but requesting higher salaries under the guise of providing for better education. Immegart and Pilecki have proposed a framework for conceptualizing four essential categories or dimensions of output: productivity, integration, organizational health, and feedback.[33] The Immegart and Pilecki model is based on a number of underlying assumptions. These are:

1. Organizational output is multidimensional, and is more than products or work performed;

2. All dimensions and aspects (measures) of output must be present to some degree in the resultants of organizational activity if the organization is to maintain itself and perpetuate its contribution to its environment. If not (that is, if any aspects of output are of a zero quantity) the organization is potentially "in trouble." Since all aspects of output must be realized through organizational activity, "zero commodities" can be appropriately regarded as pathologies;

3. Conscious attention must, therefore, be given by an organization to maintaining at, and/or increasing all aspects of output to, a maximal level. Maximization of organizational output cannot be left to chance or happenstance, but rather must be programmed into ongoing organizational activity;

4. Increasing or maximizing any aspect of output is at the expense of other aspects of output. Of course, increased efficiency or effectiveness in regard to a

category of output enables energy to be diverted toward maximizing other aspects of output. However, since an increase in either can be realized only up to a point, there is ultimately some cost. It could also be argued that by attracting more energy, output maximization could be facilitated. Thus, output maximization does require conscious effort; it costs something, and ultimately, if not initially, maximization of any aspect of output may be at the expense of other aspects of output.

5. The greater the extent to which any output dimensions or aspect (measure) is present in organizational outcomes, the more open (dynamic) is the organization.[34]

When considering the practical costs of gearing up the system for change, boards and administrators often overlook the sunken costs of initial development. When these are brought into the open, the response may be that the changes cost too much. For a clear consideration of alternatives, they should examine the consequences of not changing, that is, the costs of continuing the present system of education, both in terms of the public's growing impatience to support it and of its well-documented inability to educate large masses of students, particularly in the inner city. A compelling and provocative concept created by economist T.W. Schultz is that of "human capital."[35] Human capital represents both an investment and a resource. However, it is not a stable resource. As Schultz comments:

. . . it is obvious that human capital, like other forms of reproducible capital, depreciates, becomes obsolete, and entails maintenance. . . .

Human capital deteriorates when it is idle because unemployment impairs the skills that workers have acquired. Losses in earnings can be cushioned by appropriate payments but these do not keep idleness from taking its toll from human capital.[36]

The schools' failure to invest resources properly in the education of students is not only mismanagement, but it represents an exponential damage that is more and more costly to correct. The long-term costs of a second or third rate education to society should be compared in the calculation to the sunken costs involved in changing it. These are rarely considered. Staffing is one of the most important inputs in schools, representing the largest budget allocation in terms of teacher salaries. The move toward relating productivity to staffing with PPBS as a method of accountability is long overdue.

Are Accountability and Governance Compatible?

Teacher groups have been quick to perceive that what some administrators meant by "accountability" was a punitive based salary schedule, rather than a method by which the total organization including themselves become "accountable" to the public for the quality of their services.[37] It has also served to raise questions about the skill levels of teachers and administrators.

What skills are professional? If skills are not related to pupil growth, what other base is more justified or more pertinent? Most teacher training consists in housekeeping skills—lesson plans, room environments, visual aids, and general psychology. Few, if any, of the skills taught in most teacher training programs can be related to specific pupil behaviors. This has led to measuring teacher differences along factors which are easily determined but have little reliability, either in predicting teacher performance or in calculating the effects of teachers upon children.

Gagne has suggested that instead of measuring values related to the efficacy of a teacher's performance, such as the college he attended, his degrees, and his years in the classroom, the efficacy itself would be measured. The "process" variables—what application the teacher makes of the materials and opportunities at hand—could be studied.[38] An alternative so clearly rooted in pupil outcomes forces the profession to confront the issue: Can we continue to be indifferent to pupil growth?[39,40]

Staff differentiation can become the vehicle by which system productivity is defined, accountability related to productivity and, in the process, a mechanism of professional governance created to protect and serve the public. For this to occur, those responsible for planning and developing staff differentiation must see the movement in a larger perspective and grasp more implications of considering it than tinkering with the salary schedule or as a ploy for collective bargaining. This leads to the most critical group in developing alternative staffing patterns—teachers—because they know the system well, comprise the largest single group of professionals in the organization, and must by definition be the implementers of the new changes. While philosophically the public or parents may be most critical, the public is usually ill-informed about how schools are operated, laws and policies, and the day-to-day mechanics of keeping school going. Only fringe groups appear to have the sustained drive to stay with a concept over a long period of time, instead of showing up at one board meeting to demand an end to high taxes. The most basic tenet is, convince the teachers and they can convince the community, or at least, not provide a base for opposition. This is particularly true in smaller communities where large numbers of teachers actually live. Community uproars about education are usually fed by information from the professional staff who have their own motives for disseminating opinion and information. In some cases where teachers have become particularly fearful or bitter, they may attempt to enter directly the political system of the community to fight against change.

Anticipating Teacher Response

Unfortunately, teachers as a group appear to most observers to lack the perspective of long-range thinking. They do not look ahead to 1980 and probe those corridors of awesome mystery. They appear more here-and-now oriented, more concerned with the immediacies of their present routines, present scheduling problems, present details of course study.[41]

In anticipating teacher response to an idea like staff differentiation, the innovator is led to a number of fields: to sociology and studies of teachers as an occupational group; to management and organizational psychology; and to statements of organized teacher groups for clues as to issues, agendas and emotional blind spots which might be avoided in laying the groundwork for staff development. Recent literature on teachers finds a common theme that teaching attracts the security oriented person looking for stability as a career hallmark.[42, 43] The same literature sadly observes that those interested in change are driven from the profession by its lack of challenge and its boring routines.[44] An observation by Hickson et al. is that the garnering of power in an organization is hindered by routinization. Routinization is represented in job descriptions, procedures, and policies. It enhances the possibility of substitution by those who could not have acquired the skills by training. "A relative decline in the power of general medical personnel in hospitals during this century is thought to be due to the routinization of some tasks, which previously presented uncertainties which could be coped with only by a physician, and the transfer of these tasks to relatively routinized subunits. . . ." The relative impotence of teacher power within school systems is thought to be related to the degree of bureaucratization. In this light teacher resistance to staff differentiation for reasons which pertain to avoidance of routinization and hence a curtailment of existing power is healthy. There is little but personal observation on this theme by spokesmen with a variety of agendas, and it remains to be documented by the types of dominant career motivations possessed by those entering elementary and secondary education at the college level. Neither AFT nor NEA has done any sustained or intensive sociological analyses of questions pertaining to who enters teaching or what types of dominant value patterns they possess. Almost all research has pertained to position papers and/or statements, and data regarding salary, fringe benefits, and quantitative organizational characteristics such as class size ratios, number of books per child, and certification requirements. Neither NEA or AFT has been instrumental in lobbying for, inventing, or proposing a significant educational reform which would seriously challenge the basic organizational structure of American public education. Initiative for educational reform has not come from teacher organizations, rather, it has emanated from the federal level and Congress, university professors, an occasional school superintendent or from critics outside of the field of education who range from those like Silberman,[45] Holt,[46] and Kohl[47] to Ivan Illich.[48] In the decade ahead the oversupply of teachers is bound to continue, and with pressures on teacher organizations the position will be that public education can be improved simply by hiring more teachers. The solution is attractive since this is the first time an adequate supply of teachers is available to realistically consider the possibility. Such a solution avoids all of the questions raised by this book about the inadequacy of the structure of schools and the current practices of not asking questions about pupil needs first. The administrator, parent, or innovator should not be overly discouraged, however, because within AFT and NEA there is disagreement about these issues and there is always the hope that a more enlightened leadership will come to the fore. More importantly, there should be optimism because field chapters of both organizations enjoy latitude and disagreement with national platforms. A strong local teachers group has more than once taken positions contrary to those of their mother organizations because they were committed to local efforts to improve the schools. Perhaps the best example of this is provided by the Temple City AFT Local. Originally skeptical and negative to the concept, the AFT President J.I. Harvey filed an open letter to Superintendent M. John Rand. It is reproduced here in its entirety because it represents a sincere response of a critical group and can be used to consider alternative methods of involving teachers at the outset of investigating staff differentiation.

AN OPEN LETTER

TO: Dr. M. John Rand, Superintendent
FROM: American Federation of Teachers, Temple City High School
SUBJECT: Kettering Project

Dear Dr. Rand:

The Temple City Chapter of the American Federation of Teachers held its regular business meeting on Thursday, September 22, 1966. The meeting was attended not only by AFT members, but by other teachers from the high school who desired the AFT to represent them in the matter under discussion. All teachers present had studied the project proposal to the Kettering Foundation, and the meeting was concerned with a critical evaluation of this proposal. It was generally felt that the overall purpose of the proposed project was excellent. It was agreed that teachers should be rewarded for teaching without having to lose contact with students. Teachers conceded that modular scheduling is a coming innovation in education, and that it is desirable for us to move in that direction in Temple City. There were, however, questions in the minds of all in attendance. It is the object of this paper to seek answers to these questions and solutions to the problems.

No Teacher Involvement in Initial Planning

Those present were concerned because the Kettering Project, whose intent is to involve the total teaching staff in the development of educational programs, did not involve teachers in its development and preparation. It was felt that had this involvement occurred, greater teacher interest and enthusiasm in the Kettering Foundation proposal would have developed. Teachers should not be asked to accept proposals that affect their teaching careers for many years, when the specifics which could have great impact are left to some future and highly nebulous decision.

Possibly many of the existing questions would not exist but for the fact that the proposal to the foundation is extremely general. Those specifics which come to mind are not included. The intent of this letter is to identify those specifics. Furthermore, this letter proposes suggestions from teachers involved in implementation of the program.

Teachers Do Not Prefer Twelve-Month Employment

The Kettering Project proposes to capture the qualified teacher's talents and to involve him in educational development. It intends to accomplish this by creating a teacher hierarchy based on differentiated compensations and responsibilities. Teachers believe that the highest qualified instructors within the district *would not* be interested in twelve-month contracts: Teachers desire time free from teaching to study independently or travel or engage in various types of self-improvement. Distinct work other than teaching, such as curriculum development, would be of value, a problem results: the positions of Curriculum Associate and Senior Teacher could not be filled by these competent teachers because they would not be able or willing to work this length of time. Consequently, most competent teachers would be forced to remain in the bottom categories.

Teachers Burdened with Administrative Chores

The Kettering Proposal was predicated on the assumption that teachers will remain in the classroom and still be willing to participate in curriculum planning and development. For this they presumably would receive more money. Any teacher doing curriculum work or other types of extra planning in addition to his teaching load would be overburdened. Obviously he would need released time to carry out extra duties. With released time he would be less in the classroom and more involved in administration. Consequently, the program's intent of requesting teachers to do the administrative tasks and still teach would be negated. If teachers are granted released time for administrative tasks, thereby doing less classroom teaching, we achieve a program no different from today's, with an administrative hierarchy added.

New Duties Give Little Time for Professional Growth

The program as presently designed discourages the career teacher for these reasons: (1) He would be faced, if he wished to advance, with a twelve-month schedule. (2) He would be severely overburdened by having to do both administrative tasks and teaching assignments. (3) He would not be free to take the advanced education he needs to keep up with his profession. (4) He would be unable to engage in extracurricular activities.

More Work Demanded for Less Pay

The differentiated compensation at first glance seems to offer the career teacher excellent opportunity for advancement financially. Actually several problems present themselves at this point. (1) 75 percent of the teachers within the district could not advance financially under the Kettering Proposal as far as they can now advance under the existing salary schedule. (2) The highest salary obtainable under the Kettering Proposal for 75 percent of the staff is $10,000. This is actually $1,500 less than would be available to the same teachers under the existing salary schedule. Since a majority of the staff would not be interested in twelve-month positions, the best teachers would be in this 75 percent category which limits them to a maximum salary of $1,500 less than is now available under the present salary schedule.

Kettering Proposal Offers Less Salary per Month

Assuming that the best teachers would desire a twelve-month contract and choose to become Curriculum Associates and Senior Teachers, it is the concern of the teachers that the per-month salary available to these positions would not be significantly more than the per-month salary now available under the present salary schedule. For example, the lowest salary for a Curriculum Associate would be $14,000 per year. To find the monthly salary, divide $14,000 by twelve. This would give the Curriculum Associate $1167 per month with a total of some twenty days' vacation. Take the same teacher on the existing schedule, assuming he is at the top. Dividing $11,500 by ten results in $1,150 per month. Conclusion: a teacher in this district at the top of the schedule makes only $17 less on a per-month basis. He has less obligation to the district than he would as a beginning Curriculum Associate, where he would be expected to teach a full class load as well as innovate, design, and create for a full twelve months without benefit of the periodic holidays and vacations. The teachers in our meeting showed considerable lack of enthusiasm for a program in which they would be required to work a great deal more for only $17 per month.

Top Teachers Make Least Amount of Money

The situation is further complicated by the fact that some of these same teachers are only Senior Teachers under the proposal, and would make still less money per month. The picture is even more discouraging if these same teachers do not care to work twelve months, but must remain as staff teachers. Their salary rate per month is considerably less.

Grandfather Clause and Inflation Promote Salary Regression

The Kettering Proposal supports a Grandfather Clause by which salaries are frozen and no one goes backward on the salary schedule. The idea of freezing anyone on the salary schedule is fallacious. Unless that individual is guaranteed an annual cost-of-living increase, he is, in effect, penalized and his salary grows less yearly.

Discouragement, Not Challenge, Faces Career Teachers

Assuming that the above problems did not exist and teachers choose to advance themselves professionally in the proposed hierarchy, problems still remain to discourage a teacher under this proposal. It is stated that there is no tenure in the two senior positions. Further, it assumes that natural attrition would eliminate people from the upper positions, leaving room for other teachers to advance. Since teachers would have to be evaluated yearly to maintain these two positions, supposedly there would be significant turnover. These conclusions are fallacious. If the proposal dignifies teaching, adequately compensates for professional services, and enhances a teaching career in Temple City School District, attrition by teachers leaving the district would be almost nonexistent. Perhaps teachers would not leave the upper positions for others to attain. The result of this could be dissatisfaction, boredom, and strong belief by a large majority of the staff that there was no opportunity in Temple City. Attrition could occur, but almost exclusively in the two lowest positions. Once promoted, an incumbent tends to retain his position. Once a Curriculum Associate or Senior Teacher, all things being equal, a teacher would retain this position. The problem facing Temple City teachers is this: the two upper positions, Curriculum Associate and Senior Teacher, would remain static. The opportunity for teachers to move into these positions appears negligible.

Uncertain Future for New Teachers

Prospective teachers looking to Temple City for a life-time career must realize that 25 percent of the positions in the upper two brackets would be filled by teachers with many years before retirement. Opportunity to gain these positions would be doubtful. A teacher considering his life's career would see himself relegated for years to one of the two lower positions; he would note the maximum of $10,000 as the most to which he might attain. Obviously, chances for advancement seem most unlikely.

No Provision for Professional Growth

The existing proposal contains further difficulties. Within each position, various steps are indicated. However, there are no indications of the procedure by which a teacher moves from step to step. There is no unit incentive built into the steps so that a teacher is encouraged to continue his education. Furthermore, no seniority is built into the ladder to entice a teacher to remain. Conceivably a teacher might begin in Temple City earning $6,000—and remain there through his career, despite having acquired a Master's degree and numerous units within his field.

No Solution to Merit Pay Problem

The Kettering Proposal does not deal with merit pay; yet all promotion is based on some type of evaluation and human judgment. Someone must evaluate and judge. The proposal does not assure teachers that evaluation and judgments are to be handled other than they have been in the past. If this is true, the proposal does not succeed in eliminating merit pay. Even if teachers themselves became involved in evaluation, no criteria exists to specify how this evaluation is to take place. How are traditional pitfalls avoided?

No Guarantee of Ethical Hiring and Promotion

Actually the problem of teacher advancement and merit pay is compounded by suggestions within the proposal. The current theory that interviews will be conducted and teachers will compete for the senior positions leaves doubt as to the administration. Who will conduct the interviews? This is not specified. On what basis will the competition take place? This, too, is not clarified in the project, even though it implies that many of these thorny issues will be worked out later. The proposal repeatedly suggests that measurements for the purpose of evaluation will be developed. Those familiar with the fields of testing and statistics know that with even the best scientific formulas, testing and accurate measurement for both reliability and validity proves extremely difficult, even impossible. The project does not provide solutions for the human element— emotional, political and social problems which constantly interfere with the progress of real talent and efficiency.

Proposed Leadership Violates Spirit and Intent of Project

A point of real consternation for those teachers meeting was the echelon of the hierarchy. The report proposes that Fenwick W. English be the secondary coordinator. Teachers analyzed his biographical data. Mr. English received his BS in elementary education, his MS in elementary administration, and some graduate units in secondary administration. However, the amount of work in secondary administration is not indicated. Mr. English's teaching experience was basically in elementary schools. He was an elementary teacher in Los Angeles School district, middle and upper-grade elementary teacher in La Canada. According to data, Mr. English has had no experience teaching high school, and no experience in administering in high school. How then does Mr. English qualify as Secondary Coordinator of the project? The philosophy of the project is that leadership and advancement in the plan is based on ability and experience. Knowing this, the group concurred that the selection of Mr. English is not in harmony with the general purpose of the Kettering plan. It was the unanimous opinion of teachers present that they could not willingly participate in this proposed teacher differentiated plan with Mr. English as Secondary Coordinator.

Project Terminology Limits Purpose and Concept

The Kettering proposal makes use of terms such as "flexibility" and "teacher involvement." If these terms are to have meaning, the program must not be rigid, and the flexibility should allow the program to meet not only the needs of youth and the district, but also the needs of teachers. If teachers are indeed as important as the program suggests, they should be consulted in every aspect of the program and its development. The following suggestions were made by the group in an effort to provide flexibility and teacher involvement: such words as "hierarchy" connote ruling group without provision for mobility. "Frozen" implies a static situation with no possibility of growth. "Attrition" implies some sort of life-death process. We suggest these words be eliminated.

Teachers Locked in Rather than Advanced

The teachers suggest that positions 1, 2, and 3 (Associate Teacher, Staff Teacher, and Senior Teacher) be made flexible. It should be permissible for a teacher to be under one program one year and another program a following year without necessarily suffering financial reverses. Thirty-two Senior Teacher positions need not be confined to thirty-two people. Possibly creative work will not be limited to those Senior Teachers. Perhaps a Staff Teacher working for ten months could perform the functions of a Senior Teacher and thus receive the remuneration of a Senior Teacher during that ten months. If extra work develops, either during the ten-month contract or during the summer, and certain teachers are interested, they should be paid on an extra-work, extra-pay basis. This is in harmony with the Kettering proposal whereby teachers are paid per differentiated activities. Extra activities should receive extra pay, but no one group of teachers should be so designated. If a quality teacher prefers to teach only ten months, then during that ten months the full range of his excellence in teaching as well as his extra effort should be reimbursed. If he prefers to work on an extended schedule, he should have this choice.

Need for Teacher Involvement and Experienced Leadership

We recommend that the present administrative hierarchy be altered. We suggest that the secondary coordinating committee be replaced by the concept of secondary and elementary committees with both teachers and administrators participating. This concept is more in harmony with the spirit and intent of the Kettering proposal, extending the philosophy of teacher involvement throughout the structure: If teachers are to carry out and support the program, then they must reasonably share in the choice of leadership.

Selection for Positions Must Be Objective

The selection of teachers for the various phases of the proposed program, and the promotion of teachers within the program, must be based on a specific objective criteria. There must be built into the selection process, adequate guarantees against personal favoritism, patronage, and choice based on a subjective rapport between teacher and recommending administrator. Evaluation must be handled in a comparable manner. Unless these guarantees can be provided, teachers cannot feel confident, adequate, and supportive. The first step in this direction is to permit secondary teachers to participate directly in the selection of a secondary coordinator.

Best-Qualified Teachers May Prefer Classroom

The proposal offers a fallacious concept—that the best teachers have been promoted beyond the children. This suggests that the best teachers were not those desiring to remain with the students and would do so in spite of salary differential. We feel that the best teachers have stayed with the children and will continue to stay, and that they have found satisfaction in this capacity despite the lack of financial reward. Financial remuneration should be added for teachers working directly with students. Unfortunately, the proposal suggests that a minute salary increase ($17 per month) be given to these teachers. Teachers deserve a lighter work load, higher pay, and more prestige for dealing directly with students. Teachers must not be pressured into administrative tasks. Ideally, teachers should teach without financial fear or anxiety, or concern for promotion, or worry over evaluation—these or any administrative procedures which beset and harry the dedicated teacher.

Retention of Good Teachers a Necessity

Temple City has many excellent teachers who should be encouraged to remain. Their retention can be assured only if position openings go to Temple City teachers. If outside teachers are hired rather than competent Temple City teachers, low morale results and the program obviously weakens. There should be no barrier to teachers in the lower echelons to prevent them from progressing with promise of a future in the district. This necessitates a program based on teacher competency rather than political astuteness.

Conclusions

The foregoing is admittedly general. We acknowledge that the Kettering project itself is general, and that details are meant to be perfected. Our teachers feel concern over details; we request that provisions be made for adequate protection from innovations that could make the program untenable. We feel that the program has merit if inequities, fallacies, and vague generalities are corrected. The purpose of this letter is to assist in any way possible.

Sincerely,

J.I. Harvey, President

Temple City Chapter, AFT[49]

The memorandum served to highlight teacher fears. At this point the district did not mount a sustained public drive to overcome the objections of the AFT. Instead, the project director met with many teachers and developed a plan enabling teachers to make the policies, procedures and details of the differentiated staffing plan cooperatively. The original strategy was wrong on at least two major counts. First, teachers had not been involved in the preparation of the proposal. This led to their fears that they were going to be "put upon" as they had been so many times in the past. Secondly, the proposal was ambiguous. Despite verbal pleas by administrators that it was ambiguous because teachers were going to be involved, suspicions arose that the administration already had something in mind and was simply going to go through the motions of involvement. Subsequently, a project steering committee was formed and complete autonomy given this body to conduct an investigation. Formal teacher representation of both the AFT and the NEA affiliate were offered so that group concerns could be addressed openly. The actions of the steering committee and its obvious independence from the administration allayed fears of manipulation. The development of concrete procedures by the teachers job analysis task force answered many of the procedural questions asked in the open letter. Almost a year later Harvey predicted "teacher acceptance if the Steering Committee so recommends." "Whatever is finally proposed will probably not be 100 percent satisfactory to me, but I'm willing to bend—a little."[50] There are two cardinal principles to guide any future development of staff differentiation:

1. Teachers must be involved in developmental activities.

Administrators should avoid at all costs the strategy of coming to teacher groups with a plan in hand, or an article from some journal saying, "let's try this." Instead, a joint meeting between parties should discuss problems by which various solutions such as staff differentiation may be considered. Much suspicion about "hidden agendas" can be ameliorated in the developmental stages about the motivation of both groups. Sufficient trust must be established here to permit full experimentation with the possibility of acceptance or change if it succeeds or fails.

2. Ambiguity should be eliminated to the greatest possible extent.

Ambiguity is necessary for creative exploration of alternatives, but not in the developmental stages when two or more groups are attempting to define problems and solutions and establish a climate of trust. If there is suspicion about the intentions of one party regarding the other, ambiguous proposals heighten the suspicions, inflame rumor, and create an artificial tension counterproductive to the investigation. All cards should be played from the beginning. All knowledge, recommendations, reservations should be openly stated. If one party feels a certain procedure will be more productive than another, it should be presented in detail. If there are "givens" due to external constraints of some sort, they should be acknowledged. The danger in this approach is that initial meetings may become too structured with the mistakes and faulty concepts of past attempts. However, given the already existing tensions, mistrust, and game-playing which tends to characterize almost all administrator-teacher-board relationships, the risk may simply be too great with too much ambiguity. The risk of too much attention paid to precedent is preferred to perpetuating a vicious cycle of fear which will lead to a sterile series of exchanging position papers from entrenched view-points. When attempting to establish a climate of trust and openness, ambiguity is an enemy. It should be avoided. Another factor which will enter into teacher response is the type of relationships which have characterized teacher/administrator dealings in the past. If the teachers have been treated with contempt or heavy-handedly, they will be more difficult to work with than if those conditions did not pertain. This will be especially so with teacher organizations who will be very sensitive to appearing to be administrative "dupes" or cajoled into betraying the interests of teachers.[51] The administrator must remember that what teacher leaders may privately admit needs changing, they may not be able to publicly endorse since they may feel they are obligated to "represent" the views of the majority of their membership. While an administrator may often express publicly views which are contrary to that of the organization, the teacher leader is much more cautious, since his base of support and authority is considerably different. In the former situation, the administrator receives his backing from occupying a position which is legally a part of the organization. He does not have to conduct a plebiscite to remain in office though he may have to be circumspect on some issues. But the teacher leader is sensitive to the fact he may be replaced if he strays too far from his membership's views, no matter how justifiable or pressing they may be. Too many administrators do not understand the politics of teacher unions and associations and attribute some of the behavior of those leaders as fence-straddling or deviousness when in fact the union or association president may have few options and is as straightforward as his situation will allow him to be. Sensitivity to this will prevent an administrator from forcing teacher leaders into public corners from which they either lose their own positions, or take premature negative stands which could have been avoided. No one knows more where teachers are than some of their insightful leaders. They are often moving quietly as fast as they dare go, sometimes faster than is often perceived.

Other Factors Determining Teacher Response

Assessing teacher attitudes toward staff differentiation suggests that a series of recommendations be made for those responsible for its development.[52]

1. Those responsible for the design, implementation and evaluation of staff differentiation programs should become aware of the already vast differentiated staff which is not recognized by most school administrators;

2. Diversity within teaching as it relates to identifying and dealing with the already differentiated staff must be encouraged;

3. The fallacy of "selling" staff differentiation solely on the basis that what teaching as an occupation really needs is to masculinize itself along dimensions of other male dominated professions must be recognized;

4. The major emphasis of staff differentiation should be shifted from structure to people as the strategy which is ultimately workable for the most lasting changes.

The already differentiated staff referred to two studies which illustrated that career patterns differ markedly depending upon whether the teacher is male or a female and whether the teacher is an elementary or secondary teacher.[53] Likewise, the wellsprings of militancy also vary on the same characteristics.[54]

Ziegler's study was based upon interviews with 803 high school teachers in Oregon. His findings are provocative and offer help in assessing teacher response toward staff differentiation.

Insofar as teaching is a feminized occupation, and if it is assumed that teaching is a middle-class occupation, then for males teaching becomes a mechanism of status change while for females it is a mechanism of status maintenance.[55]

Ziegler systematically bridges his data with a convincing case that males at the high school level become progressively dissatisfied with their jobs, become progressively job alienated and resistant toward change.

Facing a crisis of authority, teachers can be expected to emphasize superior-subordinate relationships and to be suspicious of change, for they prefer that their professional world be structured so as to minimize risk-taking and to maximize established authority.[56]

Ziegler contemplates the results of the traditional system in terms of staffing.

That male teachers should develop antiestablishment attitudes is understandable, but has resulted in high schools staffed with teachers who do not like their work, who espouse an ideology of discontent, and who reject the educational orthodoxy of the educational establishment.[57]

The alienation of males is not exclusively confined to the secondary level, but also manifests itself at other levels. Top-salaried elementary school males were found to be almost as militant as high school males. (See Table 2.) Males were less satisfied with teaching than females, were more militant but interestingly enough, more positive to staff differentiation than females.

Staff differentiation does not have universal appeal to teachers at all points on the standard salary schedule. The data suggested that it is generally most appealing to teachers on the first and second salary levels and, top salaried high school males and to secondary teachers generally. Males at the middle salary levels appeared to be the most negative toward change and to staff differentiation of the males collectively.

Secondary females are more positive towards change, have less need for job security and are more positive toward staff differentiation than their elementary counterparts. Elementary females are the least open to change, the most job dependent and the least supportive at the top salary levels to staff differentiation. They are, however, the most content with teaching.

Higher salaries for teachers are not necessarily a palliative for militancy, nor will they produce more job independence (lower need for teacher job security) or openness toward change and innovation. The data illustrated that middle and top salaried teachers found more perceived conflict with the administration than beginning teachers. A correlation coefficient was calculated between teachers perceiving high conflict with the administration and the total dependent variables which revealed that such conflict (militancy) correlated negatively with a positive teacher response to school innovation, feelings regarding team teaching, need for newer teaching methods, and a low need for job security. Teachers with high conflict scores also correlated negatively with the degree to which faculty meetings were productive, perception of school climate being "open," perception of school system being "open," ability to talk openly with the administration, and with staff differentiation as a needed concept in education.[58]

TABLE 2

A Rank Order Summary of Salary Level and Perceived
Teacher Conflict with the School Administration

Pay Level	Sex	School Level	Conflict with Administration	SD	Number
3	male	high school	1.846	.801	13
2	male	high school	1.561	1.000	57
3	male	elementary	1.500	1.049	6
2	female	high school	1.333	.966	21
3	female	elementary	1.222	1.202	9
1	male	high school	1.218	.854	55
2	female	elementary	1.205	.942	73
1	female	high school	1.185	.962	27
2	female	junior high	1.100	1.165	20
2	male	elementary	1.086	.818	35
1	female	elementary	1.014	.945	208
2	male	junior high	.967	.928	30
1	male	elementary	.870	.891	54
1	male	junior high	.762	.756	63
3	male	junior high	.750	.886	8
3	female	high school	.750	.500	4

Earlier in Temple City, a study found elementary females, particularly primary females to be most opposed to staff differentiation.[59] The sex and militancy correlation was also documented by Cole.[60] "The comparative reference groups of men had higher prestige occupations than teaching, thus creating relative deprivation among male teachers and a willingness to support the union movement."[61]

Implications of the Data

Of the two organized groups of teachers, AFT and NEA, more rank and file support for staff differentiation may be found in the AFT because the union is masculinized, though its official position is far more negative than the NEA's. While males are more militant, they are not necessarily more negative toward staff differentiation than nonmilitant teachers. Elementary females are relatively satisfied with teaching, but the most negative toward staff differentiation of any group of teachers. Since staff differentiation, at least in Generation I models, offered to teachers the opportunity of increased status, it is not surprising it is more appealing to men than to women. Generation II models do not offend females as much; since they are rooted in client analysis, they bypass the objections regarding teacher hierarchies which the union leadership found so threatening to union solidarity, and the models offer increased salary differentials which men equate with satisfaction with teaching. Ziegler found this to be true particularly at the beginning with male teachers. English found beginning males also positive towards staff differentiation.

Principals and Supervisors—Middle Management

The sudden emergence of teacher power and their ability to bargain at the top of the organization, leaving the principals and other middle management positions to enforce what has been negotiated, has thrown middle management groups into a state of confusion. Some principals' groups have or are considering bargaining with the board of education as separate entities.[62] Principals talk about "role erosion."[63] Such erosion is linked to an adverse effect on children. At the nub of the argument stands the unstated assumption that supervision is necessary because teachers don't know how to teach. While the assumption is not true, particularly with the modern preparation of teachers, if it were, one hundred years of supervision has failed to upgrade it. When teachers are struggling to find a professional status in the educational organization, they naturally resent the assumptions of a group of people who maintain they are not professionals.

The typical secondary school teacher is a college graduate who has studied courses in general education together with the subject fields in which he expects to teach. Such limited preparation for teaching itself means that teachers begin their careers with incomplete professional training which must be supplemented by continuation of their education inservice.[64]

When teachers do speak, as for example a survey of 15,020 teachers in California by the Senate Factfinding Committee which noted:

Complete consistency was demonstrated throughout regarding the value to teachers of assistance by educational specialists, whose duties are to offer advice, guidance, and assistance to teachers. The inference can clearly be drawn, regardless of the type of district considered, that teachers feel strongly that the place for educational specialists, outside the classroom seems to be nil. . . .

The very positions whose sole function is to assist teachers to do a better job of teaching are considered by teachers to be of doubtful assistance in most cases, and actually harmful to the teaching situation in some. As stated before, the contribution of the educational specialist would be more welcome by teachers if they, too were teaching.[65]

The supervisor is an obsolete role in American education. No matter how it is construed, a superior/subordinate relationship devoid of real competence differentials is artificial and arbitrary and inevitably falls back upon authoritarianism for sustenance. This in turn causes more resentment.

Much of the "downtown" staff of middle-sized and large city school districts continues to support an archaic and self-defeating force of supervisory personnel which teachers greatly resent and which is a major area of contention. The teacher has changed and so has the need for supervisors. Yet the educational superstructure still insists they are necessary. The bureaucracy is unable to accept the new teacher and his new competence. The organization is unable to welcome the desire by teachers for more involvement in decision making as a sign that the profession is maturing. Rather than react arrogantly and negatively, the organization should make sure that teachers assume the responsibilities concomitant with their newly found authority.[66]

The strategy of principals and supervisors to cloak their roles behind children and cry out that erosion will downgrade the quality of education in the schools is to maintain that the old assumption of teacher incompetence is true at all costs. It is to continue the kind of attitude which brought about the problem in the first place. The fact is that principals and supervisors lack the senior skills to be considered superior teachers by teachers themselves. The lack of an esoteric knowledge base which has and will continue to plague efforts to

differentiate the classroom teacher's role has proven to be the perplexing dilemma for principals and supervisors. For supervisors, there
do not appear to be many alternatives. Many large city school systems have begun the movement toward abolishing the position.
[Perhaps the mass firing of middle management personnel in Phila-
delphia some years ago represents the most dramatic.]

The following are three recommendations regarding the principalship in a differentiated staff:[6][7]

1. That the present role definition of the principalship is changing, both by a
shifting base of teacher expertise and through militant teacher action in bypass-
ing the middle management levels in negotiating agreements with the superintendent and the board;

2. That the present or traditional role of the principal as kind of jack-of-all
trades, keeper of the keys, master teacher and evaluator is obsolete because it
rests on an assumed validity of the teacher's role at the base of the pyramidal
organizational structure; teacher need for self-governance challenges the authority base of a structure which was founded on an unprofessional view of the
teacher;

3. That improvement in the performance of the principalship lies not in
further streamlining the position itself, but by adjusting all the roles to encompass new competencies and redefining internal relationships so that specialization can occur at the lowest possible levels in keeping with diagnosed and specified requirements for students;

There is a place for the principal in the schools of the future. He may
not do what many do today, but there will always be a need for
leadership. The core of leadership skill and expertise, however, will
change as field needs change. The present role of the principal is
largely fallen into an effete cluster of responsibilities. To regenerate
the potential of the principal's role, the entire role hierarchy needs to
be reshaped. To refuse to recognize the need for change is to invite
the creation of an alternative in which there is no place at all for the
principal. Schools can run without principals. They will not run very
well without leadership.

Community Involvement and Response

Education is a highly complex undertaking. To understand an educational
program well enough to evaluate it in terms of specific criteria requires interest
and effort to an extent not demonstrated by the vast majority of citizens in

Jackson County or elsewhere. Under such circumstances, vital decisions are made by the electorate on other grounds.[68]

The educator who wants to involve the citizens of his community in an intimate examination of the merits and problems of staff differentiation and its implications will be disappointed. Citizens neither have the large doses of time nor the sophistication necessary to form a cohesive group or the nucleus for a sustained movement toward internal organizational reform.[69]

Goldhammer and Pellegrin performed a sustained analysis over a five-year period of Jackson County and its ups and downs in school board elections, superintendent turnover, and various issues.[70] They concluded that "educational issues are usually not of vital concern to lay citizens unless they are tied to larger community issues."[71] During the late sixties, school administrators in Temple City, California, made a sustained effort to enlist community involvement and support for staff differentiation. The experience in Temple City closely parallels that of Jackson County. Staff differentiation was not an issue in Temple City until it was linked with the possibility that after outside funding it would require community tax-based support. The issue of taxes overshadowed the educational implications of staff differentiation. For example, one candidate for the board of education was asked what she thought was the greatest problem facing the school district.

We share the common problem of increasing costs of education, compounded by narrow tax base of bedroom community. Lack of strongly defined guidelines plus ambitious experimental programs are expensive. Constant change in administrative personnel has an unstabilizing effect, interrupting smooth continuity of educational programs. Expediency instead of order is the rule.[72]

In a small community, since administrators often build up coteries of followers, changes in administrative positions, whether linked to innovation or not, become emotional and political issues. Aspects visible to citizens, such as changes in school boundaries, taxes, the number of administrative positions, turnover, and physical appearance of buildings, can "swallow up" more complex, less visible but more far-reaching instructional changes. It is often difficult to ascertain if substantive issues are taking on emotional overtones and getting lost in the noise or if emotional issues take cover in substantive ones.[73]

In an attempt to secure a parental response from which some measure of consistency could be ascertained, the semantic differential format was utilized. A note was sent home with each student requesting the cooperation of the parents in the survey and explaining the format of the semantic differential. This format is illustrated below in Table 3.[74]

TABLE 3

Example   Flexible Scheduling

sweet	__ :	__ :	X :	__ :	__ :	sour
	5	4	3	2	1	
cruel	__ :	__ :	__ :	X :	__ :	kind
	1	2	3	4	5	
sacred	__ :	__ :	X :	__ :	__ :	profane
	5	4	3	2	1	
worthless	__ :	X :	__ :	__ :	__ :	valuable
	1	2	3	4	5	
pleasant	__ :	X :	__ :	__ :	__ :	unpleasant
	5	4	3	2	1	

TOTAL 16 points

Each student enrolled at the pilot school was given two test forms, one for father and one for mother. Of a potential 1,302 parental responses, assuming two parents for each child, 467 forms were returned. Of these, which represented approximately 35 percent of the total parent population, 95 were filled out incorrectly and rejected for processing. Three hundred seventy-two forms were sent to Los Angeles County for processing (28 percent) and 2 percent were further rejected in the scoring process. A final total of 332 individual responses were processed, representing approximately 26 percent of the total parent population at Oak Avenue. Ten forms were returned with letters expressing inability to understand what was desired or expressing displeasure with being asked to give information of this type in the format provided.

Analysis of Data

A preliminary examination of parent and student attitudes regarding the twelve variables revealed the following:

1. Parents were more positive toward the Oak program than were the students. Parents scored higher than the students in ten of twelve areas.
2. Significant differences in attitudes between the two populations occurred over the items "school," "learning," "homework," "library," and "unscheduled time." In all but the last item, parents were more positive than the students.
3. Parents were positive (above the mean) in every area. They were less positive than their children on two items, "flexible scheduling,"· and "large group."
4. Parent responses closely paralleled the students'. The two lowest items indicated by students were "large group," and "homework." These same items were the two ranked lowest by parents (though still above the mean).
5. Parent-student attitudes indicated congruity with parents generally more positive.

Sending home the inventories provided a substantive base to parents who already disagreed with either the direction of the school district, or with those who were concerned about the costs of schools and education. The following comments were taken from notes sent back to the school by some parents.

To whom it may concern:

I feel that the attached questionnaire is idiotic and completely without relevance to my opinions of your school and its program.

The money wasted on such nonsense is typical of the entire "school" operation. Such waste is reflected in my tax bills and this only serves as a reminder to me of how my money is "used."

This questionnaire is a waste of school tax money. The excess administration we have in this school district is also a waste of money.

My husband and I are not filling out the survey sheet that our child brought home. We feel that such a survey is unnecessary. We are not sending our children to school to be analyzed but to be educated. Furthermore, I am sure that the money spent for such a survey could be put to better use.

Finally, the editor of the local community paper attempted to summarize the objections in comments she had heard.

We hate to keep picking on you, Mr. English, sir, but now we're hearing from Cloverly School parents who are objecting strenuously to this "evaluative instrument" you're sending out in an effort to determine parental reaction to innovation at that school.

They don't mind being questioned but they do mind being asked to decide whether a resource center is more sacred than profane or more sweet than sour, plus the similar choices which escape us at the moment.

Yes, Mr. English, they understand the reasoning behind this type of test but they feel they're big enough so you don't have to play games with them.

We submit you'd get a better response, in terms of numbers, and a lot less static, if you'd set up your questions in the following way, using suitable educational jargonese, of course: Check one—The library center is (1) lousy___ (2) mediocre___ (3) fair___ (4) great___ (5) terrific___ .[75]

An analysis of data gathered earlier at Cloverly school by a staff questionnaire asking parental response on a "satisfied-dissatisfied" basis netted only an 8 percent greater response. However, a straightforward type of Gallup poll, while less reliable perhaps, would not provide the fodder (a substantive base) on the part of those who already find fault with the schools. Questions of statistical reliability do not mean much to parents and may be reasonably sacrificed where the data obtained is not that critical to decision making, or where reasonable estimates may be made regarding parental feeling instead of going to the formal preparation of a respectable testing instrument in professional terms.

Parental Involvement in Goal Setting

A citizens' group in Temple City designed a questionnaire (Figure 35) to solicit community response in goal setting for the schools. The questionnaire is shown on the next several pages. Approximately a 30 percent response was obtained after the questionnaire had been sent to every registered voter in the school district (approximately 7,000). Citizens ranked various areas according to their importance. The results are shown in Table 4.

The item listed as most desirable to omit was that of "comparative religions." Earlier, the school district had attempted to involve citizens in the establishing of performance objectives. Citizens involved in the formulation of the goal-setting inventory said that was too complicated for most parents to understand. When it was pointed out that putting the goals into actual operation meant that such

FIGURE 36

DEAR CITIZEN:

One of the responsibilities of local control of education is the opportunity and advantage
of the citizens to have a major voice in the operation of the school system.

We would like to know what you would like to have taught in our schools; what emphasis
you feel should be placed on the content; and what priority you would like
placed on the various items in relation to the entire curriculum.

We are, therefore, asking your help in improving education in Temple City by filling out
this questionnaire and adding any suggestions, comments, or evaluations you
may have. A report will be published when the questionnaire information has been summarized.

Your assistance will be greatly appreciated.

Thank you very much.

Dave Wood

Dave Wood, Chairman
Citizens Curriculum Study Group | PLEASE RETURN WITHIN TWO WEEKS |

IF YOU DO NOT WISH TO BE IDENTIFIED, THIS SECTION MAY BE REMOVED BY TEARING ON PERFORATION

PLEASE DO NOT PUT YOUR NAME ON THIS QUESTIONNAIRE.

Check each of the items you think are important in describing yourself.

☐ Parent with one or more children in Temple   ☐ Parent with one or more children in private
   City public schools. In grades   K-3 _____   schools. In grades   K-3 _____
                                    4-6 _____   4-6 _____
                                    7-8 _____   7-8 _____
                                    9-12 _____   9-12 _____

☐ Parent with no children in school   ☐ Student in Temple City public school

☐ Retired   ☐ Student in private school

☐ Educator   ☐ Renter

☐ Employer   ☐ Homeowner

☐ Employee   ☐ Other - Specify

INSTRUCTIONS:

Rate each item 1 to 5 by circling your choice   EXAMPLE: Physical fitness
of numbers. This will show the importance you
place on each item in relation to entire   Weight lifting   1   2   ③   4   5
curriculum (Kindergarten to 12th grade).   Acrobatics   ①   2   3   4   5
                                                          Team Sports   ①   2   3   4   5
                                                          Basketweaving   1   2   3   4   ⑤

objectives had then to be done without citizen involvement, they
simply shrugged their shoulders saying it was a "professional responsibility." How such goal consensus can be related to staff differentiation remains abstract, except that roles and the ranking of roles
may parallel teachers who function in the basic skills and occupational preparation areas. Salaries and related personnel costs may
then also parallel such emphases. Whether that will make any differ-

QUESTIONNAIRE ON EDUCATIONAL GOALS

AREA I - CITIZENSHIP PREPARATION

UPON GRADUATION THE TEMPLE CITY
HIGH SCHOOL STUDENT SHOULD HAVE:

	Greatest Emphasis	Secondary Emphasis	Moderate Emphasis	Minimum Emphasis	Omit
A knowledge of the responsibilities and rights of an American Citizen....	1	2	3	4	5
A clear perspective of the culture of Temple City	1	2	3	4	5
An awareness of the varieties of cultures in the United States	1	2	3	4	5
A knowledge of American Heritage	1	2	3	4	5
A knowledge of America's relationships with other countries	1	2	3	4	5

AREA II - OCCUPATIONAL PREPARATION

UPON GRADUATION, THE STUDENT SHOULD
HAVE HAD:

Opportunities for vocational training for direct employment	1	2	3	4	5
Appropriate course work to meet public and private university entrance requirements	1	2	3	4	5
A broad choice of electives	1	2	3	4	5
Career Counseling	1	2	3	4	5
Academic Counseling	1	2	3	4	5

AREA III - BASIC KNOWLEDGE

UPON GRADUATION, HIGH SCHOOL STUDENTS
SHOULD BE PROFICIENT IN:

English	1	2	3	4	5
Reading	1	2	3	4	5
Composition	1	2	3	4	5
Arithmetic	1	2	3	4	5
Science	1	2	3	4	5

AREA IV - CURRENT ISSUES

THE TEMPLE CITY STUDENT SHOULD HAVE
THE OPPORTUNITY TO INVESTIGATE CURRENT
ISSUES AND TRENDS IN SUCH AREAS AS:

Moral Values	1	2	3	4	5
World Religions	1	2	3	4	5
Political Systems	1	2	3	4	5
Economic Systems	1	2	3	4	5
Human problems	1	2	3	4	5
(e.g., labor, pollution, technology, race, social changes).					

AREA V - SELF UNDERSTANDING

THE TEMPLE CITY STUDENT SHOULD HAVE
A KNOWLEDGE OF:

	Greatest Emphasis	Secondary Emphasis	Moderate Emphasis	Minimum Emphasis	Omit
Getting along with people	1	2	3	4	5
His academic potentials	1	2	3	4	5
His emotional strengths and weaknesses	1	2	3	4	5
The physical body	1	2	3	4	5
The importance of family life	1	2	3	4	5
The importance of continuing education in a changing society	1	2	3	4	5

AREA VI - EXTRACURRICULAR ACTIVITIES

ALL TEMPLE CITY STUDENTS SHOULD HAVE
THE OPPORTUNITY TO PARTICIPATE IN:

Competitive athletics	1	2	3	4	5
(e.g., intramural, interscholastic sports)					
Performing arts	1	2	3	4	5
(e.g., band, chorus, theatre)					
Student activities	1	2	3	4	5
(e.g., student government, newspaper, clubs)					

RANK THE FOLLOWING AREAS FROM THE MOST
IMPORTANT "1" TO THE LEAST IMPORTANT "6".
This will show the relative importance you place on each
AREA of curriculum.

EXAMPLE:	Physical fitness	2	(next most important)
	Art	3	(least important)
	History	1	(most important)

AREA I   CITIZENSHIP PREPARATION   _____
AREA II   OCCUPATIONAL PREPARATION   _____
AREA III   BASIC KNOWLEDGE   _____
AREA IV   CURRENT ISSUES   _____
AREA V   SELF UNDERSTANDING   _____
AREA VI   EXTRA – CURRICULAR ACTIVITIES_____

YOUR COMMENTS ARE APPRECIATED:

(please write on other side)

ence to the 70 percent of the citizens when taxes rise also remains conjectural. It does, however, provide the board of education and the administration with data on which to make priority decisions, since such decisions must be made regardless. The lack of sustained parental interest in their schools remains a problem. Undoubtedly, it is complicated by the fact that schools are no longer easily intelligible to the layman. It is no easy matter to translate a school budget, or

TABLE 4

Temple City Citizens Response to Educational Goals

Area		Citizen Ranking
I.	Basic Skills	1
III.	Occupational Preparation	2
VII.	Self-Understanding	3
II.	Citizenship Preparation	4
VIII.	Science and Technology	5
VI.	Contemporary Issues	6
V.	Cocurricular Activities	7
IV.	Cultural/Intercultural Understanding	8

understand how certification procedures inhibit teacher utilization, or how legal decisions can affect teacher tenure or teacher rights. The sophisticated technology which is visible to citizens is confusing and foreign. The emergence of powerful teacher unions who deal directly with boards of education and negotiate changes behind closed doors, which must later be explained, leaves parents with the feelings of uncertainty. Rising costs, student militancy, complicated jargon, and a growing feeling of parental powerlessness are the panoply under which many educators are attempting to bring about the often invisible changes in school structure which are rarely questioned by citizen groups. To expect citizen support may be asking too much. It is no wonder that some administrators have succumbed to the description of staff differentiation as a tool by which money may be saved, costs held or even reduced, in order to build even a modicum of parental interest in organizational reform. Such an approach then insures an almost automatic negative response from groups within the school system, particularly teacher unions. When faced with a choice, the serious educator must choose to deal first with intra-organizational problems and groups and second with parental groups. With the latter, communication must be preventative, that is, prevent the spread of rumor, supply facts in any possible ways, and reassure parents by involving them on a more personal basis by counseling with them about their children.

The right wing critic will be most difficult to deal with during times of innovation. Charges of "experimenting" with children, excess costs and federal control may fan the flames of anxiety. Educators operate in an organization which is extremely sensitive to public opinion and direct control by a community. Board meetings may witness an angry mob confronting the elected representatives demanding immediate changes in a return to the status quo. The schools may be viewed by some citizens as a bastion of the past which should be immune to change in order to preserve the "good" and the "true." O'Neill offers some insight in this conflict.

For individuals dispossessed by the increasing shift to science and professionalization and resentful of an increasingly technicized and professionalized world few things could be more therapeutic than a crusade against a learned profession replete with an attack on the value and usefulness of technical know-how itself. After all, if the old ways are succumbing elsewhere, they can at least be protected within the schools where public control remains guaranteed.[77]

Charges by some parents that schools are too permissive or progressive, that student's aren't mature enough to make decisions for themselves, that the function of the schools relates to tasks involving memorization and "disciplining the mind," and charges of dogmaticism among schoolmen may be symptoms that the schools are making significant changes towards greater improvement and sophistication. It should be understood that if professionals are to be leaders there will be casualties among that leadership. The old model of the successful administrator as one who kept everybody happy and ran a "smooth ship" no longer is adequate as a test of leadership ability. While the technological gains of society make overwhelming demands on its social institutions, social change itself will be heavily resisted. The administration should really anticipate resistance and deal with it rather than reacting when it occurs. To move from a reactionary administrative pattern to an anticipatory pattern will demand significant and extensive planning. In this sense, the mode of the administration is not to prevent conflict (which is impossible) but to anticipate it and deal with it directly when it occurs. An old military saying captures the spirit, "A good general may be surprised, but he is *never* taken by surprise."

Intervening in a School System

To bring about staff differentiation within an ongoing school system, the person responsible will have to intervene in that system. Knowledge of intervention itself in human organizations is a prerequisite for a successful implementation, particularly in large school systems. Proposals or books which advocate the implementation of staff differentiation without a thorough understanding of the dynamics of change must depend mostly on luck (which is rarely better than 50-50).

Argyris has summarized the qualities needed by the interventionist as well as anyone. He prescribes that the interventionist must have confidence in his own intervention philosophy; he must possess an accurate perception of stressful reality; he must accept the client's attacks and mistrust; he must trust in his own experience of reality and he must invest in stressful environments experiences which promote organizational and personal growth.[78] Perhaps the most critical on-site behavior of the interventionist may best be described as "character congruence." Basically, this means that what the interventionist says, he says to all parties within or without the organization, thereby promoting openness of response and trust. The interventionist may not say it in the same way, knowing that with some parties, a crisp, forceful approach may lead to rejection and withdrawal, thereby leading to a closed climate. Interventionist behavior calls for an in-depth knowledge of how certain behavior affects other people and the development of an intuitive sense of candor and honesty which brings people together.

The interventionist, whether he is from the inside or the outside of the organization, should also possess a fundamental knowledge of organizational power and organizational dependencies. Thompson has defined the source of power in an organization as a response to uncertainty or contingency.[79] This view is also shared by Hickson, et al.

Uncertainty itself does not give power: coping gives power. If organizations allocate to their various subunits task areas that vary in uncertainty, then those subunits that cope most effectively with the most uncertainty should have the most power within the organization since coping by a subunit reduces the impact of uncertainty on other activities in the organization, a shock absorber function.[80]

Power in complex organizations should be viewed as positions of subunit coalition, leading to coalition management. Unidimensional intervention strategies may fail because various subunits were not viewed as operating in a network of dependencies and counter-dependencies, instead of functioning in the pyramidal line/staff organizational chart. "Perhaps today's authority hierarchy is partly a fossilized impression of yesterday's power ranking," comments Hickson.[81]

A Guideline for Intervention

The following guideline represents some thoughts about experience gained in implementing staff differentiation in at least two distinct school systems on a longitudinal basis, and several others in a consultant capacity.

1. The most potent force going for the innovator lies not in force or counter-force, but in preventing the type of reaction in the organization which makes force (coercion) or other responses which are damaging (thus leading away from truth seeking and reducing the ability to perceive reality and thus problem solve) necessary. This means that the innovator must perceive what is going on in the organization accurately and plan for various types of coalition responses to various types of stimuli. In some cases plans must be made so that certain types of responses never occur, since if they do they set in motion a set of counter-forces which ultimately lead to the destruction of the innovative idea. Options for the use of force are more open to the defenders of the system than the innovators.

2. The system is resilient; it can fight back or absorb the change without changing itself; almost everyone has some stake in the status quo, including the innovators;

3. People react to change emotionally and the mixing of personalities and change rationale is often unavoidable;

4. Organizational change will have an impact upon the environment since no organization lives in a vacuum. This may set into motion a series of forces over which the organization has little, if any, control.

5. Unless the innovators can ultimately link to key line positions, the innovation may die a slow death by being allowed to become fenced off from the rest of the system.

All of the wishing to the contrary, and with due respect to rugged individualism, our society is controlled by organizations and institutions. We are vitally linked to each other by institutions and these form a delicate network which is highly interdependent. Individuals may belong to a variety of groups, formal and informal, within organizations. There may be secretaries and custodians, drinkers and nondrinkers, Rotarians and Lions, coffee klatches, lunchtime diet clubs and the superintendent's "kitchen cabinet." The fabric of an organization is represented in its groups and the basis for their formation. Some groups can be changed or abolished, others cannot; they simply exist. In planning an intraorganizational change, assume nothing, plan for everything and anticipate the ridiculous. Sustaining the initial thrust for change means detailed and extensive planning in which possible reactions and options open to the organizational defenders are anticipated. The impact of planning is that the change is introduced and sustained in a manner in which the defenders find it difficult to oppose. The innovators can shape the change so that certain conditions which would result in a violent backlash may be avoided or minimized. Planning may inhibit the formation of stronger coalitions which may isolate, neutralize, or defeat attempts at organizational change.

Critical Questions To Ask in Formulating a Strategy of Change

1. Determining the Interplay of Forces and Peculiar Local Antecedents

a. Does past history indicate how the critical audiences to be affected react to change? If so, how do they react? How has change been proposed and introduced before?

b. Has past change been imposed, mandated, developed cooperatively, by default (accident)?

c. For each of the above in item b, how have the critical audiences reacted?

d. What are the coping mechanisms of those affected by change? What strategies have been used in the past? How successful were they in promoting or defeating change?

e. How does or did timing of the change occur? What happened; were there events which could reoccur? If so, which ones?

f. How dry is the underbrush? What unsettled issues, working conditions, grievances, past animosities are lying around waiting to be sparked? Do some of those need to be tackled first before staff differentiation is introduced?

g. What are the power capacities of the critical audiences, i.e., how much counterforce can they muster on the decision-making organizational pressure points? Can they collectively negate the change at any one point?

h. What has been the ability of past innovators (internal or external) to withstand various forms of counterpressure? What support is there for change at the middle administrative levels?

i. What peculiar local conditions, issues, problems could be incorporated, resolved, or attached by focusing on staff differentiation as a possible solution?

j. What kind of official and public backing is available? How strong and influential is it?

k. What critical conditions of the audiences to be affected and/or changed are unknown? Can they become known? How?

2. Determining the Right "Mix" of Staff Differentiation Variables

a. How sluggish is the organization in adopting past change?

b. In light of item "a" how much of a dramatic impact is necessary to shake the organization loose of some of its preconceptions about problem solving?

c. Which organizational subunits can become partners for new coalitions? What factors or forces would promote this movement?

d. What is the sophistication of the critical decision-making managers? How much will they risk in decision making and how much counterpressure can they take?

e. Has the organization developed any capacity to respond quickly with key personnel? Who comprises the key skills and what group contains the dominant personalities?

3. Selecting a Change Strategy for Differentiated Staffing

a. The major efforts of mapping a change strategy have to be placed on *prevention* because once certain counterforces are mobilized it may be too late. The plans should anticipate the creation of counterforce, with specific strategies aimed at not creating the conditions which will lead to the mobilization of counterforce, at least not in strength to overthrow the innovation.

b. Some counterforces are already mobilized on the scene; the relative strength of these groups needs to be determined, the extent to which various groups might merge and under what conditions might this be possible. Conditions should be calibrated like a PERT: (1) the most optimistic, (2) the most pessimistic, and (3) the most likely.

c. A series of change strategies which contains events and activities should be calculated, beginning with the introduction of the concept under one set of conditions and carrying through the implementation of the change under the same conditions based upon a set of assumptions about those conditions. Each step of change alternatives should be considered to the extent that situational conditions may be altered. All the alternatives (range of decisions) should be anticipated to decide whether the same change strategy should be followed or abandoned.

d. After the plotting of the change strategies, a set of tactics may be developed which are aimed at creating certain conditions so that a change strategy may be most effective in bringing about the introduction of the innovation. Tactics should take into consideration what is known and unknown, the conditions under which the counterforce operates most effectively, such as ambiguity, fear, and rumor, and the ability of the innovators to monitor the counterforce (from formal statements to the grapevine). A change strategy should be calculated in terms of outcomes, that is, what products or processes would happen with implementation of the change. This provides the strategy with a termination point. After the implementation of the change, the innovation team should be abolished in order to avoid being added to the bureaucracy.

Implementation Problems

Towards the close of the federal Program School Personnel Utilization for staff differentiation, the seventeen funded projects met to discuss mutual problems encountered in implementing staff differentiation. The number one dilemma was that of evaluating the effects of changing a staffing pattern on student learning. The project directors were not even sure that the two could be related at all. Some were openly troubled by the lack of any method of assessing the effects of much money and effort on altering some of their school system's staffing patterns on anything but teacher morale. The sad fact confronted the directors that there were no available staffing theories from which to frame empirical hypotheses to try and arrive at some form of assessment. A nagging feeling grew that relying on the time worn assumption between teacher morale and student learning was hardly a defensible position.

Staff differentiation is a cogent case for all professionals who believe that solutions to teacher problems are necessarily directly or indirectly linked to pupil outcomes. Staff differentiation appears to be an *enabling innovation;* that is, it permits things to happen within a new structure founded on assumptions of flexibility rather than rigidity. It may be impossible to be evaluated directly, except as it was selected to *enable* specific formations of staff and students to form and re-form to achieve specific, measurable outcomes. Staff differentiation may be assessed, then, on whether the objectives for which it was established were achieved. In the past, there was an absence of specific objectives for either pupils or teachers. Assessment became a matter of trying to measure how an alteration of a staffing pattern might effect organization. This approach may be impossible because work specialization tends to follow the existing divisions of labor within the organization and merely represents a refinement of that division. Such distinctions may be impossible to assess on the recipients of those services, particularly on the standardized pre and post type of assessment models used so heavily in educational research.

A school system is ongoing. It cannot be stopped. All of the variables within the system cannot be controlled. Isolating the staffing pattern and its effects upon the system is exceedingly difficult, particularly with the confusion over means and ends. There is also ambiguity regarding allocation and utilization. Allocation, the assignment of staff on the basis of various formulae and assumptions underlying those formulae, most often influences the manner in which staff are used. Utilization is a matter of finding the most efficient relationship between work outcomes, work tasks, and people needs. Some work tasks are not met simply because the method by which teachers are allocated subsumes an actual task analysis based upon pupil need. To this extent pupil needs go begging. Allocation can be separated from utilization to the extent that there is flexibility in allocation. If substitutions can be made for staff allocation, staff can be assigned flexibly.

An example is provided in Haven's staffing unit equivalent model in Figure 37, in which a staffing unit is examined in terms of other personnel services it may purchase.[82] It may also be observed that flexible assignment (allocation) does not necessarily mean that staff

FIGURE 37

Haven's Staffing Equivalent Model

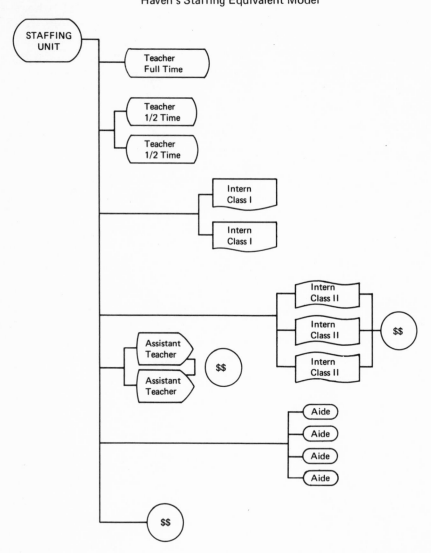

will be used flexibly. Ignoring pupil needs and designing static teacher-pupil groups which exist in more or less permanent fashion across a school year negates whatever advantages may be derived from flexible allocation. The relationship between allocation and utilization appears to be that allocation determines the degree of flexible utilization to the extent allocation prevents flexible utilization by mandating static ratios of professional staff based on static student groups. Allocation practices are often lodged in legal provisions which make them extremely difficult to change.

Weiss and Rein discuss various types of evaluation strategies for "broad aim" programs.[83] A broad-aim program is defined as:

a program which hopes to achieve nonspecific forms of change for the better, and which also, because of their ambition and magnitude, involve unstandardized, large-scale interventions and are evaluated in only a few sites.[84]

Weiss and Rein advocate three types of evaluative designs based upon the fact that the innovation is a broad-aim program. These are: process-oriented qualitative research, historical research; or case study or comparative research. These three designs should be employed when it is difficult to select satisfactory program criteria or to specify precisely outcomes of the intervention. When the situation is essentially uncontrolled, the treatments are not standardized, and the design is limited in the information it can produce.

Provus has attacked the problem directly by framing an evaluation design which is free from the classical experimental design conditions.[85] The basic tenets of the Provus approach are that it is not necessary to wait three to five years before any evaluative judgments may be made about a new program, that evaluation activity does not get in the way of program activity, and that experimental design, "is irrelevant to evaluation until a program is in its final stages of development."[86] The Provus evaluation paradigm breaks an innovation into three parts or stages. The first stage is the input stage, the second, the process stage, and the final, the output stage. During the input stages, evaluation consists of assessing various types of inputs (staff qualifications, facilities, media, etc.), in the process stage various types of transactions (students, staff etc.), and in the last stage the degree to which terminal objectives have been realized. The Provus model offers an approach to innovations being implemented in an ongoing school situation. This avoids the problem of premature analysis in which an innovation is not fully assessed before judgments are made as to its value and continuance.

FIGURE 38

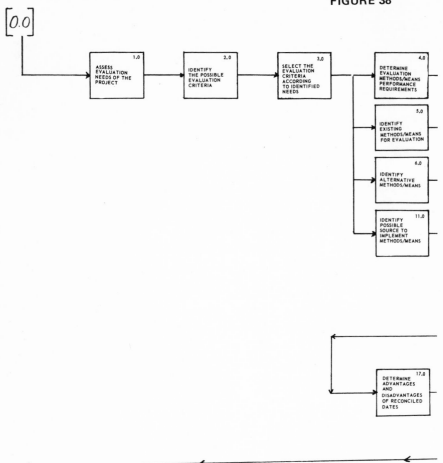

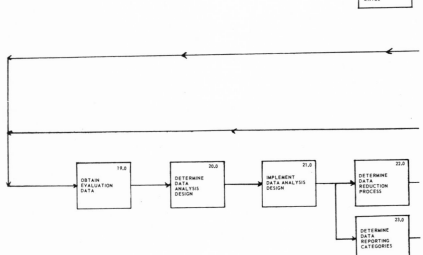

Melton's Generic Evaluation Model

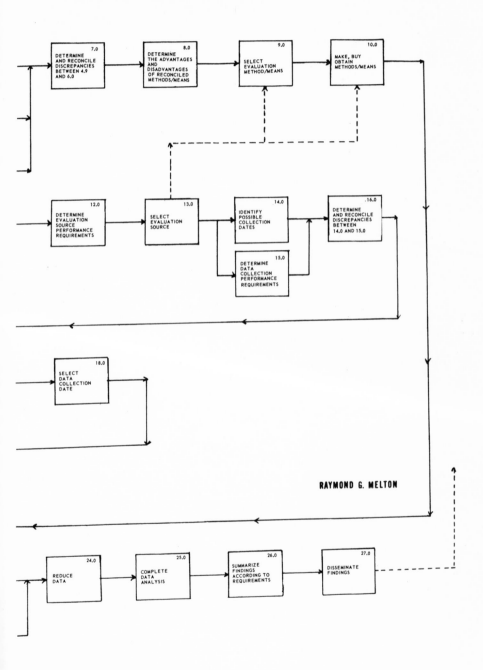

RAYMOND G. MELTON

English, Frase and Melton (Figure 38) made a case for not abandoning experimental or quasi-experimental design completely in the evaluation of staff differentiation.[87] They underscored an argument employed by Campbell:[88]

In the present political climate, reformers and administrators achieve their precarious permission to innovate by overpromising the certain efficacy of their new programs. This traps them so that they cannot afford to risk learning that the programs were not effective.[89]

English strongly advised Canadian teachers not to agree to participate in any study of staff differentiation unless there was a tight evaluation design.

Teachers should insist upon such evaluation requirements being developed before they agree to participate in any study or plan. Furthermore, they should make it public that other conditions notwithstanding, they cannot condone the piloting of an innovation for which it may not be possible to determine how much more effective it is with children than the one it might replace after experimentation. They should make it clear they will fight to protect the child in this regard. In such cases, implementation proves nothing more than an alternative (for which we have little data if it is better or worse) can be implemented. The efficacy of the alternative itself is thus never actually tested, only the ingenuity and the perseverance of the innovator is tested. Thus, the wrong thing is tested and the wrong conclusions reached.[90]

Implementation In Perspective

Much of what was developed in the early days of staff differentiation was purely arbitrary. Models came from educated hunches and intuitive judgments. Those who have picked up on the literature since that time often attribute more science to those decisions than they merit. The fact is that guidelines from research were then, and are today, rather meager. This is because research must follow action, or there would be little to research. There is danger that the same mistakes made then will be made again if readers do not carefully scrutinize all the available evidence. The problem is accentuated since some of the initial efforts by educators in this area have not produced much growth or insight into what they attempted, and they are still bound by the same rationale and the same solutions.

There are theorists and dreamers and pragmatists—those who bent reality to suit their theories, those who were never concerned much with reality, and those who demanded proof before they would reconsider their biases. Implementation is a tough business, and highly intuitive. We do know something now about staff differentiation. It has grown with other technologies and a number of people in the United States who have actually had field experience with implementation can show how better models based on hard data and sounder theories may be implemented more successfully than their predecessors.

Implementation has not, however, produced an abundance of ardent supporters, nor dramatic upgrading to pupil learning, nor instant breakthroughs for the more knotty problems of educational productivity, nor full professionalism for the teaching cadre. Dwight Allen used to remark that only a bold step had any chance of making a dent upon the educational establishment. After approaching almost a decade of developing staff differentiation, we are just beginning to understand how to be bold. We are assuming it is not too late.

SUMMARY FOR SECTION I

Section I has dealt with differentiated staffing from a *general* rationale, to a discussion of generic aspects of school staffing, and concluded with an overview of problems of school system intervention and implementation. Section I provided the groundwork for future research and development of the concept. It pointed out the need for developmental theory, the importance of theory, and related the emerging theoretical issues to larger issues involving organizational theory and behavioral science findings on organizational change.

Like so many other innovations, much of what has been learned was derived from trial and error, and the author made a serious attempt to raise questions which should be examined prior to further work on developing more sophisticated and learner sensitive staffing patterns. Early rationales for staff differentiation were reexamined and critiqued. Models were reviewed and the response by organized teachers to staff differentiation was analyzed. Future field implementation was clearly dependent upon understanding the forces at play, and why teachers have reacted negatively, particularly at the national level.

The chapters were concluded by drawing upon the author's personal experience as a project director and consultant in the area of staff differentiation, particularly with large city school systems, where DS has been, to date, less than meeting the dreams of its proponents. The general issues and ideas discussed in Section I should provide an excellent backdrop for an actual on-site examination of the case studies presented later in the book.

Footnotes

1. Seymour B. Sarason, *The Culture of the School and the Problem of Change* (Boston: Allyn and Bacon, 1971).

2. See "A Report of the Leadership Training Institute, School Personnel Utilization," offset, School of Education, University of Massachusetts, June 1971. 8 pp.

3. Gordon L. Lippitt, *Organization Renewal* (New York: Appleton-Century-Crofts, 1969) p. 145.

4. See Lawrence Feinberg, "The Clark Plan: Uneasy Truce Exists," *The Washington Post*, October 5, 1970 and "What Is Going On in Our School System?" Editorial, *The Washington Post*, September 1, 1971, p. A18.

5. Condensed and revised from Fenwick W. English, "A Tentative and Proposed Plan for Developmental Activities Towards Staff Differentiation 1971-72 for the Washington, D. C. Public Schools: An Open Memorandum," xeroxed, July 22, 1971, 12 pp. The memorandum followed several working sessions with school district officials and a meeting at union headquarters with the board president, a fellow board member, the superintendent, and the consultant.

6. Arnold S. Judson, *A Manager's Guide to Making Changes* (New York: John Wiley, Inc. 1966), p. 41.

7. Paul R. Lawrence, "How To Deal With Resistance to Change," *Harvard Business Review*, 47, January-February 1969, pp. 41-100.

8. For a good example of this approach see James Lewis, Jr., *Differentiating the Teaching Staff* (Parker: New York, 1971).

9. For an excellent review of this trend in American business and industry, see John Kenneth Galbraith, *The New Industrial State* (New York: Signet Books, 1967). Galbraith's discussion concerning the creation of the "technostructure" was compared to the movement in education toward staff differentiation in Fenwick English, "The Differentiated Staff: Education's Technostructure," *Educational Technology*, 10:2, February 1970, pp. 24-27. The reason for the change is hypothesized also by Warren G. Bennis and Philip E. Slater in *The Temporary Society* (New York: Harper Colophone Books, 1964).

Note Bennis and Slater, "Democracy becomes a functional necessity whenever a social system is competing for survival under conditions of chronic change." p. 4.

10. Tom Burns and G.M. Stalker, *The Management of Innovation* (London: Tavistock, 1961).

11. Ibid., pp. 105-6

12. For an outstanding application of the principles of organic structure see Al Haven, "The Emergent Leader Concept of Staff Utilization," offset, Top of the World Elementary School, Laguna Beach Unified School District, Laguna, California, 1970, 15 pp.

13. Burns and Stalker, *Management*, pp. 121-122.

14. Richard Beckhard, *Organization Development: Strategies and Models* (Reading, Massachusetts: Addison-Wesley, 1969).

15. Letter by Hugh J. Scott, Superintendent to William H. Simons, President Washington Teachers Union, December 15, 1971, 1 p., xeroxed.

16. Gayle Tunnell, "Rating Plans Now Threaten Job Security," *The Washington Post*, May 30, 1971. See also in the same issue "The Average Teacher is Pretty Average."

17. For a complete review of PERT see Desmond L. Cook, *Program Evaluation and Review Technique: Applications in Education* (Washington, D.C.: Department of Health, Education, and Welfare, Office of Education, 1966).

18. Ibid., p. 21.

19. Douglas S. Vance, "A Model for Balanced Staffing," unplublished paper, Office of Elementary Education, Mesa Public Schools, Mesa, Arizona, September 1970, 5 pp.

20. Raymond G. Melton, "Fremont Junior High School Needs Assessment Model," mimeographed, Mesa Public Schools, Mesa, Arizona, 191 pp.

21. Roger A. Kaufman, "A System Approach to Education: Derivation and Definition," *AV Communication Review*, 16:4, Winter 1968, pp. 415-24.

22. Roger A. Kaufman, "A Possible Integrative Model for the Systematic and Measurable Improvement of Education," *American Psychologist*, 26:3, March 1971, p. 252.

23. This following section was taken almost wholly from Fenwick English, "Utilizing Some Principles of Programmed Instruction As a Forcing Function to Change School Staffing Patterns," *NSPI Journal*, 10:2 March 1971, pp. 6-9.

24. Bert Y. Kersh, "Programming Classroom Instruction," *Teaching Machines and Programmed Learning*, II, Robert Glasser, ed., DAVI-NEA, 1965, pp. 321-70.

25. Fenwick W. English and James K. Zaharis, "How To Build A Model of Staff Differentiation," offset, Mesa Public Schools, Mesa, Arizona, published by the Center for Differentiated Staffing, Claremont Graduate School, Claremont, August 1970, 38 pp.

26. Wretha W. Wiley and Sidney A. Fine, "A Systems Approach to New Careers," W. E. Upjohn Institute for Employment Research, Kalamazoo, Michigan, November 1969, 37 pp.

27. Phelps Wilkins, William Draper, Connie Bickford and Jay Johnson, "Proposal for Support in Research and Related Activities to Complete the Holmes School Needs Assessment and Differentiated Staffing Projects," mimeographed, Holmes Elementary School, Mesa Public Schools, November 1970, 19 pp.

28. For further reading on task analysis, see H. M. Harmes, "Task Analysis," Florida Department of Education, Tallahassee, Florida, 1971, 60 pp., and Clifton Chadwick, "Task Analysis for Differentiated Staffing," mimeographed, Florida School Staffing Study Department of Education, Tallahassee, Florida, 9 pp.

29. H. Thomas James, "The New Cult of Efficiency and Education," Horace Mann Lecture, 1968 (Pittsburgh: University of Pittsburgh Press, 1969), p. 37.

30. Ibid., pp. 40-41.

31. Thomas J. Hagerty, "Forecast for School Meetings—Cloudy," The Milwaukee Journal, July 25, 1971, p. 6.

32. For a review of noncriterion referenced efforts to assess school productivity, see Maureen Woodhall and Mark Blaug, "Productivity Trends in British Secondary Education," Sociology of Education 41:1, Winter 1968, pp. 1-35.

33. Glenn L. Immegart and Francis J. Pilecki, "Assessing Organizational Output: A Framework and Some Implications," Educational Administration Quarterly, 6:1, Winter 1970, pp. 62-76.

34. Ibid., pp. 68-69.

35. T. W. Schultz, "Investment in Human Capital," Economics of Education, M. Blaug, ed., (Baltimore: Penguin Books, 1968), pp. 13-33.

36. Ibid., p. 28.

37. Taken in part from Fenwick English and James Zaharis, "Are Accountability and Governance Compatible?" Phi Delta Kappan, 42:6, pp. 374-75.

38. Robert M. Gagne, "Policy Implications and Future Research: A Response," in "Do Teachers Make A Difference?" Washington, D. C. Office of Education, 1970.

39. English and Zaharis, Accountability, pp. 374-75.

40. Much of the impetus behind performance based certification of school personnel is an attempt to arrive at a more precise definition of professional skills. See "Performance Based Certification of School Personnel," Joel L. Burdin and Margaret T. Reagan, eds., Eric Clearinghouse on Teacher Education, Association of Teacher Educators Washington, D.C., February 1971, 140 pp.

41. Sandford Reichart, Change and The Teacher: The Philosophy of a Social Phenomenon (New York: Thomas Y. Crowell, 1969), p. 8.

42. See the September 15, 1969, issue of U.S. News and World Report with an interview with James D. Koerner, pp. 48-51 entitled "How Schools Can Get Better Teachers."

43. Francis Keppel, *The Necessary Revolution in American Education* (New York: Harper and Row, 1969) pp. 92-93.

44. See D. J. Hickson, C. R. Hinings, C. A. Lee, R. E. Schneck, and J. M. Pennings, "A Strategic Contingencies' Theory of Intraorganizational Power," *Administrative Science Quarterly*, 16:2, June 1971, pp. 216-29.

45. Charles Silberman, *Crisis in the Classroom* (New York: Random House, 1970).

46. John Holt, *How Children Fail* (New York: Delta Books, 1964).

47. Herbert R. Kohl, *The Open Classroom* (New York: Vintage Books, 1969).

48. Ivan Illich, "Schooling: The Ritual of Progress," *New York Review of Books*, December 3, 1970, pp. 20-26.

49. J. I. Harvey, "An Open Letter to Superintendent M. John Rand," ditto, Temple City Schools, Temple City, California.

50. Mike Stover, "Teachers Worry Over Outcome of New Project," *Temple City Times*, June 4, 1967, p. 1.

51. For good insight into teacher behavior and the administrative power structure, see Norman J. Boyan, "The Emergent Role of the Teacher in the Authority Structure of the School," *Organizations and Human Behavior: Focus on Schools*, Fred D. Carver and Thomas J. Sergiovanni, eds., (New York: McGraw-Hill, 1969), pp. 200-11.

52. Fenwick W. English, "Assessing Teacher Attitudes Towards Staff Differentiation," Unpublished Ph.D. dissertation, Department of Secondary Education, Arizona State University, September 1971, p. 193.

53. Harmon Ziegler, *The Political Life of American Teachers* (Englewood Cliffs: Prentice-Hall, 1967).

54. See also Jerome J. Rottier, "Analysis of Teacher Satisfaction with Organizational Expectations of Differentiated Staffing," unpublished doctoral dissertation, Department of Educational Administration, University of Wisconsin, Madison, Wisconsin, May, 1971.

55. Ziegler, *Political Life*, p. 16.

56. Ibid., p. 27.

57. Ibid., p. 27.

58. English, "Assessing Teacher Attitudes," pp. 185-87.

59. Fenwick English, "Final Evaluation of the Differentiated Staffing Project for the Project Steering Committee and Administrative Staff," dittoed, Temple City Schools, September 1968, 15 pp.

60. Stephen Cole, "The Unionization of Teachers: Determinants of Rank-and-File Support," *Sociology of Education*, 41:1, Winter 1968, pp. 66-87.

61. Ibid., p. 87.

62. This trend will be accelerated by the move of the NEA to expel administrators in its recent Con Con proceedings. See *NEA Reporter*, 10:6, September 1971, a special issue on Con Con.

63. NASSP Newsletter, "Rights and Responsibilities of Principals," 14:4, May-June 1967, p. 1.

64. Harl R. Douglass, Rudyard K. Bent, and Charles W. Boardman, *Democratic Supervision in Secondary Schools* (Boston: Houghton Mifflin, 1961), pp. 7-8.

65. "Let Us Teach: An Analysis of the Helpfulness of Certain Aspects of the School Program to Classroom Teaching," (Sacramento: Senate Factfinding Committee on Governmental Administration, California State Senate, 1965), p. 8.

66. Fenwick W. English, "The Ailing Principalship," *Phi Delta Kappan*, 40:3, November 1968, pp. 158-61.

67. Fenwick W. English, "The Crises in Middle Management: Pressures for Change in the Principalship," Address before the National Academy of School Executives, American Association of School Administrators, Kansas City, Missouri, October 1970, 14 pp. See also Phelps Wilkins, "The Effects of Differentiated Staffing On The Role of the School Principal," mimeographed, Mesa Public Schools, Mesa, Arizona, May 1971, 24 pp.

68. Keith Goldhammer and Roland J. Pellegrin, *Jackson County Revisited:* A Case Study in the Politics of Public Education, (Eugene, Oregon: Center for the Advanced Study of Educational Administration, 1968), pp. 87-88.

69. The closest group of parents to such sustained action was organized in New York City. See Ellen Lurie, *How To Change the Schools: A Parents' Action Handbook on How to Fight the System* (New York: Random House, 1971).

70. Lurie, *Change the Schools.*

71. Ibid., p. 88.

72. *Temple City Times,* "Election Campaigns Now in Final Days," April 13, 1969, p. 1.

73. For a more detailed discussion of this idea see Richard E. Walton. *Interpersonal Peacemaking: Confrontations and Third-Party Consultation* (Reading, Massachusetts: Addison-Wesley, 1969).

74. Fenwick W. English, "Analysis of Partial Return on Parent Attitude Inventory of Oak Avenue," mimeographed, Temple City Schools, Temple City, California, April 14, 1969, 4 pp.

75. Helen O. Schrader, "Frying Pan," *Temple City Times,* May 25, 1969, p. 3.

76. For a good historical and enlightening analysis of how certification practices came into being, see Lucien B. Kinney, *Certification in Education* (Englewood Cliffs: Prentice-Hall, 1964).

77. William O'Neill, *Readin, Ritin, and Rafferty: A Study of Educational Fundamentalism* (Berkeley: The Glendessary Press, 1969), p. 120.

78. Chris Argyris, *Intervention Theory and Method* (Reading, Massachusetts; Addison-Wesley, 1970), p. 149.

79. James D. Thompson, *Organizations In Action* (New York: McGraw-Hill, 1967), pp. 128-30.

80. Hickson, *Contingencies Theory*, p. 219-20.

81. Ibid., p. 218.

82. Al Haven, *Emergent Leader.*

83. Robert S. Weiss and Martin Rein, "The Evaluation of Broad-Aim Programs: Experimental Design, Its Difficulties, and an Alternative," *Administrative Science Quarterly*, 15:1, March 1970, pp. 97-109.

84. Ibid., p. 97.

85. Malcolm Provus, "Evaluation of Ongoing Programs in the Public School System," *Educational Evaluation: New Roles, New Means*, 68th Yearbook of the National Society for the Study of Education, Ralph Tyler, ed. (Chicago: University of Chicago Press, 1969), pp. 242-83.

86. Ibid., p. 282.

87. Fenwick English, Larry E. Frase, and Raymond G. Melton, "Evaluating the Effects of Implementing A Differentiated Teaching Staff: Problems and Issues," mimeographed, Arizona-Mesa Differentiated Staffing Consortium, Mesa, Arizona, November, 1971, 17 pp.

88. Donald T. Campbell, "Considering the Case Against Experimental Evaluations of Social Innovations," *Administrative Science Quarterly*, 15:1, March 1970, pp. 110-113.

89. Ibid., p. 111.

90. Fenwick English, "How To Negotiate A Differentiated Teaching Staff in the Collective Bargaining Process: A Practical Precis for Teacher Negotiators," xeroxed. Paper submitted to the Canadian Teachers Federation, Ottawa, Canada, November 1971, 17 pp. For a review of Canadian problems with staff differentiation, see L. M. Hunt, "Differentiated Staffing—Implications for Canadian Education," mimeographed, address given to the Canadian Teachers' Federation Western Region Conference on Staff Utilization, Saskatoon, Saskatchewan, November 12, 1971, 16 pp.

Section II:

Case Histories and Models of Differentiated Staffing Projects

Section II describes the case histories of four projects to train teachers, funded by the Office of Education's School Personnel Utilization program: Adams High School in Portland, Oregon, Mary Harmon Weeks and Martin Luther King, Jr., Junior High School in Kansas City, Missouri, and Sarasota County School in Sarasota, Florida.

Some of the issues that emerged from the Adams project were the nature of curriculum changes, the daily functions of team leaders, the problems of teacher supervision, and the routines of students and staff schedules. Both the strengths and the weaknesses of the total school's program illustrate the problems the staff encountered as it attempted to fuse instruction, research, and training for teachers—compatible school goals that are mutually support-ive, but often not incorporated systematically in a staffing program.

Kansas City's approach to differentiating the staff of an inner city element-ary and junior high school is also useful in understanding the interplay among teacher roles and the more complex relationships among administrators at the central office and school buildings. Turnover of central city administration inner city projects, which had an impact on issues in the school, and conflicts with the teacher's union highlight this case study. Of particular interest are the nature of the principal's role at the school developing the differentiated staffing program, the relationship of that school to the central administration, and the nature of the teacher groups coming to grips with new decision-making responsibilities.

The Sarasota public schools participated in the overall flexible staffing program of the Florida State Department of Education. According to adminis-trators in the county office, tampering with the staffing design meant modify-ing the total traditional approach to instruction. This particular case history details the issues involved in a county's confrontation with organizational alternatives, the cooperation of the teachers' association, the development of a staffing model and its modification, the allocation of staff units per school, the problems of teacher transfer from schools not participating to those participating in the staffing modification, the financial limitations, and the use of teacher committees.

The unique contribution of the Mesa story is the development of a new conceptual base for a differentiated staffing program: the development of staff needs was premised on an analysis of student needs. Each school was asked to participate by a Request For Proposal (RFP). Schools specified their objectives, outcomes, time frames, and costs. Much of the effort was built upon the already established innovations funded under ESEA, Title III. Some of the central features of the project included training details, work plans, model building and staff strategies, early identification of potential problems, job descriptions, and fluid pay structures.

Each of these case histories reveals a different story, a better approach to the problems of staff development and improvement of student learning. They also show a soundness in the theoretical base of differentiated staffing, and that changes in training towards flexible staffing are workable in practice. In Sarasota, because of intensive staff participation, there was a sense of "proprietorship" among teachers. In none of the projects was there displacement of incumbent teachers. In all, there was an early commitment to voluntary participation.

The variety of administrative viewpoints about differentiated staffing—of the superintendent, project director, school coordinators, and principal— testify to the diversity of perspectives, yet uniformity of commitment in the case studies. A general conclusion from these histories might be that most of the deficiencies of the project in whatever site existed because of deficiencies in the early planning stages that were not corrected until later.

5 The John Adams Differentiated Staffing Model

Al Dobbins

John Parker

Patricia Wertheimer

The model of differentiated staffing that exists at John Adams High School in Portland, Oregon, was developed by a group of educators hired by the Portland Public Schools to plan and run a high school that would provide a major new approach to secondary education. The planners decided that reorganizing staff roles and responsibilities was an essential factor in implementing the new program.

Adams is not the only Portland school to use differentiated staffing. The model has been extended to the Portsmouth Middle School, which shares with Adams the resources of a federal grant for staff differentiation training. However, because Adams has been operational for one year longer than Portsmouth, and since the writers are two of the original Adams planners, the ensuing discussion applies only to the high school version of the model.

The two most frequently cited claims in support of staff differentiation are that it will help a system conserve its scarce resources and that it will provide additional incentives to keep competent teachers in the classroom. As important as these arguments are, however, they are not the reasons behind the Adams model. Rather, our specific staffing pattern evolved as part of a comprehensive plan to confront some of the problems plaguing inner city schools. We tried to create a school that would not be characterized by the anonymity and impersonality so typical of large schools, and therefore decided to subdivide Adams into smaller units. We saw the compartmentalization of knowledge into various subject matter disciplines as artificial and unrealistic, and we established a broad, interdisciplinary course called "general education." We objected to the negative effects of grouping students on the basis of age, attitude, or academic ability, and this led to the decision to teach general education to groups of students of mixed ages, backgrounds, and abilities. We deplored the rigid and impersonal attitudes characterizing adult relationships within many schools and tried to create an institution where students would see adults working honestly together, openly dealing with their differences. We decried the inadequacies of university and college programs in teacher preparation and research, and sought both to conduct training programs and to carry out research in a field setting. As a natural consequence of these decisions about goals, atmosphere, attitudes, and instructional strategies, we saw the need for new adult roles to be established within the school, arranged in new patterns. The specifics of the patterns and the problems in implementation are the subjects of this chapter.

STAFFING THE MODEL

The Adams staffing model resembles the structure of the teaching hospital, with training and research implicit within its goal of care and instruction of its patients, the students. The assumption is not only that research and training are compatible with instruction, but also that all three goals are mutually supportive. Training and research conducted in a school setting should result in the improvement of instruction, since a constructively critical professional atmosphere would pervade the institution. Furthermore, far more useful research and training would take place in the school than in a university or laboratory, because schools and children would be a day-to-day reality for research and training to take into account.

We established a staffing pattern that identifies differentiated roles both vertically and with a horizontal component. At the heart of the pattern is the team of instructors organized along hierarchical lines. They are supported by specialists in supervision, research and evaluation, and curriculum development. In short, the model called for not just a career ladder but a career lattice or matrix (Figure 39).

FIGURE 39

Sample of the Adams Differentiated Staffing Model

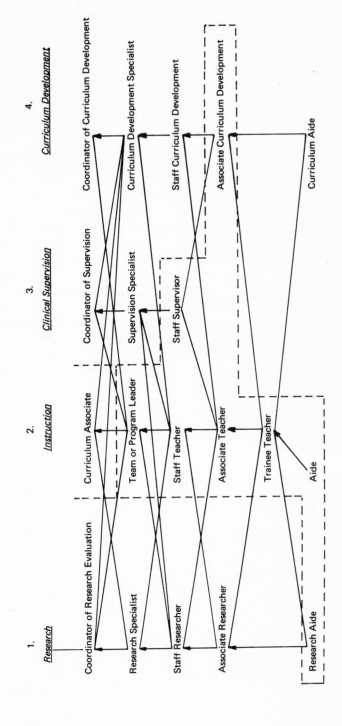

Conventional or vertically differentiated staffing models often resemble the instructional component of our model (line 2). Positions requiring the least developed instructional skills and competencies are manned by aides or other paraprofessionals. Those demanding the most sophistication are the senior or master teachers whom we call "curriculum associates." In these areas, the Adams model is probably indistinguishable from many other creative staffing patterns throughout the country.

The operational features unique to our model become clear through an examination of the curriculum for which we are staffed differentially and through the specifics of team organization and operation. Teams were established at Adams to teach "general education," the only required course (except for health and physical education). General education includes language, arts, social studies, math, and science. Most teams consist of a leader, two or three experienced teachers, and a number of trainees working toward certification. Team members have different academic backgrounds, thereby bringing to each team the perspective of several disciplines. Each team is responsible for approximately 200 students, grades nine through twelve. A typical team meets with half of its students for ninety minutes every morning, and with the other half in the afternoon. Working closely with such resource persons as a counselor, and a social worker, each team is responsible for designing, developing, implementing, and evaluating its own problem-centered, interdisciplinary course of study.

The overall aim of the course is to provide students with a base of knowledge and to help them develop a set of communication and inquiry skills that will enable them to function creatively and humanely in a society where the only constant is change. Students are involved in setting policy and selecting topics for team study. They are taught to collect and interpret data, do analytical and critical thinking, and make decisions.

Although each team has its own unique style, they all retain certain things in common, such as participating actively in the training responsibilities of the school, giving the trainees limited instructional roles commensurate with their skill, competency, and level of comfort. A supervisor assists these trainees in planning and organizing their instruction and provides feedback on their teaching effectiveness. The supervisor holds one of our horizontally differentiated staffing positions.

Second, teams seek empirical data to assess program effectiveness and optimize decision making, for important issues affecting team governance confront students and teachers alike. Being new, the general education program is not without major conceptual and operational problems. Researchers, i.e., teachers trained with special skills at data collection and interpretation, are needed to develop new ways to collect information about student learning and attitudes. Although standardized test data are regularly used, the researchers are given the task of developing new measures of performance, with emphasis upon nonobtrusive instruments. In these ways a team-based researcher is essential.

In the spring of 1971, then, a typical Adams team would be described according to Figure 40.

IMPLEMENTING THE ADAMS DIFFERENTIATED ROLES

The staffing pattern outlined in Figure 39 represents a far more comprehensive and detailed model than the actual team organization shown in Figure 40. To date we have attempted to staff only some of the roles in the broader model. However, those that were filled have been in operation since Adams opened in 1969, and we have learned a great deal about the promise and problems inherent in each of

FIGURE 40

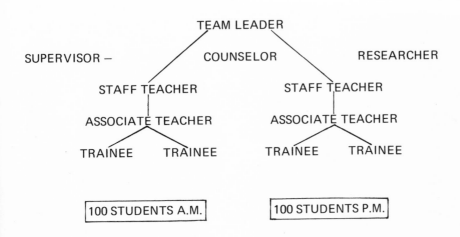

these. We turn now to a discussion of the specific responsibilities assigned to each functioning role within a career line, and an analysis of the potential of each.

Curriculum Associate

More than any other, this role has undergone metamorphosis in the program's two years. Originally, Adams opened with four curriculum associates (CA), each fulfilling similar responsibilities. In the second year the number of CAs was cut to three, and each became specialized and distinctive. The present structure, described below, applies to the most recent set of role descriptions.

The *curriculum associate for instruction* works directly for, and is responsible to, the vice principal for curriculum. His role includes (1) providing support services to all team leaders and department chairmen (program leaders); (2) providing technical assistance in the planning and implementation of interdisciplinary instructional units; and (3) evaluating the performance of all team leaders and department chairmen.

The role of curriculum associate for instruction has been troublesome from the first. It initially encompassed the responsibilities of providing overall interdisciplinary curriculum development leadership for a "house" (two teams of teachers and students); closely cooperating with the team supervisor; providing back-up supervisory services for trainees encountering instructional difficulties; carrying out routine house disciplinary and management functions; and teaching an average of one class per day.

But practice has thoroughly confounded the original role conception, for a number of reasons. The CA attempted to carry out conventional responsibilities in a new setting that rejected many conventional school expectations, i.e. an inner city school commited to cross-grades and cross-ability grouping; an institution struggling to individualize and humanize all relationships; a school that places a great amount of responsibility for learning in the hands of the students; an organization seeking to involve as many individuals—teachers, students, and administrators alike—in the processes of decision making; and a public school heavily involved with preservice training for many new professionals.

As commendable as these features were, they nonetheless required enormous amounts of time, imagination, resources, and patience. Often there were no precedents for setting policy, carrying out a given task or handling a myriad of other problems. CAs as key decision makers early became overloaded with unfulfilled tasks. We had initially assumed that the administrative functions of a house leader might take a quarter of a CA's time; but the accounting for students' routine class schedules and attendance problems became far more time-consuming than anticipated. The ticklish situations emerging within a racially desegrated but unintegrated school were exhausting. The CAs soon were seen as— and acted like — administrators and disciplinarians.

For a number of reasons the remaining components of the job—curriculum leadership, support for training, and teaching— mainly went by the boards. Despite the fact that each person filling this role had exceptional competencies and strengths, there was not sufficient training given to equip the CAs to fill all the areas of need. Neither school planners nor the CAs yet fully understood the nature of the role.

Second, the activities the CAs did undertake were obviously so important that no one seriously thought of curtailing them for the sake of the other assignments. The task of management, which for the most part the CAs performed superbly, were critical to the school's very operation.

Third, an unfortunate but probably unavoidable amount of confusion and inefficiency resulted from designing a school that rejected established—and arbitrary—ways of treating students. "Decentralized decision making," "freedom of choice," and "humanizing the atmosphere" can be frustrating and painful in practice, however laudable in theory.

The structure of the school has since changed markedly. Some of the administrative functions that CAs were doing have been centralized. Training responsibilities have been focused more on the supervisor, and additional university-appointed personnel are assisting in the training processes. The team leader, whose role is discussed later, has assumed far more responsibility in the area of curriculum development.

The curriculum associate role has, in fact, evolved into three variants, only one of which resembles its original. These role variants are more viable for their occupants, and more helpful in solving many of the school's problems. For instance, there is now a CA for administration who reports to the vice principal for administration. He handles problems of discipline, provides in-service training in race relations, and supervises school-wide social and athletic activities. There is also a CA for student services who is accountable to the vice principal for special projects, but whose work cuts across administration, training, and instruction. He directs the Record Center operations (an administrative task), is responsible for two aide training programs (a training task), and is responsible for a "reentry program" for students returning from juvenile detention facilities (an instructional task).

Team leaders

John Adams High School has eight team leaders (TL), each of whom heads up a team of teachers, trainee teachers, and students from all grade and ability levels. The team meets to study "general education," the interdisciplinary course taught in lieu of the traditional English-social studies-general mathematics-basic science requirements. Working with each team are a counselor and, periodically, a social worker and a social worker trainee. The TL reports directly to the CAI and is responsible for the following: (1) to lead the planning, instruction, and evaluation of his team's interdisciplinary curriculum; (2) to supervise the teaching performance of all members of the team (he is *not* expected to provide in-depth supervision of trainees); and (3) to establish and maintain a program to periodically inform the parents of the student members of the team about their program plans and progress, and to receive parent feedback.

Unlike that of the CA, the TL role has been strong and viable, though not problem-free. From the first, teams have coalesced into instructional units, and the students have been able to identify with their specific teams—initially as the critical group within a given house, and subsequently as the primary organizational unit within the school. The leadership exerted by the various team leaders contributed materially to these accomplishments.

It should be noted that, in the case of the CAs at Adams, the role occupants have persisted, while the role itself has undergone constant change. The team leader role, on the other hand, has remained more stable than the CA role, but has seen a rapid turnover of occupants: three of the original four CAs still are at Adams, while only two of the original eight team leaders remain.

Each team leader is responsible for team direction management and leading the work of interdisciplinary curriculum development. However, each team has evolved unique qualities that distinguishes it from the others. For example, one team groups students by "learning style," which refers to such characteristics as the individual's ability to manage his own education, his level of skills and abilities, his facility with abstract thinking, and his interest in personal projects. Another team develops widely different learning tasks among the different team sections, depending on teacher and student interest in a given topic. A third primarily stresses community problems, service opportunities, and projects. Yet another follows a more conventional, academically oriented program.

Each team leader needs management and organizational skills unfamiliar to most high school teachers. What is more, although some skills are needed by all team leaders, certain team-leading skills (such as running a substantially community-based, project-oriented team) represent unique and extraordinary competencies. Some of these team leader tasks are so complex that we have been unable to develop a training program to instill the necessary skills.

Day-to-day activity at Adams is often spontaneous. Since curriculum development is continuous, teachers and students alike are regularly confronted with a remarkable variety of challenges. (Many Adams students must face an interesting and possibly frustrating new dilemma: Which of the attractive alternatives available to them should they select on a given day?) The team leader is charged with managing his team's instructional program. In doing so he must be attuned to the goings-on of the different sections within his team and the activities and opportunities generated by other teams as well—a more formidable charge. A guest speaker, an important major film, or a field trip from one team may well be helpful to the students on another team. The responsibility of always being informed confronts team leaders with an exhausting and endless series of tasks. The problem is exacerbated by accountability: Where is every student at a given time? What is each doing? Is a specific task useful and appropriate to both the individual and the team?

As unwieldy as the job of team management is, and as intellectually unrewarding as team and student accountability is, the team leaders at John Adams, by and large, welcome the opportunity to fulfill within their team setting some of the qualities of the school-within-a-school. They argue with considerable passion that the benefits of warm, close, personal relationships among teachers and students within a team—relationships that emanate from students and teachers working together as individuals—are well worth the strain of the job. Indeed, they feel deeply that the nature of these relationships more than offsets the stultifying impact of bigness and impersonality encountered so often in inner city and suburban high schools.

Beyond management, team leaders have an enormous responsibility to spearhead the daily development of the broad program of the general education course with its enormous scope. Virtually any contemporary or historical topic or issue may become the subject for analysis and study.

To lead interdisciplinary curriculum development and implementation successfully, a team leader must get a group of teachers from diverse academic backgrounds to agree on a set of philosophical assumptions about what and how students should learn. Moreover, there is no set curriculum guide, nor is there any precedence by which to be guided vis-à-vis this type of problem- or issue-oriented program. It is a heavy challenge to develop a course that is both intellectually respectable and sufficiently encompassing to accommodate the range of interests and abilities of an inner city student body. The curriculum development responsibilities of the team leaders are demanding indeed.

Adams High School, like so many others in this country, works within an economy of scarcity: there simply aren't enough resources to do the job. As a result, team leaders are constantly engaged in tugs of war among themselves, with other departments in the school, and with the administration to acquire additional resources, whether in the form of teaching personnel, time, space, supplies, equipment, or funds. When the sought-after resources fail to appear as is often the case, team leaders find themselves frustrated.

Despite the enormous demands placed on team leaders and the frustrations incumbent in the job, we believe the role of team leader is basically sound. Nevertheless, it is being modified so that in the school's third year we find teams of different sizes with formats substantially different from one another. Variations occurred as experience taught leaders and their teams what specific form of curriculum they were capable of generating. However, a sense of continuity has come from the fact that team personnel have stabilized, as many teachers remain with groups they find comfortable and compatible, and many students continue with their same teams.

Staff Teacher

Each team has two to three certificated teachers with different academic backgrounds. The staff teachers' responsiblities are: (1) to teach on a general education team; and (2) to participate in day-to-day curriculum development within the course.

Associate Teacher

The role of associate teacher was originally defined in such a way as to give teachers in their first, second or third year of teaching somewhat more limited teaching responsibilities than the staff teachers. As associate teachers they would assume greater responsibility as they gained—and demonstrated—greater competency as team teachers. Indeed, supervision and carefully prescribed in-service training would theoretically enhance the associate teacher's development. In practice, because of the complexities of interdisciplinary instruction, the degree of responsibility shouldered by associate and staff teacher alike has been indistinguishable. In our case the role distinction is meaningless.

Trainee Teacher

Each general education team operates with at least one intern trainee, as well as two student teachers. The intern might be any of three kinds. The first might be a person working on a Master of Arts in teaching (MAT) degree; the second, a teacher corpsman; while the third might be a member of the Portland Urban Teacher Education Project, an Adams-based, federally-funded project operating in nine Portland District schools.

The student teachers who come to John Adams are resident only ten to twelve weeks of the year, and come from any of three or four regional institutions. Due to their short affiliation, they are unable to take on the functions of team members as fully as are the interns. Nevertheless, in time they assume responsibility for teaching at least two sections of a general education team, as well as teaching elective courses in their special areas.

Supervisor

Since before the opening of Adams school, we have maintained that teacher training conducted in a field setting could be more effective than that typically carried out at a university or college department of education, and that such a training program would provide a realistic induction into the profession and to the benefit of trainees and students alike, help reduce the adult-to-student ratio of the school and of the teams as well. However, a commitment of school resources is required in order to sustain an extensive and effective training program.

In the first year of the school's differentiated staffing operation, supervision of trainees was spread over three roles: two coordinators of training, four CAs, and eight TLs. Responsibility and accountability were somewhat unclear, and with the press of other tasks, supervisory relationships to trainees were unsatisfactory.

Subsequently, this arrangement has been greatly improved. One overall coordinator of teacher education took the place of the previous two, primary supervisory responsibility was removed from both curriculum associates and team leaders, and we finally did get to inaugurate the staff supervisor role. Training programs, supported by federal funds, were set up to train these staff supervisors within a twelve-month, eleven quarter-hour sequence of supervision courses taught by the coordinator of teacher education at Adams and authorized through Oregon State University.

By the second operational year, therefore, the two main supervisory roles were the following:

Cordinator of Supervision

This position is filled by a person of vice-principal rank responsible for selecting and placing all interns and student teachers, providing back-up supervision and support for trainees encountering instructional or personal difficulties, and training staff supervisors.

Staff Supervisor

Four teachers interested in expanding their professional experience into the field of teacher education have received assignments as part-time supervisors. They have participated in two full summer training institutes conducted at Adams in conjunction with a limited summer school for the disadvantaged. Most of the supervisors work as General Education staff teachers for half of the school day, and supervise the trainees the other half. Some trainees have the good fortune to be members of the same team as their supervisor, while others work with trainees from other teams.

The responsibilities of the staff supervisor are to (1) supervise the day-to-day teaching of his assigned trainees, whether interns or student teachers; (2) to team-teach a seminar in teacher education;

(3) to participate in a supervisory training program; and (4) (on a part-time basis) to meet the same responsibilities as other staff teachers.

The training staff was much better organized to handle its tasks in the second year than the first. Weekly staff meetings were built into the middle of the school day (a crucial achievement in a school with nearly 100% space utilization). At these meetings the various supervisors, instructors, administrators and researchers of training focused on short range problem "cases," planning and articulation of the various training seminars and long range planning and program evaluation.

The role of staff supervisor is far from being fully evolved. It is difficult to attract and retain the most talented teachers, given the appeal of competing team and program leadership opportunites. The dialogue about who can best help a beginning teacher—team member or outside specialist—continues unabated. Building a new educative role which is rewarding and useful to all concerned takes time, resources and experience. To legitimize the role in the long run there needs to evolve some sort of certificate program, presumably competency-based.

Coordinator of Research and Evaluation

As with the coordinator of supervision, this position is filled by a person at the level of vice principal, whose responsibilities include (1) directing the collection and organization of data required both for decision making by the school governance bodies, and for the school district and area administration; (2) providing periodic assistance to different teaching teams on their problems of information collection and interpretation for program evaluation; and (3) training the staff researchers in school-based research and evaluation competencies.

Staff Researcher

Parallel to the supervisors, the Adams faculty has four staff teachers who are also research and evaluation specialists. Most staff researchers teach half of every day and meet their researcher responsibilities the remainder of the time. To them fall such tasks as surveying student and parent attitudes toward the new curricula, the collection of data on student achievement (based on standardized instruments as well as devices developed for our specific programs), the design of evaluation of programs in Planned Program Budgeting System (PPBS) terms.

Some of the functions involved in research and evaluation require close working relationships with teachers, such as in eliciting objectives and determining criterion levels for these indicators. Others are best realized in their own separate quarters, such as instrument development and data analysis.

It proved unrealistic to expect the differentiated staffing specialists in research and evaluation to be competent in all these areas, despite the efforts of our specialists.

A wiser solution would be to separate the personnel involved in the interpersonal aspects of research and evaluation from those involved in the specialist aspects and to have the specialist teachers assigned to teams engaged mainly in the specification of objectives, in the collection of data and in the interpretation of those data to the team while operating as a liaison to a special staff of instrument developers and data analysts.

Another major problem was the inclination of teachers to regard evaluation as identical with testing. Some teachers wanted to wash their hands of the entire affair by having the evaluator come in and do "his thing." This permitted the rest of the team to avoid engaging in the hard thinking about how to evaluate what they were doing.

The evaluation specialists rapidly found that their major role was not so much one of data collection and interpretation as of attempting to get the team to think in evaluation terms. We are quite convinced that until the members of the team get into the habit of using data, evaluation specialists cannot perform their role.

Evaluation as a specialized service breaks down if it is not possible to provide good instruments for rapid assessment of teachers' special interests, or if the feedback time for analyzed data is over-long. Despite our efforts to assign personnel to the task of research and evaluation, there has never been a separate budget, adequate data processing facilities, or adequate access to specialists in the area of instrument development or data analysis to achieve this. Given the impossibility of providing systematically collected and interpreted data to many people in the building, our major effort became one of educating teachers to use such data independently.

Horizontal differentiation has real limits. The instructional area of a school is continually strapped for personnel, and to take more personnel from this segment of a school and to assign them to research and evaluation is feasible only if there is some direct payoff to instruction. We found that our efforts to increase the numbers of teachers involved or trained in evaluation naturally led to the expectations that they could be released from some of their teaching duties for work of this type. This will never be possible with the present funding levels of schools. It was our feeling after two years that the best approach is one of training a number of teachers in a very limited set of the skills of evaluation, namely those interpersonal skills mentioned earlier, and to train them to be liaison people to a small staff of specialists, rather than to train them in the details of research and evaluation itself. However, we did not have time to discern fully what skills are essential to the liaison role.

UNIQUE PROBLEMS IN IMPLEMENTATION

In common with many American schools engaged in staffing innovations, Adams encountered a number of problems, some of which are discussed elsewhere in this book. Others are endemic to the Portland scene. Their very uniqueness makes them attractive for discussion, for they may illuminate some additional difficulties inherent in launching innovative programs.

The "Colonialism" Syndrome

The colonialism syndrome cuts across all plans and programs at Adams. The Adams planning team, which in turn became the administrative staff, came to Portland from the East Coast. We saw ourselves as outsiders delighted to find such a hospitable educational climate. Others, however, viewed us at best as colonialists, and at worst as self-seeking carpetbaggers. We were given a great deal of autonomy in the planning and implementation of many new programs, including differentiated staffing. At the same time, however, our assumptions about decentralization and delegation of responsiblitiy required a great deal of input from teachers, as well as parents and students. Indeed, any effective program of staff differentiation requires strong grass roots decision making and support. Thus, we found ourselves operating both at a psychological and ideological disadvantage.

The "Superstar" Syndrome

The vast majority of the faculty of John Adams were recruited from other secondary schools in Portland. Many were articulate, independent, and anti-establishment in their viewpoints and energetic in their teaching style. In coming to Adams, each had to undergo a transformation from being an isolated but highly competent teacher to one of many able teachers in a group; from a style of operation characterized by independence to one requiring cooperation; in short, from being an isolated superstar to a member in a large galaxy of superstars. For many the adjustment was difficult. The effective functioning of teams staffed according to differentiated roles and responsibilities demanded changes in many teachers which were trying, indeed.

Resource Limitations

While the resources made available for the innovations Adams attempted to inaugurate (including differentiated staffing) were greater than those for many high schools, they were insufficient. The Portland Public Schools had budgeted for the planning team to work for a year before the school actually opened. The school was allocated additional staff and supplies for the first year in operation beyond what it might normally be granted, but all too soon found itself on a regular district budget, while laboring to develop new programs in staffing, training, and curriculum development. At Adams we initiated an array of changes because we assumed that if change was to be effective, it would have to be comprehensive. Considering the amount of additional resources necessary to mount such an operation, should a district launch major programs when revenue is limited? Our view is that a school system should *not* do so, unless there are substantial funds available for a long-time period.

This is not meant to suggest, however, that the progress of innovations should not be monitored, nor that personnel need not be financially accountable. On the contrary, the decision makers should constantly seek the best information available on project problems and achievements, and changes should be made on the basis of those data. As long as there is a reasonable degree of confidence that the new programs will meet their objectives, the additional resources should be made available.

Maintaining Horizontal Differentiation

From the outset we have argued that the specialty areas of supervision, research, and evaluation were important to instruction and that these functions are best carried out in a school setting. At Adams we demonstrated our belief in this notion by assigning and training regular school personnel who would otherwise be in the classroom, to positions in these areas. Such a horizontally differentiated staffing pattern makes for more effective teaching, and gives an extra bonus of career satisfaction to the involved.

However, when resources become scarce, it is difficult to justify keeping these positions filled out of the instructional budget of a school while class sizes escalate.

Ideally, other solutions could be worked out: schools of teacher education might allocate faculty positions to joint appointments, say, as clinical professors. But these staffing patterns raise new problems, such as establishing creditability with regular school personnel. Furthermore, universities and colleges, also experiencing a financial pinch, are reluctant to commit resources as enrollment drops and funds diminish. Suffice it to acknowledge that a horizontal differentiated staffing pattern is vulnerable in times of economic difficulties.

CRITIQUE OF THE ADAMS STAFFING PATTERN

The ultimate test of any staffing pattern should be the extent to which it increases organizational effectiveness, expands the satisfaction of and career opportunities of the faculty, and creates a climate conducive to learning. The following section contains an assessment of the Adams staffing pattern, according to these three criteria.

Organizational Effectiveness

To be defensible, a staffing pattern must enhance an organization's capacity to function effectively. In many institutions this criterion suggests rapid communication, clear delineation of responsibility, and accountability. For others it means faculty involvement in decision-making—an increasingly important morale and efficiency factor. A team structure whose members have differentiated responsibilities seems to help create both. However, we found that the process of shared decision-making at the team level was not easy because, though there was willingness to participate, difficulties were generated by divergent philosophies among the teachers.

The problem of efficiency was exacerbated at the school level, for the very same reasons, as well as those of administration. Informing different teams so that teachers and students thoroughly understand and discuss the complexities of issues and the implications and consequences of alternative choices is an exceedingly difficult and time consuming task which can limit efficiency. If a school does a poor and inconsistent job in sharing decision-making (and for many circumstantial reasons Adams has not fared especially well in this area) the faculty may become demoralized and embittered. However, if done carefully, a school will operate with a faculty characterized by high morale, high energy output, and greater productivity.

Career Line Satisfaction

Theoretically, the opportunities for professional growth and development in a differentiated staffing pattern are quite attractive and the Adams model, which allows for horizontal as well as vertical movement, maximizes this characteristic. For example, an individual might enter Adams at any point in the Matrix and proceed either vertically or horizontally, as his career goals and/or opportunities direct, and as he gains specialized skills and competencies. He might begin as an aide, for example, working part time while pursuing a Bachelor's Degree, then receive certification through the intern training program, and begin his probationary teaching as an associate teacher. With many role models in view, he might take school-based exploratory courses in research-evaluation, gain competence as an associate researcher, and divide his time between instruction and research within the school. As time passed, he might undertake work in the field of curriculum development as an associate curriculum developer, and eventually, as a program leader. Thus, he would have developed capabilities in a variety of educational specialty areas and shouldered additional responsibility, all the while maintaining an instructional role in the school.

The components of the Adams model have not actually been operational long enough for anyone to enjoy such professional advancement. However, nearly a dozen professionals have been trained for one of the horizontally differentiated specialty areas, and over 200 preprofessionals—aides, interns, social worker trainees, and student teachers—have gained experience through some aspect of the Adams staff training program.

The Climate for Learning

Since most schools correctly want students to improve in intellectual competence they attempt to enhance learning by creating a climate of academic excellence. In this regard, Adams is no exception. However, we also place great emphasis on the affective climate of the school, for we consider it a crucial factor too often overlooked in schools today. We are distressed by the negative atmosphere of many schools which causes too many students to feel unwelcome. Many schools seem neither congenial for children nor helpful in their quest for learning. The so-called hidden curriculum— that implicit set of rules and regulations which govern the relationships between children and adults and among adults themselves—we suspect has a great deal of impact on how children feel about themselves, about learning, and about the values of adult society. Translated into staffing theory, our assumption is that relationships among adults in a school, planned and unplanned, conscious and unconscious, are significant to what students learn. Most staffing models are organized primarily on "what" the school instructs, perhaps on "how" it does so, forgetting that the structure itself teaches students a great deal that is significant to instruction; in other words, the medium of schools and the staffing pattern itself deliver a powerful message.

Consequently, we tried to create a set of relationships within the faculty and the entire school community in which to achieve two objectives: to encourage a sense of purposeful inquiry and learning among students, and to establish feelings of mutual respect among students and teacher alike. Active student participation in educational decision-making and such preconditions as freedom of movement, the opportunity to select courses, and genuine friendliness between students and teachers[3] highly influence school climate.

Data generated by study of the Adams school climate led to some perplexing, tentative conclusions. Adams students say they feel good about attending and they like the freedom and sense of responsibility they are given. At the same time, they achieve neither better nor worse than they might if such innovations were not present, according to certain standard performance measures. Thus, although the school climate seems somewhat more positive than in many, more traditional schools, there is no clear improvement in academic achievement from that of regular schools.

While we are pleased with the school's climate, it is difficult to ascertain the extent to which this positive climate can be linked to the staffing pattern. Many factors tend to influence climate for learning. The egalitarian spirit of many faculty members, the informality of dress, the first name relationships between students and teachers and involvement of students in curricular and governance decision making—now seem far more consequential. Grouping students of all ability levels and ages in the same team, a team-taught, problem-centered curriculum and the opportunity for independent time are also influential. However, as the staffing pattern at Adams contributes to these factors, it is a positive feature of the school.

CONCLUSION

The Adams program presents an extremely broad and comprehensive set of educational innovations, involving not only differentiated staffing, but major curriculum development, experimentation in shared decision-making, a school climate characterized by freedom and openness, and teacher training and research. Adams is a different kind of school, not as a consequence of one program in staff reorganization, but because of the impact of many discreetly applied variables.

Sorting out such roles as curriculum associate and team leader, and assessing the overall impact of the innovative staffing pattern have been trying indeed. Nonetheless, we remain convinced that these efforts are worthwhile and have contributed to the positive aspects of Adams High School.

---

1. Patricia A. Wertheimer, "School Climate and Student Learning," *PDK*, May, 1971.

6 History of the
Sarasota Model

Gene Pillot

The business of education is to develop the learner's ability both to find answers to his questions and to ask the right questions for his particular needs. In the spring of 1968 the board and staff of the Sarasota, Florida, Public School System found themselves to be somewhat like the shoemaker's unshod children. The need for qualitative change in the system clearly existed, but the answers—and even the questions—were not so obvious to the educators. They had an obvious need for a better salary schedule and pupil-teacher ratio. However, it was beginning to appear that achievement of those benefits would not necessarily result in a better product—improved learning. A study of organizational alternatives began, and the first phase ended a year later in May 1969, with the board-approved recommendation to develop and implement a model of differentiated staffing.

The three-year project, 1968-69 through 1970-71, consisted of three major parts, each a school year in length: (1) a preliminary study of organizational alternatives; (2) the design of a model for Sarasota County; and (3) a one-year pilot implementation. Evaluation of the model design and preliminary implementation was conducted during the second and third years.

The first important decision was made at the beginning of the project: The study would be conducted by the staff and representatives of the Sarasota County Teachers Association working in close and continuous tandem with the school staff—an effort proved so successful, it should be stressed as a prerequisite to developing a new staffing pattern. The professional literature is replete with examples

229

of resistance to change and suspicion of its effect, on the part of professional associations and unions. Continuous substantial involvement by the teachers' association in the Sarasota study made them equal partners in recommendations and decisions, and co-owners of the results.

The first year was spent examining programs that either had been implemented as pilot projects in other school systems, or presented in the literature as theoretical models of alternative approaches to staffing and organizing for instruction. The Temple City and Kansas City pilot schools[1] were visited; the literature was carefully consulted; and several regional and national conferences on differentiated staffing were attended by administrators, teachers, and local professional association representatives.

During this time it was decided that participation in the study would be open to the staff at any of the local schools, *but would be voluntary.* This important commitment to voluntary participation ultimately became one of several basic guidelines for implementation of differentiated staffing in Sarasota. At the end of the first year, four elementary and two junior high schools[2] were represented in the study.

By spring, 1969, preliminary conclusions and recommendations were prepared:

1. Differentiated staffing was an innovation of substantial promise and should be tried in Sarasota.

2. A model should be designed during 1969-70.

3. Participation in the design and implementation by any school staff should be voluntary.

4. A central steering committee should be formed to represent all departments of the school system and act as an official advisory group to the school board.

These recommendations were approved by the school board in May 1969, and the second phase of the three-year study began.

Concurrent with the first year of the Sarasota study, the Florida State Department of Education had begun examining the concept of flexible staffing. In 1968 legislation was passed directing the State Commissioner to undertake such a study, and a School Personnel Utilization grant was awarded his department under the provisions of the Education Professions Development Act. This was to be implemented in Sarasota and two other Florida school systems. The grant provided the basic funding for the design of the Sarasota model during 1969-70. The study which led to the design of the model was undertaken as a doctoral dissertation at the University of Florida[3], in conjunction with a team of seven local educators representing the six pilot schools and the central office.

conjunction with a team of seven local educators representing the six pilot schools and the central office.

Early in the model development, the third major local decision was made, providing the basic philosophy of the model: The design of the model would provide the mechanics for any school staff to implement a pattern of differentiated staffing autonomously within certain criteria of minimum consistency. That is, the personnel of that school would be able to create the school model that best fitted their needs and philosophy from a general school system model. So the system model was designed in two sub-models. The staffing sub-model provided both a vertical and horizontal differentiation of professional and paraprofessional positions, with broad job specifications based upon an empirical analysis of tasks performed in the instructional process. The implementation sub-model provided a formula for allocating a number of staff "units" to each school, and assigned a unit value to each of the positions in the staffing sub-model. The school would be limited to the positions and job specifications provided and could only staff to the extent afforded by their unit allocation. Thus, each school staff could autonomously design their school model by selecting any staffing pattern of positions from one sub-model, but would have to "pay" for that staff by using the units allocated and charged for each position. This smorgasbord approach to differentiated staffing at any volunteer school made possible implementation in an entire school or in one or more departments or grade levels.

As the model was developed, the components were field tested in one department in each of the pilot junior high schools. At this stage, a fourth basic decision was made which proved to be a major factor affecting the spread of differentiated staffing to other schools: no teacher would be involuntarily transferred to provide a vacant unit. This limited implementation of the model at any school to the extent that a staffing pattern could be developed from the system model using units made vacant by staff attrition or growth.

The concurrent development of conceptual design and field testing resulted in the completion of a system model comprised of the two sub-models described above with a faculty board as the decision-making body at each school; and a set of basic job specifications as guidelines for the selection, performance, and evaluation of staff. The model was implemented during 1970-71—the third year of the study—in four of the six original pilot schools. It was at this time that the three earlier major decisions became significant: (1) autonomy and minimum consistency would be inherent in the model successfully tested; (2) the policy of voluntary participation resulted in complete implementation at one junior high school and in just one department at a second junior high school, providing the opportunity to test and compare full and partial implementation; and (3) no one would be involuntarily transferred to fill a staff unit which forced limited or no implementation at four of the pilot schools. The first administrative problem had been identified.

The eagerness of the differentiated staffing people at Sarasota to implement the program caused problems resulting from insufficient preplanning and preparation. As could be expected, other problems emerged during the trial period, mostly of an administrative nature.

INSUFFICIENT CURRICULUM-BASED DESIGN

The Problem

The major weakness identified in this pilot project was the design of the staffing sub-model with a foundation insufficiently based upon the goals and objectives of the school system. It was prepared after completion of a comprehensive task analysis, and the professional and paraprofessional staff positions were identified according to the levels of necessary tasks. These tasks were clustered into job specification according to the level of skill, training, and experience needed, and the degree of influence the position was expected to have. However, the fact that the task analysis was essentially arbitrary weakened the design. Early in the first pilot year of full implementation, it became evident that role differentiation between positions was not always clear; and that it was not always possible to organize the curriculum that the differentiated staff was implementing in a manner consistent with the staffing pattern. This resulted in some imbalance of professional and paraprofessional staff and their loads.

In one notable example, a junior high school mathematics department had staffed with four professional teachers, three teacher aides, and eight senior high school student assistants working one hour each. A traditional staff would have consisted of six professional teachers. This department had planned to differentiate the activities and modes of instruction consistent with the new staffing pattern. However, designers of the differentiated staffing model had not adequately considered the curriculum, and the mathematics curriculum had not been sufficiently reorganized into large group, small group, and individualized activities. Thus, four professionals were unnecessarily overloaded, while the teacher aides probably were not utilized to their maximum potential.

The Solution

Early in the first implementation year experience in the pilot schools proved that a model of differentiated staffing should be based upon a task analysis sequentially developed from goals to staffing pattern. The process is not unique to programs involving differentiated staffing, but the importance is magnified if a flexible staffing organization is superimposed on an inflexible curriculum consisting of traditionally organized courses. The remedial approach by the Sarasota staff took six major steps:

1. writing of all courses of study in terms of student performance objectives. These objectives specified the behavior that the learner was expected to attain as a result of his experience, and the evaluative criteria by which their achievement would be measured;
2. listing of specific activities pertinent to the objectives;
3. classifying the activities according to appropriate modes of instruction;
4. classifying the activities and modes of instruction according to the training, skill, and experience needed to conduct them;
5. clustering the classified activities into several sets, each of which constituted a logical job specification for one individual; and
6. reorganizing the positions on the staffing sub-model to conform to the several job specifications developed.

Since 1968 the entire instructional staff had been involved in an inservice education program concerned with the definition, recognition, and writing of behavioral objectives. The preparation of courses of study in terms of learner behavioral performance objectives could not be undertaken and completed in a single year. Had the Sarasota study not been started two years before differentiated staffing became fully operational in the pilot schools, it would have been impossible to complete the remedial work in curriculum design without another year or more of restricted development of the total flexible instructional program. It is strongly recommended that a careful examination of the goals of the school system be undertaken as the first step for any district considering differentiated staffing. The goals, stated as much as possible in objective and measurable terms, should constitute the basis for the major step described above.

Only then can the staff prepare a taxonomy of instructional activities that leads to a staffing pattern adapted to the needs of that school district. If a differentiated staffing model is designed otherwise, it will be no more than an artificial arrangement not unlike the proverbial cart placed before the horse. Efficient utilization of the staff, flexibility in instructional techniques, and commensurate positive change in learning outcomes could occur only through fortuitous happenstance.

The recognition that the written curriculum, the modes of instruction, the school schedule, the software and hardware, and the staffing pattern are directly related and interdependent follows naturally from the study described. This experience caused Sarasota educators to abandon the limiting label of differentiated staffing for their project and substitute the more adequately descriptive term *flexible instructional organization.*

There must be flexibility in all phases of the school's instructional program if the learner's needs are to be met, and in a format appropriate to those needs. Flexibility must be implicit in the very design of the model, and the staff, administration, and school board must keep their model of differentiated staffing—flexible instructional organization—fluid. Feedback from the early planning and implementation stages must be conscientiously sought, and applied when acceptable to changes in any phase of the program. Everyone involved must be comfortable with change. A static innovation is merely an unimproved substitution for the older model organization.

SOME PROBLEMS IN THE MECHANICS OF THE MODEL

Inhibition of Growth

Involuntary transfer of teachers from a pilot school for the sole purpose of expanding the staff differentiation was prohibited very early in the study—a personnel policy considered more important than the speed of implementation of a staffing model at any school. Testing the model's capability of being applied partially in a school or department, and expanded as vacancies in the staff occurred was basic. With the optimum model for a school on paper, the implementation would be gradual much as newlyweds furnish their home as their budget permits. Of course a newly established school, or one with a substantial number of vacancies would be able to implement complete flexible staffing much sooner, just as affluent newlyweds could move right in with all their furniture at once.

Staff of several pilot schools, convinced of the potential for improved organization, were eager to become fully operational. There was no question of the soundness of the philosophy that professional responsibility to personnel precedes a hasty implementation policy.

Ironically, the concept that had been successfully introduced contained an inherent deterrent to its own growth. During the first year of full implementation, two of the early pilot schools, unable to implement any significant part of their staffing model, gradually lost interest in the program and withdrew from direct participation. Departments in other schools, not among the six original pilot schools, had become convinced of the merits of flexible organization and staffing, and prepared their school models. Often they were unable to implement the optimum model because of insufficient vacancies on the staff.

By the summer of 1971, the end of the first full implementation year, there was still no adequate solution. The national surplus of teachers and accompanying lack of openings reduced the number of peripatetic teachers in the Sarasota staff. In addition, budgetary restrictions prevented the allocation of additional teacher units that would normally have accompanied enrollment growth. In some cases, staff allocations were reduced.

However, several efforts were made for improving the capability of a school or department to implement flexible staffing:

1. The school staff was encouraged by the school board, administration, and differentiated staffing steering committee to proceed with partial implementation. This was done by four of the six original pilot schools and departments in two other schools.

2. Uninterested members of existing staffs were encouraged without pressure to request transfer to other schools where vacancies in traditional staffing existed.

3. The principal and faculty board were encouraged to hold the vacancies which occurred until they had determined the best application toward their optimum flexible staffing model.

4. Schools on two contiguous campuses combined for flexible staffing in one or more departments, using vacant staff units more efficiently in the larger organization.

5. When critical to the continuation of a pilot program, some additional units or fractions of units were assigned to "grandfather" one or more staff members at a given school. (Carry them with their regular salary through the transition period.)

6. Special project funds, when permissible, were used to supplement staff.

Careful consideration must be given to provide the mechanics that will enable the differentiated staffing program to become operational while concurrently protecting the individual teacher. There is a point at which the balance must tip in favor of the instructional organization expected to provide maximum efficiency and yield optimum learning—the purpose of education.

Financial Limitations

One of the original concerns that motivated the Sarasota study of differentiated staffing was its financial limitations. In common with most boards of education in the nation, this one was faced with annual requests for an improved teacher salary schedule, and limited operational funds. They directed the staff to study alternative ways to compensate teachers commensurate with their performance, instead of by simple across-the-board raises based only upon degrees and experience. The spectre of merit pay with its undesirable aspects came up for discussion. Fortunately, differentiated staffing was investigated and accepted very early. The positive aspects of merit pay were included. Though saving money is not one of its goals, differentiated staffing is not expected to cost more than traditional staffing once it is implemented. The unit structure of the implementation sub-model at Sarasota was designed to provide that quality. The staff costs of first pilot programs were compared to the estimated costs of ordinary staffing in non-pilot schools. This revealed a basic conceptual arithmetic weakness in the unit system. The unit values assigned to various staff positions were based upon the mean salary of all classroom teachers as an index point. Other differentiated staffing positions were charged as a fraction of a unit, or more than one unit, dependent upon the median salary to be paid in the new staffing position. As an example, a staff teacher was charged at one unit, while a directing teacher—comparable to a senior teacher in other models—was charged at one and one-quarter units. It was presumed that the total staffing costs would be affected by some law of averages. This was the case in large pilot projects, and with minor adjustments, the unit value scheme proved to be sound in application as well as theory. However, costs in pilot programs in single departments were somewhat inflated over traditional staffing costs. Since major importance was given in the entire model to a capability of implementation in any part of a school, a solution was urgently needed.

Major Transitional Costs

During the first pilot year, this was carefully studied and several interrelated problems were identified. Partial implementation usually resulted in a staffing pattern top-heavy with staff teachers, and understaffed with paraprofessionals. Again, basic parts of the philosophy of the Sarasota model conflicted—the proscription against involuntary transfer and the determination to encourage voluntary partial implementation of differentiated staffing. The answer was "to grandfather" some staff members. School systems undertaking a program of flexible staffing should be prepared to assume some additional costs during one or two transition years. These extra costs directly attributable to staff salaries need not be outsized, however, if the model is carefully built, and should not occur at all in large pilot schools, newly opened schools, or where staff vacancies equal at least one-fourth of the total staff size. After one or two years of operation, adjustment of personnel should permit a school or department to fully implement its optimum staffing pattern. At that stage the cost of a differentiated staff will not differ significantly from that of a traditional staff in the same setting. What *will* differ is the number of adults well qualified for the roles they fill in the instructional process. In one Sarasota pilot school sixty-two adults comprised a staff which formerly consisted of forty-five certified personnel. Of the sixty-two, thirty-seven were certified. The marked difference was that the differentiated staff was being more efficiently utilized. Paraprofessionals were performing most of the non-professional tasks formerly undertaken by certified teachers whose time was now freed for professional tasks. The total salary dollars were distributed commensurately, making it possible for the professional teacher to earn a professional salary without leaving the classroom.

Two other major transitional costs in the Sarasota implementation were found to be unavoidable: an inservice education program for members of the staff in pilot projects, and the provision of minimally necessary equipment and building remodeling. These were major in the sense of importance more than in gross dollars. The local experience would suggest that these additional costs of the stages of operation are inevitable if all the interrelated components of flexible organization for instruction are provided.

Inservice Training

During the summer preceding the pilot implementation year, a two-phase inservice program was conducted for the staffs of the pilot schools. The first two-week session held immediately after school closed was attended by leadership personnel, and was devoted primarily to organization of staff, facilities, and scheduling of the individual school projects. Also at that time, a preschool workshop was planned for the entire staff of each pilot school. Again, the emphasis was on planning and preparation for the administration of the pilot programs. Some attention was given to the human relations of the new organization and to the development of flexible, individualized curriculum. This workshop emphasis proved to be the reverse of the need. The costs of an inservice program, however, will exist for these several needs regardless of the order, and will continue throughout the first several operational years. School systems developing projects in differentiated staffing should plan inservice programs in model design and development, implementation mechanics, interpersonal relations, facilities and equipment planning, and most importantly, curriculum development.

Curriculum Development

Any innovative school district should attempt to supplement the inservice budget with other funds. This was done locally by coordinating curriculum development for flexible instructional organization with a major system-wide study of behavioral objectives and writing of courses of study behaviorally. Other components in the total inservice education program were written to help meet the needs of the differentiated staffing pilot schools in human relations, basic subject area updating, and planning for selection and use of materials and equipment.

Materials and Equipment

The provision of materials and equipment in resource centers was the fourth of the major transition costs which included grandfathering staff allocation, curriculum development, and inservice education.

The main media center, already a part of each pilot school, was used to house materials and equipment that were either too expensive or unnecessary to duplicate; or were generalized in content, such as basic reference collections. Some materials, books, and equipment were moved from the main media center to the decentralized resource centers, where their use by students and staff would be facilitated and increased.

In a program of flexible organization for instruction, centers had to be provided in which individual work could be done by students, and in which materials related to the courses of study and coordinated with large-group and small-group instruction were available. These centers were decentralized from the main media center and placed in each major subject. They housed books, audio-visual equipment and materials, and software prepared by the staff or purchased commercially. Their cost included the facility in which they were housed as well as the equipment and materials.

The facilities were often classrooms remodeled by partitioning or removing partitions, but in some cases, were portable classrooms on the school campus. As in most school districts, Sarasota classroom space was limited and often not available for decentralized resource centers, so efficient scheduling and minor remodeling of classrooms for large group and small-group instruction freed some space for resource centers.

As examples, a regular sized classroom was partitioned to house two separate small groups instead of the entire space being assigned to a large one; while two contiguous classrooms were opened into one room that housed a large group. Similar modifications successfully used in the early differentiated staffing programs in other school districts provided a model for Sarasota. All remodeling was done at a relatively low cost.

Equipping the resource centers was an evolutionary process in the Sarasota pilot schools. Materials that were specific to a subject area or discipline were purchased gradually over several years as annual budgets permitted. Small special allocations given each of the pilot schools in their first year were not sufficient for more than basic beginnings for the resource centers. A technique learned from study and visitation of earlier pilot programs in other parts of the country was the preparation of audio and video tapes, filmstrips, slides, and other materials by the staff in lieu of those which could be purchased from commercial outlets. These could be provided for the cost of the raw material, and had the added advantage of absolute and direct relationship to the instructional program.

The reader interested in establishing similar resource centers should not overlook donations as a source of supply, particularly for books. Students, parents, teachers, and other members of the community often will contribute books that will significantly speed up building a usable collection in the center.

Nor should donated time and materials be overlooked in other areas of need. Local citizens are often willing to assist in minor remodeling, and occasionally, a highly interested parent-contractor will donate labor or even materials to larger facilities projects. In this manner, a very fine storage building was provided at a Sarasota school. If the community is adequately informed about the differentiated staffing project, they will recognize that it promises a more efficient and effective utilization of all the resources of the school system, and they will support it fiscally as well as philosophically.

ADJUSTMENTS IN THE MODEL

Earlier in this paper, the need for flexibility in the model—as well as in the instructional organization—has been stressed. In the Sarasota model, it was discovered during the 1970-71 pilot year that the staffing sub-model had two major weaknesses: there were arithmetic errors in the unit indices that caused some inflation in staff costs, and the job specifications were inadequately developed. These problems were considered by the central steering committee and the administration, and an *ad hoc* sub-committee appointed to study and recommend appropriate adjustments in the staffing model.

In the unit index system described earlier in this chapter the staff teacher was fixed as the index point and charged as one unit—the values of all other positions were related to the staff teacher. Essentially, the unit value of any position was proportional to the median salary of that position divided by the mean salary paid system-wide to teachers. For example, if the directing teacher's median salary was $10,500 and each classroom teacher's mean salary was $8,400, the unit index value would be 10,500 divided by 8,400, or 1.25. This arithmetic was applied to all positions on the differentiated staffing models, and yielded the following index values: consulting teacher or principal teacher—1.50; directing teacher—1.25; staff teacher—1.50; instructor—.75; resident intern—.50; instructional assitant—.50; and teacher aide—.35. Thus, all unit values were indexed to the school system's mean salary for classroom teachers. Application of those unit values was expected to satisfy the basic requirement that flexible staffing should not cost significantly more or less than traditional staffing. That principle is mathematically sound if the unit values are correct. The error discovered in the Sarasota model was simply arithmetic, and rather easily corrected after committee examination. What is important is the *concept* of a unit index scheme rather than the simple allocation of a gross number of dollars for staffing. Obviously, if a dollar allocation is made consistent with the school system's budget for traditional staffing, and the cost of any school's staff limited to that amount, inflation cannot occur in employing a differentiated staff. Then why not use that method? When members of an administrative or faculty board (often called a "senate" in other models) are selecting an individual for a particular position on the differentiated staff, they should be free from any consideration except his qualifications. If a dollar price tag is attached, the selectors may be tempted to employ a candidate who is basically qualified, but not quite as outstanding as one who would qualify for more pay under an existing differentiated staffing salary schedule. Conversely, if both candidates would be charged to the school's budget at exactly the same unit value, the board is free to recommend the better candidate with no temptation to save dollars. It will be apparent to the reader that the approach using a straight dollar-type budget format could easily result in providing a larger, but lower salaried staff—an apparent advantage and bargain. Since assigning to each member of the staff the tasks that are most appropriate to his training, experience, and skill is fundamental to flexible staffing, employing other than a person with the best available level of those three qualities will lower the quality of the instructional program. Differentiated staffing is designed to use staff economically by assigning tasks to those appropriately trained and experienced, and is intended to pay staff members accordingly.

The problem of unit values, overall dollar costs, and placement on a salary schedule would not have been as significant if the second weakness in the Sarasota model had not existed—the lack of adequately developed and discrete job specifications. In the local mode, the need for better role development existed to a much larger extent among the professional positions on the staffing sub-model than with the paraprofessional positions. The duties assigned paraprofessionals were often specific and tangible. The paraprofessionals were responsible largely for clerical, technical, and monitorial tasks. The required input for their particular jobs was easily described and the output easily measured. It is less easy to describe and evaluate the teaching act. Thus, it was more difficult to prepare job specifications for the professional roles in the Sarasota differentiated staffing model. Since a task analysis of the learner objectives of the school system is a prerequisite to writing job specifications, each member of the professional staff should contract to meet an appropriate responsibility in the learning process in specific terms of output, and should be evaluated in those terms. The professionals' job specifications then would consist of a statement of the expected results. Salaries paid to those staff members and the length of service in that differentiated staff position would depend upon their performance in terms of the expected output.

At the end of the third year of the Sarasota project and the first full year of operation, job specifications were still largely in terms of input and were tied essentially to traditional salary schedules differentiated according to vertical hierarchy levels.

Therefore, the two major weaknesses discovered in the staffing sub-model and the adjustments completed or sought after the third pilot year were modifications temporarily needed in what has been called a first generation model of differentiated staffing.[4] The need identified in the Sarasota project (and not yet met) is to evolve a second generation model—one in which staffing, scheduling, equipment, materials, and facilities are all based upon structional objectives written in terms of learner behavior; and one in which the staff contracts, and is held accountable for performance. The concept of the differentiated staffing innovation is *inseparable from modification of the total traditional approach to instruction.* It merges inevitably with other major innovations and interests of public school educators in the early seventies, such as behavioral objectives, open concept facilities, performance contracting, and accountability.

EVALUATION

An effective evaluation of the instructional process in relation to the input—accountability—is made in terms of how will it meet its objectives. Programs and activities must be evaluated on the same basis. Often an inadequate program evaluation results from the lack of behaviorally-stated objectives for which the program was prepared initially. This was a significant problem encountered during the first year of complete implementation of differentiated staffing at

Sarasota. As the evaluation of the pilot year was being written, it became evident that it would be largely subjective, presenting observers' opinions on the effect of the flexible organization; for although the observers were well qualified to judge differentiated staffing and compare its/ implementation to earlier traditional organization, they could not present evidence of first year success or failure because the objectives of the pilot program had not been stated — an oversight caused by eagerness to become operational, magnified by inexperience. There can be no justification for the absence of specific objectives, for if they are not known before the project is developed, there is no purpose for the project.

Early in the second year of implementation, the expected outcomes were clearly delineated, including the proposed implementation; the expected effect it would have on attitudes and morale of staff and students; administrative changes to be completed, such as shared decision making; role differentiation; salary differentials; and the first statements of the minimum acceptable increase in learner achievement. The latter should be a direct result of the behavioral objectives stated in each course of study, and is the ultimate purpose of the new instructional organization. It is also most difficult to prepare. Even after measuring the year's growth in student achievement, the evaluators may not know how much to attribute to the flexible organization, or whether the objectives were the right ones in the first place. It may be unimportant to know whether the organizational mechanics were cause or catalyst, but continued subjective examination will soon uncover the positive factors. The latter is a matter of professional experience and expertise. The Sarasota staff learned that innovation carefully planned and implemented is a prerequisite to accountability.

HUMAN RELATIONS

Though largely subjective, the first-year evaluation was by no means unimportant. Several significant problems were discovered that could have caused the program to lose support of many of its staff. These were human relations problems that particularly affected decision making, peer and super- or sub-ordinate evaluation, work loads, and role definition. Opinionnaires answered anonymously, and individual interviews conducted by an external evaluator pointed out administrative discrepancies between perceptions in regard to how participants felt about the project. Staff teachers, instructors, and paraprofessionals frequently stated that their recommendations were not consistently represented by their directing teacher who sat on the decision-making faculty board. Investigation substantiated this concern, but pointed to no purposeful neglect by the directing teachers. New to their role as decision makers, they were unconsciously looking to the principal for decisions as they had done in the previous traditional staff organization. Simply bringing the problem to light cautioned both principal and directing teachers to assume roles more consistent with the design of the faculty board. Directors of differentiated staffing projects in planning and development stages would do well to make training for decision-making an early inservice requirement.

Evaluation of super-ordinates, peers, or sub-ordinates was a new experience for most classroom teachers involved in flexible organization as they had never been responsible for rating other teachers in an official manner and, although they knew they were to evaluate their colleagues, the actual experience was for many somewhat traumatic. The Sarasota staff concluded that little could have been done to foresee the emotional problem inherent in evaluation, but the process could have been made more effective and less fearsome if some techniques of staff evaluation had been presented early in the year in a formal inservice program. Furthermore, the lack of specific objectives again affected a part of the differentiated staffing project. Job specifications were not adequate and did not include statements of specific achievements expected by personnel.

This same deficiency gave rise to two related problems—work loads and role definition—neither of which would have developed to as large an extent if job specifications had been clearly outlined and agreed upon in advance.

SUMMARY

In general, the preliminary philosophy of the Sarasota model of flexible instructional organization was upheld by examination of its pilot implementation. The staff is convinced that the nationally stated principles of differentiated staffing are sound in theory and workable in practice: a career ladder to enable teachers to remain in the classroom with continuing rise in both status and pay of their profession, shared decision-making to provide maximum expertise and commitment to the administrative operation of a school, optimum efficiency in the utilization of professional competency, and flexibility and individualization in the organization for instruction. To these, the Sarasota project developers and participants added an administrative approach to staff differentiation in their model which provided for autonomous selection of a staffing pattern at a school or department, while maintaining a minimum fiscal and personnel consistency system-wide. The Sarasota experience demonstrated that such a model was workable; and that it could be implemented in an existing staff in part or in total without displacing incumbent personnel. The Sarasota staff offer this as their most significant contribution.

The early and continuous imvolvement of the local teachers association, the organization of a central steering committee with strong advisory power, and the commitment to voluntary participation by a school staff in the flexible staffing program are presented as prerequisite to understanding and acceptance of differentiated staffing by all school system staff, *and a sense of proprietorship by those participating.* The preliminary belief of the Sarasota planners that those were essential to success has been strengthened by the local experience and a comparison of it to several projects in other parts of the country.

Finally, the reader is directed back to a review of the early problems encountered in the pilot program in Sarasota. It can be seen that they were the result of deficiencies in planning and preparation, or were the natural growing pains to be expected in major change. None were deficiencies inherent in the concept of flexible instructional organization—differentiated staffing.

Footnotes

1. Oak Avenue Intermediate School, Temple City, California; Mary Harmon Weeks Elementary School, Kansas City, Missouri.

2. Gocio Elemetary School; Gulf Gate Elementary School; Tuttle Elementary School; Venice Elementary School; Sarasota Junior High School; Venice Junior High School.

3. Gene M. Pillot "A Conceptual Design of a System Model of Differentiated Staffing." Doctoral Dissertation, University of Florida, 1970.

4. Fenwick W. English, Arizona-Mesa Differentiated Staffing Project, Arizona State University, Tempe, Arizona.

7 Everything Could Be Up to Date in Kansas City

Miriam Simon

In 1968 citizens of Kansas City, Missouri, dedicated a unique school building, the design and intent of which was tradition-breaking in every way: politically because it put the finest of its 99 schools for its 76,000 students in an all-black, densely populated, somewhat underprivileged area in the central city; educationally by introducing the highly-touted innovations of independent learning, individualized instruction, modular scheduling and open-space concept all under the umbrella of differentiated staffing; and architecturally by combining an elementary and a junior high in one windowless, fully carpeted, air-conditioned unit. The architect originally had planned for shared auditorium, gym and resource facilities, hoping for economic advantages and freer exchange between faculty and students. However, by the time the school's personnel involved in the planning had finished, all that was left of unity was a common tunnel rarely used.

This aloofness was reinforced when the unit was named. The school board considered the schools as two and, in the tried and true Kansas City tradition, named them after dead, reputable, but very different citizens (perhaps foreshadowing future developments): Mary Harmon Weeks, for whom the elementary was named, was a northern white P.T.A. gentlewoman who lived for 89 years and will be remembered by few, and Martin Luther King, Jr., the name given to the junior high, was a grandson of a slave, lived a brief 39 years and will be remembered through history.

The central office administration was only slightly less traditional than the school board. There was fairly firm support for the project, although it always depended on a few individuals. The key individual in the beginning was Donald Hari, who, in four years as assistant superintendent in charge of instruction, brought into being a whole central city innovational complex of which the two schools were part. It was mainly his pressure on the school board, personnel, and teacher agencies that brought about the changes needed to get the project started.

Kansas City in 1968 was a scene of student, community, and racial protest. At the Weeks and King schools there were three superintendents in two years. When the new superintendent came in the fall of 1970, all but one of the assistant superintendents who had served since the project started were gone and the position of assistant superintendent in charge of instruction had been eliminated from the table of organization.

Dr. A. Odell Thurman and Miriam Simon were named Education Professions Development Act director and coordinator, respectively. They set as their main goal the diffusion of decision-making policies to the teachers in regard to all future training, staff selection, role definition, student learning needs, etc.

The question was, would previous decisions made by an advisory committee form a base or a barrier to future teacher decisions?

Two key decisions had been made before the schools opened: selection of the differentiated staffing model; and selection of staff to fill jobs described in that model.

The broad-based advisory committee that designed the staffing pattern and instructional modes for the two schools—assuming a common student body and a common community—saw few differences in the needs of the two buildings. The new categories of personnel, with carefully delineated job descriptions, qualifications and salaries, with slight exception, were a singular pattern, as were training and evaluation plans.

Both at Weeks and King the project was intended to make better use of teacher time, talent and energy through differentiated staff assignments according to teachers' competencies. It provided for the in-service development of teachers to assume new roles. It was hoped that differentiated assignments would allow each teacher to develop a career pattern which reflected his own capabilities, professional preparation, and perception of student needs.

The original plan stated that both schools would be organized for team teaching, with each team including a senior instructor or team leader, one or more instructors, associate instructors, an intern student teacher and a paraprofessional. The design for teaching schedules at both Weeks and King would permit teachers at least one period during each day for planning and give them an opportunity to work together during the school day to develop new curricula relevant to the needs of students in central city schools.

The role of the principal in the implementation of the project was crucial, but the elementary school principal saw differentiated staffing as the tool to maximize all other instructional objectives, while the junior high principal saw it as one component in a long list of variables he needed to put together to make his school function. The difference of priorities and perceptions was critical in the future program development of the staffs in the two schools.

But it was not as simple as that. The junior high presented more complex problems from the beginning.

The paper pattern fit perfectly for the elementary school (see Figure 41). But, although it looked as good in print, it never worked for the junior high (Figure 42).

Once the decision was made to assign responsibilities on the basis of subject areas in the junior high, myriad questions arose. It is clear from deletion-filled files that there was a great deal of indecision about which areas of responsibility should go to a coordinator and which to senior instructors. One wonders why alternative staffing models were not explored at this time, with responsibilities being specialized and teams made interdisciplinary or grade level, rather than departmental. Had this been done, the fate of the project might have been different. As it was, staffing along subject matter lines never facilitated much improved instruction.

Dr. John A. Nelson, Jr., University of California, Santa Barbara, who conducted a brief functional analysis of the Kansas City project for School Personnel Utilization, reported in April, 1971:

> Both schools have similar elements in their formal structure; there are, however, some operational differences. The elementary school is less hierarchical, while the junior high school still maintains a considerable amount of traditional administrative structure. As a result the junior high school staff looks relatively less like a group decision-making body.

This is an accurate observation, and the reason for the operational differences stemmed both from the principals' diverging views and from the subject matter focus in the junior high.

FIGURE 41

Differentiated Staff Organization for Mary Harmon Weeks Elementary School

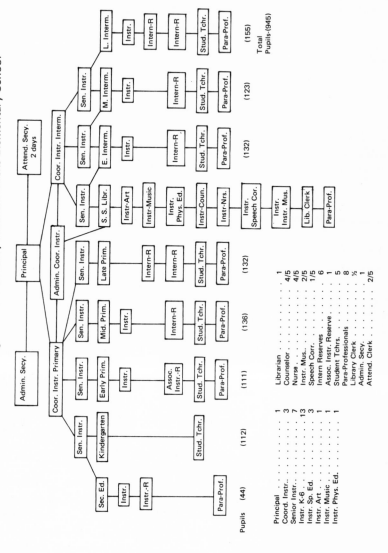

Principal	1
Coord. Instr.	3
Senior Instr.	7
Instr. K-6	13
Instr. Sp. Ed.	3
Instr. Art	1
Instr. Music	1
Instr. Phys. Ed.	1
Librarian	1
Counselor	4/5
Nurse	4/5
Instr. Mus.	2/5
Speech Corr.	1/5
Intern Reserves	6
Assoc. Instr. Reserve	1
Student Tchrs.	5
Para-Professionals	8
Library Clerk	½
Admin. Secy.	1
Attend. Clerk	2/5

FIGURE 42

Differentiated Staff Organization for
Martin Luther King Junior High School

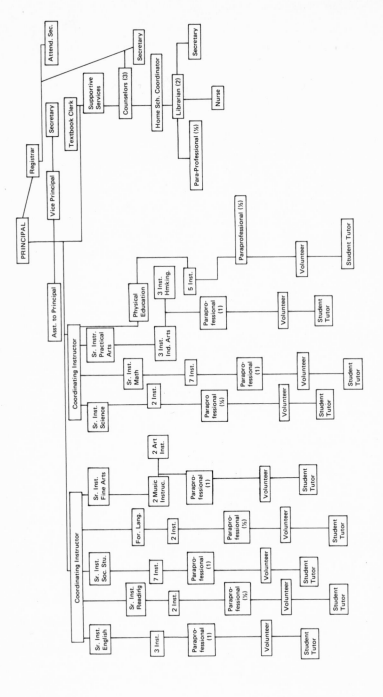

Because the elementary principal considered the staffing an enabling device, he hammered away at personnel until he got "enablers" for his leadership positions. He also built his schedule around daily planning time for each team, believing this to be creative or "enabling" time.

On the other hand, the junior high staff always complained about the unqualified people they got "from downtown." For their part, the personnel office pointed to the junior high file as a document of indecision in staff selection. "I know big city systems can be faceless," one man said, "but it just isn't true in this case. We could never get information as to what kind of people they wanted there."

It was probably the subject matter focus that led to the vertical hierarchy in King Junior High. The coordinating instructors—knowing that they could not be "master teachers" in each and every subject area for which they were responsible—totally rejected this concept. Instead, with no one offering alternative suggestions, they gravitated toward the front office and, in a voluminous list of duties compiled at the end of the first year, showed over 80 percent of their activities to be administrative. That year over, future attempts to change their roles became fruitless.

In most cases, senior instructors are the stereotyped "department heads" who, as members of an instructional council, make decisions which they pass on to their teams.

The varying sizes of the teams made joint planning an impossibility in the junior high when that was not a priority. But it was this planning time insisted upon by the elementary principal that proved the vehicle for group decision making.

His suggestions for team planning time are in Appendix A. In addition, he created a complex communications system of committees that insures decision making across team lines (Figure 43).

As a result, his teachers became the decision makers with regard to hiring, firing, and replacement of personnel, space utilization, assignment of students, time, and materials, and in-service activities. A detailed "Revised Organization" report from the school at the end of 1971 listed in great detail personnel recommendations. The last paragraph reads:

The recommendations we have made are in keeping with the philosophy of the Differentiated Staff in that all principal parties were involved in the implementation and refinement of the above suggestions. All of the recommendations came from many source suggestions throughout the initial two years of operation. We, the staff of the Mary Harmon Weeks elementary school, are

enthusiastic and committed to the philosophy and approach of the Differentiated Staffing Plan and feel that the true involvement of staff in all planning and
implementation of program has made significant gains in improving the educational climate for both staff, pupils, and parents of the Mary Harmon Weeks
school community.

Originally, the training plans were identical, but again, differences
in emphasis soon became noticeable.

FIGURE 43

Team Interaction Chart — Differentiated Staffing
Mary Harmon Weeks Elementary School

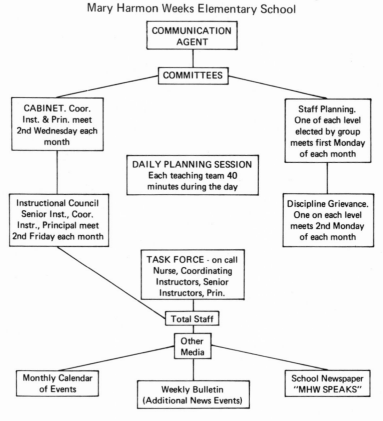

In the summer of 1968, before the schools opened and before federal funding, the school district conducted a three-week workshop for both staffs. The elementary school staff, having decided to use its structure as the tool to accomplish all other things, spent much time on team roles and responsibilities.

The workshop held for the junior high, with no priorities, tried to "cover all pertinent aspects" with strong emphasis on modular scheduling. Small group, large group, and independent study were frightening new concepts. The consultants were unanimous in their stressing students' needs, different modes of instruction, etc. — but mainly it was a time of desperate production of work sheets to go with traditional texts to be prepared for students on unstructured time. Differentiated staffing was barely discussed.

The following summer, the four coordinators went to sensitivity sessions: two to Bethel, Maine, and two to the University of Missouri.

Further orientation to modular scheduling, innovative curriculum and differentiated staffing was afforded both staffs during 1969-70 when about thirty teachers from each school took field trips to sites throughout the United States.

While King was putting forth all its effort just to meet each day as it came, Weeks was in a position to move forward. As one of three innovative schools opened in 1967-68, Weeks was assigned a research assistant from the local school district's Department of Research and Development for program evaluation. Though also offered to King, this research never took place. Thus was lost important feedback that could have provided (as it did for Weeks) team development during these two crucial developmental years.

Dr. Mary Meehan of this department, in working with Weeks Elementary School, identified those elements they considered important for evaluation. Half of the evaluation effort was geared to measure achievement and pupils' attitudes and opinions. The other half—key to developing group decision-making—was evaluation of planning sessions and staff reactions to the experimental situation. Senior and coordinating instructors soon were made aware they "were doing most of the talking" and, by May the observer could report that more team members spoke with increasing frequency and brevity.

Another assist to Weeks was that early in its development the coordinating instructors were instructional-oriented rather than administrative minded. The coordinator of the intermediate department, a former principal and research assistant, presented Jerome

Bruner's materials, "Man: A Course of Study," through in-service sessions for his teachers, to encourage teachers to help students organize ideas, shape, and stimulate thought. Evaluation by the research department stated:

During 1969-70, the teachers under the leadership of the instructional coordinator attempted the difficult task of learning both the content and processes required for *Man: A Course of Study* as they taught the unit to their students. Now that some strengths and weaknesses of the first year's experiences have been identified, the second year could be the time to identify with greater precision the desired pupil behaviors and to develop effective approaches to their evaluation.

Second year training was to be based on teacher decisions with attention being paid to Phase II of the project: Curriculum Development.

After a UNIPAC workshop in August, 1970, Weeks Elementary School decided to take one segment of its curriculum at a time and re-do it completely, setting up performance criteria and developing learning tasks for each level of achievement, the mathematics curriculum first. In October, the total staff attended a two-day workshop with consultants from Cherry Creek, Colorado, and the local school district. During the school term, teams designated their staff development day to develop skills and behavioral objectives for this mathematics curriculum in detail. In June they held a five-day write-in workshop using those staff members selected by the staff for their organizational and writing ability to edit, rewrite and reorganize those materials produced by the staff, the materials to be field-tested and refined in the following year.

There was no follow-up to the UNIPAC workshop at King. Other decisions had to be made first.

Fenwick English, Project Director, Arizona-Mesa Differentiated Staffing Consortium, Arizona State University, reported local school impressions after an U.S.O.E. inter-project visitation on December 14, 1970:

1. The training program has been very successful at Weeks Elementary School. Teachers appear to be committed, dedicated and enthusiastic. Overall, the staffing pattern fits nicely into the overall school program and is complimentary to its objectives. Weeks is a good model of how further specialization at the elementary level can upgrade and offer an exciting educational program.

2. The program at Martin Luther King, Jr. Junior High has been less than successful. The major problem does not appear to be that of differentiated staffing but rather a problem in the utilization of unstructured time by pupils on the flexible schedule. This, in turn, has a marked effect on school climate and atmosphere and has resulted in lowered staff morale and high fatigue.

The faculty welcomed Dr. English's report. It gave added impetus to a small group who had already completed a plan to reduce, eliminate or restructure (preferably the latter) student unstructured time either within blocks on flexible scheduling or without flexible scheduling.

They then proceeded to take the following steps:

(1) Through small group meetings they secured solid staff commitment to adopt new schedule changes.

(2) Through the Leadership Training Institute (LTI) at the University of Massachusetts arranged a teacher exchange to get other technical assistance for their problems. The principal and the co-ordinating instructor who, sensing the need, had emerged as "change agent," traveled to Portland, Oregon, a site with similar concerns and problems, to correct the situation. While in Portland, they had also a productive visit with Harold Wik, Project Director, in Beaverton. On the other end of the exchange, two team leaders from Portland visited King Junior High, at the same time serving as consultants for a two-day workshop to work on team objectives and team planning.

With unstructured time eliminated and with team planning time available for all teams, attention was now directed to another of Dr. English's observations:

The school attempted to create a modern educational program without adequate financial support. The material backup is very ordinary and is still very much a basic text-book based program. While differentiated staffing is a reality to some extent, it has not resulted in differentiated instruction. Teacher behavior is still aimed at groups for the most part and could only be described as very traditional. The operational methodology of the staff is not congruent with the aims of the school, its schedule, nor its philosophy.

Differentiated roles do not appear to be based upon a systematic needs assessment of the King students, nor do they appear to be very responsive or flexible.

In view of these findings, an extensive plan was developed. The E.P.D.A. project staff decided to set aside King's share of the 1970-71 E.P.D.A. grant to establish the Martin Luther King Hot Idea Fund based somewhat on Dr. English's performance-contracting ideas. Proposals were invited to fund special student-teacher learning projects that would differentiate teacher instruction based upon an assessment of student needs.

The E.P.D.A. coordinator spent a week meeting with teams, in the King building, helping to draft proposals.

A giant step away from the traditional text was taken by the math department when it ordered two programs: *Individualizing Mathematics* by Addison-Wesley and a multi-media program by Educational Progress Corporation. After attending a workshop in Louisville, Kentucky, conducted by Dr. Foley (one of the authors of the Addison-Wesley program), one of the teachers conducted training sessions for the math department on how to individualize instruction.

Responding to vocational needs of students, several teachers had practical proposals to make: "Buy me some motors and tools and I'll offer a course in small engine repair to those students who can use that skill for summer employment," said a young welding teacher. "Buy me some materials on personal typing and shorthand and teach me how to make transparencies and slides, and I'll have girls ready to work this summer," promised a business education teacher. The English department said "if we knew more about media, we could differentiate instruction." They, along with the business education teacher, attended a media workshop. The whole industrial arts department attended a "World of Construction Workshop" in the summer and with the purchase of materials is now the only junior high school in the state of Missouri to participate in this project for the 1971-72 year. A social studies team agreed to try an urban action project to get students out of the classroom into the community to study sociology where it happens.

Changes became apparent in the school. Elimination of unstructured time obviously helped the morale of students and teachers. Ensuing proposals showed that teachers were in touch with what students need and wanted only to be encouraged in meeting them. Through retraining and providing necessary time and materials, instruction could be differentiated at the teacher level.

But the issue of differentiated staffing still remains where it was.

Weeks has a well-developed in-house appraisal procedure worked out in which the staff itself selects personnel and decides how it is utilized. If any staffing pattern is to work at King, there has to be a distribution of power to include the teacher. The staff needs to decide all together what the goals of the school are and how to reach them as a team.

One objective of the school personnel utilization program of differentiated staffing was to attract and hold competent teachers in these central city schools. The senior instructor was the staff member directly responsible for supervising student and beginning teachers. Vicarious and actual training has been attempted in the first three years of the program, with better results in the elementary school than in the junior high. In the last year of funding, a systematic ongoing experiential workshop for training more effective supervising teachers is being conducted for the senior instructors by Mid-continent Regional Educational Laboratory. This training is being correlated with training in research and development procedures for coordinating instructors.

Persistent recruitment efforts, at the elementary level, have resulted in a full complement of student teachers each semester, with cooperating colleges now beginning to fight for spots. Similar help is being given King, to try to establish the same resource. All the aides in both schools are in the Career Opportunities Program. This has proven most beneficial to the staff at Weeks. (King may again regard it merely extra trouble.) The Kansas City Junior League has adopted King for its volunteer project and their help will be given to the school to see if this proves beneficial.

Steps are being taken by the project staff to develop a closer liaison with the University of Missouri at Kansas City through adoption of the King-Weeks complex as a staff development school in order to share what has been learned and use more expertise in further development of concepts only barely tried.

What, then, is the future of the Kansas City Differentiated Staffing project?

In the beginning when Dr. Hair moved both the central office and the board of directors to adopt a differentiated pay scale for seven levels of staff at an extra cost to the district of more than $80,000, he avoided the American Federation of Teachers' objections to "merit pay" and "vertical hierarchy" by bluntly stating that the extra pay was for extra time for extra-instructional duties. The union, which is the bargaining agent, agreed to differentiated staffing in the two pilot schools, but went on record as opposing any further implementation until the goals of effective utilization of professional staff had demonstrated a genuine benefit to the students in these schools.

These schools, as all schools in the project nationally, are finding it necessary to specify what aspects of a staffing pattern affect student outcomes. The elementary school has evidence that differentiated staffing can be an effective tool in enabling instructional improvement, with its students' reading scores now higher than those of students in surrounding schools.

To demonstrate inner system transferability of differentiated staffing, the elementary school principal, in the spring of 1971, applied for a job of principal at a traditional school with the stipulation he be allowed to differentiate the existing staff, and in the belief that, through utilization of differentiated staffing, any faculty, by the rearrangement of teacher time and talent, could improve pupil outcomes and its own development. However, suffering from consecutive levy defeats and facing budget cuts, the school district did not respond.

While the union points to King Junior High as an example of unsound hierarchical arrangement, it does not mention Weeks Elementary as it continues to use differentiated staffing as a negotiable item in its demands for increased financial and welfare benefits for teachers and paraprofessionals.

There are much broader benefits to students and teachers accruing at Weeks Elementary School under its differentiated staffing, both for the present and future. The question is, will these broader benefits be transferred to the rest of the system when a slightly less traditional board sits with the yet unimpressed union to contemplate a new budget in the face of its most recent levy defeat?

APPENDIX A

MARY HARMON WEEKS SCHOOL

Suggestions For Team Planning Sessions

As we begin our third year at Mary Harmon Weeks, we find that our emphasis is on curriculum improvement and the team planning necessary for such improvement to take place.

We suggest that each team work out their planning sessions to include the following:

MUSTS In Each Week's Planning
1. Presentation of subject area plans to the team
2. Evaluation of activities
3. Organization and scheduling of activities
4. Consideration of individual and group learning problems

5. Preparation and planning of materials and activities by individuals
6. Preparation and planning of materials and activities by Specialist-teams
7. Staff development activities

ALSO INCLUDE When Applicable
1. Reports from Cabinet, Instructional Council and Committees
2. Discussion of Special Events (Assemblies, Testing, Schedules, etc.)

It is also suggested that a schedule of planning be set up in which two days are used for planning and evaluation, one day for Staff Development and two days for individual and Specialist-team planning. Many teams used this type of organization last year.

APPENDIX B

Sample Schedule For Weekly Planning Time

Day	Members Involved	Major Emphasis
Monday	Total Team	Evaluation of previous weeks' activities. Discussion of individual pupil and group learning problems.
Tuesday	Specialist-teams or Individuals	Lesson planning Materials preparation Interteam visitation Supportive service visitation
Wednesday	Total Team	Staff development activities (Resource Center Orientation, Unipac Workshop follow-up, other in-service activities)
Thursday	Specialist-team or Individuals	Same as Tuesday
Friday	Total Team	Planning, organizing, scheduling next week's activities

The following specifics will assist us in implementing this plan for improving the effectiveness of team planning. During the month of September, each team will schedule with Mrs. Rowan time for in-depth orientation to new materials and equipment in the Resource Center.

Other scheduled staff development activities will include Unipac Workshop follow-up, coordinating instructor's summer institute follow-up, and work with team Teaching Modules, a semi-programmed course for in-service improvement of skills required for team teaching.

Interteam visitations will be scheduled beginning in October. This visitation will foster dissemination of ideas within our program. These visits can occur at planning time or any other time when staff members are free of team responsibility and will continue through-out the year.

In order to assure continued and improved communication and correlation of curriculum with the members of the supportive services team, beginning in September, each senior instructor will be scheduled to meet with this team at its planning time at least once a month. Supporting service team members will be scheduled to visit and meet with other teams.

There is need for paraprofessionals to regularly be a part of team planning. This will be worked out and scheduled according to each team's requirements.

Each Senior Instructor is asked to make out an agenda for the Monday and Friday total-team planning session and to provide copies for each team member and the Coordinating Instructor. These should be filed, in order that a complete record of the team's activities may be built.

Attached is a sample form of the agenda which Senior Instructors may use, as we begin our sessions this year. Teams may desire to revise it as needs arise to fit specific situations.

Edythe Darton
Aurelia Johnson
Earle Kenyon
Eugene Wolkey

Team Planning Agenda

Team _____   Date _____

I. Presentation of subject Area Plans
   A. Immediate
   B. Long-Range

II. Evaluation

III. Organization and Scheduling

IV. Reports

V. Consideration of Individual and Group Learning Problems

Suggested Reading

Bhaerman, Robert D. "Several Educators' Cure for the Common Cold, Among Other Things—or—One Unionist View of Staff Differentiation," *Quest Paper No. 7,* Washington, D.C., American Federation of Teachers, 1971.

English, Fenwick W. "Interim Report On-Site Observations and a Report of Findings of the Martin Luther King, Jr. Junior High School-Kansas City, Missouri," Arizona-Mesa Differentiated Staffing Consortium, Mesa, Arizona, December 1970.

Hair, Donald, and Hazlett, James A. "A Plan for Differentiated Staffing: Mary Harmon Weeks Elementary School and Martin Luther King, Jr. Junior High School," Public School District of Kansas City, Missouri, November 1968.

Meehan, Mary. "The Evaluation of C. A. Franklin School, James School and Mary Harmon Weeks School: Progress Reports for 1968-69," Research Department of the Public School District of Kansas City, Missouri, October, 1969.

Meehan, Mary. "A Report on a Simulation Exercise and Related Activities for the Evaluation of Pupil Learnings, in *Man: A Course of Study* by Jerome Bruner," Research Department of the Public School District of Kansas City, Missouri, October, 1970.

Nelson, John A. "Kansas City, Missouri, Differentiated Staffing Project: a Functional Analysis," Santa Barbara, California: University of California, April, 1971.

8 The Mesa Model: Generation II

James Zaharis

The main thrust of the Mesa project is to prove the feasibility of a different conceptual base for a differentiated staffing hierarchy. The premise is that a static hierarchy of teaching roles cannot be based on the needs of pupils, for when needs change (as they will if instruction is effective), roles, too, must enjoy the capacity of change. The Mesa approach is to create a fluid model whereby teaching roles are defined by particular pupil needs in a particular building. When these needs are met, through a performance contract, the roles end.

Teaching tasks are related to pupil needs via an on-going needs assessment of pupils. Roles are differentiated horizontally, but they do not assume a hierarchy until a specific set of objectives—the learning situation—and time frame are established. The scheme also allows for the formation and re-formation of various sub-hierarchies. At the expiration of the time frame (which is in the form of a performance contract) any ranking of position reverts to a horizontal position until a new set of objectives in a new time frame has been negotiated and accepted.

A fluid arrangement of roles demands a fluid pay structure and a different method of allocating resources when specific outcomes are achieved. This has resulted in the notion of internal educational performance contracting now peculiar to Mesa. Each school responds to the Request for Proposal (RFP) with a school bid that specifies the objectives, results, outcome, time limits, and cost of reaching their objective.

The RFP assumes that no one set of differentiated skills is any more valuable than any other until specific objectives and a time frame are established. There are no salary ceilings, and staffs create and manipulate the salary mechanism within the context of the "bids."

The Mesa training program has therefore emphasized the acquisition of staff "process" skills such as group dynamics and other conflict resolution techniques, inquiry and other more technical skills, such as continual model building, curriculum planning, altering schedules and changing time/space configurations in meeting RFP specifications.

There is no generic Mesa model to which all schools must comply or train. Training is aimed at preparing an entire school staff to develop the process skills to continually prepare their own models of staff differentiation. Mesa sees differentiated staffing as a means to an end. No *a priori* administrative decisions have been made about what type and kind of positions shall be in the model or their ultimate worth. Such decisions are left to the determination of the individual staffs when they are a part of a strategy to reach specified objectives in given time limits. It is hoped that this continual analysis of pupil need and teacher behavior will engender the establishment and maintenance of a contract between a staffing pattern and client needs. Since clients are site-specific and individualistic, staffing patterns must also be specific if they are to be responsive.

DEVELOPMENTAL ACTIVITIES

The Mesa School District had a three-year history of innovation in sections of the school district. A regional Elementary and Secondary Education Act Title III center was located in Mesa and this had produced a grass roots interest in innovation. A symposium in differentiated staffing (DS) was initiated in the summer of 1969. Key local and state administrators, professors, and teacher association officers were asked to enter into dialogue with the consultants during the two-day seminar. Conceptual cobwebs were cleared away regarding the original DS idea. The end result was a general interest in DS and awareness on the part of the training institutions, state department of education and education associations. A real commitment was made by the leadership of the Mesa School District to seek funds for implementing this concept in cooperation with Arizona State University Department of Secondary Education, Southwestern Co-operative Educational Laboratory (SWCEL) at Albuquerque, New Mexico, Mesa Community College, and Casa Grande elementary schools. The rationale for the consortium was:

1. Each member has a different approach, responsibility, and perspective that may be utilized to achieve the overall goals.

2. Unless there is a consortium effort such as that by Education Profession Development Act, the result will be a fragmented effort.

3. It allows for the concentration of institutions and their re-sources on the problems of assessment of student needs, and subsequent training and more effective utilization of personnel in the staffing of public schools.

4. It gives freedom and latitude to move in alternative directions, and provides a responsive relationship among all participants.

5. It has the necessary components for developing an idea from conception through planning and implementation.

6. Its broad base helps dissemination and implementation of training models because of commitment at each state of development by every kind of educational institution.

The consortium idea had its strengths and weaknesses. In retro-spect it is extremely difficult to make real institutional change when there is the commitment of only a few persons in one department. Distance was also a problem for the SWCEL personnel. The Casa Grande schools' teacher association voted not to participate or allow a pilot school. The major responsibility for the implementation of the project fell to the Mesa schools.

In January, 1970, a district-wide conference was held for all personnel on differentiated staffing with two special consultants, Fenwick English and James Olivero, as well as key teachers from Temple City, California. The major documents on differentiated staffing were given to every teacher in the district for reading prior to the conference.

In the spring of 1970 schools interested in becoming pilot schools for differentiated staffing were asked to apply for consideration. The application form stated the goals of the project and suggested preliminary activities for school staffs prior to final model develop-ment (Zaharis, 1970):

1. We need to gather data about students, teachers, and parents of each school, including
   a. achievement scores,

   b. attitudes of parents toward school and what they want their children to accomplish there,

   c. population characteristics,

   d. direction over all students and teachers,

   e. definition of the curriculum objects for students, their grade levels, etc.

2. What should a differentiated staffing model do?

   a. define outcomes

   (Don't attempt to define roles at this point)

3. What don't you want the model to do?

4. This is the time for mapping out the performance objectives you want from your students, teachers, and curriculum, and from this we will go back and design a staffing arrangement to meet these objectives.

Criteria Upon Which Schools Who Want To Be Involved in Pilot Project Will Be Judged:

1. Demonstrated past efforts with other innovative programs, projects, proposals, etc. These efforts may have involved team teaching, Educational Television, programmed instruction, application of media to classroom instruction, use of teacher aides, team leaders, etc.

2. Demonstrated staff commitment and involvement in deciding whether to apply. Staff members should realize that change will be difficult at times. Change produces the necessity for scrutiny of practice, and scrutiny of your school staff will be increased. These factors will be offset to some degree by increased application of the project's resources to the schools selected as pilot models. Another aspect of commitment will be *time*. Staffs should understand that while stipends will be made available for part of the training, and much consultant help will be available for work in small groups, there will be other occasions which cannot be anticipated or always remunerated.

Six schools demonstrated interest in the project, four applied and three were selected. Fremont Junior High, Holmes Elementary, and Lincoln Elementary. Teachers were given an opportunity to transfer if they desired; none did. In general Holmes and Fremont had young, innovative staffs, and Lincoln was the second most tenured staff in the district.

Each staff was given ten video tapes on various elements of differentiated staffing, along with a study guide and final test. These increased everyone's understanding of terms and the function of a staffing pattern within the total configuration of a school operation.

During the month of May a steering committee was chosen with representatives from each school. Their function was to help the project administration become sensitive to the climate of the schools, as training was underway, and to help establish the necessary components of the first summer training. With the steering committee's guidance the first summer training schedule was designed with the following specifications:

Skills Necessary for Achieving Goals of Summer Training

It is apparent that if we are to specify what should happen with students, teachers will need to be trained to engage in an extensive and somewhat detailed negotiation with the Board of Education over contracts. Skills needed include:

1. Ability to specify student outcomes precisely in the cognitive, affective and psychomotor domains so as to become accountable for student progress.

2. Ability to "package" curricula in ways which optimally meet the unit objectives in the time limit required for maximum student achievement.

3. If all children are to achieve some "baseline" skills and knowledge, teachers will have to be trained to respond or subcontract diagnostic skills in various subject areas to other teachers at other schools in order to take maximum advantage of limited manpower.

4. Ability to assess adequately and accurately student learning within the required dimensions. Good background in tests and measures, and other methods of evaluation (since teacher-made tests will probably be used because of the nature of the short units involved).

5. Ability to discuss professional problems adult-to-adult, and to assign both professional personnel and students to work groups.

6. Ability to assess the relative contributions of staff members in order to meet the "contract" specifications; and to assess each other's contributions when the unit is completed.

7. Ability to negotiate contract specifications with the Board of Education; extensive dialogue sessions regarding performance with another group of adults or lay citizens.

8. Ability to cost and quantify key variables related to contracting with the Board of Education regarding pupil behavioral change.

The training schedule had to be developed with an eye toward the common and unique needs of each school. Remember, the emphasis was on *building* a model with their skills based in their needs, not on learning a preconceived model.

Training Climate

The following taken from the complete project profile indicates the necessary conditions under which training can be attempted. They. are offered in the hope that other schools and systems appreciate the process of participation and re-thinking objectives necessary for developing new staffing patterns.

Creative human action, the kind and type necessary to accomplish the goals set forth in the Arizona-Mesa Differentiated Staffing Project, cannot occur in an atmosphere of mistrust, hostility, or fear. Research provides abundant evidence that if any of those elements are substantially present people will not reveal their feelings. Consequently games are played, appearances are managed, but little changes.

In order to establish the appropriate climate for the concerted push necessary to realize the summer EPDA objectives, certain ground rules should be established. These will promote the development of a climate in which the necessary cooperative action can be developed and expressed. The characteristics of this climate may be summarized as follows:

1. Full and free communication among project staff members (also consultants, observers);

2. Reliance on open consensus in managing conflict, as opposed to coercion, oppression, or compromise;

3. Influence based upon competence rather than on personal whim, politics, or formal power;

4. Respect for norms that permit expression of emotions as well as professional behavior;

5. Acceptance of conflict as a natural phenomenon to be coped with willingly and openly rather than suppressed.

It will be the goal of the project staff to create and to monitor the development of an open climate in which interaction and the development of ideas can be jointly examined, challenged and fostered. From time-to-time the project staff will ask the participants for written expression of their feelings and thoughts in order to ascertain whether the open climate desired for productive work is in fact a reality.

Project Goals

General Goal: To specifically improve pupil performance of the Mesa Public Schools' program.

The Mission: To develop a more flexible and responsive staff deployment model.

Goal Inhibitors	*Goal Facilitators*
Mechanistic, artificial learning environment	Stimulating, client-centered, inquiry-based programs
Sterile, non-assessable curricula	Performance curricula with validated needs assessment design and criteria
Inflexible staffing patterns	Flexible (fluid) staffing patterns
Lack of role specialization	Role differentiation
Inadequate materials	Expanded material support system
Lack of paraprofessional support system	Expanded/differentiated paraprofessional support system
Inadequate funds	Procurement of outside funds
Lack of program accountability	Mechanism for school system accountability
Inflexible facilities	"Open-space" buildings

The EPDA Project Aims to:

1. Develop a more flexible staffing model peculiar or unique to each school;
2. Develop a system of staff-board accountability generic to all schools.

The Desired Objectives

1. A new staffing model which
   a. Is client-centered (roles are based on defined student objectives and centered on tasks to be accomplished from defined student needs);
   b. Creates a model in which roles are fluid (that can be changed in relationship to one another as the tasks change and student needs change);
   c. Fosters a humanistic school climate conducive to learning;
   d. Promotes a shift from teaching per se, to the management of learning;

e. Provides a means whereby teachers can develop a career in teaching as in other professions and be paid commensurate with what they may earn as administrators if promoted;

f. Provides a criterion of teacher salary which reflects responsibility and performance of students rather than solely time served or units accrued.

2. A system of accountability is developed whereby all those responsible to the public for the education of children may be related to the growth and development of the student (the client);

a. Performance outcomes expected of students (and validated) are defined as baseline criteria for the schools;

b. A system of contracting is developed whereby the professional staff is accountable for the expenditure of an agreed upon number of resources to educate children in a specific way and which will include personnel, time, materials, and related sub-contracted services desired.

Limitations

Limitations	*Tentative Solution*
1. Insufficient development funds	1. Obtain funds from interested agencies
2. Lack of time for staff to plan	2. Provide staff planning time with adequate incentives
3. Absence of training program to meet actual staff needs	3. Have pilot staffs define own needs
4. Lack of expertise	4. Develop training program for staff and obtain expertise via consultants
5. No community support	5. Involve the community in facets of training program, and disseminate facts via community organs
6. Lack of ability to predict if new models will perform better and meet specified criteria	6. Field test models for performance specificity and revise where necessary
7. Lack of procedures for developing contracting specifications	7. Devise procedures and stimulate/revise

Limitations (cont'd.)	*Tentative Solution (cont'd.)*
8. Insufficient teacher association involvement	8. Involve association on steering committee and training program
9. Lack of general staff understanding and support	9. Disseminate project results to general staff; conduct total staff needs assessment/readiness survey to determine staff understanding
10. Inability to determine if expansion is desirable.	10. Develop criteria of desirability to determine if expansion is warranted; involve those with interest in outcome.

Each participant was given a complete system analysis profile for each of the two major objectives. At this point there was still a great deal of mistrust. The fear was that project administrators had some preconceived model of staffing hidden under the table. To establish a level of trust, all information was made public.

BUILDING THE FIRST MODEL

A semi-programmed booklet was developed by English and Zaharis (1970) entitled *How to Build a Model of Staff Differentiation,* wherein the authors' chief interests were in

1. Assessing the benefits from various organizations—the attempt was made to emphasize that schools must be client-centered—and

2. Defining the complexity of a task by analyzing its a) job depth—the range of tasks which must be performed by a job incumbent, and b) job scope—the range of application of the tasks in the whole organization for which the job incumbent is responsible.

A fourteen-step process was undertaken for constructing site-specific models in the Mesa Schools. Note that pupil needs and objectives are specified prior to the analysis of teacher tasks. This assures the building of teacher roles that are sensitive to student need. Previously most models had been constructed from a sample analysis of present teacher functions. The question was never asked whether these new roles are necessary for assuring student success based on need. This step represented a real breakthrough in the rationale for establishing school staffing patterns. The following sequence was used for building the model in this project.

1. *Identify pupil performance objectives.* List in detail what the students need to know, feel, and be able to do at the end of a given period of time.
2. *Outline primary teacher tasks* to meet the pupil objectives.
3. *Group teacher tasks* on the basis of like teaching skills for achieving the objectives with disciple (subject) cohesiveness or cross discipline relationships (inter-disciplinary).
4. *Sequence the primary work tasks,* giving priority according to student entry skills as to what should be learned first.
5. *Develop secondary work tasks* to accompany primary work tasks.
6. *Group work tasks into homogeneous clusters* by skills and begin to relate to possible teacher roles.
7. *Relate skill cluster areas to hypothetical teacher roles.* "Play" with the roles. Arrange a set of tasks and create roles to match them. Juxtapose the roles, move them about, take hypothetical problems with students and ascertain how practical the roles are. Does such staff expertise exist? Could some roles which will be heavily used be further divided for greater pupil efficiency?
8. *Develop first set of staff roles into a pattern.* Relate them to time and space. Would facilities have to be changed? What about the paraprofessional support system needed? How would curriculum have to be altered? Is the media base adequate?
9. *Evaluate the staffing pattern.* After sketching the staffing pattern out and noting three or four main tasks and skills for each role (in global terms) use the following criteria for a first check:
   a. Is it client-centered?
   b. Do roles relate specifically and concretely to tasks?
   c. Is it flexible? Can it respond to the changing needs of pupils?
   d. Is it centered on primary work tasks? Does the natural ordering of roles use as its base a sequence based upon work priorities rather than an artificial ordering via authority relationships?
   e. Are controls of the patterns transactional, i.e., do all members of the unit, including the leader (principal) determine the structure, the responsibilities, and the goals of the unit; the norms governing its operation, and the standards of performance?
   f. Will the staffing pattern provide opportunities for intrinsic rewards for teachers based upon their desire to help children, be close to children and see children progress? Is group cohesiveness planned?
   g. Are all the above characteristics operational within the limits defined by the larger organization?

h. Do cooperative relationships exist between the members to accomplish the objectives, the tasks?

i. Has the interdependence between members and sub-groups of the team been planned for? Do they exist?

j. Do the members of the team possess the necessary skills to accomplish the objectives; if not, how can the skills be acquired?

10. *Rewrite the staffing pattern.* Take a second "cut" on the roles. Develop some rough job descriptions. Pay some heed to mechanics and nitty-gritty at this point like scheduling, record-keeping, etc.

11. *Refine the staffing pattern.* Have team members act out some typical situations. Evaluate the simulated effects.

12. *Develop job indices.* Spell out precisely how and under what conditions certain roles are to realize pupils' objectives. Under what conditions are role priorities determined, changed and decided upon?

13. *Operationalize staffing pattern.* Using a "force-field" analysis, decide how to implement the staffing pattern, noting barriers, obstacles, etc.

14. *Decide when to evaluate.* Each model should have built-in provisions for feedback and a preliminary determination of when and how changes are made in the model after implementation. Criteria may be developed on which to judge the efficacy of what was accomplished.

It became apparent that future training should be defined by the staff in order to meet their identified goals, rather than being developed by the project administration's assumptions of what they thought was needed. This evaluation provided the needs assessment basis for the RFP bidding format for internal performance contracting. This new process of allowing schools to define their own methods, means and training procedures for reaching project goals has provided a more individualized training program. It also gave real ownership of the differentiated staffing model to the teachers. This transition of ownership is crucial to any innovation that is to go beyond the talking stage.

ORGANIZATIONAL DATA GATHERING

One of the problems of any innovation is the "hothouse effect"—surfacing of personnel problems once dormant but magnified by external pressure to produce. A differentiated staffing pattern demands an easy (or free) atmosphere in which emotions' can surface and problems can be openly solved. It was evident that many of our staff did communicate well with children, but that they couldn't talk with other adults. "Hot data" or emotion-charged feelings were unable to surface, making group decision-making very difficult. When a decision *was* made there was little commitment to it. Therefore it became imperative to introduce techniques to "flush out" the personal problems in order to resolve them. Two of the techniques used were "intergroup building" and "organizational slice."

Intergroup Building

This is a useful technique by which two groups experiencing some difficulties in communication or working relationships identify problems and initiate procedures by which they may be resolved. It is a fact of life in organizations that everyone is part of the problem. There is a tendency for groups to place the blame on others, the ambiguous "they;" but intergroup building makes both groups realize that all are part of the problem.

Problem Identification and Procedure

Step 1. A "match" is made when both groups have identified the same problem in relatively the same intensity and give it more or less equal importance. The groups should proceed over the two agendas identifying the items which both agree upon. These should then be prioritized.

Step 2. "Gaps" or "mismatches" occur when one group is oblivious to the concerns of another. Incongruity of the two lists should be identified. Gaps should be filled in cooperatively so that the one group may receive a first-hand accounting of the feelings of the other.

Step 3. Identify "intensity differentials," which are made when one group is more agitated about a problem than the other. Each group should identify where it thinks the others do not realize its deep and pervasive feelings. This, too, should be openly communicated. Meetings should continue until one side feels it has reached a point where it understands intuitively and emotionally what the other is saying.

Step 4. Draw up a composite list of problems after a consensus is reached as to the order of importance of the problems. This is prioritizing.

Step 5. Analyze symptoms and causes, as mistaking one for the other creates "mismatches." Though group members identify the symptoms of a problem and earnestly seek a way to solve it, they cannot do so if the dimensions of the problem are not fully realized. The best way to differentiate causes from symptoms is to examine each one to determine if like responses occur elsewhere, and whether there would be any more problems if the responses were somehow removed. If the answer is yes (the problem didn't go away), only the symptoms have been dealt with and the cause remains. As an example, a staff complains of fatigue and pressure. The cause of the fatigue may not be a long working day or extra duties, but anxiety due to the ambiguity of some roles, which places a strain on existing role relationships. Dealing with symptoms only simply delays solving the problem, for anxiety manifests itself in many ways, and will surface again in another form.

Be wary of jumping on symptoms too soon. Search for deeper meanings and clues. Scrutinize each agenda item for deeper questions: Is that really the problem? Will its solution eliminate the underlying bad feelings? If not, have we fully identified the problem?

Step 6. Consider problem-solving strategies by sitting down and seeking solutions. Problems are usually varied and complex and must be solved by a combination of solutions. Before leaping to the problem-solving stage, all strategies available should be considered.

Step 7. Consider various problem-solving strategies, but select those which are specific. Strategies must contain answers to the questions of *who, what, when,* and *where* to be acceptable. Otherwise problems are only identified, not resolved.

For example, the problem of lack of involvement is tackled by having a group member "form a list by Tuesday of those wishing to be involved in curriculum development to be presented on Thursday to the faculty meeting."

Step 8. The action agenda is prepared as the final step. It outlines the specific steps, personnel and work required to solve the problems identified.

Step 9. Make an evaluation which asks whether the problems were ameliorated, and if not, what went wrong. Consider whether it was incorrect diagnosis, or, if the problem was identified correctly, a bad solution picked. Be sure enough solution strategies were considered, and reflect upon new questions possibly arising.

Organizational Slice

This method samples personnel in an organization from top to bottom. Data is gathered from a vertical slice of the organization at the school level as viewed from the position of a principal, tenured teacher, new teacher, secretary, custodian, student, and parent. The data is usually collected by interview and compiled into a format that can be discussed by the members receiving group. At this point the receiving group (which was the entire school staff) begins to seek a clear definition of the problem and separates symptoms from causes, seeks alternative solution strategies and develops an action agenda. This technique allows for good "emotional data" to be fed back to the main body to get a better feel for the psychological climate and perception of problems held by personnel.

Sample Data

The following data represent such emotionally tinged remarks. They were taken exactly as spoken.

1. "This staff hasn't developed a real *esprit de corps*. The new people should watch their silent language. New people inferred that older people should somehow know these things. Some of the new people were very blase about the summer AV, now they are taking an AV course."

2. "We are troubled by a kind of blind idealism. There are kids here who aren't taking advantage of the opportunities."

3. "With the change in administration, staff leadership was abolished, some people who used to be in the know are now adrift."

4. "All I hear is money. Money isn't the real reason for our problem."

5. "The word here is 'frustration.' We bring on our own frustrations."

6. "The older teachers need to realize that the younger teachers have something to say. I personally feel intimidated."

7. "There is a campus-wide problem this year with students."

8. "We all depended on our principal too much to do our work."

9. "There are a lot of individualists here. We spend a lot of time describing problems but we don't do anything about them."

10. "The younger staff got sucked in. We had a false sense of our own sophistication."

11. "We were praised so much that we got complacent."

12. "The teacher leadership here doesn't rest on much. We should call it like we see it."

Problem Definition

Many problems are not solved because of imprecise definition. Therefore, in order to provide more concrete insights into the statement of the problem, a technique called "problem definition" is used. This technique, while labeled the same as one previously, is much different in application and emphasis. It indicates difficulties, then elaborates on the conditions present that make the situation a problem. After the problem conditions have been defined it should be projected as to what conditions will still be present if the problem is solved. From these first two steps a change strategy must be formulated in order to seek a solution to the original problem:

1. Administrator states problem and problem indicators.

2. Assessment of personnel involved is taken and individual, team, or school profiles are noted.

3. A list is made of conditions under which problems would be solved.

4. A formalized change strategy is built with specific assignments made.

Data for Problem

1. Problem: Principal observes, "Our teaching teams are not working well."

   a. The teaching teams are not planning well enough;

   b. There is a lack of complete trust and openness between members of teams;

   c. There is not close enough correlation within the teams on such items as student grouping;

   d. The teams have not adequately assessed pupil needs;

   e. If the teams have assessed pupil needs, there is not much evidence of a change in teacher behavior;

   f. There is still a very uneven level of total staff commitment towards the school;

   g. In some cases we have self-contained classrooms functioning with the "open space" concept which is an anachronism;

   h. The students are manifesting staff frustration with the above problem.

Problem Indicator I: The teaching teams are not planning well enough. Conditions indicating the presence of good team planning and the solution of the problem are:

1. Teachers would know what members were doing individually and in groups, there would be no surprises from day to day such as two teachers planning to use the same room for conflicting activities.

2. There would be total team input rather than domination of the input by one or two teachers on a team. Teachers would not complain of unaccepted feelings or reluctance to make themselves heard in planning sessions.

3. There would be greater awareness by teachers of the need for more teacher-teacher and teacher-pupil dialogue, and more meaningful verbal interaction at both levels than is now occurring.

4. Within the discipline teams there would be more staff cohesiveness that is, a more *articulated* curriculum for children in the area involved.

Problem Indicator II: There is a lack of trust among team members. Conditions which point to a proper attitude of mutual trust are:

1. Team members would openly display a feeling of mutual confidence, thus bring about full participation and cut down on hostilities.

2. There would be less discontent on the part of qualifications placed on them.

3. Teachers' undue suspicions of pupil motives and behavior (which always increases bad pupil behavior) is cut down.

Problem Indicator III: The teams have not adequately assessed pupil needs. There has been an adequate assessment of pupil needs if

1. The instructional program in a discipline area would not be designed prior to assessing pupil needs; the program would fit the student and not the other way around.

2. The emphasis is on assessing pupil needs and constructing learning experiences based upon those needs, not using pupil needs as the central focus for determining instructional sequencing and pacing.

Problem Indicator IV: There is little change in teacher behavior, despite assessment of pupil needs. Indications that there had been a change in teacher behavior as a result of needs assessment are:

1. The program would follow the assessment and there would be a design for systematically sampling pupil attitudes and using it as a major input in determining teaching.

2. A variety of instructional modes would be present and obvious.

3. Groups would not be of a permanent nature; they would be continually grouped and re-grouped on the basis of reach achievement.

4. Pupils would have a direct say in the selection of much of what they learned.

5. More pupil diversity of response and participation would be encouraged.

6. There would be more utilization of various types of instructional resources.

7. There would be more chances provided for students to exploit learning resources, including the teacher as a resource.

8. Pupil success would be emphasized more on a regular, planned basis. Teaching would begin where students actually were, and not where they were presumed to be.

9. Teacher behavior would not be so much aimed at producing convergent thinking as divergence and creative responses on the part of students.

10. Assessment of pupil growth in all areas would occur regularly and periodically on a planned basis by the team. This forms the data base for the next unit planning.

Problem Indicator V: There is a very uneven level of total staff commitment towards the school. If the proper commitment exists, the following are true:

1. The good of the school is placed above personal agenda items.

2. A majority of the staff can agree and function as a total body.

3. An *esprit de corps* exists that precludes faculty cliques, splinter groups or isolates.

4. There is good cooperation among teams and departments and individuals when limited resources are involved.

5. There is the presentation of a "unified front" when the school as a totality is involved in activities.

6. There is a high degree of teacher sharing and intra-staff feedback.

7. There is an "even load" commitment within teams; a few don't always get stuck with most of the work.

Problem Indicator VI: There is open space but self-contained classrooms are functioning within it. Conditions indicating good utilization of the open space are:

1. There would be no permanent single-teacher-per-class organization on a permanent basis over an extended period of time within the open space.

2. There would be flexibility of group and teacher assignments within the open space.

3. Teachers would stress group fluidity with purpose and many varied experiences for students.

4. The role of the teacher is that of facilitator and guide, rather than full-time director or lecturer.

5. The role of pupils in open space is active, involved and direct. The role of teacher is that of guide and shaper of activities and resources towards pupil needs.

Problem Indicator VII: Students are mirroring staff frustration. If students are free from this, and are learning and productive, they

1. Exhibit a high degree of motivation for learning;
2. Have fewer conflicts with the staff;
3. Perform less vandalism and have less disrespect for staff;
4. Show more tolerance towards each other;
5. Show more perception of self-worth; and
6. Commit less absenteeism and class-cutting.

It is essential that this process of examination be undertaken periodically in order to "flush out" the normal tensions and frictions that arise during the implementation of an innovation that demands cooperation.

Fall Training

It became clear that systematic planning skills were going to be necessary to perform a complete needs assessment of each school and specify what amount of resources would be required to meet an identified need.

The trainer was Roger Kaufman, Educational System Analyst at United States International University, San Diego, California, and the process was system analysis and a tri-level needs assessment model.

Needs Assessment

Kaufman's tri-level needs assessment model. A need is defined as "a measurable discrepancy between what is and what should be." And since problem solving must start with an assessment of needs, needs must be viewed from many viewpoints, chiefly from those of the student, of the educator, and of society. Needs assessment helps prevent us from making unwarranted assumptions.

The definition of "system" is "the sum total of separate parts working independently and together to achieve a required outcome."

There are two parts to the system model. Blocks 1 and 2 in Figure 44 are *system analysis* or *problem identification*. These report *what* is to be done. Blocks 3 through 5 report *system synthesis* or *problem resolution*. This reports *how* to do it. Experience has shown that too many of our innovations start off at step 4 and, therefore, usually become another passing fancy because they never solve an actual problem.

Needs may be identified through a process called *needs assessment* wherein all discrepancies are identified relative to a given area (such as within a specified school district or a community) and priorities placed on each of the needs relative to one another. This needs assessment procedure will increase the probability of obtaining valid needs and thus relevant problems which will allow educators to reduce, or eliminate true and validated needs.

THE REQUEST FOR PROPOSAL: THE PROCESS OF BIDDING

This internal performance contracting phase of the project allowed the project administration to model the bidding procedure with each school, for real monies, for the accomplishment of training goals.

The project administration developed a request for proposal (RFP) and issued one to each school. Schools were allowed two

FIGURE 44

Six Step System Problem Solving Model

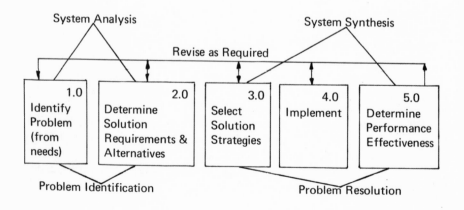

weeks to develop bids to be submitted to the evaluation panel comprised of the project directors, directors of secondary and elementary education, and president and president-elect of Mesa Education Association.

REP Format

INSTRUCTION SHEET FOR TEACHERS

Background

The Mesa differentiated staffing project calls for school staffs to submit "bids" (RFP) to the Board of Education to educate their students to achieve specific outcomes.

This RFP closely parallels what teachers will be deliberating with the Mesa Board of Education later in the spring. However, it is chiefly confined to teacher objectives to attain the goals of the differentiated staffing project.

Read these instructions as a guide in preparing your "bid" on the project RFP. The RFP spells out what should be in your "bid" to reach the objectives of the project.

Recommended Procedure for Preparation of Bid by School Staffs.
1. Faculty nominates staff steering committee to perform the task of coordination (can be faculty senates if they have already been elected, or an appointed committee of faculty senates);
2. Faculty staff steering committee performs task of data gathering and writing staff "bid", securing staff consensus and negotiating bid;
3. Faculty staff steering committee performs staff liaison with entire school staff during "bid" implementation and in representing the staff on other formal on-going deliberations with the project staff such as:
    a. Deliberating on-going changes in the original objectives should progress indicate objectives which are unrealistic or need alteration (see RFP for specification of tolerance limits);
    b. Receiving and presenting staff grievances of the staff during the time it is functioning under the conditions of the "bid";
    c. Working with the staff as an evaluative body of consultants, project management and direction, public relations to explain the program to the press and community, set up visitation

procedures and other on-site evaluation procedures by outside persons or agencies;

4. Faculty staff steering committees should be elected and serve staggered terms so that a portion of the group is continually replaced, but that enough experience is retained to give continuity.

5. The entire school staff should set criteria of selection by which teachers are elected to the staff steering committee; MEA building representatives may have an automatic seat as either voting members or an ex-officio representative of the MEA.

Guidelines for the Request For Proposal (RFP)

DIRECTIONS: Guidelines for RFP's are to be used in the preparation of staff "bids" for project resources to meet the following objectives:

1. To complete the pilot school's staffing model with the following components:
    a. A well-defined horizontal level of role specialization which contains at least *three* distinct roles;
    b. The illustration of at least three plans by which horizontal roles may form a vertical hierarchy in relationship to one another and are subsequently abolished when specified pupil objectives have been met;
    c. A cost-defined training component based upon role specialization and costs of implementation.

2. The development of a general needs assessment model for the total school utilizing the Kaufman system approach and from which future bids will be designed and deliberated.

3. The clear linkage between the proposed staffing model and the needs assessment model (not the needs assessment itself).

Other parts of the Mesa RFP included sections on evaluation, bid format, guideline format and submission details, notes on the content of the training program, and specifications of procedures for satisfying grievances.

A sample series of budget items and proposed staffing model for one of the schools submitting a bid is given in Figure 45.

Fluid Staffing Model of Holmes School

Due to the fluidity of the model, roles must be generic. However,

FIGURE 45

Bid Budget

Objective I

Selected staff members will complete a needs assessment model, including a function and task analysis, and develop a *pert* for completion of the needs assessment.

Calculated Cost

4 substitute teachers @ $20.00 x 2 days =	$160.00
1 secretary @ $2.00 hr. x 4 hr. =	8.00
24 teachers @ $4.00 hr. x 4 hrs. =	384.00
4 teachers @ $4.00 hr. x 8 hrs. =	128.00
Total	$680.00

Objective II

Selected staff members will develop a teacher directory which will list:
1. Present expertise
2. Desired expertise
3. Other information deemed necessary by the staff

All staff members will help critique the final draft.

Calculated Cost

25 teachers @ $4.00 hr. x 3 hrs. =	$300.00
(non school time)	
Secretary @ $2.00 hr. x 4 hrs. =	8.00
5 teachers @ $4.00 hr. x 6 hrs. =	120.00
Total	$428.00

Objective III   Part A

Selected staff members will develop and/or select limited instruments to measure:
1. Self Direction
2. Self Respect
3. Attitudes toward school
4. Other affective goals

Said staff members will be trained to administer and interpret results.

Calculated Cost

Travel 3 teachers @ $160 =	$480.00
Room and Board 3 teachers @ $12.85 =	38.55
Ground Transportation =	20.00
3 Substitute teachers @ $20.00 x 1 day =	60.00
3 teachers @ $4.00 hr. x 7 hrs. =	84.00
Total	$682.55

Objective III   Part B

Selected staff members will develop and/or select instruments to diagnose psychomotor deficiencies. Said staff members will be trained to administer and interpret results.

Calculated Cost

Travel - 3 teachers @ $168.00 =	$504.00
Room and board 2 teachers @ $12.85 =	25.70
Ground transportation =	14.00
2 teacher substitutes @ $20.00 x 3 days =	120.00
Total	$663.70

Objective III   Part C

Selected staff members will develop and/or select diagnostic and evaluative instruments in math skills, language arts skills, social studies skills and science concepts. Said staff members will be able to administer and interpret results.

Calculated Cost

6 substitute teachers @ $20.00 x 3 days =	$360.00
Total	$360.00

Objective IV	*Calculated Cost*	
Selected staff members will develop instructional packets organized within a three dimensional framework. The three dimensions shall consist of a value base (Rucker), a problem solving method and an integrated content area vehicle.	Travel - car 900 mi. @ $.10 mi. =	$ 90.00
	Meal & lodging $30.00 day x 3 days x 6 teachers =	540.00
	1 secretary @ $2.00 hr. x 16 hrs. =	32.00
	24 books @ $6.00 each =	144.00
	6 substitute teachers @ $20.00 x 2 days =	240.00
	6 teachers @ $4.00 hr. x 16 hrs. =	384.00
	Consultant (Ray Rucker) 1 day x $100.00 Expenses $75.00 =	175.00
	Total	$1605.00

Objective V	*Calculated Cost*	
Selected staff members will develop at least one flexible time-space model.	4 substitute teachers @ $20.00 x 4 days =	$320.00
	1 consultant @ $100.00 day x 1 day + $75.00 expenses =	175.00
	Total	$495.00

Bid Preparation	*Cost*	
Project steering committee will complete bid proposal within the alloted time.	3 substitute teachers @ $20.00 x 3 days =	$180.00
	Total	$180.00

	Projected cost	$5094.25
	10% Bonus	509.43
	Grand total	$5603.67

some roles are necessarily more constant than others, although their importance within the hierarchy will change. The following roles occur regularly within the framework of the model.

Coordinator, whose role is to develop a systematic, workable relationship among the variables of time, space, people, and resources.

Diagnostician, who must develop and/or obtain diagnostic instruments in the cognitive, affective, and psycho-motor domains, and must administer these instruments and compile and interpret the results to proper personnel.

Researcher, who does continuous research to help determine alternate methods/means that will meet specific requirements as determined by the needs assessment.

Strategist, who, given the inputs from the diagnostician, coordinator, and researcher, selects the best methods/means available to meet the assessed needs.

Implementor, who bases his implementation of the program with specified learners on information obtained from diagnostician, researcher, and strategist, and follows through with the program until desired outcomes are reached.

Evaluator, whose role is to assess the methods/means used in meeting the needs of the learners, and who administers evaluative instruments and then interprets the results, and must recognize areas where program improvement is necessary.

A Teacher Directory

When developed, the Teacher Directory will be aι important part of the model. Its purpose will be to facilitate the assessment of in-house expertise and specific short-range goals of individual staff members. From this information, selection of personnel to fill the various roles can be determined. The information will also be used to determine staffing limitations and to supply the school with information upon which criteria for future staff selection can be built.

This particular project was one of the most successful. It demanded accountability, but allowed teachers control of the resources to accomplish chosen ends. The project administration estimated this procedure increased the internalization of the idea by at least six months. The solutions to goals were developed by teachers, ownership of each model developed was theirs, and it was based on the needs of the children, faculty, and parents of that area. What the project had taught was a *process* for defining a model based on identified need. This is a long term skill that can be responsive to changing needs.

The bidding procedure took place in two rounds:
1. First the schools stated their objective and submitted their bid. The evaluation panel stated it was acceptable and put conditions on some of the objectives (i.e., if staff meetings were held an identifiable product had to be completed). Bids were cut at this point because they were 30 percent over resources. A statement was let to each school indicating the conditions set by the panel and the new dollar amount to which they had been cut.
2. Second round each school submitted its altered bids. (All were accepted.)
3. A 10 percent bonus factor was provided if all schools met their objectives within the specified time limits (two of the schools did).

Second round of bidding

In the Spring of 1971, $8,000 was "let" to the pilot schools to accomplish the following objectives:

1. Completion of a validated needs assessment model.
2. Performance of an actual needs assessment based upon the model.
3. Submission of a complete summer training program based upon the identified needs.

This round of bidding was accomplished with little difficulty. The teachers felt comfortable with the idea of internal performance contracting and had already become very proficient. A straw vote indicated all three pilot schools would favor this kind of procedure for the total school resources. It seems that if the teacher is asked to be accountable they must have some control of the reward and control system of the organization. It is presumed in this project that accountability and governance are bedfellows and in fact must be instituted concurrently (English, Zaharis, 1971).

This second round of bidding facilitated a product-oriented summer training effort, based upon student need. In short, a differentiated training program had accompanied the development of a differentiated staff.

BASELINE PLUS COMMISSION: A FLUID PAY STRUCTURE

As the project began to assess different ways of remunerating teachers for performing different tasks of differing complexities, the concept of salary-plus-commission emerged. It allowed for a baseline salary that provided teacher security, but allowed for extra responsibilities by using the reward system of the organization to pay instructors that developed materials and methods to meet student needs identified in the needs assessment. It was felt that experience and graduate credit were important to salary considerations. We have to assume under this salary plan that there is better teaching going on if a teacher has an MA +30 and fourteen years of experience rather than a BA +30 and four years of experience. This is difficult to prove and provides no leverage for the organization to put dollars into areas of identified student need. It also provides the teacher with only one commitment level: a regular contract. The determination of this project was to conceptualize a way for dollars to be responsive to student needs and based in some percentage on student objectives. The following ideas were developed as a first cut at modeling this kind of reward structure.

Fremont Model of Baseline and Commission

General Conditions. Those in leadership positions will be paid an extra training stipend for the major activities involved. These will be equated on a *performance basis;* that is, job descriptions are written in performance objectives. Pay is based upon meeting the performance objectives of the job description. The positions will model the differentiated staffing project goals of "salary commission"; that is, salary will be equated at a baseline figure for the acceptance of the additional responsibilities ($250) and the remainder equated on a performance basis. Instructional leaders may sub-contract on commission objectives to other team members or other teachers in other schools. Tentative plans at the present time call for a total stipend of between $1000 or $1500 for each position. Those in such positions are not department chairmen; rather, they are "supra" department chairmen. They will encompass broader power, responsibility, and accountability than department chairmen. It is anticipated that some restructuring of the school day in terms of tasks and functions for the instructional leader position will be necessary. On the following pages the responsibilities of these positions will be described.

Instructional Leaders

Tentative Generic Job Description for Instructional Leader of Humanities, Sciences, and Applied Arts

I. Material resource development

Baseline
The instructional leader will perform a simple needs assessment of his teaching team to include the following:
a. subject area (discipline) and basic discipline competency;
b. methods of inquiry within and peculiar to the discipline;
c. methods of analysis within the discipline;
d. methods of mediating the major ideas within the discipline into pupil objectives;
e. analyzing teacher needs based upon their abilities to perform the above;
f. individualizing instruction utilizing proper teacher techniques within the discipline.

The needs assessment will include at least two outside observers (ex: a counselor and a teacher from another school). All subsequent leadership activities will be based upon this needs assessment.

A. *Products based upon the team needs assessment: baseline*
   1. The team leader (based upon the team needs assessment) will produce as baseline products the following:
      a. at least two teacher work guides of not more than ten pages incorporating major suggestions to the team for improvement in:
         1. curriculum content and the major or representative ideas to be learned;
         2. instructional methods and modes appropriate to the objectives;
         3. teacher effectiveness in meeting learner specified objectives;
         4. improvement of teacher effectiveness through monitoring techniques such as Flanders, Iota, etc.;
         5. improved scheduling techniques or grouping towards specific objectives;
         6. specific plans for evaluating;
         7. direct instructional service for instructional leaders.
      b. Initiate and maintain a teacher file for each member of the teaching team to include the following:
         1. short and long range plans for professional growth;
         2. needs and growth as observed by the instructional leader and the principal; and
         3. specific plans arrived at jointly for improvement.

Commission

The instructional leader will produce at least two teacher guides in addition to the baseline each quarter to meet the previously defined criteria of team leadership and organization leadership.

II. Team Leadership

Baseline

The instructional leader will produce at least two total department time/space models which will contain the following components:

a. specifications as to time percentage spent in small group, large group, and independent study which matches instructional objectives;

b. at least 20 percent of the time for the time/space models will include provisions for teacher planning time;

c. the time/space models will include a definition of materials, equipment, and future needs for both material and equipment, within the two models.

Commission
The production of four additional time/space models, with at least three coordinated with a total school schedule, equipment utilization, and facility utilization.

III. Coordinating Leadership

Baseline
The instructional leader will develop utilization schedules appropriate to the coordination of facilities, equipment, student time, and material deployment, to be judged effective by the fact that not more than twelve to fourteen complaints are received each semester by the senate of each department.

Commission
The instructional leader will work with other leaders and develop at least two total time/space schedules projected on a three-year growth plan which include school goals, training, budget development, hiring and teacher deplacement policies and procedures. At least one such schedule shall be implemented each semester and not more than twenty-five complaints by teachers shall be registered with the Senate regarding adequate coordination.

IV. Quality Control

Baseline
The instructional leader will develop the following:

a. two pupil attitude inventories administered once each quarter of the school year to assess pupil attitudes regarding the teaching and learning within the discipline. No more than 40 percent of the students inventoried will be dissatisfied in any one area;

b. pupil achievement will indicate that at least 50 percent of the pupils are progressing according to expectations; 20 percent above expectations; 20 percent below expectations and 10 percent unknown or missing; the instructional leader will select, determine and report this achievement data based upon validated instruments (teacher-made or standardized).

Commission

a. Not more than 5 percent of the students surveyed on the pupil attitude inventory indicate that their needs are not being met or that they are unhappy;
b. Pupil achievement data will indicate that 60 percent are progressing at or above expectations, 30 percent are achieving above expectations, and only 10 percent below expectations. Criteria and instruments are to be defined by the instructional leader.
c. Not more than 5 percent parental complaints are registered for any one quarter regarding any aspect of the discipline involved (lack of learning, poor attitudes, lack of understanding between pupil-home-teacher regarding assignments, report cards, etc.).

In-service

Baseline

The instructional leader designs and implements an in-service training program which is:

a. based upon the previously defined needs assessment;
b. based upon each teacher completing a personal/professional growth plan which is harmonized with the total area needs assessment;
c. matched with the school's total needs;
d. includes new teacher orientation and aide training;
e. includes parent information meetings and community involvement.

The instructional leader performs at least three major in-service activities around the activities noted above each semester. At least 70 percent of the teacher involvement rate will increase. The instructional leader will design the evaluative instruments for providing the above data.

Commission

The instructional leader sees to it that at least 70 percent of the teachers complete the first phase of the personal/professional growth plans by the end of the year. He performs an additional five in-service meetings pertaining to the above topics per semester with at least 80 percent of the teachers indicating that they experienced substantial professional growth. He develops at least two *quasi* programmed guides for teachers on the team for professional improvement.

V. Humanistic Learning Climate

Baseline

The instructional leader works to create with his teaching team a humanistic learning climate to be judged by a panel of three outside experts on the following criteria (once per quarter and all criteria must be met at least one of the four quarters):

a. the degree and type of pupil involvement;
b. the degree of pupil-initiated conferences with teachers;
c. the overall cleanliness of the school;
d. the evident enthusiasm for learning on the part of the students;
e. the degree to which pupil work is exhibited;
f. the degree of high interest projects arising from pupil needs;
g. the discernible respect between teachers and pupils;
h. the informal sessions between pupils and teachers;
i. a lower absentee and vandalism rate;
j. fewer discipline problems and types;
k. a high degree of faculty esprit, leadership and sharing;
l. a low degree of teacher cynicism; and
m. use of human relations skills in teaching (such as TET, etc.)

Commission
The instructional leader is able to secure consensus on the part of the observational team each quarter for the entire year that such conditions are present and improving each time.

This tentative job description of the instructional leader is an example of the development required for each of the instructional leaders, and is subject to revision as the school year progresses. But it is only one example of the development each project must undertake as its program matures.

VI. Problems Encountered

The following problems of the differentiated staffing project encountered in Mesa are documented for the benefit of other educators contemplating similar projects. Not all of the problems occurred simultaneously, but each is serious enough to merit consideration.

1. Fatigue factors were underestimated. The staff, (especially during the school year) was overworked. Substitutes were hired, but the positive effect of substitutes was overestimated. The project staff would recommend overhiring for a one year period in order that staff may be utilized during school time.
2. The "Sophomoric Complex" was a problem with our young innovative staffs. They overestimated their own capacities, which made them difficult to teach in workshops. When this attitude

was worked through the "roof fell in." They tended toward extreme conditions in morale, either very high or very low. Maturity and solidarity came after going through this process.

3. Staff composition should be a mixture of young and old. Diversity of experience is a definite asset for growth. Two of the pilot schools did not have this ingredient, and it tended to magnify problems.

4. There is a tendency for the innovation to become "fenced off" from other schools and policy-making groups. Linkage must be planned for and made early in the project with district leadership encouraging it, or an isolated innovation will occur.

5. The bidding procedure encouraged competition which was healthy, but there is a tendency for this feeling to go too far and the goal becomes that of winning a particular bid rather than meeting special needs. Guidelines in the RFP establishing baselines of funding and making bids relate directly to needs assessment must be developed for precaution.

6. The "hothouse effect" occurs in an innovation such as this and it demands a continual processing of the tensions and people problems that arise. The stress and ambiguity levels are much higher and this magnifies any existing or even dormant problems.

THE FUTURE

The concept of differentiated staffing is undergoing a healthy self-analysis and is therefore in a state of growth and change. More than ever the relationship of staffing patterns, as a part of school structure that meets a child's needs, must be explored and the relationship known. The Mesa approach is one level of the evolutionary process of this idea. At the time of this writing it appears that this project's major contributions are:

1. Emphasis of defining students' needs before building teacher tasks.

2. Internal performance contracting model to allow teacher governance and flexible resource allocation and pay plans.

3. Comprehensive planning through system analysis.

4. The fluid hierarchy, where teacher roles are in a vertical relationship for a particular set of needs within a defined time frame. This avoids over-specialization, loss of morale, and insures a more responsive faculty.

5. It shows more than ever that differentiated staffing is a

process, not a product. It is a means to an end and therefore the only thing that can be left with a staff is a process by which they can construct a differentiated staffing model based upon their own identified need.

Suggested Reading

Differentiated Staffing, the Mesa Approach. Pamphlet, Mesa Education Association document, August 1971.

Differentiated Staffing Proposal submitted by Mesa Public Schools, November 1969.

English, F. W., and Zaharis, J. K. "Are Accountability and Governance Compatible," *Phi Delta Kappan,* February 1971.

English, F. W., and Zaharis, J. K. "Complete Project Profile," unpublished paper, June 1970.

English, F. W., and Zaharis, J. K. "How to Build a Model of Staff Differentiation," unpublished paper, July 1970, p. 38.

English, F. W., and Zaharis, J. K. "Staff Differentiation the Right way," *Arizona Teacher* 60:2, November 1971, pp. 6-9, 35.

Mann, Peter B. "Differentiated Staffing: The Second Generation," *Arizona Teacher* 59:2, January 1971, pp. 13-17.

Zaharis, J. K. "Application for Consideration as a Pilot School for Differentiated Staffing," unpublished paper, April 1970.

Zaharis, J. K. "Performance Contracting: Problem Definition and Problem Resolution," unpublished paper, March 1971, p. 35.

INTRODUCTION TO

SECTION III

Easily the most combustible issue in any differentiated staffing project was the question of differential salaries. Although advocacy in favor of differentiated staffing is often thought to be a ploy of educators against teacher unions, the following transcript from the House Appropriations Subcommittee for HEW and the Office of Education for the fiscal year 1972 gives an indication that similarly favorable advocacy by Mr. Daniel Flood, chairman of that committee is also espoused by congressional representatives. Dr. Sidney P. Marland is Commissioner of Education and Dr. Don Davies is Deputy Commissioner for Development.

TRANSCRIPT
FROM HEARINGS, HOUSE APPROPRIATIONS COMMITTEE, FISCAL YEAR 1972

PROVIDING SALARY INCENTIVES IN TEACHER SCARCITY FIELDS

MR. FLOOD. I am still following the same line of attack here.

With the analogy to the business world, wouldn't paying higher salaries be a much, much better way to attract teachers into the shortage fields? Of course, it would wouldn't it?

DR. DAVIES. This program——

MR. FLOOD. Wouldn't it?

DR. DAVIES. Salaries provide a good incentive. The teaching profession in most school districts does not provide for that kind of incentive field by field. The first point——

MR. FLOOD. We have had some testimony to the contrary here from two of our friends in the last couple of days that in many States there are provisions that do provide such incentives. I think Mr. Michel was developing that point.

295

The fact that there are stepups of incentives by grades in different places for this kind of thing.

DR. MARLAND. I think we concluded that was an occasional condition. The record would show this is not common.

MR. FLOOD. Why shouldn't it be?

DR. MARLAND. Because the practice in the school system is to recognize virtually all teachers according to rank and grade, according to their training and years of service. It is rare that there is an exceptional salary afforded.

MR. FLOOD. Why don't you do something about that? You have the cart before the horse perhaps. Maybe you should educate somebody else besides the disadvantaged. Maybe there are a lot of other disadvantaged people in State capitols that should be educated, and the Department of HEW has such tremendous confidence in the States all of a sudden. They seem to be derelict.

DR. DAVIES. One of the programs supported by this budget makes it possible for school districts to try to pay different salaries for different levels of teaching assistance, regular teachers, master teachers, paraprofessionals and to pay those people differently because they do different kinds of jobs. This has been much more acceptable both to the school boards and teachers than any kind of a system which says that this third-grade teacher is going to make more than this science teacher, or that this special education teacher is going to make more than this vocational education teacher. We are providing development work in 30 different places for school systems that want to adopt a more differentiated way to pay them.

MR. FLOOD. Maybe instead of talking to school boards you should talk to teacher unions. I have heard a great deal about them. All unions would be delighted to discuss this kind of thing with you, Any union I know.

DR. DAVIES. We talk quite a little bit with them.

MR. FLOOD. Good.

Although clearly the economic principles governing teachers' salaries need fuller development, Sharpes outlines a few of those principles applicable to teacher salary differentials.

The problem of actually financing a differentiating staffing program is offered by Krumbein in his development of a financing model. He explores dollar costs and "opportunity costs." His main hypothesis is that the re-allocation of resources could enable a district or school system to embark upon a differentiated staffing program. The limitations of the financing model affect the transitional phase of a district's development, not later compensation efforts. Krumbein assumes that the school is already committed to implementation of differentiated staffing.

In the third chapter in Section III, Frinks describes the development of a competency-based exercise to arrive at a new staffing design. He defines task analysis and used a flow diagram based on student and staff needs to isolate the flow of tasks. The importance of a competency-based approach strengthens the ability of teacher and learner alike to express desired results. He describes in detail the various levels of performance criteria, from student through teacher certification and performance assessment systems. He enlarges on the roles of state education agencies and state legislatures in that process.

DeBloois reports on the status of recent experiments in differentiated staffing projects, especially those funded by School Personnel Utilization (SPU). He describes his conceptual model, the components of which relate to self (individualism), interpersonal relations (collegiality), professional commitments (professional disposition), decision making (workflow structures), and policies of the institution (perpetuation structures). In analyzing twenty-three school districts and nearly 1,000 educators, DeBloois describes a high degree of unanimity on most aspects of the model. Some conclusions from the evaluation are tentative; many are disappointing. But generally educators were more receptive to experimentation and more enthusiastic in their jobs after SPU funding and participation.

The federal program of SPU with approximately nine million dollars over three years, supported over thirty school systems to develop training models for differentiated staffing schools. Sharpes, in the final chapter of this book, describes through the eyes of a student of the federal educational establishment the problems and issues of administering federal educational policy. Some of these issues, which he encountered in his administration of SPU, were: fear of federal control, the defense of government spending to the bureaucracy and the public, the role of the professional and community participants in educational reform, teacher union practices and policies, the posture of the Administration in Washington towards education, and a host of others.

Concepts relating to finances and cost, performance-based program development, evaluation, and the federal investment will hopefully complement for the student or practicing administrator the selections from the case histories of Section II and the theories and rationale from Section I.

9   Competitive Teaching Wages

Donald K. Sharpes

The Committee for Economic Development supports this view:

> Teacher salaries are commonly based on seniority and the accumulation of college credits. We regard this as a serious block to the recruitment and retention of countless competent teachers and to eliciting the best efforts of teaching staffs. The variety of talent, preparation, and competence required for effective and efficient teaching justifies differentiated pay scales, which in our opinion would overcome this block to improved instruction. [1]

The committee's statement continues by recommending a reconstruction of teacher compensation:

> We urge school boards, school administrators and professional teachers' associations to undertake a reconstruction of the basis for teacher compensation to bring pay scales more in conformity with the functions, responsibilities and performance of teachers. Such pay scales should also take into account the shortages in certain teaching skills. [2]

Wage rates even among teachers differ tremendously. The average wage for teachers is as hard to define as the average teacher. A teacher at the top of the salary schedule in an affluent area may be making above $15,000 a year, whereas a beginning teacher in rural or disadvantaged area may be making less than $4,500. These differentials in wage are based on two considerations—length of time as a teacher and length of time as a teacher in a particular locality.

School costs are rising faster than the growth of the economy. The overwhelming proportion of public expenditures for schools—over 60 percent—is for teachers' services. The aggregate rise in school costs is largely because of the exponential rise in teachers' salaries.

There will be a corresponding slackening of school expenditures as new building construction and funds for new teachers' salaries go down and as student enrollment levels off in the coming decade. It is doubtful whether additional appropriations will raise the schools' effectiveness and productivity. If economic trends continue, any increase of funds given to schools in their current conventional and procedural format will likely not insure significant qualitative benefits.

The key to cost-efficient school expenditures will probably not be technological hardware, the architecture of buildings, or the refinement of curricula innovations, but more likely the recognition of teacher effectiveness and a corresponding differentiation of teacher pay.

If schools are to retain competent career teachers, then they will have to create new salary differentials and new categories for recognizing widely differing teacher abilities. The present standardization of teacher classification, certification, and salary schedules does not acknowledge individual teacher differences. Making teacher salaries uniform is an unfair practice to teachers of uncommon ability.

The average annual salary for instructional staff members in regular public elementary and secondary schools in 1968-69 was $7,835.[3] The total cost for this instructional staff of 2,122,000 equaled $16.6 billion. The estimated projected cost for a total national instructional staff of 2,330,000 was $22.5 billion (in 1967-68 dollar value). The average annual salary of a teacher in 1977 will be $7,677.

EQUAL WAGE FOR EQUAL WORK

Let us look at a case of wages paid to a particular category of teachers mostly alike in skill, effort, and competency. We are interested in wages in relation to cost of living and will therefore speak in terms of money units whose purchasing power of goods is constant at a particular place and time, for example, in 1975. The law of diminishing returns suggests that when we add more labor to the same natural resources we tend to diminish wages and productivity.[4] Consequently, if we simply add more teachers to the teacher labor market and increase their wages to take into account the increased cost of living index, we are satisfying the law of diminishing returns.

There is a counter law to the law of diminishing returns—the law of increasing returns, which also governs the economics of mass production. As the birth rate continues to decline, the number of teachers needed will be less.

Within the ten-year period from 1968-69 to 1978-79 there will be an increase of only 208,000 regular teachers in public elementary and secondary schools. Within an equal time span—the period 1957-58 to 1967-68—766,000 teachers were needed in public elementary and secondary schools. Though the number of teachers needed is diminishing annually, the problems of teacher turnover, mobility, and loss continue to plague the profession. The paradox is that there is less of a total increase of teachers needed, even while there is a need for replacing teachers who abandon teaching.

THE LAW OF WAGES

There will be more teachers in the future than necessary. According to Marx such a situation would be enough to depress wages to the level of a subsistence minimum. On the contrary, however, real wage rates will not fall to a minimum subsistence level. Rather, unemployment will increase. Consequently, we establish an important principle: if there is genuine competition in the teacher labor market there is no necessity for wages to fall to a minimum subsistence level.

There is a more pertinent and urgent reason why teachers as workers fight for higher pay. They do not usually fear unemployment. Nor as professional people do they fear the amount of work they may be given, since they do not generate a product. What they do feel is that, as professionals, they are not being paid competitive wages. Again this suggests that the law of increasing returns is in effect. The economy of mass production is not keeping constant the wage increase that teachers could make elsewhere, given the skills they presently have.

To a particular group of teacher-workers, especially those with special skills and status not now being currently utilized in schools, the introduction of technological change may pose a threat.

UNEMPLOYMENT VS. LEISURE

There are two considerations in the increase of teacher competencies and skills and in the number of teachers needed in the future to maintain the educational enterprise as we now understand it: unemployment and leisure. In the near future there will be an equilibrium necessary for a constant number of teachers to maintain a constant number of schools. In other words, there will be a fine balance between the number of graduates coming from teacher training institutions and the number of teachers necessary to maintain the schools. However, there will also be an increased amount of leisure time for those teachers currently employed. The professional labor market, however, is not the same as the ordinary labor market. It is questionable, then, whether teachers who are on higher differentiated salary schedules will opt to spend more leisure time at their profession than those who are not. This is particularly true since time is usually increased for differentiated positions.

Let us consider the case of a teacher who, because of differential competencies, has been offered a higher salary to work in the district and is free to choose the amount of time that he spends at his work. On the one hand, he is tempted to work extra time because he thereby increases his professional skills. Suppose also that schools will operate twelve months a year with vacations spaced intermittently. The tendency for the higher paid teacher will be to spend more time on the job. For him each hour of leisure time becomes more expensive. He is tempted to substitute extra work for leisure. In other words, although there may be a conflict between what economists call "substitution-effect" (a worker substituting extra work for leisure) and "income-effect" (the consumer buying more goods), there is also a person who is driven less by financial ambitions and more by the desire for achievement and keenness for his profession.

In other words, professionals work hard because they want to achieve and because they enjoy what they do. Therefore, the teacher who enjoys teaching the most will—in a differentiated staffing salary program—also have the opportunity for making the most money, and he will be making more because he will work harder and be rewarded for doing what he enjoys most.

DIFFERENCES IN LABOR QUALITY

The salary or labor market will always group teachers into certain classifications for purposes of determining wages. The classifications are progressive steps on the wages or salary ladder. A teacher's classification depends on time spent in teaching, among other things. Assuming a program of staff differentiation, there may still remain many categories of labor. Wage rates will have a diversified spread. The competitive wage between what a teacher can make in a large metropolitan area, for example, and what local industries are offering for technical writers will have a large influence on whether or not career-oriented teachers will remain long in the teaching profession.

A differentiated staffing program will offer competitive wages within the teaching profession. Moreover, there may be several differentiated staffing programs within an urban area, any one or all of which can offer challenge to the lure of business or industry in competitive wages at the higher salary levels.

DETERMINATION FOR COMPETITIVE WAGES

If people and jobs were all alike there would be no wage differentials. However, when teachers are all alike and some of their jobs different, there will be a tendency to equalize the differentials in wage. If teachers are different in skills and in training, and if there is recognition that some are better teachers than others—and if there is mobility among the higher paid teachers—assuming a differentiated staff—then there will be an equilibrium or a standard pattern of wage differential determined by the general supply and demand. In other words, those districts or local education agencies that run differentiated staffing programs will have identified the better teachers and adjusted their salary schedules accordingly. But once those better teachers are recognized by the rest of the educational community, their general pattern of wages will be determined by supply and demand.

The teaching profession has simply never recognized the tremendous qualitative differentials among its teaching members. As a result, teachers are—in the phrase of the economists—a noncompeting group in the labor market. They do not compete with each other within the system. The competition for their services is outside the school in the commercial world. If the wages of a plumber were to become $50,000 a year, we can be sure that some teachers would quit and learn the art of plumbing. In a large metropolitan area the collective bargaining procedures for determining the teacher salary schedule will be subject to (whether or not it is in active consideration) what nearby industries are paying for trained mathematicians, liberal artists and social scientists.

COLLECTIVE BARGAINING AND MARKET IMPERFECTIONS

School systems do not slash their teachers' salaries. They freeze them. Teachers who have high recommendations and are not especially attached to a particular district will soon move to where expectations for high pay will be realized. For the system that does not systematically review its salary schedule, recruitment of new teachers with even the same quality will become increasingly difficult, and there likely will be a slackening off in performance of those teachers who remain.

The ultimate weapon of the teacher in conjunction with the union is the strike. In every other strike of labor against management, the worker makes the sacrifice of loss of pay in order to achieve higher benefits in the long run. The teacher strike does not conform to that model, because the state law requires that children attend school a fixed number of days a year. The teacher withholds his services, but really does not lose either working time or salary, since schools remain open by law, regardless. In other words, he will recover, days lost on a strike and in addition receive the benefits and rewards of the strike. His risk is minimal.

The options are protecting the teacher and his family from rising prices. He is protecting the investment he made in his education and is attempting to protect himself as a member of a profession that has not addressed itself to differentiating its teaching responsibilities. The teachers' strike is a predictable response given the state of the inflationary economy and the inability of schools to make the profession competitive with other professions and within itself.

However, some innovative school systems have attempted to confront the problem of differential pay for differential service and have shown signs of being responsive to the individualization of teacher performance. Some of these schools and systems have been described elsewhere in these pages. The success or failure of their refinement, of their reform of differentiating teachers' salaries, and of their offering a new measure of quality pay for quality teaching will likely depend on the willingness of administrators and schools to change present practices. Precedents to similar domestic concerns dealing with personnel practices, employee relations, and salary adjustments indicate that these problems are solvable.

Footnotes

1. *Innovation in Education: New Directions for the American School,* Committee for Economic Development, Research and Policy Committee, July 1968, p. 49.
2. Ibid., p. 80.
3. These and the following statistics were taken from *Projections of Educational Statistics to 1977-78,* Department of Health, Education and Welfare, Office of Education, (Washington, D.C.: U.S. Government Printing Office, 1968), pp. 84-85.
4. Consult Paul A. Samuelson, *Economics: An Introductory Analysis,* (New York: McGraw-Hill, 4th ed., 1968) pp. 544.

10   A Model for the Financing of a Differentiated Staffing Program

Gerald Krumbein

INTRODUCTION

In any society where resources are limited, competition exists among the various agencies of that society for use of those resources. When the resources are human, the competition becomes especially severe. Although there is no shortage of teachers at the present time, the education profession is still faced with the problem of making itself occupationally alluring to highly qualified and competent personnel. While traditionally it has offered the prospective employee a great deal of security, education has not provided a means whereby the professional can advance in the organization and still remain in the classroom. If a teacher is given a promotion, he may become a supervisor, consultant, dean, department chairman, curriculum coordinator, principal, counselor, or superintendent. Upon receiving a promotion, he will rarely, if ever, remain a teacher. This is unfortunate, for we have constantly maintained that the most important part of the educational process occurs in the classroom. Yet salaries, status, and prestige rise in direct proportion to the distance the professional moves away form the teaching function and contact with children. One result of the failure of education to provide a means of professional advancement within teaching itself has been the tendency for the most competent personnel to seek more favorable positions both in and out of the profession, invariably removing themselves from the classroom. A corollary of this reward and incentive system is that there is usually more skill and competence displayed by teachers who occupy the middle, rather than the upper section of the salary schedule. Thus, to a great extent, the best teachers, or those who would ordinarily be at the top of the schedule, have been promoted away from teaching. The relationship between competence and time on the job is not the straight line that the salary schedule assumes it to be (Figure 46). It can be more realistically represented by a curve (Figure 47).

FIGURE 46   FIGURE 47

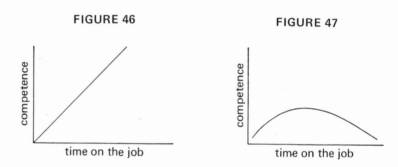

Hence a major problem is to provide a way for the teacher to continue growing professionally and still be in contact with students.

One solution to this problem may rest in the establishment of the concept of staff utilization known as differentiated staffing. John Rand, the superintendent of Temple City, California, a pioneer in this field, defines differentiated staffing in the following manner:

> Teachers are not treated the same. They may receive additional remuneration for increased professional responsibilities, which means change in their roles as teachers. These new responsibilities imply increased training and time on the job, and implicit in the concept of advancement is professional competence as a teacher, however it is measured. Teachers are not chosen to be paid more simply for continuing to perform their same functions. They are paid more for assuming increased responsibilities in the instructional program. They are selected on the basis of their experience and qualifications for the job by a professional panel and are retained only as they are able to perform adequately in their capacities. [1]

---

1. M. John Rand and Fenwick English, "Towards A Differentiated Teaching Staff," *Phi Delta Kappan*, January 1968, pp. 264-265

In other words, teachers are given different duties and responsibilities based on their levels of performance and competence. Experience and degrees alone will not qualify a teacher for a higher position in the differentiated hierarchy. The emphasis is placed on individuals assuming their different roles, responsibilities, and salaries based on the differences in their backgrounds, personalities, interests, and levels of competence and training. These roles run the gamut from high to low responsibility, and teachers are placed on this continuum according to the contributions they are able to make towards the achievement of the school's educational objectives. Their salaries are commensurate with the responsibilities they assume.

This is by no means a camouflaged merit pay system, although merit pay also involves differentiated salaries. In the merit system, the level of compensation is based only on the degree of "competence" displayed by the teacher. It rewards those individuals who have shown themselves to be superior to their colleagues, even though they all may perform the same tasks and have the same training. This judgment is usually a poor one and may not have any empirical basis. Merit pay attempts to discriminate among equals. Differentiated staffing does not. It rests on the premise that teachers are, and should be, unequal and provides higher salaries only for those individuals who assume additional responsibilities.

THE PROBLEM OF COST

Accompanying the rise in tax dollars that have been spent on education in recent years is a demand by school administrators for more attention to the principles of economic efficiency, such as that of "opportunity cost," which suggests that when a decision is made as to how some productive resource will be allocated, the opportunity of using that resource in some alternative way is no longer possible. The most obvious productive resources of the educational system is the teacher. Yet the teacher spends a great deal of the time performing non-teaching monitor tasks which could be executed less expensively, and possibly more efficiently by other types of personnel. The fact that the alternative educators have consistently chosen involves a large opportunity cost violates all the principles of sound economics. Among other things, differentiated staffing aims to concentrate all the teacher's time on teaching.

The 1970's have brought an end to the teacher shortage. However, the use of the differentiated staff is becoming more and more widespread, as educators search for ways to make education more effective and efficient. Unfortunately, like most innovations, the introduction of differentiated staffing is likely to be accompanied by an increased level of expenditure for personnel on the part of the school district.[2]

Because of the relative newness of differentiated staffing, little is known about what it costs. School districts either assume that they can alter their staffing patterns with little or no change in operational cost (ignoring the entire question of cost), or they may attempt to make decisions with no knowledge of the financial implications.

If a school district receives an adequate federal or foundation grant to cover the added cost of a differentiated staffing program, it may have little or no financial problem. However, there are many districts that may wish to inaugurate such a program, but cannot afford to do so. Thus, in the absence of outside subsidy, the school district may be forced to raise the money locally if it wishes to innovate. But overburdened taxpayers are becoming increasingly less willing to vote increases in the tax rate, and militant teacher organizations are demanding that any extra funds be allocated to teacher salaries. The result is that there is little or no money available in most districts to finance innovative programs.

This chapter is designed to accomplish two major objectives for the school district in this position. The first is to examine the dollar costs a district may incur during the transition from a traditional to a differentiated staff. The second is to explore a model which may enable a district to meet these extra transitional costs locally without either exceeding its budget ceiling or sacrificing any instructional time.

In particular, the author explores the hypothesis that the reallocation of resources, both human and financial, may enable the school district to introduce a differentiated staffing program. The data is designed to test the assumption that the reduction of the school district's highly paid professional staff, combined with a corresponding increase in the number of less expensive paraprofessionals, will result in the district's possessing more adults per student at less cost, with no loss of instructional time. It is further hypothesized that the savings that would result from the reallocation of resources from

---

2. For a more complete treatment of the costs of the personnel involved in the creation of a differentiated staff, see Gerald Krumbein, "How To Tell Exactly What Differentiated Staffing will Cost Your District," *American School Board Journal,* May 1970, pp. 19-24.

certificated to paraprofessional personnel could be used to offset the transitional costs of the differentiated staffing program.

The author assumes that the school district has already committed itself to the philosophy of differentiated staffing and is only searching for a way in which to finance the innovation. The conclusions reached are thus limited to this beginning or transitional phase and do not purport to deal with the actual differentiation and compensation of the certificated staff of a seasoned, on-going project.

The need for information of this nature is greatest among those school administrators who are faced with the problem of either initiating or implementing an innovation such as differentiated staffing. Although the model presented here will not be applicable to every potential project in every school district, it should have some implications for most districts which are contemplating the transition from a traditional to a differentiated staff.

PROCEDURES

In order to discover whether or not the use of paraprofessionals could enable a district to save enough money to cover the added cost of a differentiated staffing program, two types of data were collected: the first isolating the tasks of a sample of secondary school teachers functioning normally in a traditionally organized sample of schools; and the second involving a sample of differentiated staffing project directors and their responses to a questionnaire concerning the financing of their projects.

The data on which the first part of the model is based were collected by questionnaire from full-time certificated teachers in nine secondary schools (grades 7-12) in five different suburban school districts. The financial information was obtained also by questionnaire from differentiated staffing project directors administering programs (in both the planning and operational stages) throughout the country.

From all of this data one sample district and one sample project are presented to illustrate how effectively the paraprofessional replacement model can operate.

The Time-Analysis Questionnaire

The time-analysis questionnaire (see Appendix A) that was distributed to the teachers was constructed to answer the following questions:

1. What functions or tasks do the teachers perform?

2. Which of these are instructional and which are non-instructional?

3. How much time do they spend performing each task or function?

4. What are they paid for performing these tasks or functions?

5. Which of these functions do they feel can be adequately performed by non-certificated, non-professional personnel?

There was no rationale or basis for the exclusion of any item on the questionnaire. On the contrary, an attempt was made to systematically include everything that the secondary teacher might conceivably do as a part of his job. Although data from elementary schools (grades K-6) were not available there is no reason why the concept of differentiated staffing cannot be utilized as well in an elementary setting as a secondary one, as the teachers working in elementary projects well know. Thus, the results should be viewed with this limitation in mind. However, I wish to emphasize this point: While the figures may be somewhat different for elementary teachers, the concept is not. Elementary teachers also spend a great deal of their time on non-instructional activities which represent a great opportunity cost to the school. The addition or deletion of relevant items from the non-instructional section of the time-analysis questionnaire (question 16A-X) would make the questionnaire as applicable to elementary teachers as it is to secondary teachers in its present state.

The Differentiated Staffing Project Questionnaire

The purpose of this questionnaire was to determine how much money a differentiated staffing project is likely to spend in its transitional stage. It was constructed to elicit five basic transitional costs: personnel, scheduling, travel, materials and supplies, and publicity. A complete copy of the questionnaire can be found in Appendix B.

The costs for each project were divided into two sections—fixed and variable. Fixed costs were those which were judged to be those which almost every differentiated staffing project must usually incur, including the project director's salary, the salaries of his staff, the consultants' salary, travel, and per diem, and teacher-training.

Variable costs are those with which projects may become involved, depending on their wealth and degree of commitment to differentiated staffing. They include: 1) the cost of substitutes to provide released time for teacher planning, 2) increased salaries for differentiated personnel, 3) travel expense for district personnel to observe other differentiated projects, 4) scheduling (computer time and personnel) if projects begin to implement flexible or modular scheduling, 5) additional curricular materials and supplies needed by the project, 6) publicity, and 7) other miscellaneous costs.

The only costs purposely omitted from the analysis at this stage were those involving paraprofessionals and their training. These are dealt with in the first section of the analysis.

All of these costs were added together (except for the amount spent on paraprofessionals) to give a total project expenditure. The result was divided by the number of students involved in the project in order to derive the amount per student that a district seeking to undergo a change to a differentiated staff might have to spend in order to accomplish that change. In the absence of any federal or foundation grant, this money would have to be raised locally.

RESULTS

The Time-Analysis Questionnaire

The time-analysis questionnaire administered to secondary school teachers (Appendix A) was constructed to provide two separate measures of total time spent on the job. The author was thus provided with an internal check on the reliability of the answers of the respondents.

The first measure, called "Total School Related Activities" (SRA), was derived by adding together all of the hours and minutes listed in answer to questions 6 through 16X. These included time spent working on schoolwork at home, in faculty meetings, parent and staff conferences, team planning, formal and informal contacts with students, and non-instructional tasks. The computation of total hours for question 6, dealing with the number of daily periods taught, was based on a fifty-minute class period.

The second measure, "Total Reported Hours" (TRH), was derived by subtracting arrival time at work (4) from departure time (5) and adding the time spent at home or at school on weekends in preparation for school (7 plus 8). The resulting figure covers total time spent at school (5 minus 4) and at home preparing for school (7 plus 8).

In other words, the first measure, "School Related Activities," called for an individual time accounting for all the activities performed by the teacher. "Total Reported Hours" involved a more cumulative estimation of time spent on the job. Theoretically, these two figures should have come out approximately equal. In fact, they did not.

The mean number of hours for SRA for District A was 61.6 with a standard deviation of 16.6. The mean number of hours reported in the TRH measure was 52.7 with a standard deviation of 9.4, a rather large difference.

Since the figures for SRA and TRH differ, the problem was to decide whether to adopt one or the other, or some combination of the two. The assumption will be made that TRH, the lower figure, is the more reasonable one for three major reasons.

1. The SRA figure, which averages out to approximately sixty hours per week, seems to be rather high. On the basis of a five-day work week, this figure averages out to twelve hours a day spent on school related activities. On the basis of a seven-day week, this is still a rather respectable total of eight and one-half hours per day. the average weekly amount of time spent at home working on school work (7) was only nine and one-tenth hours, leaving the rest of the time (52.5 hours) to be spent at school. This averages out to about ten and one-half hours per day at school. Thus, there is a daily two-hour block of time unaccounted for if the SRA measure is utilized.

2. SRA was computed by adding together questions 6 through 16X. This represents a large number (forty-three) of individual measures. Even a small overestimation of from ten to fifteen minutes per week on each item would magnify the total weekly error to one approaching ten hours. On the other hand, TRH only involved four items (4, 5, 7, and 8). It would take a significant and more easily detectable error on these four items to add up to ten hours per week.

3. Examination of the standard deviation for both SRA and TRH reveals the greater variability in SRA (16.6 as opposed to 9.4). Thus, more teachers seem to agree on Total Reported Hours rather than Total School Related Activities. For these reasons, TRH will become the time criterion to be used for this analysis.

Table 1 illustrates the percentage of time spent on non-instructional tasks by teachers of academic and non-academic subjects in the District A senior high schools (see question 16A-X). The academic disciplines include English, social studies, math, science, and foreign language. The non-academic subjects include business, physical education, home economics, art, music, and industrial arts.

TABLE I

Percentage of time spent per week on non-instructional tasks (NIT) by senior high school teachers of academic and non-academic subjects

	ACADEMIC	NON-ACADEMIC	AVERAGE
Total Reported Hours	54.1	50.0	52.7
Number of Non-Instructional hours	14.1	12.0	13.4
Number of Non-Instructional hours expressed as a percentage of Total Reported Hours	26.1%	24.0%	25.4%

Approximately one-fourth (up to 25.4) of the teacher's total time is spent executing non-instructional tasks.

THE COST OF NON-INSTRUCTIONAL TASKS

These tasks are not only expensive in terms of time, but in terms of money as well. The average yearly salary for the teachers in District A is $11,318. Using a 177-178-day school year (35.5 weeks), the average weekly salary for the teachers in District A can be derived. If this average weekly salary is divided by the total number of hours reported, the result is a figure which represents a dollar expenditure per unit of time (one hour) for both instructional and non-instructional activities. Table 2 illustrates this expenditure per unit of time for District A.

TABLE 2

Dollar expenditure per unit of time for instructional and non-instructional activities for District A

Average yearly salary	$11,318
Average weekly salary	$318.82
TRH	52.7
Expenditure per unit of time	$6.05

These salary figures are probably generalizable at least to the State of California. There is a relatively small difference between the average yearly salary of District A ($11,318) and the average salary of all secondary public school districts in California for the year 1970-1971 ($11,741).

Thus, for every hour per week a teacher spends typing a ditto, sitting in a study hall, or monitoring a playground, it costs District A an average of $6.05. The average yearly cost to District A of the non-instructional activities performed by each teacher is $2877.99. This figure is derived by multiplying the dollar expenditure per unit of time (one hour) by the average number of weekly hours spent on non-instructional activities. The result, or the cost of non-instructional tasks per teacher per week, is then multiplied by 35.5 which represents the weekly length of the teaching year (177-178 days). (See Table 3.)

TABLE 3

Per teacher cost of non-instructional tasks (NIT) per hour, per week, and per year for District A

NIT hours per week	13.40
Hourly cost	$6.05
Per teacher cost of NIT per week	$81.07
Per teacher cost of NIT per year	$2877.99

By carrying this process one step further, the total yearly cost to the district of non-instructional tasks can be computed. The average cost of non-instructional tasks per teacher per year is multiplied by the total number of teachers in the district, as is shown below in Table 4.

TABLE 4

Total yearly cost to the district of non-instructional tasks (NIT) performed by teachers in District A

Per teacher cost of NIT per year	$2877.99
Number of teachers	589
Yearly cost of NIT to district	$1,695,136

Logically, the next step is to derive a figure which represents the cost of non-instructional tasks expressed as a percentage of the total budget. This process is relatively straightforward for a secondary district such as A. But a problem exists for the elementary district (K-8) or the unified district (K-12) that needs this percentage. In order to derive it, it is necessary to adjust the budgets of these elementary or unified districts to isolate the total amounts which are spent for the education of elementary (K-6) and secondary (7-12) students respectively. Since school business offices are unlikely to possess these figures, the adjustment can be done artificially using the following procedure. The example figures are from the California State Department of Education.

The total expenditure per unit of (Average Daily Attendance (ADA) for the State of California for both elementary and secondary students for the years 1962-63 to 1969-70 was examined. These figures were obtained from a publication entitled *California Public Schools, Selected Statistics, 1969-1970*, published by the Bureau of Administrative Research and District Organization of the California State Department of Education. On the basis of the figures presented in this document, the dollar expenditure per unit of ADA was projected to the current year, 1970-1971. This was accomplished by the use of a weighted mean percentage of increase to predict the amount of expenditure for 1970-1971. The weighting was achieved by assigning a value of one to the figure for 1962-63, and so on. This was done in order to make the more recent figures count more heavily in the average. Thus, for 1970-1971 the state average total expenditure per unit of ADA was $776.65 for elementary students and $1010.49 for secondary students, a ratio of 1:1.318. The entire series of figures is shown in Table 5.

To illustrate how this ratio can be used, let us look at another district which we shall call District B. District B has 82 teachers of which 27 are secondary (708) and 55 are elementary (K-6). There are 1642 students, of which 407 are secondary and 1235 are elementary. The total budget for District B is $2,089,255.

Using this ratio of 1:1.318, an adjusted budgetary figure was derived which represented the expenditure for secondary schools only. For example, out of a total budget of $2,089,255 spent for the education of 1235 K-6 students and 407 seventh and eighth grade students in District B, $632,640 is spent on secondary students. This figure was computed using the following procedure:

1. The number of secondary students (407) was multiplied by 1.318. The resulting figure represents the total number of secondary "units" (536.4).

TABLE 5

Total expenditure per unit of ADA projected for 1970-1971

ELEMENTARY   SECONDARY

Year	Dollar Amount	Increase Over Previous Year	Dollar Amount	Increase Over Previous Year	Ratio of Elementary to Secondary
1962-63	394.34		607.11		1:1.5395
1963-64	414.40	.0508	630.92	.0392	1:1.5224
1964-65	447.39	.0796	680.45	.0785	1:1.5209
1965-66	482.56	.0786	722.03	.0611	1:1.4962
1966-67	524.27	.0864	762.62	.0562	1:1.4546
1967-68	563.99	.0757	808.75	.0604	1:1.4339
1968-69	640.37	.1354	880.03	.0881	1:1.3742
1969-70	700.59	.0940	944.72	.0735	1:1.3484
1970-71	766.65	.0943	1010.49	.0696	1:1.318

2. The number of elementary students or "units" (1,235) and the adjusted number of secondary "units" (536.4) were added together. The total was 1,771.4.

3. The total budget of the district, $2,089,255, was divided by 1,771.4 in order to arrive at a per unit cost. This per unit cost equalled $1,179.40.

4. The per unit cost, $1,179.40, was then multiplied by 1,235 elementary units, and 536.4 secondary units respectively, totaling $1,456,499 (elementary) and $632,640.16 (secondary).

Although these figures only add up to $2,089,139 instead of $2,089,255, the discrepancy can be explained by rounding out the figures that occurred throughout the computation.

With these figures, it is possible to derive the percentage of the total budget of the district that is paid out yearly for the performance of routine, non-instructional tasks. The percentage for District B is 14.28 percent. For District A the percentage is 10.27 percent. These figures are illustrated in Table 6.

TABLE 6

Percentage of the budget paid out for the performance of non-instructional tasks (NIT) by secondary teachers.

	DISTRICT A	DISTRICT B
Total budget	$16,507,350	$2,089,255
Total number of teachers	589	82
Number of secondary students	12,742	407
Number of secondary teachers	589	27
Total adjusted budget	$16,507,350	$ 632,640
Per teacher cost of NIT per year	$ 2,877.99	$ 3323.51
Total cost of NIT by all teachers	$ 1,695,136	$ 89,735
Cost of NIT expressed as a percentage of the adjusted budget	10.27%	14.18%

THE USE OF PARAPROFESSIONALS

One solution to this problem, which will be explored in this chapter, is to free teachers from having to execute these non-instructional tasks by hiring paraprofessionals, such as aides, clerks, secretaries, and technicians of various kinds to fulfill this function.

It is important to know whether teachers feel that paraprofessionals can perform these tasks competently. Question 17 of the time-analysis questionnaire asked teachers to indicate which of the items in question 16 they felt could be adequately performed by trained, non-certificated paraprofessionals. (The figures in Table 7 illustrate the responses to this question.) It should be noted that the responses given by the teachers in District A were quite conservative, and that the true percentages for all teachers may be quite a bit higher.

THE PARAPROFESSIONAL-REPLACEMENT MODEL

In order to illustrate what this use of paraprofessionals can mean to a district financially, District A will be used as an example once again. The following figures should be kept in mind:

TABLE 7

Percentages of teachers in District A who feel that non-instructional
tasks can be performed by paraprofessionals

	TASK	n=138 A
A.	Yard duty (e.g. recess)	96
B.	Bus duty	94
C.	Monitoring corridors or washrooms	92
D.	Straightening or decorating rroms or labs	80
E.	Monitoring study halls	86
F.	Monitoring athletic events	80
G.	Supervising at student activities or dances	73
H.	Supervising the cafeteria or lunchroom	90
I.	Filling out weekly attendance forms	86
J.	Transcribing grades	78
K.	Calculating grade-point averages	61
L.	Grading objective or standardized examinations	86
M.	Monitoring college board or psychological examinations	78
N.	Typing tests or dittoes	90
O.	Running off and collating dittoes or mimeo material	92
P.	Passing out materials	98
Q.	Taking inventory of supplies	86
R.	Ordering and obtaining supplies	66
S.	Collecting money for student events	86
T.	Reading announcements	86
U.	Monitoring homerooms	81
V.	Taking daily attendance	88
W.	Operating audio-visual equipment	84
	Median	86

Total number of teachers: 589

Cost of non-instructional tasks per teacher per year: $2878

Total yearly cost to the district of non-instructional tasks performed
by teachers: $1,695,136

Percentage of time spent on the performance of non-instructional
tasks: 25 percent

Average number of non-instructional hours per week per teacher:
13.4

The number of paraprofessionals needed to complete all of the non-instructional tasks that teachers generally perform can be found by figuring the total number of weekly hours needed, which can be computed by multiplying the total number of teachers (589) by the average amount of time spent on non-instructional activities per week (13.4). The result is 7,893 hours per week.

An assumption will be made that paraprofessionals will work daily from eight in the morning to four in the afternoon, or a forty-hour week. By dividing 7,893 by forty, the total number of paraprofessionals is derived at 197.

Table 8 shows the cost of these paraprofessionals figures for an hourly wage of two dollars, three dollars, four dollars, and five dollars.

TABLE 8

Cost to the district of paraprofessionals at varying hourly wage rates

Hourly wage of paraprofessional	$2.00	$3.00	$4.00	$5.00
Daily cost per paraprofessional	$ 16	$ 24	$ 32	$ 40
Weekly cost per paraprofessional	80	120	160	200
Yearly cost per paraprofessional	2840	4260	5680	7100
Total yearly cost to the district	559,480	839,220	1,118,960	1,398,700

If certificated teachers in District A spent 25 percent of their time on non-instructional tasks (see Table 1), and if paraprofessionals are to fulfill these duties, then it is reasonable to assume that the district can operate successfully with 25 percent fewer teachers. How the district chooses to accomplish this is its own concern. One way might be to let natural attrition take its course. Other personnel could then be shifted to fill the vacancies that occur. This might take more than one year to accomplish in a period when jobs are scarce. However, the process can be begun at any time and does not have to be completed within one year.

District A, with 12,742 students and 589 teachers, has a student-teacher ratio of 21.63 students to each teacher. Decreasing the number of teachers by 25 percent to 442 would increase this ratio to 28.83 to one. However, the addition of 197 paraprofessionals to replace the 147 teachers would *decrease* the adult-student ratio to 19.94 to one. Therefore, even though there are fewer certificated teachers per student under the new arrangement, there are more adults, and the possibility of each child getting more individual attention.

As was illustrated in Table 4, the total yearly cost to this district of non-instructional tasks performed by the teacher is $1,695,136. Should these tasks be executed by paraprofessionals, a substantial savings could result. Table 9 illustrates this savings based on the hourly salaries of two dollars, three dollars, four dollars, and five dollars.

TABLE 9

Potential savings to the district by substituting paraprofessionals for certificated teachers in the performance of non-instructional tasks (NIT)

Hourly wage of paraprofessional	$2.00	$3.00	$4.00	$5.00
Yearly cost to district of teachers performing NIT	$1,695,136	$1,695,136	$1,695,136	$1,695,136
Yearly cost to district of paraprofessionals performing NIT	559,480	839,220	1,118,960	1,398,700
Possible saving to district	1,135,656	855,916	576,176	296,436

Thus, even paying the paraprofessionals five dollars per hour or $7100 per year, the highest wage, the result is a considerable saving of almost $300,000 for District A. This has been accomplished with no loss of instructional time, a decrease in the adult-student ratio, and the possibility of increased individualized attention and instruction for each student.

In addition, the total savings at the various salary rates can be divided by the number of teachers and students to compute a per teacher and per student saving. These possible savings are shown in

Table 10 below. They range from $89 per student and $1928 per teacher if paraprofessionals are paid $2.00 per hour, to a saving of $23 per student and $503 per teacher if paraprofessionals are paid $5.00 per hour.

TABLE 10

Possible savings per teacher and per student by replacing 25 percent of the teachers with enough paraprofessionals to perform their non-instructional tasks at wages of two to five dollars per hour

Hourly Wage	$2.00	$3.00	$4.00	$5.00
DISTRICT A				
Total savings	$1,135,656	$855,916	$576,176	$296,436
Per teacher	1928	1453	978	503
Per student	89	67	45	23

The research on which this chapter is based has shown the average per teacher and per student savings to be somewhat lower than those indicated above. Accordingly, since they are derived from a much bigger sample, these average figures are the ones that will be used henceforth. They are illustrated below in Table 11.

TABLE 11

Average per teacher and per student savings

Hourly wage	$2.00	$3.00	$4.00	$5.00
Per teacher saving	$2169	$1675	$1181	$686
Per student saving	79	61	43	25

However, there is a great deal of evidence that most paraprofessionals earn not five dollars per hour, but somewhere between two and four dollars per hour. In fact, some school districts, such as Berkeley or Sunnyvale, use volunteer aides from the community who are paid nothing for their services. In these instances, the possible savings would be even greater.

Thus, there is the possibility of a considerable savings per student if paraprofessionals are used to perform the non-instructional tasks which do not demand the skills of certificated personnel. If these savings can be applied to the added costs of the differentiated staffing projects, it may become economically possible for more districts to attempt the process of differentiation.

THE TRANSITIONAL COST OF THE
DIFFERENTIATED STAFFING PROJECT

In order to find out what these additional costs were, several projects were surveyed. However, for purposes of illustration and brevity, only one of those sample projects will be highlighted as an example. It includes 175 teachers, 2500 students, and has schools in both the planning and operational stages for differential staffing.

On the questionnaire sent to the project director (see Appendix B) it was reported that the paraprofessionals in the district were paid an hourly wage of $3.00. This means that there is a possibility of a per student saving of $61.00 per year based on the figures presented above in Table 11. In order to ascertain whether or not this per student saving was sufficient enough to offset the cost of the differentiated staffing project, the following method was used.

The analysis was begun by dividing total project expenditure into the two basic sections which were defined and explained earlier in the chapter. These were the fixed costs and the variable costs. The total fixed cost of this sample project was $81,570. The per student fixed cost came to $32.63. In the variable cost category, the total was $47,280, while the per student cost was $18.91.

Table 12 shows the total and the per-student expenditures in the fixed cost category. Table 13 shows the total and per student expenditures in the variable cost category.

Thus, the total expenditure for this project was $128,850, and the total per student expenditure to the nearest dollar was approximately $52. These figures were derived by adding together the fixed and the variable costs.

THE RESULTS — SAVINGS OR DEFICIT?

It is obvious, then, that the transition to a differentiated teaching

TABLE 12

Fixed Costs

	TOTAL	PER STUDENT
Project director's salary	$26,000	$10.40
Staff salary	20,500	8.20
Consultants' salary	1,800	.72
Consultants' travel expenses	1,150	.46
Teacher training costs	32,120	12.85
Per teacher training costs	184	
TOTAL	$81,570	$32.63

TABLE 13

Variable Costs

	TOTAL	PER STUDENT
Cost of substitutes	$4,500	$1.80
Increment in salary	9,500	3.80
Travel	4,000	1.60
Scheduling costs	3,000	1.20
Materials and supplies	25,000	10.00
Publicity	700	.28
Miscellaneous	580	.23
TOTAL	$47,280	$18.91

staff can involve a considerable expenditure to most districts. Consequently, the decision to embark on this course is one that should be preceded by careful study.

Financing this innovation by grants, raising taxes, or teachers volunteering to take salary cuts to finance the program are not particularly feasible for the large numbers of districts that have expressed an interest in differentiated staffing, but the alternative that may be feasible involves the use of paraprofessionals.

An integral part of a differentiated staff is the paraprofessional who is employed in an auxiliary role and assists the teacher in many ways. By showing how the judicious use of paraprofessionals can free funds for differentiated staffing, and illustrating the cost structure through a sample of differentiated staffing projects, this chapter presents one technique which a school district might employ in order to pay for a differentiated staffing program, and obtain the paraprofessionals required for the program all in one step.

In this illustrative differentiated project, the total per student cost is lower than the possible saving per student based on the paraprofessional wage paid by that project. The project reported a paraprofessional wage of $3.00 per hour, which allowed it to save $61.00 per student. The cost of the project was only $52.00 per student. Thus, in this case, the use of paraprofessionals not only pays for the innovation, it starts the district down the road to differentiation. In addition, there is an $11.00 per student surplus which can be used within the project for additional personnel or materials, or which might even be used to lower the district tax rate.

Assuming that the differentiation of teaching roles, combined with an increase in paraprofessional use, is likely to lead to more individualized instruction, it is logical to hope that individualizing instruction will enhance the learning potential. Should this occur, there will undoubtedly be greater demands made on the curriculum, as students begin to expect more and better classes and a higher quality of instruction. The school will have to develop some rationale and technique for coping with this potential problem. In addition, the school must develop some way to determine whether or not the lower ratio of adults to students is as effective educationally as the higher ratio of professional teachers to students.

Several psychological issues would also have to be resolved, such as how the introduction of paraprofessionals will

1. change the teacher's perception of his own role?

2. affect the teacher psychologically seeing others perform tasks that were once his own?

3. affect the student's perception of the role of the teacher?

4. give rise to psychological problems from the student-teacher-paraprofessional interaction?

Several problems of a sociological nature should also be researched, such as:

1. What are the classroom interactional patterns of behavior between the professional and the paraprofessional?

2. What effects will the introduction of paraprofessionals have, if any, on the relations among teachers, and also between teachers and students?

3. What implications and/or consequences will the utilization of paraprofessionals have for the organizational pattern of the school?

4. What will be the effect of the paraprofessional on the student's perception of the teacher as an authority figure?

Perhaps the most perplexing political problem would be that of making the model attractive to teachers in general, and to the teacher associations and unions, in particular. It is likely to be an extremely thorny problem to convince the teacher that he may be able to do as effective a job with a class size of forty-five students and one or two aides as he can with twenty-five or thirty students and no aide. In addition, the teachers' groups will undoubtedly look upon this model with great disfavor, since its implementation would severely limit the number of positions available to certificated personnel and contribute to the general scarcity of teaching jobs.

Research will hopefully provide the answers to the above questions, for some steps must be taken, even though they may be drastic. The education profession is struggling through a financial crisis which is severely taxing its ability to grow and to develop. If this model can help a school district to alleviate some of its economic problems, it should be thoroughly explored as a possible alternative.

While this model can prove to be of great benefit to the creative district which would like to, but for economic reasons is unable to innovate, it is not proposed as being a panacea for all the ills that plague the education profession. As Winston Churchill once cautioned: "This is not the end. It is not even the beginning of the end. But it is, perhaps, the end of the beginning."

APPENDIX A

Teacher Time Analysis Questionnaire

The purpose of this questionnaire is to find out what a secondary school teacher does throughout the day, and how much of his or her time is spent on performing both instructional and non-instructional duties. All answers will be held in the strictest confidence. Please do NOT put your name on this questionnaire.

1. Is your present assignment junior or senior high school?   _____
2. How many years have you taught?   _____
3. What subject do you teach?   _____
4. What time do you usually arrive at work?   _____
5. What time do you usually leave work?   _____
6. How many periods per day do you teach?   _____
7. How many hours per week do you usually spend working on school work at home?   _____
8. How many hours do you spend on weekends working at school?   _____

9. How many hours per week do you normally spend in the following kinds of meetings? (If they are monthly activities, please use
the following conversion table.)   _____

       1 hour per month   =   15 minutes per week
       2 hours per month =   30 minutes per week
       3 hours per month =   45 minutes per week
       4 hours per month =   1 hour per week

A. School faculty meetings
B. PTA meetings   _____
C. Departmental, faculty senate, building meetings, other than
above   _____
D. District curriculum planning meetings
E. District in-serivce meetings   _____
F. Out-of-district in-service meetings   _____
G. District professional organization meetings (e.g. teacher as-
sociation, union)   _____
H. Other (specify)

_____   _____

_____

10. How many hours per week do you spend in parent conferences?
   A. In school   _____
   B. Out of school _____   _____
11. How many hours per week do you usually spend in school,
outside of class, preparing for classroom teaching?   _____
12. How many hours per week do you spend in team planning?   _____
13. How many hours per week do you usually spend conferring
with counselors, psychologists, administrators, other staff members, etc. about instructional matters?   _____
14. How many hours per week do you usually spend in informal
classroom situations with students before or after school, during
prep periods, etc.? Include activities such as tutoring, but not
corridor or bus duty.   _____
15. How many hours per week do you usually spend socializing
with other teachers in school? Include informal meetings but
exclude the lunch period.   _____
16. How much time per week do you usually spend on the following activities?   _____
   A. Yard duty (e.g. recess)   _____
   B. Bus duty   _____
   C. Monitoring corridors or washrooms   _____
   D. Straightening or decorating rooms or labs   _____
   E. Monitoring study halls   _____
   F. Monitoring athletic events   _____
   G. Supervising at student activities or dances   _____
   H. Supervising the cafeteria or lunchroom   _____
   I. Filling out weekly attendance forms   _____
   J. Transcribing grades   _____
   K. Calculating grade-point averages   _____
   L. Grading objective or standardized examinations   _____
   M. Monitoring college board or psychological examinations   _____
   N. Typing tests or dittoes   _____
   O. Running off and collating dittoes or mimeo material   _____
   P. Passing out materials   _____
   Q. Taking inventories of supplies   _____
   R. Ordering and obtaining supplies   _____
   S. Collecting money for student events   _____

T. Reading announcements _____
U. Monitoring homerooms _____
V. Taking daily attendance _____
W. Operating audio-visual equipment _____
X. Other (specify) _____

_____ _____
_____ _____

17. Which of the above tasks do you feel can be adequately performed by trained, non-certificated paraprofessionals?

(Please circle the letters that apply)

A   B   C   D   E   F   G   H   I   J   K   L

M   N   O   P   Q   R   S   T   U   V   W   X

18. If there are any tasks mentioned above that you feel CANNOT be adequately performed by trained paraprofessionals, please state your reasons below.

APPENDIX B

Differentiated Staffing Questionnaire

TO: PROJECT DIRECTOR

This questionnaire is an attempt to define the transitional costs of moving from a traditional to a differentiated staff. Please fill in the figures that apply to your project. If your project combines costs listed under different headings on this questionnaire, please make a note to that effect. Please note that I am not interested in dividing the expenditures into those provided by the state or government, and those provided locally. I only need the total amounts expended in the categories provided.

PERSONNEL COSTS

1. Salary of project director _____
2. Total salary of project director's staff _____
   A. Number of staff members _____
   B. Salary of each _____
   C. Number full or part time full ____ part _____
3. Total salaries of outside consultants _____
   A. Number of consultants used _____
   B. Amount of time spent consulting _____
   C. Hourly or daily salary _____
4. Total salaries of differentiated personnel over and above the traditional salary schedule (Differentiated salary minus traditional salary) _____
   A. Number of personnel on project _____
   B. Amount of time spent _____
   C. Daily or hourly salary _____
5. Total salaries of substitutes to allow for released time for teacher planning _____
   A. Number of substitutes used _____
   B. Number of hours worked _____
   C. Cost per hour of substitutes _____

6. Total teacher training costs   _____
   A. Number of teachers involved   _____
   B. Amount of training time   _____
7. Total salaries of paraprofessionals (secretaries, clerks, aides, etc.)
   ADDED under the differentiated staffing program.   _____
   A. Number of personnel added   _____
   B. Hourly, weekly, monthly, or yearly wage — specify _____
8. Costs of training program for paraprofessionals NOT ACCOUNT-
   ED FOR in question No. 6   _____

SCHEDULING COSTS
1. Do you anticipate a change in scheduling (e.g. modular scheduling) to accompany your differentiated staffing program   YES   NO
2. Cost of computer usage (time & personnel)   _____

TRAVEL COSTS
1. Total amount of reimbursement of consultants' travel expenses   _____
   A. Number of consultants used   _____
   B. Travel from where to where   _____

2. Expenses of district observation teams to other differentiated
   districts, meetings, institutes, etc. (total)   _____
   A. Number of individuals involved   _____
   B. Travel from where to where   _____
   _____

COST OF MATERIALS & SUPPLIES
1. Audio-Visual equipment (over that already possessed by the
   district)   _____
2. Other curricular materials for project   _____
   _____ $ _____
   _____ $ _____
   _____ $ _____

PUBLICITY COSTS
1. Surveys of staff, students, and community   _____
2. Publicity about project   _____
3. Miscellaneous — e.g. federal proposal, etc.   _____

OTHER COSTS
(Include any expenditures not already mentioned)
_____   _____
_____   _____
_____   _____

1. Which of the above figures have been based on estimates rather
   than actual costs?   _____

2. On what basis were the estimates made?
3. How big is your total school district?
   A. Number of schools   _____
   B. Number of teachers   _____
   C. Number of students   _____
4. How big is your differentiated staffing project?
   A. Number of schools involved   _____
   B. Number of teachers involved   _____
   C. Number of students involved   _____

11 Focus on Competency-Based Educational Systems

Marshall Frinks

The last decade has produced an ever growing concern for instructional personnel utilization in our school systems. This concern is evidenced in an increasing emphasis by local education agencies on in-service education programs for teachers, as well as a search for more effective utilization patterns for these instructional personnel that might enhance the teaching-learning processes. To summarize this movement, one might simply state that, over the past ten years, educational decision makers have become increasingly concerned with having an output-oriented education system rather than the traditional input-oriented system. They are concerned with the competencies which a student should possess after having gone through that system, and instructional personnel who possess the competencies to facilitate the learning processes of students to achieve those objectives.

This shift in emphasis raises several questions in the minds of many educators and lay people. First, do we in fact have the knowledge required to succeed in this transition, or can we, indeed, ready ourselves for such a change? Is the attitude of our teacher training institutions flexible enough to prepare future instructional personnel for an output-oriented school system when traditionally preservice preparation has been geared toward input? Can we use traditional staffing patterns as the facilitator of the competency-based program? Will regulatory responsibilities impede or support competency-based education? Responses to these questions at this point are not without qualifications; however, the momentum of the behavioral trend cannot be ignored.

Defining a Competency-Based System

Those educators who are developing the output-oriented systems find that defending the need for a competency or performance-based educational program is somewhat easier than providing a precise definition for such a program. Current usage of the phrase "performance-based" or "competency-based" may have a variety of meanings throughout the nation, but the characteristics of this movement are essentially the same, whether the term is applied to teacher education and certification or student learning programs. Basically, a competency-based program would include: prespecified performance objectives (competencies); techniques for assessing the achievement of those performance objectives; and decision making regarding training needs based on successful mastery of performance objectives.[1]

The terms "performance-based," "competency-based," and "criterion-referenced" are used synonymously by many educators to describe various programs bearing these three characteristics, although the interpretation and development of their techniques may vary.

An example of one technique that is used in the process-product development is *task analysis*. The purpose of task analysis is to identify everything that has to be done by the system to facilitate the attainment of the specified learning tasks. (Bela Banathy describes an instructional system that substantiates the need for identifying learning tasks prior to assigning resources.[2]) Performing an analysis will enable the developer to identify a hierarchy of instructional activities in an orderly and logical manner. One of the products of the analysis will be the specified individual skills and knowledge needed as a basis for building a meaningful staff development and utilization design.

It is not the intention of this chapter to deal specifically with the techniques of task analysis. There are several excellent sources, e.g., Fine and Wiley; Jackson; and Kaufman, to whom the reader might refer for specific technical information.[3] A caution should be expressed at this point, however, for task analysis is a fairly complex and sophisticated approach to teacher job design, and should not be taken lightly by the practitioner. To illustrate the nature of the technique supported by this writer and others, the subsequent flow diagram (Figure 48) and explanation were developed during a recent

FIGURE 48

Conceptual Design for Implementing Task
Analysis Based on Assessment of Needs

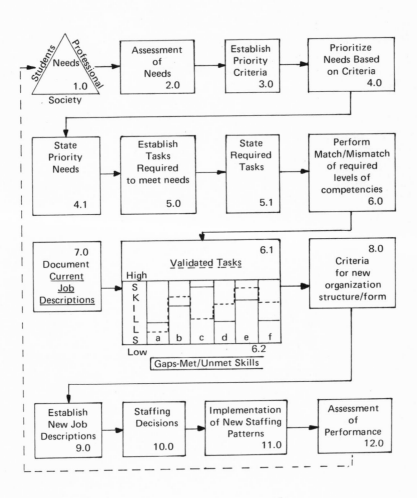

Office of Education sponsored task force meeting on task analysis by DeBloois, English and Frinks.[4] The conceptual design, which is needs assessment based, begins by validating identified needs, setting criteria for prioritizing needs, and proceeds through the process of matching present job descriptions with teaching tasks as related to priority needs, to statements of required performances, establishment of new job descriptions, staffing decisions, implementation and reassessment. It is the statements of required performances for all instructional personnel and the establishment of new job descriptions that imply the use of differentiated staffing patterns that are competency-based.

The use of the task analysis techniques, as illustrated, is intended to reduce the possibility of a predetermined staff design prior to the completion of a valid needs assessment, the establishment of required tasks/jobs to be performed, and the determination of skill levels necessary to complete required tasks. It is the process that is followed to legitimize the staffing patterns required that will be indicative of a competency-based consideration.

Why a Competency-Based Approach?

Considered in the most general terms, a competency-based program is an examination in the most specific terms of the questions: *Where are we? Where are we going?* and *How do we get there?* It calls for the establishment of performance requirements and the design of measurements to determine when and if these desired outcomes have been met. It insists upon a consideration of the techniques which can and should be used to accomplish the agreed-upon objectives. Competency-based education, then, is a process-product combination that is strengthened by the ability of both the teacher and the learner to express desired outcomes in a diffused decision-making situation. It belies the "all things to all men" appearance of teaching and learning, and permits the resources of a system to be directed toward appropriate and accountable ends. It makes explicit the competencies which are to be acquired and the criteria which are to be applied in assessing whether or not those criteria have been met.

Competency-based programs presuppose a systems approach to education which, despite its emphasis, insists upon a greater degree of personalization of learning than many of the traditional programs now in use.

Designers of such programs have little option but to personalize both the teaching-learning and the assessment process, for the demonstration of the ability to effect desired educational outcomes is always situation specific. Competence in a prospective teacher becomes measurable in terms of the ability of that teacher to bring about a specific outcome for a specific child or set of children who have specific characteristics and who are operating in a specific teaching-learning context. How much more sense it makes to concentrate on the ability of the teacher to bring about growth in children rather than to be preoccupied with what the teacher knows about teaching. Extensive involvement by all of those related to the educational processes in the establishment of desired outcomes will do much to assure legitimate personalization of the teacher-learner relations.[5]

Goal Setting and Objectives

Goal statements and objectives are essential in the definition or redirection of an educational system, whether one may be considering a statewide or building-level unit of this system. The establishment of overall goals translated into specific objectives serves to keep the criteria for achievement in focus. However visionary, these objectives must establish without question the desired outcomes of the educational community involved in terms which are specific enough to measure whether or not these goals have been or, in fact, can be attained in terms of the personnel and fiscal resources available. Goals should be broad enough to be direction-setting statements of ideal conditions of the educational system which may serve to define the arena in which the educational enterprise of the state, for example, will operate. Within an individual school, however, goals should be specific enough to measure in terms of long and short range objectives and should serve as guidelines for planning and programming the time and resources of the smaller educational community. Realistically, if you don't know what it is you are trying to do, there is little way to measure if, in fact, you've done it.

Differentiated Staffing and the Competency-Based Movement

The concept of staff differentiation is in essence the utilization of those competencies which have been identified by an educational assessment of the resources of a particular school community. It is essentially a matching of the strengths of staff members with the functions and tasks which must be performed to achieve the agreed-upon goals of the individual school. The differentiation of responsibilities and assignments of personnel follow as a logical outgrowth of a systematic approach to education.

In seeking to implement positive change within an educational system, leaders would do well to begin by focusing their attention on the aspects of input, process and output. *"Input* encompasses the provision, allocation and assignment of resources, both human and material. *Process* concerns the application and utilization of these resources in ways which will produce change in students or staff. *Output* is the behavior resulting from the process (behavior is used here in the general sense to include any observable student attributes which are the concern of the school.)[6] Staff differentiation or flexible staff organization, then, is the utilization of the available personnel resources on the basis of their skills, interests and personal motivations, in order to achieve the specified learning outcomes for the particular student population involved.

In order to work effectively, a differentiated staffing pattern cannot be superimposed upon a school, but must grow out of and reflect the needs and the resources of the individual school community. It should provide each member, regardless of years of service, with assignments best suited to his talents and abilities. An educational needs assessment, performance objectives for students, flexible scheduling, compensation for services which would be commensurate with levels of instructional and organizational responsibilities, and provisions for self-correction are all characteristics of a differentiated approach to staff utilization, as well as characteristics required of a competency-based program. As these new programs and approaches are designed, new functions will be called for and new roles will have to be developed. A comprehensive task analysis conducted with future needs in mind is likely to suggest not only the realignment of present personnel, but also the development of newly defined jobs. All of these roles may not fit within the traditional framework of the existing school design. In-service education, then, becomes an integral part of any reorganization plan.

Traditionally, in-service education has been the responsibility of the employee (teacher) of a school; however, when a school system makes the transition from an input to an output-oriented educational system, it then becomes the responsibility of the employer (school system) to provide appropriate in-service training programs for the instructional staff which are designed to help the entire school community meet the needs or goals which have been mutually agreed upon. It is only logical to assume that if the school conducts a search for the answers to "where are we" and "where do we want to go," it should be just as vitally interested in providing the experiences necessary for the "how we are going to get there" portion of the program.

The shift from an input to an output orientation also implies that the employer should recognize the need for a shift from an evaluation system of its employees for dismissal purposes to an instructional assessment system which would provide for diagnosis and prescription prior to in-service programs used for upgrading employees. This should also reduce the attrition rate to retain competent teachers in the system.

If widely adopted, differentiated staffing could stimulate the remaking of the education profession, since it raises issues about all phases of performance relating to both teaching and learning. Dramatic changes in teacher education institutions will be required to meet the demands of these new staffing arrangements which are performance-oriented. By abandoning the concept of all teachers as interchangeable parts, more specialized training can be brought about by focusing on specific roles. If beginning teachers, career teachers and auxiliary personnel are to be prepared for many of these specialized roles, they will need the flexibility to move through new experiences in more universities, and state education agencies and practicing teachers will be called upon to work together to define these new roles and to design specific models for their application to meet the needs of individual situations.

The Competency-Based Movement in Relation to the State Educational System

If we no longer accept the current uniformity of structure in our school systems for achieving the highest level of performance from the students upon which it is imposed, then the search for acceptable alternatives becomes imperative. Consequently, when a competency-based education system is viewed as an alternative replacement for the traditional system which has limited accountability in the areas of teaching-learning processes, it would be appropriate to place the alternative in the right context and proper perspective in relation to the statewide educational system. The illustration that follows is intended to provide the reader with one perception of the "people" dimensions of a state education system—the student performance criteria, the teacher performance as it relates to the specified student performance criteria, and the required preservice and inservice training based upon levels of competencies needed. The reader should note that as in all system approaches, to which the competency-based approach lends itself, the desired outcomes or educational goals are paramount. Each one of the four dimensions illustrated is, or should be, affixed to some quality assurance control of the state education system, whether it be managed by the state education agency, the local education agency, or both.

The focal points of Figure 49 are the stated educational goals. Goal statements are necessary, though they may appear to have little usefulness other than to provide a general structure for the educational system prior to stating the system's desired outcomes. How-

FIGURE 49

Competency-based Education System Dimensions

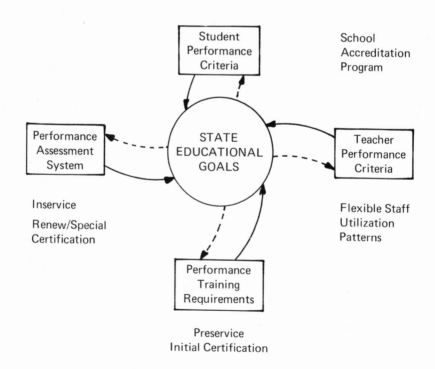

ever, these general statements provide the direction in which the system moves as it operates on a day-to-day, year-to-year basis. Goals in the case of the "people" dimension of the educational system provide the impetus for student development, teacher assignments based on the observed needs of the learner, minimum pre-in-the-service training essentials, and the diagnosis and prescription of attainable teaching skills.

Student Performance Criteria are intended to operationalize what students should achieve or acquire during their formal learning program. Learning objectives should be developed or adopted in student behavioral terms with sufficient clarity to permit measurement of student progress toward achievement of the goals of the educational system. The student performance criteria or objectives must be the basis for the development of not only the instructional program or learning tasks, but also the instructional support program. It is the characteristics of these instructional programs that imply *who must do what.*

Teacher Performance Criteria, analyzed functionally, determine the tasks or jobs that must be done to accomplish the instructional objectives. The product of the analyses then results in the "WHAT's" that must be accomplished, consistent with the student performance criteria. The wide range of skills and interests needed by instructional personnel to complete the prescribed tasks/jobs implies that teacher assignments be based upon the needs of the learners, and that the form or organizational structure follows functions. Thus, preconceived notions about traditional staffing patterns facilitating the learning criteria that are based upon needs prove to be ineffective. Some form of flexible staff utilization (differentiated staffing) is required in the competency-based approach. Statements of differentiated student objectives coupled with differentiated teacher assignments should result in a concise set of statements focused upon improving the school's product—the student. Many educators who are dealing with the competency-based education system are confronted with a number of teacher accountability questions. One such question, "Should a teacher's success be measured by his ability to bring about certain kinds of pupil outcomes?" prompts the consideration of *what skills are required and what training essentials must be met?*

Performance Training Requirements based upon skills needed by instructional personnel to complete the prescribed tasks/jobs places increased emphasis on the use of performance-product criteria and less emphasis on the traditional application of the knowledge criteria for preservice training. The implications for this shift are for teacher training institutions to seek the approval of state authorities to have the freedom to develop creative approaches to preservice and continuing preparation programs for educational personnel. To assure quality in teaching standards, program approval should be more than the transference of paper work from one agency to another. Along with the transference of much of the authority from the state regulatory agency to the teacher training institution which would allow creativity, as well as greater accountability in teacher preparation approaches, must also go a commitment to closer working relationships among the state, the colleges, and the local school districts.

On a recent study completed by the writer, state education agency personnel responsible for teacher education and certification expressed an attitude that preservice and in-service education should become a part of a continuum, with certification serving as only a formality to establish the point of growth in a teacher's educational process.[7] Under these conditions, the state credentialing agent would become just one of a series of checkpoints in a teacher's progression toward full competency. Renewal and advanced/specialization certification should increasingly become the responsibility of the local school district, training institutions, and the professional associations working hand in hand. Differentiation in staffing levels and responsibilities, as well as continuous skill training, must of necessity be situational and reflect the needs of local educational systems. The approach suggested by the writer would recognize that competence is more than a quality that exists in isolation or at a minimum level; competence should depend at least in part upon the local teaching situation. The intention is not to shift the legal authority for the educational system away from the state level, but to focus upon perhaps changing roles for educational agencies at all levels.

Performance Assessment Systems are systems of diagnosis and prescription for retaining and retraining educational personnel. The performance assessment system is a notion that will renew and shift the inservice responsibility within a state education system from the employee to the employer. This idea would thus become a requirement of a competency-based educational system. The development of a system for performance assessment begins with the identification of the skills and knowledge which teachers are expected to possess as they are related to the learning structures. These skills are first validated, i.e., demonstrated to be relevant to the goals teachers are expected to attain in the teaching-learning process. The establishment of required levels of competencies makes the process of screening for training and assignment of personnel for the various positions in the staff utilization mode more efficient.

In an endeavor to place greater emphasis on provisions for competency-based, output-oriented educational systems, and to move away from the traditional idea of minimum essentials, an attempt should be made to develop quality assurance controls in the context of the total system on the basis of desirable student performance. The controls/standards should be developed to stimulate total involvement and utilization of a system approach to the teaching-learning processes.

The State's Role in Direction Setting

The provision for public education is constitutionally a matter for the state governments. The ultimate responsibility for the well being of the educational system of a state resides, therefore, with the state education agency, under the general administration of the chief state school officer, subject to the rules established by the state board of education and the state legislature.

Traditionally, the role of the state department of education has been one of unilateral regulation. A recent study by this writer has revealed movement away from this authoritarian position, however, toward a service and consultative role.[8] There appears to be strong evidence of an emerging leadership among state education personnel who have the confidence and knowledge to effect change through a sharing of the responsibilities for direction setting. Increasingly, there seems to be less emphasis on inspection and more emphasis on improvement through cooperative action by educators at the state levels and those in the field.

This same study revealed that each of the twelve change characteristics commonly associated with the competency-based movement is currently being dealt with to some degree by the leadership personnel within the fifty state education agencies.[9] As a group, these leaders of the teacher education and certification sections of the state agencies felt that teacher training institutions, teacher advisory councils and professional organizations were also involved to some degree in the competency-based movement.

The states of Florida and Washington, both of which are attempting to implement performance-based teacher certification, have encouraged teacher training institutions to develop training programs employing performance criteria. A number of states, in fact, have already taken leadership roles in encouraging and implementing competency-based teacher education and certification. Others have chosen to approach the redefining of their educational system from an accreditation-standards point of view. These movements vary; however, common to all is the attempt to utilize objective performance criteria as a standard of measure. A sizable number of these states have committed their resources to the development of the areas of individualized instruction, a field-centered approach to teacher education, the use of feedback, and the development of consortia arrangement among local school districts. Exemplary programs are currently being developed throughout the nation, but to date no one state has yet made operational an entire system.

As these programs continue to develop, state education agency leaders will be increasingly challenged to provide expertise relevant to the local systems they serve. State education agency resources must provide, directly or indirectly, that expertise which is not available elsewhere.

The Importance of the Legislature

One major source of the educational community's power to effect change is their influence on the state legislature. Too often the role of the legislature is neglected in discussion of educational change— yet few other agencies have as much influence on the schools. A legislative mandate for school curriculum or standards has few competitors for the top of the list of actions that produce basic alterations in school operations.

While the legislature may not be the best place to establish detailed educational policy requirements, most new proposals for changes in educational policies must come before the legislature if for no other reason than to obtain funding. Through their power to establish teacher certification standards and specify curriculum, legislatures influence who will teach what in addition to determining the amount of money educators will be granted to accomplish their goals.

The magnitude of the strength and expertise of an effective working combination of the profession, university representatives, and state education personnel is staggering. It is somewhat surprising that educators have failed to utilize this combined source of power to any degree in the past; unfortunately there are more examples on record of in-fighting within the profession as a whole than of results of effective coalitions. For too long the politicians have been isolated from the educators, and the educators have talked mostly to themselves. Undoubtedly this area of influence has implications for new and more trenchant relationships for the future.[10]

CONCLUSIONS

The past decade has seen the emergence of a trend toward participatory decision making on the part of teacher education institutions and members of the profession generally. (Evidence supporting this trend can be found in the approved program approach, cooperation and planning across institutional lines, teacher advisory councils, professional practices commissions, and professional standards boards, and an increased interest in relevant and meaningful teacher-learning experiences both in preservice and in-service education programs.) It is the writer's opinion that the search for quality in education will continue and gain momentum as educators strive toward professionalism through accountability. Sharing must become a trademark of the profession, not only in the relationships of ideas among members of the profession within their own cities and states, but also across state lines and beyond established boundaries.

Personnel in state education agencies will have to accept the idea of a partnership among various institutions and agencies on matters relating to change, for the spark for significant changes in the educational programs within the state is likely to come from any one of the several agencies within the state. Realistically, it would be impossible to designate any one of these as "the leaders" in all states. By the same token, effective strategy would make it inadvisable to attempt to create a single pattern of operation among the fifty states.

One thing is abundantly clear—continuing state and federal funds must be made available for educational research. All too often pressures for instant improvement together with the conditions of insufficient time and inadequate resources can crystalize practices prematurely. There must remain those within the educational community whose task it is to examine with unblurred vision the innovations as well as the traditions. There must be a place for those who question as well as for those who promote, for those who hold back as well as for those who forge ahead; for the advent of change for change's sake without hard-headed inquiry may only build a different set of vested interests which may or may not be an improvement over those which already exist.

No one in the field of education can deny the need for a focus upon a more competent educational system, or that the questions of transition must be confronted in an orderly, unbiased exploratory manner. It is the writer's opinion that those developers of the competency-based approach have both the need and transition in mind.

Footnotes

1. Fred Daniel, "Performance-Based Does Not Mean Teacher Education Program Is Good — It Just Means It Is Easier To Tell," State of Florida, Department of Education, Tallahassee, unpublished discussion paper, September 1971.
2. Bela Banathy, *Instructional Systems* (Palo Alto: Fearon Publishers, 1968).
3. Sidney Fine and Wretha Wiley, *A Systems Approach To New Careers*, 1969; Vivian Jackson, *Task Analysis: Designing New Careers Programs*, 1971; Roger Kaufman, *Task Analysis In Educational Planning* (a chapter from unpublished book, publication date pending), draft copy, 1970.
4. Michael DeBloois, Fenwick English, and Marshall Frinks, "Conceptual Design For Implementing Task Analysis Based On Assessment Of Needs," unpublished discussion notes, 1971.
5. H. Del Scholock, *BEPD, NCERD, and Teacher Education That Makes A Demonstrable Difference*, "The Power of Competency-Based Teacher Education," U. S. Office of Education, July 1971.
6. State of Florida, *Plan For Educational Assessment In Florida: Final Report*, Department of Education, Tallahassee, March 1971.
7. Marshall L. Frinks, "An Analytical Study of Teacher Certification Processes As Perceived by Leadership Personnel Within the Teacher Education and Certification Sections of the Fifty State Education Agencies with Special Emphasis on the Development of the Performance-Based Movement," unpublished doctoral dissertation, University of Massachusetts, Amherst, June 1971.
8. Ibid.
9. Ibid.
10. Ibid.

12 Bifocals for Differentiated Staffers: A Report on the Status of Flexible Staffing Experiments

Michael DeBloois

Why We Need To Evaluate

As innovations go, differentiated staffing is getting well along in years; yet it has had a most difficult time resolving a youthful identity crisis. A number of educators have been using the term for half a decade or better now, but are still grasping for an adequate definition of the concept. It is not uncommon to hear a staffing innovator attempt to identify what he considers to be flexible staff-use goals by listing a series of strategies for initiating educational change. This confusion of goals with change strategies seems widespread even in groups claiming more than a passing familiarity with staffing innovation. As a result, we find individuals implementing a change strategy, then prematurely viewing their task as having been accomplished. Thus, titles are often changed and job descriptions are rewritten, but the goal of changing teacher and student behavior is seldom realized.

In describing one aspect of differentiated staffing, the use of aides and paraprofessionals, educators often speak in terms of hiring personnel to free the classroom teacher from lower order tasks so he may spend more time in instructional activities. Once the aide is hired, that aspect of staff innovation is considered accomplished. An

343

assessment of whether the paraprofessional is indeed performing an educational maintenance function, and whether the teacher is spending significantly more time instructing, seldom follows. There is a world of difference between the two positions. The first emphasizes the strategy (the means), while the second zeros in on the objective. Paraprofessionals are hired to increase the amount of time spent in instruction. It is the increased teacher time in instruction, not hiring the aide, which represents the accomplishment of that aspect of differentiated staffing. A similar critique could be made for other elements typically considered part of the concept such as vertical hierarchies, group decision making, and differentiated salaries.

All of this raises the problem of knowing what someone actually means when he states his school recently implemented differentiated or flexible staffing.

Hundreds of schools over the past five years have claimed to have adopted a differentiated staffing pattern. However, upon analysis, they were found all along to have a traditional/innovative spectrum. It is very unsettling to observe how different they are in operation while claiming to work toward the same goal. In many cases, the dissimilarities which can be found between the school claiming a differentiated staff and a neighboring school making no such claim, exist only in the minds of the respective administrators, or on the paper models filed away in the principal's office. The problem is widespread; once this author even found himself caught up in it. Innovators are called upon to describe what they plan to do so often, and they want to see it done so badly, that sometimes they picture it prematurely as already having been accomplished. They seem to be trapped in a tyranny of innovation—that involuntary spiral with its own vocabulary and requirement to "keep the faith" and support innovation at all costs, including one's perspective and sometimes even one's integrity—only later to find themselves supporting claims impossible to document. It is something other than blatant misrepresentation and is usually relatively innocent, and normally harmless. But it does take its toll in a credibility loss among colleagues who know the claims are not founded in fact, and has serious implications on the staff's receptivity toward future innovations.

In a sense, this might be considered a form of innovational astigmatism; people simply get too close to the subject and perceptions of reality become fuzzy. Since this nearsightedness is a problem encountered by all educators at one time or another, the need for the role of the evaluator, a practitioner of educational optometry, is made clearer. The analogy has additional meaning. A preacher or a policeman is not called in, neither is a judge nor an accountant, but an optometrist who can help identify the problem, without condemnation or punishment and suggest appropriate prescriptive measures to resolve the situation.

Gene V. Glass (1969, p. 5), offers a useful description of the role of the evaluator by comparing it with the role of a researcher. Research activity is conclusion oriented, in search of scientific "truth," and empirical verification. Evaluation activity, on the other hand, is decision oriented and directed toward assessing worth or social utility. The goal then, of an evaluation is to provide the educational specialist with a clearer perspective of his work, and a body of information (gathered in a systematic manner) which he can use as a baseline for better decision making.

What Is It that Needs Assessment?

The evaluator of a flexible staffing effort is immediately faced with the dilemma of providing appropriate and relevant data for educational decision makers. A search for data gathering guidelines leads the evaluator to study organizational theory and other literature related to flexible staffing to discover what the main elements of the staffing concept are. In doing this, he finds that he has returned to the beginning point of this article: he is in search of an adequate definition of the concept. Before evaluation can provide decision makers with meaningful information, the goals associated with flexible or differentiated staffing must be identified and interrelated in some consistent and logically meaningful fashion.

A recent evaluation of differentiated staffing projects by personnel in the Evaluation Training Center at Florida State Unviersity had as its theoretical base a Conceptual Model of School Personnel Utilization (DeBloois 1970). This model defines the concept of flexible staffing and interrelates the various components employed in the definition (see Figure 50). At the most general level, the conceptual framework identifies variables of input, process variables, and outputs of product variables which schools must act upon when attempting staffing innovation.

At a level of greater specificity, the model identifies the components of staff-use which relate to a staff member's regard for self (Individualism); the degree and quality of interpersonal interaction which exists (Collegiality); and the professional commitments which guide the actions of individuals on the staff (Professional Disposi-

FIGURE 50

A Conceptual Model for Evaluating
Organizational-Structural Innovations

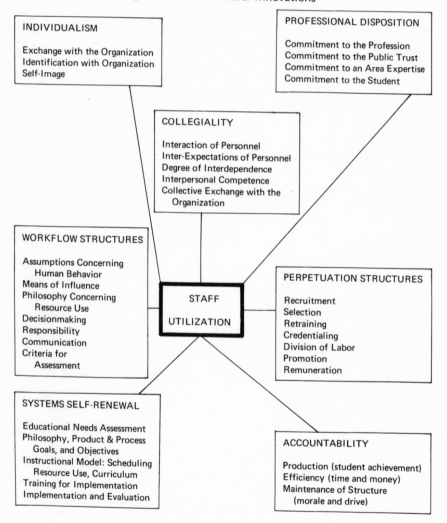

INDIVIDUALISM

Exchange with the Organization
Identification with Organization
Self-Image

PROFESSIONAL DISPOSITION

Commitment to the Profession
Commitment to the Public Trust
Commitment to an Area Expertise
Commitment to the Student

COLLEGIALITY

Interaction of Personnel
Inter-Expectations of Personnel
Degree of Interdependence
Interpersonal Competence
Collective Exchange with the
    Organization

WORKFLOW STRUCTURES

Assumptions Concerning
    Human Behavior
Means of Influence
Philosophy Concerning
    Resource Use
Decisionmaking
Responsibility
Communication
Criteria for
    Assessment

STAFF

UTILIZATION

PERPETUATION STRUCTURES

Recruitment
Selection
Retraining
Credentialing
Division of Labor
Promotion
Remuneration

SYSTEMS SELF-RENEWAL

Educational Needs Assessment
Philosophy, Product & Process
    Goals, and Objectives
Instructional Model: Scheduling
    Resource Use, Curriculum
Training for Implementation
Implementation and Evaluation

ACCOUNTABILITY

Production (student achievement)
Efficiency (time and money)
Maintenance of Structure
    (morale and drive)

tion). Also identified are the operations which enable the accomplishment of institutional goals such as communication, decision making, and implementation of decisions (Workflow Structures); and the policies established to recruit, employ, train, retrain, and reward the instructional and support personnel required by the institutional mission (Perpetuation Structures). Finally, the model describes the system an institution employs to monitor its goals of the program (Accountability).

This framework describes the flexible staffing concept by hypothesizing a developmental spectrum for each of these variables. Almost any form of staff-use can be located somewhere along the spectrum representing each variable. The seven variables themselves are believed to be comprehensive enough to include all varieties of the innovation currently being attempted. Thus, a staffing innovation which focuses on vertical hierarchies and salary differentials, or one with a focus on the interpersonal dimensions, as well as most varieties lying somewhere in between, can be described in relation to the common variable of the conceptual model and may be evaluated in any one or all of those variable areas.

The conceptual model proved to be adequate as a framework for studies of flexible staffing carried out by the Evaluation Training Center and shows promise as a factor in the theoretical development of the flexible staffing concept.

Guidelines for Evaluation

An evaluation of a flexible staffing project must begin with a rather comprehensive definition of the concept such as provided by the conceptual model. The evaluator must demonstrate an understanding of the developmental process, including the changing concerns of a staff as they pass through the various levels or phases of development. Even small staffing innovations cause ripple effects which are felt throughout the school organization, and an evaluation must be prepared to provide decision makers with data concerning the impact of the innovation on all the subcomponents of the system.

Any planned change or innovation in education requires a staff to take certain concrete actions on the basis of deliberate decisions which were made after a formal or informal evaluation of a known condition and an examination of plausible alternatives to that condition. Educational developers have been making changes in schools for years on an intuitive-informal evaluation base. An evaluation paradigm should offer a means of formalizing this intuitive process. It must combine the relevance of the developer's approach with the explicitness and rigor of a more scientific approach.

The paradigm developed and used in the Florida State University evaluation was designed against these criteria. It places emphasis on formative evaluation and reflects a philosophy which holds that the ultimate purpose of evaluation is the improvement of education. It postulates that an educational program can be improved in a more direct and immediate way than through a singular approach of summative evaluation. Furthermore, the information collected in a formative assessment can be used for the interpretation of product data gathered in subsequent summative evaluation efforts. Instruments and procedures have been developed by the FSU team to operationalize each of the paradigm steps.

Focusing on the variables of the conceptual framework, and based in a general developmental model, the FSU Evaluation Paradigm consisted of the steps listed below. These six steps correspond to developmental stages through which all staffing innovations, formally or informally, must pass.

Goal analysis is the first step of the FSU design. The evaluation focuses on a project's early goal setting efforts through an analysis of its flexible staffing goals. The intent here is to *analyze goals* and provide the people who wrote them with information pertaining to their clarity, specificity, and consistency which is relevant to goal revision. Goals are also submitted to a test of relevance to determine whether they reflect the needs and priorities established by the staff.

A process evaluation for planning and decision making constitutes the second step of the paradigm. Included in this step in an *analysis of the process* of goal selection and other decision-making processes. Personnel in the schools are surveyed to determine whether they feel decisions are being made by appropriate people in the organizational structure and to what extent they feel they influence decisions. In addition, they are asked to what extent they would like to change their role in the decision process and whether they feel the various decisions being made are of a high quality.

The model evaluation is not unlike the goal evaluation. An analysis is made of the staffing model proposed by the project. Here, the evaluator is concerned with whether a model exists or not and whether it adequately describes what was intended. A second issue is one of providing a description of the particular staffing model in terms of variables common to all flexible staffing efforts.

Evaluating the installment plan is the next step of the paradigm. This component attempts to make explicit the strategies and techniques which staffing innovators intend to use to install a staffing model. Here the evaluation focuses on the consistency of the plan with the model and with school goals. Also of importance in this step are the considerations of the legality, legitimacy, practicability, and the balance of the plan.

The evaluation of the installation process has three major objectives: to monitor the implementation of the installation plan, to provide information needed for improving decisions during the installation stage of development, and to document the extent of installation which has taken place.

The evaluation of outcomes is the final step, and is a type of summative evaluation which focuses on the products of an implemented staffing model at a given point in time. These products are related to changes in the organizational structure, levels of knowledge, attitudes, and skills existing among the staff. The organizational climate, assessed as well as unanticipated, nevertheless indicates significant outcomes of the staffing installation.

Since the intent of this chapter is to focus on a description of the current status of flexible staffing rather than on the details of evaluation, methodology, the specifics of instrument design and validation, and the steps of data processing and interpretation will not be discussed. Interested readers may check the report of the study for these methodological and statistical treatments (Beard, DeBloois, and Foster, 1971).

What Aspects of Flexible Staffing Are Receiving the Most Attention?

The FSU study involved some 976 educators, 94 percent of whom represent schools or districts which were funded by the U.S. Office of Education for training their personnel to implement a differentiated or flexible staffing model. The other 6 percent made up the control segment of the study. These individuals were employed by twenty-three school districts, geographically distributed from Northern Washington state to Miami, Florida, and from Southern California to New York City.

Three instruments were administered in all but five of the projects. An intensive on-site evaluation, in addition to the administration of these three instruments, was made in five projects.

All elements of the conceptual model of staff-use were represented in each of the instruments. On two of these scales, a staffing perception and a staffing receptivity questionnaire, twenty-one items were included to represent flexible staffing situations, and ten items represented conventionally staffed schools. On a third scale, which was designed to measure the importance the respondents placed on various staffing goals as well as their perceived level of implementation, twenty-seven items representing the areas of the conceptual model were included.

An interpretation of the data gathered through these instruments indicates what staffing foci exist throughout eighteen projects. How far this might be generalized is not entirely clear. However, due to the geographical representation of the sample, and because the projects included a relatively representative mix of urban and suburban schools in both high and low socioeconomic neighborhoods, members of the FSU team felt that broad generalizations were not inappropriate.

Several points are evident. The study demonstrates that the personnel in the project schools agree most with statements taken from the Perpetuation Structures area of the conceptual model. This variable emphasized policies concerning recruitment, employment, division of labor, training, and remuneration. Eighty-eight percent of the respondents agreed that hiring paraprofessionals as classroom assistants is typical of a school having flexible staffing. Eighty-seven percent of the respondents were in agreement that the employment of teachers on the basis of their special interests and special abilities as well as their certification status was typical of flexible staffing. Providing in-service training which may lead staff members to increased instructional responsibility and increased pay was also an area of general agreement (eighty-one percent).

Individuals in the flexible staffing project schools rated the element Collegiality as being nearly as important to the flexible staffing concept as Perpetuation Structures. Eighty-six percent agreed that solving instructional problems through a group process involving teachers was central to the concept. Eighty percent agreed that teachers assuming responsibility for helping solve school problems was an important characteristic of flexible staffing. Seventy-six percent agreed that teachers interacting with administrators as peers, though their responsibility differed as to type and amount, was also a central factor.

The element of Accountability was of major importance according to the combined perceptions reported in the questionnaire. A full ninety-one percent of the respondents indicated they considered a periodic public explanation of school objectives and the degree to which they were being achieved as typical of a staffed school. Seventy-eight percent believed the concept included occasional surveys of parents, and the public, to obtain their opinions about school policies and objectives. Obviously, both sides of the accountability coin were perceived to be key factors in the flexible staffing concept. Nearly eighty percent of those surveyed indicated a flexible staffing situation was one where teachers were encouraged to attain their own career goals, even though these may differ widely in a staff, without leaving the classroom for advancement into administration.

As a whole, the body of administrators surveyed seemed to possess a better understanding of flexible staffing concepts than the group of teachers. Administrators were also slightly more receptive of the concept than were teachers. Both the teachers and administrators in schools where staffing flexibility was being planned for, or had already been achieved, scored higher on the perception and receptivity scales than personnel in conventional schools. As a result of in-service efforts, it appears that instructional personnel in staffing project schools have more positive attitudes toward the concept of flexible staff use, and are also more knowledgeable than teachers in nonproject schools. This indicates a degree of success in their staff training objectives. There were some discrepancies, however, Eighty-three percent of the teachers in flexible staffing projects felt that giving up individual classroom autonomy in favor of team solutions to instructional problems was an element of flexible staffing; but they were less receptive (seventy-four percent) when asked if they wished to work in a school where this was actually the case. Apparently, the group surveyed was convinced by the rationale of flexible staffing, though somewhat less enthusiastic about actually participating in shared planning and direction of classroom instruction.

In a similar vein, sixty percent of the teachers agreed that in a flexible staffing situation a teacher's activity would be governed by written instructional goals while only fifty-one percent wished to work in a situation where written goals governed the instructional behavior of the teacher.

When asked which of the twenty-seven goal statements provided in the instrument was most important, and for which they had carried out at least a limited degree of implementation, teachers and administrators serving as members of project planning committees gave some unexpected responses.

The planning committee members in all of the eighteen projects listed the goal of "making effective use of available resources within the existing staffing structure by providing teachers with adequate nonprofessional help" as being most important. Two-thirds of these planning committees considered the following goals, listed in order of importance, as being very important:

1. Differentiating staff responsibilities based on a breakdown of educational and instructional tasks.

2. Providing each child with learning resources appropriate to his individual needs.

3. Relating differentiated responsibilities to salary differentials.

4. Providing continuous and relevant inservice training based on instructional objectives established by the staff.

5. Insuring that decisions are influenced by individuals who will be called upon to implement them.

6. Increasing the staff's professional commitment to the student.

7. Improving interpersonal relations skills in the schools.

Three of these goals which were given high priority relate to the Perpetuation Structures identified in the conceptual framework; two others relate to Collegiality, and the remaining two represent the Professional Disposition and Individualism dimensions of the model.

This list of ordered goal statements is similar to the list of staffing elements teachers perceived to be aspects of the flexible staffing concept. The ratings indicate that project staffs consider the structural aspects of the concept to be most important. The elements of group process, communication, and involvement are close runners-up.

What Staffing Variables Are Being Neglected?

The responses of committee members indicating which goals they considered unimportant, are also of interest. These include:

1. Involving the professional teachers' organization in the planning and execution of inservice training programs for its members.

2. Gradually transferring credentialing authority from the state to the professional teachers' organization.

3. Disseminating information concerning flexible staffing experiences in the project schools to nonproject schools in the district.

It appears that the promise found in much of the literature, that flexible staffing will be a tool for the improvement and strengthening of professional organizations for teachers, is far from being realized. An instrument designed to measure the Professional Disposition dimension of the conceptual model (observed professional practices) which was used in the five on-site evaluations, indicates a low level of professionalism (as defined in the model) in those project schools. The preferred professional practices measure (attributes which a teacher feels a professional should have), was considerably higher. This indicates that teachers agree with the aspects of the Professional Disposition dimension but do not perceive these to exist in their schools.

The literature of flexible or differentiated staffing abounds with recommendations of performance-based promotion schemes for teachers; where the teachers who demonstrate qualities of competency above that of the average teacher, are given additional responsibility and increased salary. An example of this is the description of the Master Teacher, or Curriculum Coordinator role which is found in many of the project's staffing models. The FSU evaluation indicates that, in spite of this emphasis in the literature, less than sixty percent of those attempting to implement the concept view this as a vital part.

In another vein, the differentiated teaching staff has been viewed as a team of instructional specialists who establish job descriptions and have major influence in the screening and hiring of subsequent additions to the team. Nearly fifty percent of the teachers surveyed indicated they did not consider this a part of the flexible staffing concept. Only forty-eight percent of the project personnel agreed that flexible staffing included promotion and advancement of teachers being tied to an evaluation of his performance by his peers, subordinates, and superiors. A similar percentage felt that pupil achievement gains should have no bearing on teacher performance ratings. Less than forty-three percent of the people responding wished to work in a school where this was part of the criteria used for evaluating teaching competence.

Although more than ninety percent of the teachers disagreed that individuals may do their jobs independently of other members of a differentiated staff, and nearly seventy percent disagreed that in such a staff each teacher would prepare his yearly curriculum outline on his own; more than sixty-five percent of those responding agreed that an individual teacher would exercise considerable autonomy in selecting the topics to be included in the courses he teaches. Obviously, the teacher engaged in staffing innovation, however willing to join in group planning at the grade level, department level, or school level, is not yet ready to give up the autonomy which for so long has been his only real source of power—being able to close the classroom door and doing that which he personally feels is best.

Trading off monies normally used for filling a teaching position in order to employ two or three aides, or to purchase instructional materials, has recently become a popular administrative application of the flexible staffing concept. When asked how they felt about this, forty-six percent of the teachers responding indicated they agreed; twenty-six percent were uncertain; and twenty-seven percent totally opposed the practice. Thus, even in the project schools where teachers are exposed to a constant stream of enthusiastic indoctrination, skepticism remains high as to whether this form of tradeoff is really in the best interest of the teaching profession, and whether it is part of the flexible staffing concept. Certainly, with the recent declaration that a teacher surplus exists in some subject and geographic areas, this staffing practice will fall under severe scrutiny.

What Is Being Implemented in the Name of Flexible Staffing?

The responses of the project committees to the FSU evaluation indicate that only three areas of the conceptual model are being implemented. Many committees claimed to have implemented goal statements that were derived in the areas of Perpetuation Structures, Collegiality, and Workflow Structures. Only one project, of the 18 surveyed, claimed to have implemented any of the goal statements taken from the conceptual areas of Accountability, Systems-renewal, Professional Disposition, and Individualism; although a number did indicate that planning was nearly complete and that implementation would begin shortly for some of these goal areas.

Six of the eighteen committees claimed to have implemented the goal of differentiating staff responsibilities. Following a task analysis, they related the various job descriptions to salary differentials. The responses of individuals from five of the project planning committees indicated they had implemented the goals of: 1) providing adequate paraprofessional assistance to teachers, 2) providing the student with learning resources appropriate to his needs, and 3) organizing a climate where groups of individuals representing the total staff can engage in collective planning and decision making.

These data suggest that when personnel from the projects involved in this evaluation speak of having implemented differentiated staffing or flexible staffing, they are referring mainly to the use of parapro-fessionals, an emphasis on individualizing instruction, diffused plan-ning and decision making, and differentiated levels of teaching responsibility being tied to salary differentials. Only a third of the eighteen projects claimed to have implemented these six goals. One-half of project committees claimed these same goals were in a planning stage and soon would be implemented. A sixth of the projects indicated these were not considered goals and no planning nor implementation had been done.

Only two project committees indicated that they had imple-mented the goal of establishing a continuous in-service training program based on instructional objectives derived by their colleagues. Twelve other committees said plans for implementing this goal were nearly complete. It appears that some of the projects may have acted prematurely. Six project committees say that they have implemented differentiated responsibilities and adopted new instructional roles, yet only two projects claim to have done any training of personnel for the adoption of new roles. One might suspect that only the titles are different in the other projects and that little role change has occurred since no training accompanied title changes.

No fewer than eleven committees indicated that plans were nearly complete for implementing three goals from the Collegiality area of the conceptual model dealing with: improvement of interpersonal relation skills among members of their staff, merging the formal and informal organization of their school, and establishing a climate which encourages interaction among personnel regardless of their position within the district.

It is generally true that flexible staffing projects have only begun to implement many of the goals they consider important. Only a small number of the projects which were evaluated have reached the point of development where they are implementing their full staffing model.

Flexible staffing project directors proved to be no different from directors in other types of projects attempting educational innova-tion in their claiming more than could really be documented. An example may serve to illuminate this point. The project directors surveyed in this study claimed that forty-nine percent of the goal statements which were very important had been implemented. On-site visits to five of these projects by the evaluation team documented the actual level of implementation. In every case, it was found that the project director and administrators typically over-estimated what had been implemented, and the teachers on the steering committee, and teachers who were involved to a smaller degree, typically underestimated what had been implemented. The level of implementation as it was documented in these projects lay somewhere in between these two extremes of estimation.

What Pressing Problems Were Perceived by Individuals in Project Schools?

A survey of participants in the eighteen projects was used to determine what pressing problems they perceived in their schools. It was assumed by the evaluation team that a good deal of overlap would occur in the problems reported, and from this, a list of serious problems for all flexibly staffed schools could be generated. This was not the case; in fact, the opposite proved to be true. Very little commonality of pressing concerns was evident. This suggests that the problems which are occurring—and every project had a lengthy list—are unique to the locale, and each independent staffing effort encounters its own peculiar set of problems. Those few problems which did begin to appear in more than one project's response form, concerned a lack of adequate facilities, inadequate materials, under-equipped resource centers, and insufficient time for teachers to accomplish their regular duties along with work related to the planning and implementation of the staffing model.

What Does the Evaluation Data Suggest?

The evaluation team from FSU made careful on-site evaluations of five staffing projects. As a result of observations made during these visits, and through the complete analysis of the data collected through the battery of instruments, statements can be made which are directly applicable to the projects visited, and perhaps applicable to other schools involved in staffing innovation.

Individuals in all of the projects visited were enthusiastic about what they were attempting. Indeed there were problems; there were even a few who felt compelled to unfurl the projects' dirty linen, but an overwhelming majority of individuals were terribly excited about their particular form of staffing innovation, and about teaching children. Data which were cited earlier indicate that individuals in project schools were more receptive to innovative staffing concepts than those in control groups. They were also observed to be more enthusiastic about the teaching/learning act than many of their counterparts in conventional schools. Teachers in five project schools scored high on an instrument designed to measure the individualism dimension of the conceptual model, which indicates flexible staffing may indeed provide for differences in individual goals among staff members.

It is not known whether students are learning more as a result of differentiated staffing; yet, how could this be an expectation at this point in time when none of the eighteen projects has actually implemented all the goals they consider to be important and essential to the success of the concept. One might realistically expect a slight drop to occur in student achievement until the new model is fully implemented. One or two of the projects were very close to the level of goal implementation they desired and will soon be able to evaluate the impact of their staffing model on student achievement and attitude levels. Most of the rest, however, have considerable development to complete before their desired treatment is accomplished. The model parts lie scattered on the table before them, and the intended product is beginning to take form, but they can't realistically expect it to function until it is properly assembled.

In almost every project expectations on staffing experiments are much too high. Once a member of a school board or a concerned parent learns an experiment is being conducted, he begins almost immediately to expect fantastic gains. Sometimes teachers in project schools also fall victim to these unrealistic expectations and become discouraged when unprecedented gains are not realized in the first month of a pilot study. A few educators, however, are beginning to realize that innovations, like flexible staffing, flexible scheduling, flexible space-use, and nongradedness, are structural innovations which alter the *climate* for learning, but do not immediately have direct impact on the learning act. The student is still responding to rather specific cues in a learning situation. Simply changing the context in which those same cues occur is not likely to change levels of achievement. Unless the cue itself is altered, few gains should be anticipated. Thus, structural innovations are likely to provide a context in which a larger variety of instructional cues may be offered the student, and ultimately have a significant effect on his achievement. Until this happens, one might look to the teacher for documenting gains in attitude, skill, and knowledge during early phases of instructional innovation. The environmental press of the school may also improve, but wild expectations in the area of student attitude are unwarranted.

Once an environment is created which frees human talent and allows a variety of expertise to come together for program planning and designing instruction, and once more kinds of different human resources are available to bring the student to this new learning interface and achieve the desired goals of learning, we can begin to look for improved student scores.

In some projects, increased achievement on the part of students, following the onset of a staffing experiment, may have been documented, but it is much too early to attempt to give the flexible staffing concept the credit. Many other factors, only slightly related to a reorganization of the teaching staff, may have been causal agents.

Students are not learning less as a result of the staffing experiment. None of the projects identified as a serious problem a drop in student achievement, nor was student morale said to have declined. In personal interviews, which were structured in advance by an interview instrument, members of project staffs cited student benefits which they felt resulted from the staffing experiment. These included more direct one-to-one instruction, more exposure to various kinds of human resources, curriculum experiences which were better planned and more adequately presented, and interaction with enthusiastic, "turned-on" teachers.

A level of rapport was observed among the various teaching roles and with school administrators, which is uncommon for public schools. Much decision making has been diffused to levels below the office of the administrator, and a climate conducive to open communication is pervasive throughout the flexible staffing effort. The instructional personnel indicate they would like even more decision-making responsibility in many areas, although they were generally satisfied with the decisions being made. There is the danger that democratization of decision making will result in more involvement, but at the same time turn out mediocre products. Involving many people in the decision process does not guarantee the quality of the decision made. Perhaps project personnel need to identify in which of the various aspects of decision making they truly desire involvement. Activities such as gathering data relevant to the decision, narrowing the range of options, testing feasibility of alternatives, might best be performed by an administrator. The act of advisement and ratification may prove to offer instructional personnel the most meaningful kind of involvement in decision making. Consensus seeking, after various options have been eliminated, is another option. Future studies of flexible staffing patterns in operation may find more viable and efficient means of decision making than are currently being attempted in the projects evaluated by the FSU team.

Contrary to pessimistic predictions, the role of the principal has not withered and died with the onslaught of flexible staffing. In the FSU study, principals were typically more knowledgeable about staffing innovations and are more receptive toward them than their respective staffs. They are enthusiastic about sharing the role of instructional leadership, and strongly support the notion of interacting with teachers and noninstructional personnel as a colleague, or a peer, with a different kind of expertise. They support informality in communication with the staff and are anxious to bury, once and for all, the artificial class distinctions among school personnel which have existed to the detriment of programs.

The concept of flexible staffing calls for a change in the role of the principal perhaps more than for any other role. The FSU study indicates that most administrators are not only accepting that change, but are accelerating the pace and increasing the scope of that change.

The models of staff utilization being designed are basically of two types: those which emphasize the Perpetuation Structures of the conceptual model, and those which emphasize Collegiality. The former are all patterned after the early Temple City model where the staff is organized into a vertical hierarchy of role descriptions. The second type of model is a process one. Here, the model sets forth the goals to be accomplished and prescribes a process from which a staffing form may emerge. The emphasis is on opening up channels of communication and developing interpersonal competence so that the planning and development of the program will be efficient and effective.

A third model, which is just beginning to receive attention, is one based on the concept of performance contracting. Although this resembles a process model, the elements of teachers receiving the necessary resources to accomplish goals, and their guaranteeing a predetermined level of performance, makes the Mesa, Arizona, model rather unique among flexible staffing projects.

Of the models of staff utilization which were studied, most seemed to lack emphasis on accountability and systems self-renewal. While the planning committees listed goal statements taken from these conceptual model areas as goals of high priority for their project, few of their staffing models, or plans for installing those models, reflected activities consistent with that need. The on-site evaluation of project planning efforts reflected this void as well.

The probability that projects will successfully implement the models they designed is greatly reduced as a result of the lack of planning in the systems self-renewal and accountability areas. Few projects have actually set up a systems approach for installing their model and for evaluating the installation process. As a result, few projects are prepared to account for their progress in terms of their original project goals and present project status. These shortcomings in the accountability and systems self-renewal areas could have harmful effects on possible continued support from local and state education agencies, which are in increasing number, turning to program budgeting and relating cost effectiveness to performance outcomes as a means of justifying developmental expenditures.

Where Should We Go from Here?

Present indications are that fewer and fewer dollars will be made available from federal funding sources for isolated innovations such as differentiated staffing. In the future more comprehensive efforts at school innovation and change will be financed through the consolidation of federal grants which, until now, have existed somewhat separately within school systems. Title III, Model Cities, rehabilitation funds, experimental schools grants, teacher training centers funds, etc., will likely be consolidated and applied toward the successful completion of one well designed and carefully administered comprehensive educational reform program.

As a result, the concept which is currently called flexible staffing will be merged into a larger effort, or will be carried out as a district, or state, level project. Whichever of the three possibilities takes place, there is an increased need for staffing innovators to carefully define their goals. They must place themselves in a position to identify exactly what they hope to accomplish by organizing carefully written performance objectives into thoughtful models of staff utilization. They must develop and execute in detail a plan for installing the set of objectives contained in the model. And they must account for their time and expenditures of money by stating what was accomplished as compared to what was desired through what level of resource utilization.

The staffing innovations evaluated by the FSU study indicate that much has been accomplished. At the same time someone who has been close to the action during the past five years would probably argue that far too little has resulted from resources which have been expended.

We must be more efficient. There is no excuse for continually having to learn through unsuccessful experiences. Enough staffing efforts have documented their failures that we needn't learn every lesson by duplicating their experiences. Likewise, we should avoid the continual reinvention of the wheel which has characterized the flexible staffing effort to date. At this point in time, there have probably been sufficient staffing goals derived, and enough models postulated, that someone desiring to attempt his own innovation need not begin from scratch. Again, there have been sufficient projects go through that agonizing process of moving from a traditional staffing base to one based on flexibility, that shortcuts are now available. Training programs need to be systematically developed and validated, so they may be "packaged" and used wherever staffing innovation is attempted. This business of each project duplicating the development of a training program in isolation is wasteful and, because of the scarcity of resources, usually results in a product which is mediocre at best. The proliferation of evaluation efforts—each developed independently and on an inadequate budget—should also be controlled through the development and validation of a design comprehensive enough to serve all varieties of staffing innovation.

The instructional staff will always be a critical variable in any program of educational reform. Certainly, the concept of differentiated staff use has provided educators with alternatives which have proven themselves viable. While staffing innovation will not stand still, nor should it, an immediate effort should be mounted which will result in a consolidation of existing knowledge and strategies, and their integration into reliable process and product models of staff use. A stronger theory upon which future staffing efforts might be based is essential. With all this, we may indeed prove the opponents to staffing innovation wrong in their recurring criticism that there is less to the concept than meets the eye.

Bibliography

Beard, J., DeBloois, M., and Foster, G.R., *An Evaluation of School Personnel Utilization Projects,* 4 vols., Evaluation Training Center, Department of Educational Research, Florida State University, Tallahassee, Florida, 1971.

De Bloois, Michael L., *A Conceptual Model for Organizational Structural Innovations,* Evaluation Training Center, Department of

Educational Research, Florida State University, Tallahassee, Florida, 1970.

Glass, Gene, V., *The Growth of Evaluation Methodology,* Laboratory of Educational Research, University of Colorado, Boulder, Colorado, 1969.

13 Administering Federal Educational Policy

Donald K. Sharpes

The early Americans escaped from tyranny, not from the traditions of a ruling class. Americans have continued to expect from the political and civil service reformers people intelligent enough to serve all the people all the time, moderate enough to be self-restraining in judgement, courageous enough to distinguish the art of statesmanship from chicanery. Perfectionists were bound to be disappointed. But students of federal educational policy have come more and more to realize that the modernization of government is a political as well as an administrative task. Although some may be frightened by the bogies of regimentation and bureaucracy, they have never experienced the dictatorial nature of bureaucracy that existed in the Old World and still is preserved in milder forms in countries where democracy is observed only among the aristocrats.

Perhaps in defiance of the bureaucracy itself, especially as reflected in federal educational programs, students of federal educational policy show themselves susceptible more to political instruction than indoctrination. Because of an enlightened educational public, there is an expansion of federal educational activities. There is also a new zest for educational reform.

Most regard the Office of Education, for example, not as a Delphic oracle of educational wisdom, but as a political institution adminstering political educational legislation. Many educators, or at least those engaged in seeking funds earnestly, recognize the Office of Education as a convenient government response to a variety of local educational needs. The sometimes general distrust of government yields to the perception that the office is perhaps nothing more than educators organized politically.

But one of the most important results of the new political realism of students of the federal educational establishment was a livelier understanding of the interdependence of short-lived attempts at educational renewal and supposedly long-ranged objectives. The objectives of the Office of Education for Equality of Educational Opportunity and programs for the disadvantaged are two examples from a wilderness of others. What did the privileges of equal educational opportunities mean to a failing sixth-grader in Biloxi, Mississippi? What did the rights of free speech and assembly mean to a teacher voicing her concerns about early sex education to the local community? Of what price was the technical and administrative competence of a superintendent committed to school reform yet unacceptable to the local teachers' union? Clearly, ancient rights were not clothed in modern apparel, and the myths the federal establishment hoped to eradicate continue to abound.

But as old myths are eradicated new ones arise. Some revolve around timeless educational issues and themes. From the perspective of a local school administrator the skeletons in the closet might include: fear of federal control, congressional legislation and appropriate authorizations, and the role of the professional and community participants in policy decisions. These issues, together with a brief historical account of the rise and fall of school personnel utilization, will serve as a backdrop for an analysis of federal educational policy making in process.

EXPANDING FEDERAL EDUCATION

Students of federal educational policy and administration of federal programs have only recently had a formal schooling. It has been only in the most recent years that the wariness of local school and state agency administrators toward Office of Education policies and procedures has been tempered by a more tolerant understanding of the political realities surrounding the administration of congressional legislation. Local school officials were once genuinely concerned about the shifts in federal power when strict policies followed stingy dollars. The dynamics of agency growth are principally exhibited in the Office of Education's expansion in the last decade. For sixty-nine years; from 1869-1939, the office was housed in the Department of the Interior. That year it employed 300 people and had a budget of $40 million. As late as 1962, the budget was only $600 million, and the staff was approximately 1,400 people. In fiscal year 1972, the office employed approximately 2,800 persons and had an appropriation of $5.35 billion.

Because in the mid-sixties Congress voted to meet deficiencies in school programs in vocational education, the training of teachers, equality of educational opportunity, and the Emergency School Assistance, the relationships between federal, state and local education was often tenuous and fragile. Reflective educators knew the broad purposes for which Congress appropriated money. They were concerned in the mid-sixties that program directives and guidelines as well as legislation would tie their hands to federal policies and exert a form of control.[1]

Authorization vs. Appropriation

Yet it is the amount of the appropriation for education, not just the diversity of management, that continues to plague administrators. The gap that exists between what the Congress authorizes for educational programs and what it makes available is a contiually widening discrepancy. A study done by the Advisory Commission of Intergovernmental Relations of 1969 federal programs with fixed dollar authorizations revealed a sizable reduction occurred in the amount appropriated from the amount authorized. Between 1965 to 1970 the appropriations fell from 80 to 65 percent. Most were domestic programs sponsored by HEW. But the greatest gap occurred in education programs. In 1970 Congress appropriated only 36 percent of the amount it authorized for federal aid to education. In 1968, the amount was equal to 60 percent. The ratio has been decreasing since then. For the fiscal year 1972, based on the appropriations already approved by the House of Representatives the actual dollar amount will be $4,684,281,000. The authorization for 1972 was $14 billion. The ratio between authorization and appropriation has decreased to 33.3 percent.[2]

The Issue of Control

The passage of the Elementary and Secondary Education Act (ESEA) in 1965 helped resolve partly the religious controversy over aid to parochial and private schools that had stymied the Kennedy administration's educational legislative efforts. That issue was again partially resolved when Senator Wayne Morse proposed in the ESEA legislation that the special purpose grants be used for "the education of the children of needy families and children residing in areas of substantial unemployment," thereby obviating skillfully the false "school" issue.

The administration of Title IV of the Civil Rights Act, for example, is always particularly ticklish. The legislation prohibits the Office of Education from funding local school systems that practice discrimination. The charges that the schools were controlled from Washington were not taken seriously by intelligent students of the new political educational realism, but they only partially allayed the fears others had of signs of federal control.

The standards set by office of education officials, in consultation with Department of Health, Education and Welfare officials and White House administration officials, for desegregation policies have not always been accepted. However, neither have the same standards been accepted by civil rights organizations. The strong, pervasive feelings about civil rights programs cloud the standards set for the administration of other financial aid programs, and the distinctions between different legislative acts in education blur the minds of the less studious. Feelings about civil rights' controversies become transferred to other programs sponsored by the office. The concern over federal control is always an alive issue.

A similar source of tension between federal and local education officials is that Congress authorized over a few years educational systems which neither local nor state authorities control. The Neighborhood Youth Corps and Youth Opportunity Centers of the Department of Labor, Head Start and the Community Coordinated Child Care (4-C) of the Office of Child Development are a few examples of programs not administered by the Office of Education and are outside the network of local and state control. These and similar educational systems which bypass local and state policy making add to the reservations some observers legitimately feel. Students of the new political educational realism expressly want the White House to appoint the Commissioner of Education to a cabinet level to coordinate all educational programs scattered throughout the government. The number is extraordinary.

The Social and Rehabilitation Service sponsors grants and contracts for demonstration programs in child welfare, juvenile delinquency, and health services to children and youth in schools. The Office of Economic Opportunity adminsters voluntary assistance programs for needy children, as well as educational services to community agencies. The Justice Department staffs a Community Relations Service as a result of the Civil Rights Act of 1964, and the Department of Agriculture has special milk programs, a national lunch program, and an equipment program to expand school food services.

None of these programs is managed by the Office of Education. Yet the array of federal domestic programs that ultimately serve children and youth is bewildering to those who must administer and manage the funds and programs.

Legislative Development

Program execution has its beginning in Congress, and any given day can witness several education bills introduced and referred to committees for consideration. The range of such bills varies according to which senator and representative introduced it, whether or not the administration supports it, and the extent of congressional support. May 20, 1971, for example, was not exactly typical but it is illustrative of the scope of bills proposed. Two bills were introduced in the Senate, four in the House, and one emerged from a House joint resolution. All were referred to various committees in both the House and Senate. Senator McGovern (D-SD) introduced Senate bills to provide additional educational benefits to veterans who have served in the Indochina theater of operations during the Vietnam era (referred to the Committee on Veterans affairs), and a bill to amend the Child Nutrition Act of 1966 to make the school breakfast program permanent (referred to the Committee on Agriculture and Forestry).

The House bills with one exception were amendments to existing laws. One bill (H.R. 8592) proposed amending the Internal Revenue Code of 1954 to allow a credit against income tax to individuals for certain expenses incurred in providing higher education—referred to the Committee on Ways and Means.

An amendment (H.R. 8596) was proposed to amend the Higher Education Act of 1965 to strengthen the student insured loan program "and other purposes." It was referred to the Committee on Education and Labor. To aid returning veterans in furthering employment, and educational opportunities, H.R. 8604 proposed amending title 37, United States Code, to apply with respect to veterans and war orphans in noncollege level educational institutions the same criteria for determining satisfactory pursuance of course work that is applied with respect to veterans and war orphans in college level educational institutions—referred to the committee on veterans' affairs.

Representative Podell introduced H.R. 8609 to improve and increase postsecondary education opportunities by providing assistance to the States for the development and construction of comprehensive community colleges, referred to the Committee on Education and Labor. Finally a joint resolution (H.R. Res. 652) of the House proposed an amendment to the Constitution of the United States with respect to freedom of choice in attending public schools. It was referred to the Committee on the Judiciary.

But the only educational legislation that will pass must satisfy a majority of Congress. As we have seen, the mere passage of legislation may not be significant, unless Congress authorizes and continues to appropriate funds sufficient to insure the continuity of the program.

The congressional route by which appropriations are made, hearings conducted, and educational legislation developed is labyrinthine. Five different congressional committees and subcommittees are responsible for educational issues—two in the Senate and three in the House. They are:

Senate Subcommittee on Education
Senate Subcommittee for Appropriations, Labor, HEW
House Committee on Education and Labor
General Subcommittee on Education of the House Committee on Education and Labor
Subcommittee on Labor, HEW of the House Appropriations Committee

But assuming legislation is enacted, that it is a compromise of issues, that it does not induce intolerable expectations, that it receives appropriations suitable to the development of a national need locally administered, the questions remain of who will share in its progress and control its destiny. Two kinds of people have been involved in federal program development and policy decisions—professional educators and resident community participants. Sometimes precipitating their own confrontations, they nevertheless share a mutual concern for the improvement of federal program implementation.

PARITY: INCLUDING COMMUNITIES

The common school, later to develop into the high school and secondary school, was one of the ways of equalizing life chances for all in the community. The equalization of ethnic differences in immigrant America was to be accomplished through an educational system which eliminated or reduced the heterogeneity of groups and made all, equally, Americans. It was a common standard among intellectuals that there ought to be a consensual, integrated and organic community that would Americanize class and caste differences. The resulting equalitarian educational systems, because of their penchant for maintaining schools apart from the main political processes of the expanding cities, perpetuated the domination of the middle-class ethic. It also widened the active participation of the educational establishment from any political experience. The upshot has been an educational system with little muscle in urban and state politics.

The community, contrary to popular opinion, is not a single, unitary phenomenon, but rather a series of discrete strands not necessarily interwoven.

Community Participation

Although few educators doubt the impact of the emerging role of community participation in educational programs, fewer community advocates have confronted the unromantic but necessarily vital concerns about economic feasibility. Will new educational programs pay for themselves or must they be eternally subsidized by the federal coffers? If they are subsidized who will reap the blessings? Will such subsidies drain equally important resources and divert leadership from related domestic activities, such as housing and health? Educational objectives cannot reasonably be satisfied apart from a comprehensive community plan which includes housing, recreation, health, and education. Educational programs sponsored by the federal government have rarely been comprehensive. They have often been planned only for a specific target population. Rarely have the effects and success spilled over into the community at large. Each program in the past has insisted on community involvement, and representativeness. Thus, federal legislation and policy makers have proliferated community and advisory groups without capturing the full spirit of the community or institutionalizing in the schools the process of community participation.

The requirement of involving people in policy making is usually frustrated by an equally fundamental characteristic of American politics—the fragmentation of those who adminster and share responsibility and authority of public services. This pattern of divergent authorities and overlapping policies makes it very difficult to realize the full benefits of comprehensive planning. Constructive educational policy seldom results from the loosely spelled-out guidelines for communities to share in policy development and from repeated confrontations with rigid educational and political positions.

Past legislation was often vague about the nature and extent of community participation. The slogan, "maximum feasible participation" from OEO's legislation, did not clarify the extent of the participation of community representatives. Recent legislation, however, exhibits a keen sensitivity to parental participation and offers precise prescriptions for selection procedures, jurisdiction, and extent of responsibility. The latest amendments to ESEA (November, 1970) details the extent of parental involvement: "Sec. 415. In the case of any applicable program in which the Commissioner determines that parental participation ... would increase the effectiveness of the program ... he shall promulgate regulations ... designed to encourage such participation."[3]

In addition, applications for any school for ESEA funds has to:

1. set forth such policies and procedures as will ensure that programs and projects assisted under the application have been planned and developed, and will be operated, in consultation with, and with the involvement of parents of, the children to be served by such programs and projects;

2. be submitted with assurance that such parents have had an opportunity to present their views with respect to the application; and

3. set forth policies and procedures for adequate program plans and evaluations to such parents and the public.[4]

The Emergency School Aid and Quality Integrated Education Act of 1971 goes even further in granting authority to the clientele of educational services sponsored by the whole federal effort.

... the Commissioner is authorized to make grants to, and contracts with ... programs and projects to promote quality of educational opportunity, through facilitating the participation of parents, students, and teachers in the design and implementation of comprehensive educational planning; the provision of services which will enable parents to become effective participants in the educational process; the conduct of activities which foster understanding among minority group and nonminority group parents, children, teachers, and school officials ... [5]

H.R. 6748, a bill submitted to provide a comprehensive child development program (a similar bill, H.R. 9081, provides for similar services), calls for the establishment of child development councils and local policy councils. "Such councils shall be composed of parents of children eligible under this Act. ... Local Policy Councils shall be responsible ... for determining child development needs and priorities in their neighborhoods ...."[6]

Professionals in the Advisory Process

Part of the disparity in understanding the new political realism noticeable in education has filtered through to those who serve as members of advisory groups to the Office of Education.[7] The limitations of the advisory groups that provide advice and serve as sounding boards are largely the misunderstandings that members have of their roles and responsibilities. Many participants in this process join in the expectation that with the distinction of serving comes the responsibility for developing educational policy of a particular program. They tend to suffer role conflict when they find that their responsibilities do not include legislative, administrative or policy changes. Their active participation in attempting to establish wholesale changes often run counter to the agendas of federal educational personnel.

Program officers in the Office of Education, responsible for liaison between the policy established for a given program, often see a similar ambiguity in their roles. Both the advisory group members and the federal program officers are unrepresentative of typical Americans in education. For the most part they hold advanced degrees, are nearly all teachers or administrators, and consequently participate in policy making in some degree in the institution that employs them. Advisory members often see the federal officers as the facilitators of their active role in helping to determine the federal government's role in education. Federal officials, who usually do participate in federal education program directives and guidelines are sometimes inattentive to the ways in which a variety of opinions can be integrated into an emerging educational program strategy.

The lack of clarity and definition at the formation of an advisory group contributes to the ambivalence of the serving members and the Office of Education personnel called upon to react to a spectrum of alternative solutions to broad policies effecting educational programs. The record of advisory councils and groups in education is sometimes characterized by the ambiguity of those who serve and those who help direct its activities.

All who have engaged in the exercise appreciate the government's attempt for expanded popular involvement in federal education decisions, but having served know something about the difficulty of implementing long-ranged objectives with short participatory shrift.

Administering School Personnel Utilization

Apart from the educational issues described elsewhere in this volume, the political realities discussed in this chapter also prevailed in the administration of the federal program that sponsored training for differentiated staffing, School Personnel Utilization. The history of the federal investment in sponsoring such projects also includes, therefore, the politics of administering any federal program.

School Personnel Utilization (sometimes confused in the bureaucracy with Surplus Property Utilization, also known as SPU) in 1970 was one of the 1019 federal domestic assistance programs administered by 57 different departments and agencies. (A sample page for SPU from the Catalog of Federal Domestic Assistance is in the appendix to this chapter).

Although for the purposes of discussion, a distinction is made between educational as opposed to administrative issues involved in the politics of administering projects in differentiated staffing, the SPU program was often engaged in splitting educational infinitives. It was too often mired in defining mechanics and procedures and not enough in substance. But by the same token, given the impetus of federal resources (money not the least among them), few schools actually began the process of synthesizing a total program of educational reform. It will not likely be known what the effort of the SPU program meant to an individual school district that did receive funds as contrasted to one that did not.

The administration of differentiated staffing, whether from the perspective of a building principal, project director or federal manager, involved the politics of planning the reform, paradoxically, of administrative practices and policies towards staffing. As difficult as "implementing" a federal program may have seemed, it was more difficult to determine the degree of commitment to flexibility in staffing. Many of the school systems remained imbedded in universal patterns of established thought. The high degree of uniformity in the stability of the organization was translated into the uniformity of function and management policies. The SPU program had no stomach nor precedent for delving into the machinery of local school politics. Yet the political behavior of those managing the schools meant life or death for the accomplishment of educational objectives and activities.

Moreover, undue significance was attached, in the politics of funding and administering the SPU program, to fiscal concerns. Managers of projects were gauged by their effectiveness in using political strategies to penetrate the mazes of government in order to obtain a federal grant—or to increase it. Often, jobs, promotions, status advancement and other inducements and blandishments swung in the balance. Energies were expended in the means and the delivery systems rather than in pursuit of the satisfaction of goals.

The SPU program was instituted for the benefit of local schools to demonstrate new and diverse approaches to staffing schools. The amount of information describing results that could be said to be significantly novel and experimental were negligible. Hence, when occasions came for federal managers to justify in detail meaningful evaluations, thereby justifying the continuance of the SPU program, little could be reported without hypocrisy. The comparatively rich potential contribution of the total, integrated effort at differentiating staffs foundered. The apparent complexity of implementing a differentiated staffing program at an individual school was marked by uncertainty of commitment. It was nothing less than what characterized any movement to shake the pillars of the closed school system and substitute educational options.

The unification of a staff development program, a package for educational personnel flexibility, was eventually blunted by the myriad of issues associated with the process of implementation. From the SPU program perspective, some of these included:

Legislative developments
federal guidelines and formats
community dynamics
local and state administrative practices and policies
ongoing school innovations, perhaps federally sponsored
desegregation policies, if any
school board relations
teacher union postures

Because at the time little agreement existed about priorities or theories to guide a school towards developing strategies for differentiating its staff, the process was treated in the same manner as any other innovation funded through the federal coffers. The limitations of this parochial mode of thinking were really a reflection of the insensitivity to all the variables that the SPU program promoted. There was an early need to analyze a vast amount of data from a scarcity of resources.

The positive degree of acceptance and consensual thinking of the 1,500 participants in the process will have significance for the teaching profession. The politics of implementing educational reform and renewal will at least be able to isolate attitudinal features important to training projects. The evaluative techniques and methodology of DeBloois described in this chapter can facilitate studies of the interaction of schools with the politics of administering at the federal level.

EDUCATION AND THE NEW FEDERALISM

Despite the larger issues in administering a federal program and the daily tasks of communicating with school project directors, federal program managers must cope with the political realities proposed by the administration. Two such issues from the executive branch of the government in the early seventies were decentralization and special revenue sharing. Any discussion of how federal educational policies are applied would not be complete without an analysis, however brief, of the administration-in-power's stance on education. The Nixon administration's themes among federal education agencies were clearly reform and innovation. However laudable, the themes were themselves incapable of increasing the government's response of the pressures to the public search for accountable sources, lack of credibility in traditional educational approaches, and nonchalance in voting-in necessary appropriations, bond issues and tax levies. Recognizing the need for revitalizing the federal-state partnership in concert with reform and innovation, President Nixon indicated to Congress that "important new areas of government decision making must be returned to the regions and locales where the problems exist."

DECENTRALIZATION

Decentralization of activities, meanwhile, proceeded throughout the ten regions. The OE established ten positions of Regional Assistant Commissioners of Education who were to exercise "administrative, technical, and programmatic direction for the review and approval of state plans, proposals, and amendments for regionalized programs." They report directly to the Commissioner. As regionalization and decentralization proceeded, the OE Washington office assumed more responsibility for issues of national educational policy and program direction, relations with Congress, the educational policy and program direction, the educational constituency at large, and planning and evaluation. The regions assumed more operational control—funds and reports, audits, technical assistance.

The concept of decentralization did not begin in 1970. It had actually been instituted twenty years earlier in 1950 to facilitate what has come to be known as "impacted aid"—School assistance in federally affected areas. Some of the activities sponsored by the National Defense Education Act (NDEA) instituted in 1958 were also decentralized. A White House Task Force on Education, following the passage of ESEA in 1965, recommended further reinforcement of regional offices. In late August of 1969, HEW began an approach destined to streamline the federal educational requirements for state assistance. A task force with the acronym of FAST (Federal Assistance Streamlining Task Force) was initiated with charges to review all Office of Education programs relating to formula and project grants and state plans—nearly $2 billion. Grouping common classes of grants, the FAST Force developed simplified ways for processing grants for OE and the state recipient.

One of the breakthroughs was an "assurance" agreement with states, providing federal law permitted, that a state agreed it would abide by all federal requirements. Each program is reviewed by OE regional offices, but the program narratives and details are held in state offices and not submitted to OE. The FAST group did much to reduce the paper flow, simplify reports, codify multiyear application, and give more continuity to ongoing programs.

In addition to the history of legislative decentralization, the FAST development, joint evaluation efforts, and state management review plans, many discretionary grant programs have been decentralized. For example, in fiscal year 1970, the funding and control of all ESEA Title III supplementary education centers was transmitted from OE to the states. This has been the intent of the ESEA amendments of 1968. However, many states were caught without the available personnel, money or resources to operate the centers, and instead converted many of them into planning centers.

Mutual planning existed between the states and OE through the regions, most dramatically, in education for the handicapped programs. The Bureau of Education for the Handicapped in 1970 stated that it was "the responsibility of each state educational agency to establish definitions of handicapping conditions to be applied within its state." Nearly $37.5 million went in 1970 for state-controlled and/or supported programs for the handicapped. Decentralization, as an ambitious government concept, found a positive and constructive illustration in the working arrangement between federal, state and local educators in developing programs and plans for the education of the handicapped.

But the whole question of decentralization is part of the larger issue of how government responds to peoples' needs. The organization of government is bureaucratic. The problems of bureaucracy are, like all the probable derivatives of its etymological roots, *stratified,* like the drawers of a bureau; *concentrated,* like the pyramidic centralization of authority; and mostly *ticklish* and *wooly,* like the later root *burra,* coarse hair. As government grows, inevitably and inexorably the problems of legislation and administration become immense. Entire departments are created solely for liaison activities. One way to reduce the paperwork of the cycle of planning, executing, and evaluating is to decentralize authority. One advantage is simply a reduction of coordination to a lower administrative unit, a state or a local agency. One disadvantage is whether or not the lower agency can efficiently administer the operation. Legislation specifiying a program, consequently, usually includes a section devoted to "strengthening" the agency's ability to administer the programs. This is not a form of control, but an approach to improve the capacity of local response. The New Federalism included both decentralized activities and sharing the revenue.

Special Revenue Sharing

Walter Heller described the use of economic policy and called revenue sharing, "per capital revenue sharing." By whatever name it is unconditional, unfettered, no-strings, unencumbered, block grant, general aid and a reapportionment of resources. As noted earlier, the generation of new revenues at the federal level, created new responsibilities at the local level, and in fact outstripped the revenues available. The problems created by new educational revenues are passed on in spawning new administrative responsibilities and new bureaucracies at state agencies and local school systems. Each new legislation or new federal program demands new coordinators and project directors. Thus, local schools grow top-heavy with administrators created by new federal resources at the very time they are forced to cut back or eliminate essential services because of dwindling local funds. There is little reconciliation of rising expenditures and limited tax bases. The pinch is felt hardest when federal funds are also reduced.

Revenue sharing, in an educational application, is a fiscal realignment that will at the same time promote national educational interests and strengthen the state agencies and local schools capacity to administer programs without undermining their willingness and resolve to do so. Heller notes: "We must move toward broader categories that will give states and localities more freedom of choice, more scope for expressing their varying needs and preference, within the framework of national purpose."[10] In keeping with the administration's policy, therefore, of general and special revenue sharing, the Office of Education in fiscal year, 1970 distributed $2 billion—over half its budget at that time—to the states in a variety of categorical accounts. The states in turn distributed funds locally. The Office of Education, in order to strengthen the leadership capabilities of state agencies and to cover planning, evaluation and other administrative costs, distributed an additional $109 million directly to state agencies.

CONCLUSION

This chapter has attempted to put in focus the mind of the federal program manager and the issues he must deal with. Foremost among these is the degree of credibility among the professional community: whether the federal officer is accepted as a governmental monitor or an educator. Thus, sometimes the posture of the federal officer is low-key, a mollification of the stern, auditor who must find the flaws in federal expenditures.

Another concern he has is how to manage all the resources of the public service agencies of the government for the benefit of projects. Much of his effort involves learning about the responsibilities of other federal agencies for individual projects, sometimes on request.

He always treads a cautious line between his role as administrator of the federal grant award and his advisory capacity to schools.

There is sometimes an impression in the public mind, especially since the exposure of the secret *Pentagon Papers*, that at the highest levels of government decision making mortal men and the calm reasoning they purportedly bring to public service are too often unreal images of harassed men coping with turbulent issues beyond their grasp. Much of that process has been described by Robert Kennedy in *Thirteen Days*. That public image may include government bureaucrats alert and trim in their conservative attire, often frustrated by the mechanics of moving any action program or policy through the elaborate gears of government.

Perhaps in any historical perspective the best policies have been those that ·endured the crucible of public debate. The irony is that most harried government officials have little time for the sheer delight of contemplation about policies. The press often characterizes the bureaucracy as faceless, without credibility, and wavering on the fulcrum of power and decision making. But however caricatured and pilloried the federal bureaucrat may be, the commitment to pursue sound and reasonable development in educational programs is strong. Their educational soundness will perhaps always be a compromise among educational constituencies. Unless exposed to the full glare of public scrutiny and debate, however, the development of federal educational policy will always end up being dialogues among bureaucrats.

Footnotes

1. Harold Howe II, "Growth and Growing Pains," *Saturday Review*, December 17, 1966.
2. Editorial, *The Washington Post*, Friday, May 28, 1971.
3. "Compilation of Federal Elementary and Secondary Education Legislation" (Washington, D.C.: U.S. Government Printing Office, 1970), p. 5.
4. Ibid.
5. S. 1557, 92nd Congress, 1st session, p. 19.
6. H.R. 6748, 92nd Congress, 1st session, p. 9.
7. Thomas E. Cronin, and Norman C. Thomas, "Federal Advisory Processes: Advice and Discontent," *Science*, February 26, 1971, pp. 771-79.
8. See Edith K. Mosher and Stephen K. Bailey, *The Office of Education Administers a Law* (Syracuse: Syracuse University Press, 1968), especially pp. 98-103 and 109-119. See also Stephen K. Bailey, *The Office of Education*

Act of 1965, in *The Politics of Education at the Local State and Federal Levels*, Michael Kirst, ed. (Berkeley, Calif.: McCutchan Publishing Corp., 1970), pp. 357-83.

9. Walter Heller, *New Dimensions of Political Economy* (Cambridge, Mass.: Harvard University Press, 1966), 203 pp.

10. Ibid, p. 206.

APPENDIX

PROGRAM TITLE	**EDUCATIONAL STAFF TRAINING—SCHOOL PERSONNEL UTILIZATION**
POPULAR NAME	SCHOOL PERSONNEL UTILIZATION PROGRAM
ADMINISTERING AGENCY	OFFICE OF EDUCATION, DEPARTMENT OF HEALTH, EDUCATION, AND WELFARE
AUTHORIZATION	Education Professions Development Act, Part C, Sections 521-528, and Part D, Sections 531-533; Public Law 90-35; 20 U.S.C. 1111-1119a; CFR 45-174.
OBJECTIVES	To recruit and train new personnel and to retrain experienced personnel for new roles in schools which provide promotional opportunities within the instructional process; and to develop training projects that enable schools to develop staffing plans which provide more economic and effective instruction for children and make maximum use of the talent available in a school system and its community.
TYPES OF ASSISTANCE	Project grants.
USES AND USE RESTRICTIONS	Part C grants may be used for fellowships for graduate study leading to an advanced degree for persons who are pursuing or plan to pursue a career in early childhood education. Fellowship funds may be used for stipends, dependency allowances and cost of education allowances. Part C also authorizes grants to institutions of higher education to develop and strengthen graduate programs for training educational personnel. Part D grants may be used for improving the qualifications of persons who are serving or preparing to serve in early childhood educational programs, or to supervise or train persons so serving. Funds cover stipends, dependency allowances and instructional costs. No fellowships are awarded for study at a school or department of divinity. EPDA funds may not be used to support regular undergraduate teacher preparation programs.
ELIGIBILITY REQUIREMENTS	1. APPLICANT ELIGIBILITY: Institutions of higher education, State departments of education, and local public educational agencies, or two or more of the above types of agencies in combination. 2. BENEFICIARY ELIGIBILITY: Present or prospective educational personnel of all types who will be trained for work in elementary, secondary, or postsecondary vocational schools.

3. CREDENTIALS/DOCUMENTATION: Where applicable, proposals must include signatures indicating approval by cooperating agencies or institutions: local education agencies applying for part D grants must have the signature of the chief State school officer indicating coordination with EPDA, Part B.

APPLICATION PROCESS

1. PREAPPLICATION COORDINATION: Proposals submitted by local education agencies must be signed by the chief State school officer, signifying coordination with part B programs.

2. METHOD OF APPLICATION: Program materials describe application procedures. Initial application is a prospectus, briefly outlining program need, objectives, and design. Following prospectus evaluation, certain applicants are encouraged to submit full proposals. In final selection, outside evaluators' ratings, geographical distribution, and availability of funds will be considered.

3. DEADLINES: Prospectuses are due August 1, 1969, Proposals are due November 1, 1969.

4. RANGE OF APPROVAL/DISAPPROVAL TIME: 90 days from the time of proposal submission. Prospectuses will be encouraged or discouraged within 60-90 days after submission.

5. APPEALS: There are no appeals procedures. Unfunded applicants will be notified of the reasons for refusal on request.

6. RENEWALS: Grants are awarded annually; proposals may be projected for more than 1 year only if (1) the project will train the same personnel for the whole time; or (2) will not succeed unless continued for more than 1 year. But continued funding is not guaranteed, and will be based on the availability of funds, a clear demonstration of need, and evidence of satisfactory performance.

ASSISTANCE CONSIDERATIONS

1. TYPE OF GRANT: Project.

2. MATCHING REQUIREMENTS: None. Applicants are encouraged to seek partial funding for the project from local and other sources.

3. LENGTH OF ASSISTANCE PERIOD: 6 to 18 months.

4. TIME PHASING OF ASSISTANCE: Payments on demand, based on quarterly estimates of need.

POST ASSISTANCE REQUIREMENTS

1. REPORTS: Interim technical reports. Final expenditure reports within 60 days of grant termination.

2. AUDITS: None.

3. RECORDS: Detailed records covering all funds expended under the grant must be kept for 5 years or until an audit is performed.

FINANCIAL AND OUTPUT INFORMATION

1. ACCOUNT IDENTIFICATION: 09-10 0294-0-1-001.

2. OBLIGATIONS: Fiscal year 1970

3. FACE VALUE OF LOANS: Not applicable.

4. RANGE OF FINANCIAL ASSISTANCE: $20,000 to $150,000.

5. OUTPUT MEASURE: Fiscal year 1969: 1,500 persons trained.

PROGRAM LITERATURE

"Education Professions Development Act, Facts About Programs for 1970-71." OE-58030; no charge. Education Professions Development Act, Program Information, School Personnel Utilization Program; no charge.

**INFORMATION
CONTACTS**

1. REGIONAL OR LOCAL OFFICE: Persons may communicate with the EPDA coordinators in the Office of Education regional offices; see the appendix for a list of addresses.

2. HEADQUARTERS OFFICE: Dr. Donald K. Sharpes, Director, School Personnel Utilization Program, Bureau of Educational Personnel Development, Office of Education.